# Higher Education
# and the
# United States Office of Education
# (1867–1953)

*by*

RICHARD WAYNE LYKES

BUREAU OF POSTSECONDARY EDUCATION
UNITED STATES OFFICE OF EDUCATION
WASHINGTON, D.C.
1975

The author gratefully acknowledges the invaluable assistance of
the following faculty members of The American University:

DR. ERNEST POSNER        DR. ARTHUR EKIRCH
DR. JOHN DEVOR           DR. STANLEY SMITH
           DR. WARD STEWART

Library of Congress Catalogue Card No. 75–619321

FOR SALE BY THE SUPERINTENDENT OF DOCUMENTS,
U.S. GOVERNMENT PRINTING OFFICE
WASHINGTON, D.C. 20402 - PRICE $2.85
STOCK NUMBER 017–080–01427–1

# Preface

It was my original intention to confine this history to the activities of the Division of Higher Education. This has been done as far as possible but in several respects I could not separate the activities of the division from the rest of the Office of Education. Therefore, this is not so much a history of the Division of Higher Education as it is an account of some of the contributions of the Office of Education to the colleges and universities of the United States prior to the creation of the Department of Health, Education, and Welfare in 1953.

The arrangement of the material is chronological since this seemed the most logical method to follow. The history of the higher education activities of the Office of Education falls into seven clearly defined periods which I have chosen to divide into five chapters: activities prior to 1911; 1911 to World War I; World War I and the 1920's; the depression years and World War II; and the post-World War II years.

In some cases it seemed desirable to violate the strict chronological sequence in order to take a topic beyond the time limits of the chapter. This I have not hesitated to do if the story gained cogency and lucidity by the procedure. As an example, in Chapter II I carried my account of the college accreditation movement and survey movement somewhat past the year 1916 when the chapter ends. I have tried to keep this procedure to a minimum. When it has been done it was only because I felt there was no better way to handle the material.

There are three sets of facts which belong to the story yet should not be brought directly into the narrative. One is the various names and assignments of the Office of Education through the years. A second is the names and dates of the Commissioners of Education and the chiefs of the Division of Higher Education. Finally, there is a list of the various locations of the Office of Education from 1867 to the present. I decided that these should be made a part of this Preface and they will be found immediately following.

*        *        *        *        *        *        *

A few words about the mechanics of the study should be made. I have used the term "Office of Education" throughout except when quoting from various sources which use the term "Bureau of Education" or, infrequently "Department of Education." Even though the Office was a Bureau for 59 years, from 1870 to 1929, I have preferred the present name for the sake of consistency.

In footnoting I have taken full advantage of such scholarly shortcuts as *op. cit.* and *ibid.* wherever possible. But I have not carried them beyond the limits of each chapter. In other words I

TABLE 1.—*Names and Administrative Assignments, Office of Education*

| Name | Assignment | Effective date and authority |
|---|---|---|
| DEPARTMENT OF EDUCATION _____ | — | March 2, 1867 14 Stat. L., Chap. 434, 1867. |
| OFFICE OF EDUCATION ___ | Department of the Interior | July 1, 1869 15 Stat. L., Chap. 176, 1868. |
| BUREAU OF EDUCATION* __ | Department of the Interior | July 12, 1870 16 Stat. L., Chap. 251, 1870. |
| OFFICE OF EDUCATION ___ | Department of the Interior | October 3, 1929 Department of the Interior Order 379, 1929. |
| OFFICE OF EDUCATION ___ | Federal Security Agency | July 1, 1939 53 Stat. L., pt. 2, Reorganization Plan No. 1 of Reorganization Act of 1939, approved April 3, 1939. |
| OFFICE OF EDUCATION ___ | Department of Health, Education, and Welfare | April 11, 1953 67 Stat. L., PL 13, April 1, 1953. |

* First called Bureau in Appropriation Act of 1870 for FY 1871.

(Compiled by author from material assembled by Mr. Charles Gately, Educational Reference Librarian, Department of Health, Education, and Welfare Library, and Mrs. Rebecca Fowler, Librarian, Department of the Interior Library.)

Table 2.—*Commissioners of Education and Chiefs of Division of Higher Education*

| Commissioner | Dates | Chief of division | Dates |
|---|---|---|---|
| Henry Barnard | March 14, 1867–March 15, 1870 | | |
| John Eaton | March 16, 1870–August 5, 1886 | | |
| Nathaniel H. R. Dawson | August 6, 1886–September 5, 1889 | | |
| William T. Harris | September 12, 1889–June 30, 1906 | | |
| Elmer E. Brown | July 1, 1906–June 30, 1911 | Kendric C. Babcock | November 9, 1910–May 2, 1913 |
| Philander P. Claxton | July 8, 1911–June 1, 1921 | Samuel P. Capen | February 1, 1914–December 1, 1919 |
| | | George F. Zook | February 1, 1920–August 31, 1925 |
| John James Tigert | June 2, 1921–August 31, 1928 | Arthur J. Klein | December 10, 1925–July 15, 1930 |
| William John Cooper | February 11, 1929–July 10, 1933 | Frederick J. Kelly | June 15, 1931–June 30, 1946 |
| George F. Zook | July 11, 1933–June 30, 1934 | | |
| John W. Studebaker | October 23, 1934–July 15, 1948 | John Dale Russell | September 3, 1946–January 15, 1952 |
| Earl James McGrath | March 16, 1949–April 22, 1953 | Buell G. Gallagher | April 15, 1952–August 1, 1952 |
| Lee M. Thurston | July 2, 1953–September 4, 1953 | (Rall Grigsby and Wesley Armstrong, Acting Heads) | August 1952–September 1955 |
| Samuel M. Brownell | November 16, 1953–August 31, 1956 | | |

TABLE 3.—*Physical Locations of Administrative Offices, Office of Education, Washington, D. C.*

| | |
|---|---|
| 1867 | 430 G Street, NW |
| 1869 moved to | 763 G Street, NW |
| 1871 moved to | 709 G Street, NW |
| 1878 moved to | 12th Street and Pennsylvania Avenue, NW (Shepherd Building) |
| 1879 moved to | 8th and G Streets, NW (Wright Building) |
| 1909 moved to | 12th Street and Pennsylvania Avenue, NW ("Old" Post Office Building) |
| 1917 moved to | 5th and F Streets, NW (Pension Building) |
| 1923 moved to | 18th and F Streets, NW (Department of the Interior Building) |
| 1933 moved to | 18th Street and Pennsylvania Avenue, NW (Hurley-Wright Building) |
| 1937 moved to | 18th and C Streets, NW ("New" Department of the Interior Building) |
| 1943 moved to | 26th Street near Constitution Avenue and Rock Creek Parkway, NW (Temporary Building "M") |
| 1948 moved to | 4th Street and Independence Avenue, SW (Federal Security Agency Building, after 1953 Department of Health, Education, and Welfare Building, North) |

(Based upon information supplied by Miss Susan Futterer, Assistant Librarian, Department of Health, Education, and Welfare Library; and information from *Education for Victory*, II, No. 7, October 1, 1943, p. 5; *School Life*, XXI, No. 2 (Special Supplement), October 1935, p. 28; XXII, No. 10, June 1937, pp. 304-305, 307; XXX, No. 6, March 1948, p. 18; and Ford, T. B., "The Educational Contributions of the U. S. Commissioners of Education, 1867-1928" (Washington, 1933, typewritten ms.), pp. 27, 40, 49, 59, 72, 82, 90).

have treated each chapter as a separate study as far as footnotes are concerned. The first mention of a source in each chapter includes the name of the author or names of authors if more than one, the complete title, the place and date of publication, and the page reference. After that, further reference in the same chapter to that source has used accepted abbreviation and terminology.

\*      \*      \*      \*      \*      \*      \*

A work, even one of this modest proportion, would be impossible without the assistance of a large number of fellow students and advisers. I owe thanks to a large number of people. Among the more helpful have been the following:

Miss Rebecca Fowler, Department of the Interior Library;

Mr. Boise Bristor, Statistician, District of Columbia Public Schools;

Miss Lee Canales, Office of Education Services, International Cooperation Administration;

Miss Elizabeth Bethel, Mr. Joseph B. Howerton, and Mr. Leo Pascal, National Archives;

Mr. Henry C. Badger, Mrs. Edna Cave, Mrs. Genevieve Dane, Mr. Emery M. Foster, Dr. Walter Gaumnitz, Mr. Carroll Hanson, Mr. Charles T. Harris, Mr. Lester Herlihy, Dr. Martin Mayes, Mr. Glenn Northup, Mr. Joseph Shea, and Mrs. Patricia Topp of the Office of Education, United States Department of Health, Education, and Welfare;

Dr. Lloyd C. Blauch, Assistant Director, Register of Retired Professors; and

Miss Susan Futterer and Mrs. Claire Tedesco, Department of Health, Education, and Welfare Library.

My very special thanks go to these people:

Miss Lora Brookley and Mr. Charles Gately, Educational Reference Librarians, Department of Health, Education, and Welfare Library, for patience combined with knowledge, and lastly

Mr. John H. Lloyd, former Chief, Reports Section, Publications Service, Office of Education, for combining an encyclopedic knowledge of the Office of Education with understanding and good-will.

RICHARD WAYNE LYKES

# Contents

|  | Page |
|---|---|
| PREFACE | iii |
| HIGHER EDUCATION AND THE UNITED STATES OFFICE OF EDUCATION | 1 |
| *Chapter I:* HIGHER EDUCATIONAL ACTIVITIES PRIOR TO 1911 | 3 |

(Establishment of the Office of Education · Commissioners Barnard, Eaton, and Dawson · Herbert Baxter Adams and the historical program · Commissioner Harris · Second Morrill Act and land-grant college specialist · Commissioner Brown · Need for specialist grows.)

| *Chapter II:* THE FORMATIVE YEARS (1911–1916) | 29 |
|---|---|
| THE DIVISION IS ESTABLISHED | 29 |

(College growth · Need for specialist · Selection of Babcock · Division of Higher Education created.)

| THE DEVELOPMENT OF AN ACTIVE PROGRAM | 38 |
|---|---|

(Commissioner Claxton · Higher educational needs · Routine operations developed · Statistics · Publications · Land-grant colleges · Field work · The "suppressed report" and accreditation · Degree mills · Babcock replaced by Capen · The survey movement including developments to 1936 · "Dollar-a-year-men.")

| *Chapter III:* FROM WORLD WAR I THROUGH THE YEARS OF PROSPERITY (1917–1928) | 65 |
|---|---|
| THE FIRST WORLD WAR | 65 |

*Page*

(General activities  ·  Contact with institutions  ·
Planning programs of the Division  ·  Committee on
Science, Engineering, and Education of the Council of
National Defense  ·  Committee on the Relation of
Engineering Schools to the Government  ·  Com-
mittee on Education and Special Training  ·  Na-
tional Army Training Detachments  ·  Students'
Army Training Corps  ·  American Council on Edu-
cation  ·  Summary.)

"NORMALCY," 1919–1928 _____     79
(Movement to establish a Department  ·  Capen replaced by Zook  ·  Educational research  ·  Junior
college movement  ·  Evaluation of foreign student
credentials  ·  Commissioner Tigert  ·  Office reorganized  ·  National surveys  ·  Zook replaced by
Klein  ·  Annual inspections of Howard University  ·
Clearing-house of research studies  ·  Formation of
National Committee on Standard Reports for Institutions of Higher Education.)

*Chapter IV:* FROM THE DEPRESSION THROUGH THE SECOND
          WORLD WAR (1929–1945) _____     99

THE DEPRESSION YEARS _____     99
(Commissioner Tigert replaced by Cooper  ·  Extensive reorganization of the Office  ·  Division of Higher
Education renamed  ·  Research activities strengthened  ·  Klein replaced by Kelly  ·  Kelly's contributions  ·  Report of National Advisory Committee,
1931  ·  Depression  ·  Growth of financial studies
·  Commissioner Cooper replaced by Zook  ·  Zook's
contributions  ·  Commissioner Studebaker  ·  The
National Youth Administration  ·  The Civilian Conservation Corps  ·  University emergency research
project  ·  Bankhead-Jones Act, 1935  ·  Report of
Advisory Committee on Education, 1938  ·  Routine
activities  ·  Accreditation studies  ·  Interdepartmental Committee on Cooperation with the American
Republics  ·  Study of graduate schools in American
democracy  ·  Activities in 1939.)

THE SECOND WORLD WAR _____     122
(Improvement over World War I  ·  Defense training
in 1940  ·  Studebaker lists Office activities  ·  Na-

*Page*

tional Conference of College and University Presidents, 1942 · Office of Education Wartime Commission · Conference at American University, 1942 · List of Office essential wartime programs · Engineering, Science, and Management War Training · Student War Loans Program · *Education for Victory* · Wartime publications · Acceleration of curriculum study · Plans for teacher training program · Reorganization in 1943 · Start of *Higher Education* magazine · Post-war planning begins.)

*Chapter V:* THE POST-WAR YEARS (1946–1953) _____ 141
(Post-war planning · Studebaker's reorganization plan · Outside opinion of plan · Kelly replaced by Russell · Report of President's Commission on Higher Education, 1947 · Fragmented Federal programs · Surplus Property Act · Veteran's Educational Facilities Program · Growth of specialization · Routine operations · Commissioner Studebaker replaced by McGrath · Reorganization · Conference on preparation of college teachers · Korean War efforts · Controlled Materials Plan · College Housing Loan Program · Russell replaced by Gallagher · Organization and functions in 1953.)

*Chapter VI:* CONCLUSION _____ 163

*Appendix I:* BIOGRAPHICAL SKETCHES OF PROFESSIONAL STAFF MEMBERS OF THE DIVISION OF HIGHER EDUCATION _____ 175

*Appendix II:* THE SUPPRESSED BABCOCK REPORT AND COMMISSIONER CLAXTON'S EXPLANATION _____ 213

*Appendix III:* A LIST OF PUBLICATIONS OF THE OFFICE OF EDUCATION RELATING TO THE FIELD OF HIGHER EDUCATION _____ 239

BIBLIOGRAPHY _____ 281

## Tables

*Table 1.* —NAMES AND ADMINISTRATIVE ASSIGNMENTS, OFFICE OF EDUCATION _____ iv

*Page*

*Table 2.* —Commissioners of Education and Chiefs of Division of Higher Education _____     v

*Table 3.* —Physical Locations of Administrative Offices, Office of Education, Washington, D.C.     vi

*Table 4.* —Historical Statistics Showing Growth of Higher Education to 1950 _____     32

*Table 5.* —Funds Appropriated to the Office of Education for Colleges and Agriculture and the Mechanics Arts _____

*Table 6.* —Appropriations Made Available for National Defense, Office of Education, FY 1941–1946 _____     124

*Table 7.* —Summary of EDT, ESMDT, ESMWT–I, ESMWT–II, and ESMWT–III (October 9, 1940—June 30, 1945) _____     132

*Table 8.* —Appropriations and Operating Costs, Office of Education _____     165

*Table 9.* —Number of Employees, Office of Education _     165

*Table 10.*—Number of Professional Employees in the Division of Higher Education _____     166

*Table 11.*—Subject Matter of Publications Relating to Higher Education Prepared and Issued by the Office of Education, 1867–1953 _____     168

# Higher Education
## and the
## United States Office of Education
## (1867–1953)

CHAPTER I

# Higher Educational Activities
# Prior to 1911

On March 2, 1867, President Andrew Johnson signed a bill which created a "Department of Education." This incident, accomplished without fanfare and almost without notice in the press of the day, brought to a close years of ceaseless agitation by many leading educators for a voice in the Nation's Capital.

In 1838 Henry Barnard, a prominent Connecticut educator and political leader, had proposed that the 1840 National Census takers gather data on illiteracy and on educational institutions.[1] He was serving as an unofficial spokesman for a large number of others who desired this information to promote education throughout the Nation. There was a feeling that a central agency to collect and disseminate information on education was badly needed.

Throughout the 1840's and 1850's proposals for some sort of national educational office were introduced before the Congress. But the troubled decades that preceded the Civil War were not conducive to the passage of legislation of an educational nature. Also, the suggestion for educational activity at the Federal level was opposed by many sincere Americans as both unconstitutional and an infringement of States rights.

This is not the place to recount the story of the fight for a National Office of Education. It has been told by other scholars.[2]

[1] L. E. Blauch, *To Promote the Cause of Education. A Review of Historic Background of Today's Office of Education* (Washington, 1953), p. 2. See also W. T. Harris, *Report of the Commissioner of Education for the Year 1902* (Washington, 1903), I, p. 893.

[2] For succinct accounts see Blauch, *op. cit.*, pp. 1–8; J. J. Tigert, "An Organization by the Teachers and for the Teachers," *School Life*, IX, No. 9. May 1924, pp. 195–196; and C. H. Judd, *Research in the United States Office of Education* (Washington, 1939), pp. 1–7. More detailed accounts are in H. R. Evans, and E. A. Wright, "The United States Office of Education" (Washington, 1939, typewritten ms.), pp. 5–31; and J. N. Rodeheaver, Jr., "The Relation of the Federal Government to Civic Education" (Cambridge, Mass., 1951, typewritten ms.), pp. 48–66.

But cutting across the years of proposal, counter-proposal, and debate, we find that in February 1866 the National Association of School Superintendents held their annual meeting in Washington, D.C. During that meeting they appointed a committee of three to prepare a memorial to Congress asking for the creation of a "National Bureau of Education." [3] This memorial, and a bill which would enable the Bureau to be established, were both given to a staunch supporter of education, Representative James A. Garfield of Ohio.[4]

Garfield presented a bill to the House of Representatives on February 14, 1866. Debate and discussion continued for more than a year in the House of Representatives and Senate. Finally, suitable legislation was presented to the Congress and was passed on March 1, 1867. The following day the President signed the organic act of establishment and a "Department of Education" was an accomplished fact.[5]

The text of the organic act is as follows:

An Act To Establish a Department of Education (Approved March 2, 1867).

Be it enacted by the Senate and House of Representatives of the United States of America in Congress assembled, That there shall be established at the city of Washington, a department of education, for the purpose of collecting such statistics and facts as shall show the condition and progress of education in the several States and Territories, and of diffusing such information respecting the organization and management of schools and school systems, and methods of teaching, as shall aid the people of the United States in the establishment and maintenance of efficient school systems, and otherwise promote the cause of education throughout the country.

Sec. 2. And be it further enacted, That there shall be appointed by the President, by and with the advice and consent of the Senate, a Commissioner of Education, who shall be intrusted

---

[3] Rodeheaver, *op. cit.*, pp. 56–58.

[4] James Abram Garfield (1831–1881) had been engaged in educational work most of his life prior to the Civil War. He had taught school in Ohio in 1849. He graduated from Williams College, Williamstown, Massachusetts, in 1856, and was President of Hiram College, Hiram, Ohio, from 1857 to 1861, probably one of the very few men to be appointed President of an educational institution a year after receiving his bachelor's degree. Following service in the Civil War from 1861 to 1863, during which time he rose from the rank of Lt. Colonel to Major General, Garfield served as a member of the House of Representatives from Ohio. He was in Congress from 1863 to 1880. In the latter year he resigned following his election to the Presidency of the United States. *Biographical Directory of the American Congress, 1774–1949* (Washington, 1950), p. 1196.

[5] D. H. Smith, *The Bureau of Education. Its History, Activities and Organization* (Baltimore, Md., 1923), p. 2.

with the management of the department herein established, and
who shall receive a salary of $4,000 per annum, and who shall
have authority to appoint 1 chief clerk of his department, who
shall receive a salary of $2,000 per annum, 1 clerk who shall
receive a salary of $1,800 per annum, and 1 clerk who shall
receive a salary of $1,600 per annum, which said clerks shall be
subject to the appointing and removing powers of the Commissioner of Education.

Sec. 3. And be it further enacted, That it shall be the duty
of the Commissioner of Education to present annually to Congress a report embodying the results of his investigations and
labors, together with a statement of such facts and recommendations as will, in his judgment, subserve the purpose for
which this department is established. In the first report made
by the Commissioner of Education under this act, there shall
be presented a statement of the several grants of land made
by Congress to promote education, and the manner in which
these several trusts have been managed, the amount of funds
arising therefrom, and the annual proceeds of the same, as far
as the same can be determined.

Sec. 4. And be it further enacted, That the Commissioner of
Public Buildings is hereby authorized and directed to furnish
proper offices for the use of the department herein established.[6]

It is significant that this Act mentions "schools and school
systems" but makes no specific mention of higher education. As
conceived and planned by its major supporters the Department
of Education was to be a research and tabulation agency concerned basically with public school education. There were only two
ways in which higher education was involved. One was in the
vague, broad terms of the clause to "otherwise promote the cause
of education." The second was in the requirement that the first
Report of the Commissioner should contain some statement of the
several grants of land made by the Congress to promote education.
This statement would largely be concerned with the Morrill Act of
1862, or the "Land-Grant College Act," which called for the dona-
tion of "public lands to the several states and territories which
may provide colleges for the benefit of agriculture and mechanics
arts."[7]

Other than these oblique references there was nothing to indicate the relationship of the new Department of Education to the
colleges and universities of the Nation. It had been established
as an organization devoted to the diffusion of information on
"popular education." It was to be a federally financed clearing
house of statistics, reports, and papers concerned essentially with

---

[6] 14 Stat. L., 434, March 2, 1867.
[7] 12 Stat. L., 503, July 2, 1862.

education on the primary and secondary levels. In short, it was a common school movement.[8]

The activities of the Office of Education prior to the appointment of the first specialist in higher education may best be told by a review of the accomplishments of each Commissioner. A student of the Office of Education wrote nearly forty years ago that "to a degree equalled, perhaps, by few other government organizations the work of the Bureau of Education has been a reflection of the personality of the commissioners." [9]

On March 11, 1867, Henry Barnard of Connecticut was appointed the first Commissioner of Education. He took his office three days later. It was an appointment richly deserved and applauded by educators throughout the United States. Henry Barnard (1811–1900) was devoted to the cause of public education. Born in Hartford, Connecticut, on January 24, 1811, Barnard had spent nearly all his life in educational work. He graduated from Yale University in 1830 and immediately took a position as head of an academy in Pennsylvania. By 1835 he was back in Connecticut as a practicing member of the bar. He served as a member of the Connecticut Legislature from 1837 to 1840 where he maintained a keen and lively interest in free public education. He was the first Secretary of the Board of Commissioners of Common Schools from 1839 to 1842. This position corresponds to a State Superintendent of Schools today. In 1843 he became Superintendent of Education in Rhode Island and the same year organized the Rhode Island Institute of Instruction, the oldest State teacher's association in the United States. Barnard remained in the Rhode Island office until 1849 when he returned to Connecticut as principal of the Connecticut Normal School and Superintendent of Common Schools.

When Barnard resigned from the latter two positions in 1855 because of poor health he started an educational periodical, *American Journal of Education*, which continued publication, except for short breaks, until 1881. In 1859 he became Chancellor of the University of Wisconsin, remaining in Milwaukee until 1861 when again his health forced him to retire. In 1866 he was well enough to return to an active position and accepted the presidency of St. John's College, Annapolis, Maryland. This was his position when he was appointed first Commissioner of Education by President Johnson.[10]

---

[8] Evans and Wright, *op. cit.*, pp. 10–11.

[9] Smith, *op. cit.*, p. 9.

[10] Evans and Wright, *op. cit.*, pp. 32–33; E. S. Harris, "Henry Barnard," *Dictionary of American Biography* (New York, 1928 *et seq.*), I, pp. 621–624;

Barnard's most serious problem stemmed from the deplorable condition of common school systems throughout the country. "The elementary schools of the North had suffered severely during the war, while those of the South were demoralized. The new West, then in the making, also needed aid in shaping its school policies." [11] So the Commissioner and his "force" of four employees (including himself), reinforced with appropriations of a little more than $24,000 for two years, would be forced to devote their efforts to this most urgent problem.

But even if there had been no such need, it is unlikely that Barnard would have devoted much attention to education beyond the secondary school level. His basic interest seemed to be the public school system in which he had done most of his work. Even while associated with the University of Wisconsin he had spent a great deal of his time in the supervision of higher and normal departments of education in the public school systems of the State. His primary attention at that time was directed at teacher training and preparation.[12]

Although Barnard, by necessity as well as desire, inclined toward giving most of his attention to the public elementary school system, he realized the need for statistical information on higher education. When he became Commissioner there was no accurate or complete list of colleges and universities in the Nation. There was no way to tell how many students were granted degrees each year, what the degrees were, or whether an institution was qualified to grant degrees at all. Indeed, it was not possible for any person in the United States to tell the exact number of such institutions of higher education that existed!

An educator of Barnard's stature could not ignore this situation. In his *First Report*, actually the only general report he was to prepare and submit as Commissioner, he stated that he planned to gather the following information on higher education:

1. The number of colleges in each State;
2. The circumstances of origin of each;
3. The conditions of the admission of students;
4. The courses of study;

---

B. C. Steiner, *Life of Henry Barnard, the First Commissioner of Education, 1867–1870* (Washington, 1919); T. B. Ford, "The Educational Contributions of the U.S. Commissioners of Education, 1867–1928" (Washington, 1933, typewritten ms.), pp. 14–26; L. E. Hartley, "A Critical Study of the United States Office of Education Since 1933" (Boulder, Colorado, 1941, typewritten ms.), pp. 18–23; and I. M. Wright, "History of the United States Bureau of Education" (New York, 1916, typewritten ms.), pp. 18–21.

[11] Smith, *op. cit.*, p. 9.

[12] Wright, "History of the Bureau," p. 21.

5. The equipment of libraries and material aids to instruction;

6. Students, professors, and graduates;

7. Endowments;

8. What the colleges profess and what they really accomplish, as well as their relations with "professional and special" schools;

9. Information on foreign higher education; and

10. Information on "professional and special schools," such as schools of theology, law, medicine, teaching, agriculture, manufactures, engineering, and mining.[13]

In addition to this schedule of information, he outlined a simple plan for reporting on the land-grant colleges as the Congress had required in the Act of 1867.[14]

This was a worthy, but ambitious, program for so small a staff. If it could have been done, the Nation would have been presented with a comprehensive catalogue of institutions which would have done much to eliminate fraudulent and bogus "colleges," and would have forced borderline institutions either to improve or close their doors. In fact, if Barnard could have assembled, prepared, and published this information it would have been an important step forward for American higher education.

Barnard had a plan for collecting information. His main reliance was to be placed upon annual reports and special replies from administrative officials, supplemented by personal visitation and conferences of the Commissioner and official inspectors. He also proposed to use information gathered at annual conferences, and to maintain an extensive correspondence with the active schoolmen of the day. Finally, he would consult the educational library which he was starting to assemble, and the daily and weekly press of the country, "both secular and religious." [15]

Barnard's *First Report,* accompanied by circulars and documents, was submitted to the Congress on June 2, 1868.[16] Along with it he submitted a special report on the condition of public schools in the District of Columbia. Barnard embarked upon what promised to be an ambitious and comprehensive publication program which would include monthly circulars, quarterly publications, and educational documents and tracts.[17]

---

[13] Henry Barnard, *First Report of the Commissioner of Education (1867– 68) with Circulars and Documents Accompanying the Same;* . . . (Washington, 1868), pp. xiii, xvii–xviii.

[14] *Ibid.,* pp. xxvi–xxviii.

[15] *Ibid.,* pp. xxii–xxiii.

[16] Rodeheaver, *op. cit.,* p. 68.

[17] *Ibid.,* p. 68; Barnard, *op. cit.,* pp. xxiii–xxvi. This report on schools is the First Office of Education school survey. Survey work is discussed in Chapters II and III, *infra.*

This *First Report* included three supplements relating to higher education which were later published as "Official Circulars." These were the initial higher education publications of the Office of Education. The first was a document of approximately 180 pages which summarized the history and development of land-grant institutions up to 1868. It was compiled largely by the Chief Clerk under Barnard's supervision.[18] Thus, in a sense, the Chief Clerk, a gentleman left unnamed by Barnard, was the first "specialist in higher education." The other publications which related to higher education were a brief summary report on "female education" and a longer study of normal schools.[19] Although these studies were largely compilations of reports submitted by those institutions willing to participate, and although they made no pretense of being definitive, they showed some interest in higher education at the national level.

Before Barnard could begin to realize his comprehensive plan of publication which would chronicle education at all levels, he found his position so unpleasant that he resigned. It was effective on March 15, 1870. The causes of this course of action were, apparently, a lack of confidence on the part of several members of the Congress and some opposition among educational administrators about cooperating in supplying information and data to Washington. The opposition of the Congress was shown by the action it took on July 20, 1868. At that time the "Department" was reduced to an "Office" and placed in the Department of the Interior effective at the start of the following fiscal year. Furthermore, as though to give further offense, the Commissioner's salary was reduced from $4,000 per year to $3,000. A later statute, effective on the same date, reduced the number of clerks from three to two.[20]

Barnard's brief tenure had been a mixed success. He had begun the publication of materials on higher education and he had given "to the schools of the country, more than any other man of his time, a conception of education as a national force." [21] Writing years later, John Eaton, his successor, emphasized Barnard's

---

[18] *Ibid.*, pp. xxvi.

[19] *Ibid.*, pp. 129–310, 369–400, 649–820. Pertinent data on all publications relating to higher education which were prepared and published by the Office of Education is given in Appendix III, *infra*. This compilation of publications should be consulted since it would be undesirable to list the nearly 800 titles in the body of the text.

[20] Smith, *op. cit.*, p. 10; Rodeheaver, *op. cit.*, pp. 69–72; 15 Stat L., 176, 1868; 15 Stat. L., 291, 1869. The "Office" became a "Bureau" in 1870. See Table 1, Preface, *Supra*.

[21] Hartley, *op. cit.*, p. 23.

contribution in awakening national interest in education and establishing a publication program which covered a wide field of educational interests.[22]

Yet, Barnard was not too well suited for the problems he had to face as the first Commissioner. His administrative policies often were vague and indefinite and his publications were, in the words of one student, "more descriptive than analytical— and superficial." Furthermore, he was somewhat lacking in the tact and political acumen necessary to get what he wanted from the Congress.[23] Believing he lacked support, a supposition not altogether groundless, Commissioner Barnard resigned. He returned to Hartford, Connecticut, where he continued publication of the *American Journal of Education*. He died in the town of his birth on July 5, 1900.

The second Commissioner of Education took office on March 16, 1870, the day following the resignation of Barnard. This gentlemen was John Eaton (1829–1906) of Tennessee. Eaton was born on December 5, 1829, in Sutton, New Hampshire. He graduated from Dartmouth College in 1854. For the next five years Eaton was in educational work, first as a school principal in Cleveland, Ohio, and later as Superintendent of Schools in Toledo, Ohio. He had long cherished a desire to enter the ministry and in 1859 matriculated at Andover Theological Seminary, Massachusetts. He was ordained in September, 1861, after having accepted a commission as Chaplain of the 27th Ohio Volunteers.

Eaton served in various capacities during the Civil War and had reached the grade of Brigadier General by March of 1865. He served as Assistant Commissioner of the Freedmen's Bureau from the end of the war in April until December 1865. From 1867 to 1870, General Eaton served as State Superintendent of Public Instruction in Tennessee. This was the position he was holding when President Grant appointed him Commissioner.[24]

Eaton had even less of a background in higher education than Barnard. In fact, it was not until after leaving the Office of Education that he held his first position in higher education. This

---

[22] Harris, *Report . . . 1902*, I, pp. 904–906 (Letter from John Eaton to William T. Harris on Henry Barnard's connections with the Bureau of Education, May 29, 1901).

[23] Hartley, *op. cit.*, p. 19; Rodeheaver, *op. cit.*, p. 69.

[24] Philip W. Alexander, *John Eaton, Jr., Preacher, Soldier, and Educator* (Nashville, Tenn., 1940, abstract of Ph.D. Dissertation); Donald L. McMurray, "John Eaton," in *Dictionary of American Biography*, V, pp. 608–609; *Who's Who in America*, IV, p. 528; Evans and Wright, *op. cit.*, pp. 42–43; E. O. Mason, "John Eaton, a Biographical Sketch" in John Eaton, *Grant, Lincoln, and the Freedman* (New York, 1907), pp. ix–xxxiv; Ford, *op. cit.*, pp. 36–40; Hartley, *op cit.*, pp. 23–25; and Wright, *op. cit.*, pp. 27–28.

was the presidency of Marietta College to which he had been elected during the latter part of his term as Commissioner. Eaton, furthermore, had no wide circle of educational friends and acquaintances like Barnard had in 1867.

The new Commissioner had several qualities that were to serve him well in his sixteen years in office. One was the administrative ability he had demonstrated in work with the freedmen during the Civil War. He also had a warm, friendly personality and understood the technique of dealing with people. He enjoyed better health than Barnard. Finally, although comparatively unknown in the educational world, he was respected and liked by President Grant.[25]

When Eaton entered his office on a March morning in 1870 he was not encouraged by the physical size of the organization that awaited him. He "found that the entire working force of this Bureau at that time consisted of two clerks, at a salary of $1,200 each, and that the rooms assigned to its use were so crowded with books, pamphlets, and desks as to be wholly unfit for successful clerical work." [26]

The fifteen annual reports of Eaton contain enough information on education in the United States to delight the heart of insatiable Henry Barnard but they did not come close to the goal which the latter had set for higher education. For example, Eaton's *Report* for 1870 records the following items of interest about higher education: a statement of need for more documentary information on teacher preparation; a study supporting an American University to be established in the District of Columbia; a location by State of 369 colleges; a listing of several theological seminaries; and several remarks on medical, law, agricultural, scientific, and commercial colleges, and military academies.[27]

This seems impressive and considering the facilities and personnel which were available it is an excellent accomplishment. But Eaton, himself, admitted that more information on higher education was badly needed. He pointed out that the report which had been prepared in Massachusetts for the use of the Office of Education almost completely ignored institutions of higher learning such as Amherst, Williams, and Tufts. What was needed, he stressed, was a "harmonious" study of education in which the whole system would be considered.[28] Statistics on colleges and

---

[25] Rodeheaver, *op. cit.*, pp. 86–87; c.f. Mason, *op. cit.*

[26] John Eaton, Jr., *Report of the Commissioner of Education made to the Secretary of the Interior for the Year 1870, with Accompanying Papers* (Washington, 1870), p. 5.

[27] *Ibid.*, pp. 62–63, 65–66, 71–76.

[28] *Ibid.*, p. 11.

universities were "necessarily imperfect" and little was known about 80 of the 369 colleges on the list.[29] The information he possessed about higher education was sketchy and incomplete.

Eaton began the classification system of higher educational institutions which was used, with minor modifications, for approximately forty years. This system consisted of dividing institutions of higher education into seven categories: colleges (i.e., liberal arts institutions and those following the "traditional" curriculum) ; theological seminaries; law schools; medical, dental, and pharmaceutical institutions; normal schools; agricultural and scientific schools; and commercial colleges.[30]

This division of institutions by type was satisfactory until around the turn of the century when more and more institutions widened the scope of their activities and increased the complexity of their functions. The system underwent modification with the advent of the *Educational Directory* in 1912. Institutions were then listed by State and territory. The names were followed by brief descriptions which contained facts on accreditation, enrollment, type of school and so forth.

Subsequent reports prepared while Eaton held office included information on higher education but a study of these reports makes it apparent that Eaton was far from satisfied with the information he had been able to obtain. He made several suggestions relative to colleges and universities showing his interest in the subject. In 1871 he proposed that colleges require a knowledge of elementary English studies; a comment, incidentally, that reflects no great credit on the standards of the day. He also urged the outlawing of hazing and stressed the need for higher admission requirements and stiffer entrance examinations.[31]

In 1872 the Congress appropriated the sum of $1,800 for the salary of a statistician. Upon appointment, this man took over the duties which the chief clerk had performed under Barnard when the initial compilation of land-grant information had occurred.[32] This appears to have been the beginning of the practice of hiring educational specialists, men and women who devote their professional talents and experience to some special field of education. The practice was slow in catching on and specialists remained few in number until the time of World War I.

The first statistician is not listed in the contemporary publica-

[29] *Ibid.*, pp. 71–72.
[30] *Ibid.*, pp. 506–529.
[31] John Eaton, Jr., *Report of the Commissioner of Education (Vol. II, Report of the Secretary of the Interior)* (Washington, 1872), pp. 28–29.
[32] Smith, *op. cit.*, p. 20.

tions of the Office of Education. However, it appears that Dr. Charles Warren, who had been appointed from Illinois on October 13, 1870, took over the duties in 1872. In June of 1880 Isaac E. Clarke of New York was appointed a "collector and compiler of statistics." Two others joined the Office in the 1880's to help with statistical work. These were Wellford Addis, appointed in 1882, and Federick E. Upton, appointed 1885. Both of these latter named individuals later served as specialists in land-grant college statistics.[33]

The incumbent of the statistical position found his hands full. In 1875, Eaton wrote about some of the problems he faced:

When the work of collecting educational statistics was begun by the Office, it was found that there was no authentic list of the colleges in the United States, or of academies, or normal schools, or schools of science, law or medicine, or of any other class of educational institutions. The lists of nearly all grades of schools are now nearly complete. Information on all other matters relating to educational systems was equally incomplete and difficult of access.[34]

It is understandable that the first statistical tables on American education should be incomplete. Gradual improvement was noticable under Eaton. By 1872 there were statistical compilations on eight kinds of schools beyond the secondary level and the following year the number increased to ten. From then on, even after Eaton left office, statistical information relating to higher education became more accurate, more detailed, and more complete.[35]

In 1871 Eaton made his first request for what can be termed "specialized assistance." He requested "an increase in the permanent force of this office, so that the different divisions may each be in charge of a competent chief. Until this is done the Bureau cannot attain that efficiency which the public expect and have a right to demand." [36]

The following year he requested "an increase of the permanent force of this office commensurate with the increasing amount of

[33] N. H. R. Dawson, *Report of the Commissioner of Education for the Year 1887–88* (Washington, 1889), pp. 1117–1120. Dr. Warren died in office on September 9, 1889. Biographical sketches of Addis and Upton who were more closely associated with higher educational activities than the others, may be found in Appendix I, *infra*.

[34] John Eaton, Jr., *Report of the Commissioner of Education for the Year 1875* (Washington, 1876), p. viii.

[35] cf. Eaton, *Report . . . 1872* (Washington, 1873), *et. seq.*, for statistical tables.

[36] Eaton, *Report . . . (Vol. II, Report of the Secretary) . . .* (1871), p. 73.

work to be done." [37] Annually, from that time on Eaton repeated his hope that more money would be appropriated so the staff could be enlarged. His request was made almost without a word change until 1879 when he rewrote the lyrics while retaining the basic melody.[38]

His efforts were partially successful for, while he never got all the staff he felt necessary, the Office grew appreciably. When he took office there were two clerks and the annual appropriation was $6,000. The "library," exclusive of volumes belonging to former Commissioner Barnard, contained less than 100 books. When he left in 1886 the staff had grown to 38, the library contained 18,000 volumes and 47,000 pamphlets, and there was an educational museum. All of these were housed in adequate quarters.[39]

When Eaton left in 1886 to become President of Marietta College, Marietta, Ohio, the Office of Education had been strengthened in academic stature as well as physical size.[40] There were still no specialists in the present sense of the word, excepting the statistician, but more accurate figures were available than before. Some 45 publications relating to various problems and topics in higher education appeared between 1870 and 1886. The leadership he imparted stimulated education at all levels from kindergarten through university.[41]

Eaton's successor was Nathaniel H. R. Dawson who was appointed by President Grover Cleveland and took office on August 6, 1886. Dawson (1829–1895) was born in Charleston, South Carolina, on February 14, 1829. In 1842 his family moved to Alabama where he lived for most of the remainder of his life. He received his education at St. Joseph's College (later Spring Hill College), Alabama, and began practicing law in 1851. He served as an officer in an Alabama cavalry battalion during the Civil War. Following his military service he returned to law practice.

---

[37] Eaton, *Report . . . 1872*, p. lxxxvii.

[38] cf. Eaton, *Report . . . 1878* (Washington, 1880), p. cci; and Eaton, *Report . . . 1879* (Washington, 1881), p. ccxxx.

[39] Alexander, *op. cit.*, p. 5; Rodeheaver, *op. cit.*, p. 97.

[40] Eaton had a long and active career in education after leaving office in 1886. He remained at Marietta College until 1891. In 1895 he became President of Westminster College, Salt Lake City, Utah. He resigned in 1899 to organize the school system of Puerto Rico along American lines for the Federal Government. While in Puerto Rico he was stricken with a form of paralysis and was forced to return to the United States. He remained active in educational writing and advisory work in Washington, D.C., until his death on February 9, 1906. (See *supra*, fn. 24.)

[41] cf. quotation from resolutions made at the 1886 meeting of Department of Superintendence of the National Education Association in Evans and Wright, *op. cit.*, pp. 45–46; and Ford, *op. cit.*, pp. 36–46.

Dawson demonstrated organizational ability and political talent while serving as President of the State Bar Association of Alabama, 1884–85, and as Speaker of the State House of Representatives, 1880–81. In 1884 he was appointed chairman of the Democratic State Executive Committee where he managed the Cleveland campaign in Alabama. He was still a member of that committee when appointed Commissioner of Education.[42]

There is little question but that Dawson's appointment was based primarily on partisan considerations. He had worked hard for the election of the first Democratic President since Buchanan and his party was thirsty for the sweet refreshment of patronage. Moreover, Dawson was a lawyer by profession and inclination. He had no practical experience as an educator except through his service as Trustee of two universities: the University of the South, Sewanee, Tennessee; and the University of Alabama, University (Tuscaloosa), Alabama. This was the full extent of his association with the profession which he was now to head on the Federal level. His qualifications were virtually nil when compared with those preceding and following him. It was not surprising that his appointment brought protests from educators throughout the land.[43]

It is somewhat ironic that Dawson's brief tenure of office, lasting just over three years, should have been marked by achievements comparable to those of Eaton, and filled with a harmony of effort that was greater than existed in the administration of Barnard. Dawson had administrative ability and his training as a lawyer doubtless contributed to his aptitude for clear and logical thinking. He was helped by the fact that he took over the Office when it had a stability and prestige not previously known. There were some experienced people in the Office, such as Charles Warren, and Dawson had the wisdom to rely upon them.

Dawson continued the policy of publishing educational statistics as supplements to the annual reports. His statistical compilations are as complete as those of Eaton during the latter's final years in office. But of at least equal, if not greater, importance were the historical studies which he sponsored and Professor Herbert Baxter Adams of Johns Hopkins University supervised, and to which he made substantial contributions.[44]

---

[42] Evans and Wright, *op. cit.*, pp. 46–47; Ford, *op. cit.*, pp. 47–48; Wright, *op. cit.*, pp. 36–38; Hartley, *op. cit.*, pp. 28–29; and Rodeheaver, *op. cit.*, pp. 97–98.

[43] cf. Wright, *op. cit.*, pp. 36–38; Rodeheaver, *op. cit.*, p. 103; and Smith, *op. cit.*, p. 13.

[44] Smith, *op. cit.*, p. 28. Smith says that "Commissioner Dawson in 1886–87 put under way a valuable series of monographs on the history of higher

During his first months in office, Dawson became convinced that statistical studies, supplemented by occasional monographs prepared without reference to any publication pattern, were not sufficient if the Federal Government wished to make any lasting contribution to higher educational development. He believed that the study of higher education should be approached systematically through a series of historical monographs.

The history of the higher education in the United States deserves organized inquiry and national attention. The origin, development, academic status, and practical usefulness, of many of our older and better institutions of learning are scarcely known beyond their own scholastic environment. Documentary and manuscript material for such educational history and statistics is abundant, although often widely scattered, as will be seen by an examination of the bibliography appended to the present sketch.

Thus in January, 1887, Dawson wrote to Secretary of the Interior Lucius Q. C. Lamar, another ex-Confederate officer now serving the Union.[45] A little later Dawson stated that the material on higher education which had been collected was sufficient for making an analysis and study of higher education. "In order, however, that definite conclusions should be reached, more time must be given to the investigation than is afforded in a single year, and in the case of many colleges special inquiries instituted." [46]

Even before he had so expressed his ideas, Dawson acted to have monographic studies prepared. He enlisted the services of young Herbert Adams of nearby Johns Hopkins to prepare the kind of study he had in mind, one combining sound historical

---

institutions of learning in the United States, the outstanding feature, other than administrative, of his term of office." Herbert Baxter Adams (1850–1901) is generally conceded to be one of the more important American historical scholars of the Nineteenth Century. He was born on April 16, 1850, in Shutesbury, Massachusetts. He attended Amherst College from which he graduated in 1872, and Heidelberg University, Germany, where he received his Ph.D. in 1876. From then up almost until his death he was associated with Johns Hopkins University, Baltimore, Maryland. He was a co-founder of the American Historical Association and its secretary for a number of years. He was the founder of the "Johns Hopkins University Studies in Historical and Political Science." Adams was the author of many historical monographs and books and was a respected and admired teacher. He died at Amherst, Massachusetts, on July 30, 1901, while at the height of his intellectual powers. (For additional information see sketch in *Encyclopaedia Britannica* (Chicago, 1958), I, pp. 147–148.

[45] Letter from Dawson to L. Q. C. Lamar, Secretary of the Interior, January 20, 1887 as reproduced in Herbert B. Adams, *The College of William and Mary; A Contribution to the History of Higher Education, with Suggestions for its National Promotion* (Washington, 1887), pp. 7–9.

[46] Nathaniel H. R. Dawson, *Report . . . 1885–86* (Washington, 1887), p. xvi.

scholarship with acute educational observation. This study appeared in 1887 identified as "Contributions to American educational history, No. 1." It was a history of the College of William and Mary, Williamsburg, Virginia. Within months Adams followed this with a monograph on *The study of history in American colleges and universities,* and the following year he, with the assistance of others, finished a second of the "Contributions": *Thomas Jefferson and the University of Virginia; with authorized sketches of Hampden-Sidney, Randolph-Macon, Emory-Henry, Roanoke, and Richmond colleges, Washington and Lee university, and Virginia Military institute.*[47]

These works on Virginia were the start of a series of histories which would appear at irregular intervals up to 1903 and would finally number 36 volumes. The first was the only one to be devoted to a single institution and the second covered most of the institutions in Virginia. The third, which also appeared in 1888, was concerned with education in North Carolina. It was followed in succession by studies of education in the States of South Carolina, Georgia, Florida, Wisconsin, and Alabama. No. 9 was a history of Federal and State aid to higher education. Then came histories of education in Indiana, Michigan, Ohio, Massachusetts, Connecticut, Delaware, Tennessee, Iowa, Rhode Island, Maryland, Louisiana, Missouri, New Hampshire, New Jersey, Mississippi, Kentucky, Arkansas, Kansas, New York, Vermont, West Virginia, Minnesota, Nebraska, Pennsylvania, Colorado, Texas, and Maine.[48]

Each study was prepared by an educational scholar, usually a faculty member of an institution of higher education in the State about which he wrote. None of the authors were members of the Office of Education although they were apparently given some payment for their work. It is doubtful if the payment equalled the effort expended. There was some unevenness in the standards of writing and thoroughness of research but in general the quality was high.

Dawson was proud of the series he launched. This is obvious

---

[47] Adams also made two contributions to Dawson's first report: Appendix 11: "The promotion of higher political education;" and Appendix 12: "University extension in England." See Dawson, *op. cit.,* pp. 743–749. Titles are capitalized as originally published.

[48] Full publication details may be found in Appendix III, *infra.* The general plan of preparation and publication by geographical area is discussed in Dawson, *Report . . . 1886–87* (Washington, 1888), pp. 19–23. See also (U. S. Office of Education), *Commissioner of Education, Department of the Interior, Annual Statements, 1887–1907* (Washington, 1887 *et seq.*), Dawson's "Statement," 1889, pp. 4–6. This statement contains a copy of a letter from Adams to Dawson, dated February 18, 1889, in which the former lists the persons helping with the project.

from reading his 1886–87 *Report*.[49] The volumes do constitute the single most important series of studies on higher education to appear prior to the establishment of the Division of Higher Education, and one of the most important done in the entire history of the Office. They deserved the praise which Dr. Harris, Dawson's successor, lavished on them. As late as 1934 they were serving as the basis of studies being made in higher education. Even today the best of them stand as models of educational history writing, and Adams' history of the University of Virginia is one of the best histories of that university available.[50]

Dawson resigned as Commissioner effective September 5, 1889. The resignation was almost certainly due to the change in the political situation and not to any shortcomings on his part as Commissioner. Benjamin Harrison and the Republicans came into power as a result of the election of 1888, and Cleveland and the Democrats went out.[51] In the short time he held office, Dawson showed that he was interested in furthering the aims of Barnard and Eaton for comprehensive statistical records and reports, and, even more important, he demonstrated a keener interest in higher education than either.[52]

The fourth Commissioner of Education was one of the most celebrated and honored educators of the day. He was perhaps even better known than Henry Barnard had been in 1867. This was William Torrey Harris (1835–1909). Harris had been born in North Killingly, Connecticut, on September 10, 1835. He studied at Phillips Academy, Andover, Massachusetts, and Yale University. He left Yale in 1856 prior to graduating and became a teacher in St. Louis, Missouri. Subsequently, Harris became principal, assistant superintendent, and superintendent of schools. He held the latter position from 1867 to 1880. His annual reports as St. Louis Superintendent of Schools earned him a national reputation as an educator and philosopher.

In 1880 Harris resigned his position and became connected with the Concord School of Philosophy in Massachusetts where he was associated with Ralph Waldo Emerson, Bronson Alcott, and other distinguished intellectuals and educational philosophers.

---

[49] Dawson, *Report* . . . *1886–87*, pp. 19–23.

[50] Smith, *op. cit.*, p. 13; David Spence Hill, *Control of Tax-Supported Higher Education in the United States* (New York, 1934), pp. 51–52; Evans and Wright, *op. cit.*, p. 47.

[51] Rodeheaver, *op. cit.*, p. 103. Curiously, Rodeheaver in his scholarly study states the following: "It appears that he resigned simply because the Republicans were now out and Cleveland and the Democrats were back in." Of course, the reverse was true.

[52] Evans and Wright, *op. cit.*, p. 47.

In addition to his connection with the Concord School, Harris continued his prolific educational writings. A list of articles, pamphlets, and books which he authored during his life appeared in the Commissioner's *Report* for 1907. It contained 469 titles and was not considered a complete list.[53] Also while at Concord Harris played an extremely active role in the National Education Association.[54]

Harris had no direct connection with higher educational institutions prior to becoming Commissioner. His major concern seemed to have been with the learning process of the child. But he had shown some interest in higher education from time to time. Possibly the most notable instance came in 1874. On August 5 he spoke before the National Education Association Convention in Detroit, Michigan, on behalf of a "national university." Harris said that the entire Nation would benefit from "the connection a national university would have with the several bureaus" of the Federal Government.[55]

Commissioner Harris took office on September 12, 1889. The difference between him and Dawson has been summarized by a student writing at a later date:

> The contrast between him and the man he succeeded was marked. Dr. Harris was a practical school man of long experience, and his appointment was hailed with enthusiasm by the educators of the country. He brought to the office wide acquaintance in the field of education, the respect of his colleagues, high ideals, and a large grasp of the problems to be met.[56]

Despite the differences, Harris did not vary sharply from the policies of Dawson, nor from those of the earlier men. He continued publishing as complete statistical summaries as possible. He also continued the promotion and publication of the "Contributions to American educational history" started by Dawson.

---

[53] Henry R. Evans, "A List of Writings of William Torrey Harris," in Elmer E. Brown, *Report of the Commissioner of Education for the Year Ending June 30, 1907* (Washington, 1908), Vol. I, pp. 37–66.

[54] Ernest Sutherland Bates, "William Torrey Harris," in *Dictionary of American Biography*, VIII, pp. 328–330; *Who's Who in America*, V, p. 828; Evans and Wright, *op. cit.*, p. 48; Henry R. Evans, "William Torrey Harris; United States Commissioner of Education, 1889–1906," *School Life*, XV, No. 8, April 1930, pp. 144–147; Hartley, *op. cit.*, pp. 29–31; Ford, *op. cit.*, pp. 53–57; and Wright, *op. cit.*, pp. 41–42.

[55] William Torrey Harris, "Collection of papers and writings assembled by Office of Education Library," Volume I, "On a National University," p. 19.

[56] Smith, *op. cit.*, p. 33. The "Dr." was the result of several honorary degrees which Commissioner Harris received (Yale, Brown, Princeton, Pennsylvania, and Jena).

Harris expanded the system of "Divisions" which existed when he became Commissioner. When he took office there had been three operating divisions: Correspondence and Records, Statistics, and Library and Museum. He added a fourth: the Division of International Exchange for the comparative study of national school systems.[57]

There was still nothing resembling any division of higher education nor, for that matter, was there any division which devoted full attention to any other level of the American educational system. Harris had retained and broadened operational activities of a purely administrative nature. He was not interested in specialization and the Office of Education reflected his personality and interests.

Just prior to the end of his first full year in office, the Congress passed and the President signed into law a piece of legislation which related directly to higher education. This was the Second Morrill Act, dated August 30, 1890.[58] It was actually a supplement to the original Morrill Act of 1862, the famous "Land-Grant College Act." The 1862 legislation granted each State 30,000 acres of land for each Senator and Representative it had in Congress. This land, or the income therefrom, was to be used to establish one or more institutions of higher education which should teach those branches of learning related to agriculture and the mechanic arts.[59]

The original Morrill Act seems to have had but slight influence on the activities of the Office of Education. This was not true of the 1890 legislation which provided for the allotment of funds to the land-grant colleges on an annual, graduated program of assistance.[60] It also laid down restrictions on the use of the funds. Section 4 required the Secretary of the Interior to certify to the Secretary of the Treasury

---

[57] Wright, *op. cit.*, p. 44; (U.S. Office of Education), *Commissioner of Education . . . 1887–1907*, Harris, "Statement," 1890, p. 3.

[58] 26 Stat. L., 417, 419, August 30, 1890.

[59] See 12 Stat. L., 503, July 2, 1862.

[60] This Act appropriated to each State and Territory the sum of $15,000 for fiscal year 1890 and an increase of $1,000 annually for ten years until a maximum amount of $25,000 had been reached. This was later supplemented by the "Nelson Amendment" (34 Stat. L., 1281, March 4, 1907). This appropriated to each State and Territory the sum of $5,000 for the fiscal year 1908 and an annual increase of the amount of such appropriation thereafter for four years by an additional sum of $5,000 until a maximum amount of $50,000 for each State and Territory had been reached. Table 5, Chapter IV, shows the annual appropriation for the period from 1890 to 1953. For more detailed discussion see George A. Works, and Barton Morgan, *The Land Grant Colleges* (Washington, 1939), pp. 8–15.

as to each state and territory whether it is entitled to receive its share of the annual appropriation for colleges, or of institutions for colored students under this act, and the amount which thereupon each is entitled, respectively, to receive . . . And the Secretary of the Interior is hereby charged with the proper administration of this law.

(Section 5) . . . the Secretary of the Interior shall annually report to Congress the disbursements which have been made in all the states and territories, and also whether the appropriation of any state or territory has been withheld, and if so, the reasons therefor.

The Secretary of the Interior delegated this task to the Commissioner of Education. It was in this way that the Office of Education found itself involved in the land-grant college program.[61] Harris immediately assumed the task Secretary John W. Noble had assigned him. He prepared a circular in the Secretary's name to the Governors of each State and Territory. This asked for information on existing schools, if they were segregated, what payments should be made, and so on. The circular was mailed on September 22, 1890. Four months later, January 19, 1891, an additional circular was mailed to the college and university presidents of institutions involved. This asked for information on how much money had been received under the Morrill Act of 1890, how it had been delegated or spent, and for what the remainder was to be used.[62] In addition to these actions, Harris caused detailed reports on land-grant colleges to be prepared and made a part of the annual reports.

As a direct result of the Second Morrill Act the Office of Education received its first specialist in the field of higher education. The statistician appointed in 1872 had dealt with statistics of all types in education but on March 2, 1895, funds were appropriated for the appointment of a clerk who would spend his full time working with the reports received from land-grant colleges and universities. The first person appointed to fill this position was Wellford Addis who was appointed a "Clerk of Class 4" to work in the agricultural college area.[63] He was succeeded by Frederick E. Upton in 1902 who was appointed "Specialist in Charge of Land-grant College Statistics." From the time of the

---

[61] Hollis P. Allen, *The Federal Government and Education* (New York, 1950), p. 189; Smith, *op cit.*, pp. 4–5.

[62] (U.S. Office of Education), *Commissioner of Education . . . 1887–1907*, Harris, "Statement," 1891, pp. 14–18.

[63] 28 Stat. L., 764, 798, March 2, 1895; National Advisory Committee on Education, *Federal Relations to Education* (Washington, 1931), II, p. 404; Biographical sketches of Addis and Upton in Appendix I, *infra*.

initial appointment there was a specialist devoted to work in land-grant statistics.[64]

Early in his seventeen-year tenure, Harris expressed his views on higher education. In his first *Report* he prepared a commentary on the fact that the colleges stressed the classics while public secondary schools were emphasizing more and more the "modern" subjects such as literature, natural science, geography, and so forth. Consequently the modern high schools were weaker in classical studies than the old type and students were finding the jump from them to college more difficult to make. As a solution, prep schools were developed to make the transition easier. Harris did not find this entirely satisfactory. He hoped that colleges would swing away from classics into more of the modern subjects. Thus, he wrote, "an inestimable advantage" would "accrue to the people." [65]

In September 1890 he wrote words of praise for the series of historical studies started by Commissioner Dawson:

> National education does not begin, as is sometimes supposed, with primary education, but with higher education. The first education was that of the princes and the clergy. Finally, the diffusion of the democratic ideas contained in Christianity makes education a gift to all men. The history of higher education in the several States affords the needed clew [sic] to the beginning of our present widely extended system of common schools. The publication of that history by this Bureau is having an excellent practical effect for good, for it is doing much to secure the necessary co-operation of the large body of highly cultured and influential men who hold in their hands the education of colleges and universities, and who are, by the very nature of the work they have in hand, somewhat skeptical in regard to the usefulness of higher institutions or bureaus that are directly controlled by the State or National Governments, it being supposed that party politics makes such governmental control uncertain in its policy and liable to be influenced by other than disinterested motives.[66]

Obviously, the fourth Commissioner was interested in higher education to some extent, demanding that its curriculum be made more practical, and that it play a more active role in the demo-

---

[64] See (U. S. Office of Education), *Commissioner of Education . . . 1887–1907*, Harris and Brown, "Statements," 1895, p. 26; 1896, p. 30; 1897, p. 34; 1898, p. 31; 1899, p. 46; 1900, p. 48; 1901, p. 44; 1902, p. 40; 1903, p. 38; 1904, p. 39; and 1906, p. 39.

[65] William T. Harris, *Report of the Commissioner of Education for the Year 1888–89* (Washington, 1891), I, pp. liv–lix (Quotation from p. lvii).

[66] (U.S. Office of Education), *Commissioner of Education . . . 1887–1907*, Harris, "Statement," 1889–90, p. 7.

cratic life of the common man. In this Harris was reflecting, or perhaps helping to formulate, the demands of the closing years of the Nineteenth Century. It was an age of expansion in higher education and Harris, as the chief national spokesman for education, was expressing the view held by many Americans that higher education was not something to be confined to the clergy and the sons of the "well born." Higher education, if it were to serve democracy well, should provide an opportunity for the competent men and women of all social strata to develop as far as they could.

Although Harris did not introduce any startling innovations in his official writings, he made certain that the annual reports and statements contained full coverage of higher education statistics. Under Dawson the policy of an annual *Statement* had been started to serve as a brief pre-*Report* digest of developments for the Secretary of the Interior and other interested persons. This was continued until 1921 when Commissioner Tigert abandoned the practice. Harris made it his practice to include summary statistical tables in his statements. Meanwhile, he made the *Report* a two-volume affair often running 2,000 or more pages. The first volume was devoted largely to articles and essays on education and educational trends, and the second to statistics. Approximately half of Volume I consisted of reports of education in foreign lands but there were several articles and studies on higher education.[67]

At the time Harris came into office it was the practice to supply figures on seven different topics: colleges and universities (liberal arts), colleges for women, schools of science, commercial and business schools, normal schools, professional schools, and the number of degrees conferred. Harris introduced a new table in his *Report* for 1888–89. This was a list of the courses of study in various institutions. As in the treatment of the other items, the approach was not interpretive or analytical. It was a purely statistical summary. However, it did demonstrate a growing interest in curriculum on the part of the Federal Government.[68] Also, after the passage of the Second Morrill Act in 1890, Harris made tables on agricultural and mechanical colleges part of his statements and reports.

Like other Commissioners Harris spent a good deal of time and effort trying to get college professors and administrators to prepare studies and essays for his reports. In this he was successful. Studies prepared by college and university officials were respected by those who would consult them. Of course, the small size of the

---

[67] Rodeheaver, *op. cit.*, p. 105; for titles of appendices see Appendix III, *infra.*

[68] Harris, *op. cit.*, II, pp. 1071–1361, 1368–1378.

Office of Education staff made it impossible for them to prepare such publications without outside assistance. It would be pointless to list the large number of contributors but examples picked at random include in the 1893–94 *Report* papers by the President of Rutgers College (University), New Brunswick, New Jersey, and a Professor from Berlin University, Germany, and in 1903 a chapter written by President Thwing of Western Reserve University, Cleveland, Ohio. Whenever possible the Commissioner obtained the assistance of the most widely accepted authority. This gave weight to the publications they would not otherwise have had.[69]

Counting the historical studies and appendices to the reports some 140 publications relating to higher education appeared from 1890 through 1906. They covered a wide variety of subject matter. There was a sharp increase in the number of studies relating to curriculum problems and developments, and an equally significant increase in the number of studies relating to special types of institutions of higher education.[70] This is an indication of the interest in the increasing specialization taking place in institutions of higher education.

Harris resigned as Commissioner effective at the end of fiscal year 1906. The resignation was probably prompted by failing health and an offer of the highest possible retiring allowance ($3,000 per year) that the Carnegie Foundation for the Advancement of Teaching could grant.[71] He retired to Providence, Rhode Island, where he died on November 5, 1909.

A student of administration who later made a careful analysis of the Office of Education wrote that Harris "displayed a degree of indifference with regard to administrative detail." Also, "Dr. Harris takes rank to-day as one of the Nation's great educational leaders, but his abilities did not extend to the management of administrative machinery. His successor, therefore, faced the task of administrative rehabilitation." [72]

Although correct to say that Harris did not contribute to the administrative growth of the organization he headed so long, his years as Commissioner show achievement in the field of higher

---

[69] See William T. Harris, *Report of the Commissioner of Education for the Year 1893–94* (Washington, 1896), Volumes I & II; and William T. Harris, *Report of the Commissioner of Education for the Year 1903* (Washington, 1905), I, pp. xxix–xxxi, Chap. V.

[70] Table 11, Chapter VI, shows the breakdown by type of publication. Appendix III lists titles chronologically and gives publication information.

[71] Evans and Wright, *op. cit.*, p. 52; Smith, *op. cit.*, p. 15.

[72] Smith, *op. cit.*, pp. 14–15.

education. In addition to the appointment of a full-time specialist in land-grant statistical work, Harris promoted several publications of value in higher education, nearly two and one-half times as many as all his predecessors combined. Under his guidance the historical study series was completed. Standardized statistical programs for higher education, including land-grant colleges, were developed and the administration of the 1890 Act successfully implemented. Harris showed that he was aware of the current trends in institutions of higher education and his personal prestige, as well as the prestige of those he induced to write for him, enhanced the reputation of the Office of Education.

The fifth Commissioner of Education was Elmer Ellsworth Brown (1861–1934) who took office on July 1, 1906. Brown was born in Chatauqua County, New York, on August 28, 1861. He graduated from Illinois State Normal University in 1881, received an A.B. from the University of Michigan in 1889, and a Ph.D. from the University of Halle-Wittenberg, Germany, in 1890. From then on his career was devoted to education as a profession. After serving as a teacher and principal in schools in Illinois and Michigan, Brown entered college work in 1892 as acting Assistant Professor of the Science and Art of Teaching, University of Michigan. Following a brief stay in Michigan he became Associate Professor, later Professor, of the Theory and Practice of Education at the University of California. He was still at California when appointed Commissioner by President Theodore Roosevelt.[73]

Commissioner Brown had a more extensive background in higher education than any of his predecessors and most of those who were to succeed him. But even though he had been in college teaching for fourteen years his work had been in the preparation of teachers for work in elementary and secondary schools. His immediate concern was not college curriculums and administration but education as applied to lower grades. However, Brown had served in higher education long enough to have an awareness of the trends and problems faced by colleges and universities on the threshold of the Twentieth Century.

Brown lacked the international reputation of Harris but he was

[73] Theodore F. Jones, "Elmer Ellsworth Brown," in *Dictionary of American Biography*, XXI, pp. 124–125; Walter Miller, "Elmer Ellsworth Brown, the New Commissioner of Education," *Southern Educational Review*, III, No. 7, November 1906, pp. 73–78; Evans and Wright, *op. cit.*, p. 53; *Who's Who in America*, XVIII, p. 406; Ford, *op. cit.*, pp. 69–70; *Elmer Ellsworth Brown, August 28, 1861–November 3, 1934* (New York, 1935); Jacques Cattell and E. F. Ross (ed), *Leaders in Education* (Lancaster, Pennsylvania, 1932), pp. 121–122; and Wright, *op. cit.*, pp. 54–55.

a more practical administrator. "In the passing of Dr. Harris as Commissioner, we left behind philosophical speculation and rational psychology, and turned more directly to a scientific method of fact-gathering by the Bureau." [74] His first task as he saw it was to increase the size of the Office so that it could widen and deepen the scope of its activities. In seventeen years under Harris the total appropriation for salaries had risen less than $9,000. Largely through his efforts, Brown saw them increase $12,000 in five years and a growth of approximately $7,000 for 1912 was largely due to his efforts although he was no longer in office.[75] Appropriations for 1905 totaled $99,941; in 1910 they were $122,200.[76] His own salary was increased from $4,000 to $4,500 and later to $5,000.[77] Larger appropriations made it possible to raise salaries, increase the staff, and improve on the publications program.

When Brown took office the staff of 51 persons were organized into five divisions: Statistics, Correspondence and Records, Editorial, Library, and Alaska. The latter had been added by Harris to deal with the growing complexity of supervision and operation of Education in Alaska, a responsibility of the Interior Department since 1884. The Division of International Exchange had ceased to exist under Harris, probably around 1903 when its functions had been absorbed by other divisions.[78]

There were three activities in higher education of particular interest to Brown. One was the establishment and operation of a national university. Another was the promotion of agricultural and technical subjects in colleges and universities, similar to the ideas Harris had advocated concerning a more practical curricula. Finally, Brown wanted an expansion of the research and dissemination activity.[79]

The five annual reports and statements prepared while Brown was in office (fiscal years 1906 through 1910) show, on one hand, a tendency to follow patterns established by his predecessors and, on the other, a more acute awareness of the problems of higher

---

[74] Ford, op. cit., p. 69.

[75] Rodeheaver, op. cit., pp. 116–117; Evans and Wright, op. cit., p. 53.

[76] Figures supplied by Mrs. Genevieve Dane, Assistant Budget Management Officer, Office of Education, from material in Budget Management Office files.

[77] Evans and Wright, op. cit., p. 53.

[78] Elmer E. Brown, Report of the Commissioner of Education for the Year Ending June 30, 1907 (Washington, 1908), I, p. 2; Smith, op. cit., pp. 5–7; (U. S. Office of Education), Commissioner of Education . . . 1887–1907, Harris, "Statements," 1902, pp. 40–41; 1903, pp. 38–39.

[79] Elmer E. Brown, "Educational Interests at Washington," Science, XXXIX, No. 998, February 13, 1914, pp. 239–246.

education in a fast-moving modern world. For example, his 1906 *Statement* contains the usual statistical tables and reports of agricultural and mechanical colleges. But in that same paper he issued what may be termed the first call for a specialist in higher education. In speaking of "lines of advance" to be followed in the future:

> Particularly in its relations with the agricultural and mechanical colleges subsidized by the National Government under the provisions of the act of Congress on August 30, 1890, this Bureau should render available to each of these institutions such information relating to the best methods of organization, experiment, and instruction as may be gathered from the experience of other institutions of similar character either at home or abroad.[80]

In order to accomplish this objective, an objective which fitted in with his desire to promote agricultural and technical subjects and take a more active role in research and dissemination of information, a full-time specialist would be required.

In the 1909 *Statement* Brown noted there was a need for "the addition of competent experts in higher education . . . with a sufficient force of clerical assistants." [81] There were, he observed elsewhere, three specialists already at work in the Office of Education: one was in land-grant college statistics; another in foreign educational systems; and a third in (American) educational systems.[82]

In 1910 he wrote: ". . . More and more it becomes clear that the activity of such specialists [as already existed in the Office], both in the collection and in the diffusion of information, can best be accomplished through visits to educational institutions, offices, and conventions in different parts of the country." [83]

By the time he wrote these words Brown had already obtained approval for a specialist in higher education. This approval and the selection of the specialist will be treated more fully in Chapter II. But the comments he made show his continuing concern over the need for specialized help. More and more specialization was required if the Office of Education was to "promote the cause of education throughout the country." It was this perception, coupled

---

[80] (U. S. Office of Education), *Commissioner of Education . . . 1887–1907*, Brown, "Statement," 1906, p. 42.

[81] Elmer E. Brown, *Statement of the Commissioner of Education . . . 1909* (Washington, 1909), p. 14.

[82] Elmer E. Brown, *Report of the Commissioner of Education for the Year Ended June 30, 1909* (Washington, 1909), I, pp. 248–249.

[83] Elmer E. Brown, *Report of the Commissioner of Education for the Fiscal Year Ended June 30, 1910* (Washington, 1910), I, p. 3.

with his constructive innovations, that made him one of the most capable of our educational administrators.[84]

Among the most important of his constructive innovations was obtaining authority for, and appointing, the first specialist in higher education. With this appointment the story of the Division of Higher Education properly begins.

[84] For concise and highly laudatory commentary on Brown's administrative ability see "A Minute of the Meeting of the Council of New York University, January 28, 1935" in *Elmer Ellsworth Brown*, p. 32.

CHAPTER II

# The Formative Years
# (1911–1916)

## The Division is Established

Beginnings are often elusive. It is hard to locate a point in history and say "Here this movement began." This is certainly the case with the Division of Higher Education.

The movement for a specialist started long before 1910. It has been noted that there was a specialist working in land-grant college statistics as early as 1895. This was a forerunner, a portent of what was to come; but was not the type needed in the Twentieth Century. The land-grant specialist often had to be a jack-of-all-trades. As late as the middle of 1909 the Commissioner confessed to a candidate for this office: "It is possible that at times it may be necessary to ask you to assist in some of the work of the Bureau." [1]

This position necessitated by the Second Morrill Act was a far cry from what many educators felt was needed for any positive higher educational program within the Office of Education. In 1901, for example, Nicholas Murray Butler called for an expansion of activity which envisioned more analytical and interpretive work than heretofore.[2] Commissioner Brown held to substantially the same belief and repeatedly requested a specialist who would contribute something other than statistical tables and reports.[3] In 1907, he wrote:

---

[1] Ltr., Clerk to the Commissioner of Education to Mr. James E. McClintock, University of Maine, June 24, 1909. (McClintock's Personnel Folder, St. Louis Records Center, St. Louis, Missouri).

[2] Nicholas M. Butler, "The Future of the Bureau of Education," *Educational Review*, XXI, No. 5, May 1901, pp. 526–529.

[3] This has been noted in Chapter I, *supra*. See also Elmer E. Brown, *Report of the Commissioner of Education for the Year Ended June 30, 1908* (Washington, 1908), I, pp. 2–3.

A specialist in higher education is needed to deal with certain special relations of the Bureau with universities and professional schools . . . The Bureau of Education was established expressly "for the purpose of * * * diffusing such information * * * as shall * * * promote the cause of education throughout the country." In pursuance of this purpose, one of the things urgently needed at this time is that it should facilitate the cooperation of these higher institutions. And to that end it requires the special services of a man of university standing in the position that I have proposed.[4]

Brown was in close touch with college and university problems. He understood, probably better than any of his predecessors, the efforts being made to standardize American higher degrees and therefore he urged the establishment of a division to act as a clearing house for the collection and dissemination of information that would further this objective. The longer he was in office, the more clearly he saw the urgent necessity for a positive, active role in higher education.[5]

Others shared similar opinions. Mr. H. R. Linville made a strong case for a Department of Education in 1909 thereby voicing the opinion of many that Washington take a more active role in education on all levels.[6] On the other hand, the Office of Education was opposed by forces that stood against any expansion of activity as an encroachment on State and local rights. These forces proved the more powerful until 1910.[7]

In the final analysis it was the changing college situation, more than anything else, that made the appointment of a specialist inevitable. It has been estimated that in 1870 there were slightly more than 52,000 Americans enrolled in 563 institutions of higher education. Based upon total population 13 of every 10,000 were college students. Less than 10,000 bachelor degrees were granted and only one earned doctorate in a research field was reported.

---

[4] (U. S. Office of Education), *Commissioner of Education, Department of the Interior, Annual Statement, 1887–1907* (Washington, 1887 *et seq.*), Brown's "Statement," 1907, p. 17.

[5] cf. I. M. Wright, "History of the United States Bureau of Education," (New York, 1916, typewritten ms.), p. 66; Brown, *op. cit.*, pp. 17–18; Elmer E. Brown, *Statement of the Commissioner of Education to the Secretary of the Interior for the Fiscal Year Ended June 30, 1910* (Washington, 1910), p. 3.

[6] Henry R. Linville, "National Leadership in Education," *Science*, XXX, No. 78, December 17, 1909, pp. 878–879.

[7] L. E. Blauch, "United States Office of Education" in Walter S. Monroe (ed), *Encyclopedia of Educational Research* (New York, 1950), p. 1496. See also Glen Edwards, "The Fight for the Bureau of Education," *Journal of Education*, LXXIII, No. 12, March 23, 1911, pp. 311–314; and Wright, *op. cit.*, pp. 62–64.

Thirty years later there were nearly a quarter of a million college students, 31 of every 10,000, and in 1910 there were 355,000 college students, 39 per 10,000. The number of bachelor degrees was increasing at a corresponding rate and in 1910, 443 doctorates were awarded in research areas.[8]

Thoughtful educators studied the move to college campuses, the swelling enrollments, and the healthy increase in the number of degrees granted on all levels. They realized that more attention must be paid to this phenomenon. Brown, drawing on his own observations and those of President Lowell of Harvard University, succinctly stated the case for a careful study of a stripling grown to giant size:

> President Lowell recently remarked that "the fact is we know very little about higher education. The whole subject is one that needs to be scientifically studied, and as yet it has received very little attention of that kind." But while this discussion has thrown much of our scholastic tradition into the melting pot, the process of remolding is going on. It lacks as yet in clear convication as to the changes which should be made. It can hardly be said that the assured and convincing leadership which is called for has yet appeared. There is need of more analytic study of the facts concerning our higher institutions, their endeavors and their performance, and still more need of constructive interpretation of those facts.[9]

Dr. John Dale Russell, who served as Director of the Division of Higher Education years later, listed three factors which were involved in the appointment of the specialist and the subsequent development of the division:

First, there was the increase in the number of colleges and universities and the growing number of students.

Second, colleges and universities were becoming increasingly complex and varied in their offerings. New courses were opening at a fast and furious rate and entire new programs of study were being developed. Students entering college were faced with a bewildering number of courses.[10] The days of the rigid classical

---

[8] See Table 4, *infra.* Statistical data are from sources listed beneath that table.

[9] Elmer E. Brown, *Report of the Commissioner of Education for the Year Ended June 30, 1910* (Washington, 1910), I, p. 5.

[10] Will Rogers spoke to an alumni group of Columbia University in 1924. In his speech he made some remarks about the number of courses available to undergraduates and, as usual, his wit contained considerable wisdom and truth: "There are thirty-two hundred courses. You spend your first two years in deciding what course to take, the next two years in finding the building that these courses are given in, and the rest of your life in wishing you had taken another course." Lewis Copeland, and Lawrence Lamm (ed), *The World's Great Speeches* (New York, 1958), p. 730.

TABLE 4.—*Historical Statistics Showing Growth of Higher Education to 1950*

| | Academic Year | | | | |
|---|---|---|---|---|---|
| | 1869–1870 | 1899–1900 | 1909–1910 | 1929–1930 | 1949–1950 |
| Number of institutions reporting _____ | 563 | 977 | 951 | 1,409 | 1,851 |
| Faculty (full-time & part-time) _____ | 5,553* | 23,868 | 36,480 | 82,386 | 246,722 |
| Total enrollment (Resident students, regular session) _____ | 52,286* | 237,592 | 355,213 | 1,100,737 | 2,659,021 |
| Total bachelor and first professional degrees awarded _____ | 9,371 | 27,410 | 37,199 | 122,484 | 432,058 |
| Total resident students to 100 of total population _____ | 0.13 | 0.31 | 0.39 | 0.90 | 1.79 |
| Institutions reporting earned doctorate degrees _____ | 1 | 38 | 37 | 74 | 130 |
| Total number of earned doctorates, 1870, 1900, 1930, 1950. (Not including professional or non-research degrees such as M.D., D.D.S., and J.D.) _____ | 1 | 382 | 443 | 2,299 | 6,633 |
| Cumulative total of earned doctorates through academic year shown _____ | 17 | 3,935 | 7,650 | 26,575 | 89,883 |

*Estimated figures.

(Compiled by author from Badger, H. G., "Higher Education Statistics 1870 to 1952," *Higher Education*, XI, No. 1, September 1954, pp. 10–15; Badger, H. G. *et al*, *Statistics of Higher Education: 1955–56. Faculty, Students and Degrees* (Washington, 1958), pp. 6–8; Eells, W. C., "Earned Doctorates in American Institutions of Higher Education," *Higher Education*, XII, No. 7, March 1956, pp. 109–114; cumulative total column compiled by author.)

curriculum were gone from many institutions and numbered in nearly all the rest holding out. Variety in curriculum offering was one thing; chaos quite another. Study was necessary to prevent the former from blurring into the latter.

Third, there was need for a national advisory group and a research body of some sort to help institutions make the optimum use of their facilities and to develop new programs of lasting value. There were no State bodies to deal with problems in higher education. Even if they had existed on a State or regional basis they would not have been able to cope with problems that were increasingly national in scope.[11]

The turning point in the effort of the Commissioner to get a higher education specialist came during the 1910 fiscal year. A small increase in the appropriation for the preceding year made it possible to pay traveling expenses for a "field force" to collect statistical information. This field force consisted of two men: the specialist in land-grant college statistics, and a newly appointed specialist in school administration. The efforts of these men were not sufficient to obtain all the information desired nor to prepare it in a useable format.[12] So in June 1910 the Congress approved Brown's request for a specialist to work in higher education thereby increasing the field force a full 50 per cent and, at the same time, obtaining the expert advice so badly needed in Office of Education higher education activities.[13] On July 1, 1910, President William Howard Taft signed Executive Order No. 1218 appointing "One specialist in higher education in the Bureau of Education." [14]

In his *Statement* for 1910 Brown showed his delight over the addition to his staff. At the same time he set forth a brief exposition of the duties he thought the new man should perform:

The Congress at its recent session provided for the employment in this office of a specialist in higher education at an annual salary of $3,000. Such a specialist has become an imperative need of the office because of the growing demand for information relating to standards of collegiate and professional education, the statistics and accounting systems of colleges and universities, cooperation in graduate studies, the opportunities afforded in this country for students from foreign countries, and many related questions. The new specialist will, moreover, visit colleges and universities in different parts of the country, conferring with their officers of administration and instruction, and will accordingly be a third member of the field force now in process of organization.[15]

[11] John D. Russell, "The Role of the Division of Higher Education of the United States Office of Education," *American Association of University Professors, Bulletin,* XXXIII, No. 3, Autumn 1947, pp. 432–433.

[12] Harlan Updegraff, "The United States Bureau of Education," *The American School Board Journal,* XLIV, No. 5, May 1972, pp. 13–15; Brown, *Statement . . . 1910,* p. 3.

[13] 32 Act of Congress approved June 17, 1910. See Walter C. Eells, *Surveys of American Higher Education* (New York, 1937), p. 33.

[14] A copy of this Executive Order is in Babcock's Personnel Folder, St. Louis Records Center, St. Louis, Missouri.

[15] Brown, *Statement . . . 1910,* p. 4.

A more detailed description of the duties the specialist would be called on to perform is given in Brown's *Report* for the same year. There were six different types of duties:

1. Collect and give out information concerning matters of common interest to our colleges and universities;

2. Improve the statistical and accounting procedures of those institutions;

3. Improve administration "to which statistics and accounting are tributary:"

4. Report and record information concerning academic and professional standards which may be required to answer inquiries from home and abroad;

5. Index current graduate studies in the United States to help further cooperation among graduate schools; and

6. Prepare such special studies and publications, and perform such other services as "may be found useful and practicable." [16]

While the new position represented a triumph of sorts for the Office of Education, it was not without some aspects that chilled the warm glow of victory.[17] Brown had requested ten specialists in a plan he had submitted to the Congress through the Secretary of the Interior. Congress had specifically granted only the one although providing funds for three others.[18] Also, the salary of $3,000 which the specialist was to receive annually did not represent any gain in appropriation. In 1909 the Office was moved from quarters it had been renting in the Wright Building, 8th and G Streets, Northwest, to a Federal building on the corner of 12th Street and Pennsylvania Avenue, Northwest.[19] This resulted in the saving of $4,000 in annual rent. So the Congress shifted the money to pay for the specialist and hire an additional clerk at $1,000.[20]

Permission granted and duties determined, the next step was to find a man suitable for the job. Brown set about this by writing to college and university officials asking for recommendations. Among those to whom he addressed inquiries were Dean James E. Russell, Teachers College, Columbia University; President Jacob

---

[16] Brown, *Report . . . 1910*, I, pp. 9–10.

[17] In a letter to Dean James E. Russell, Teachers College, Columbia University, June 13, 1910, Brown wrote "It is now practically certain that we shall get our $3,000 Specialist in Higher Education. This modest event marks an epoch in the history of the Bureau." (Babcock's Personnel Folder, St. Louis Records Center, St. Louis, Missouri.)

[18] D. H. Smith, *The Bureau of Education. Its History, Activities and Organization* (Baltimore, Md., 1923), p. 16.

[19] See Table 3, Preface, *supra*.

[20] Edwards, *op. cit.*, p. 313.

Gould Schurman, Cornell University; President Charles R. Van
Hise, University of Wisconsin; President Benjamin Wheeler,
University of California; President A. Lawrence Lowell, Harvard
University; President Arthur Hadley, Yale University; and
President Clark Sanford, Clark College.[21]

A large number of names were suggested by this distinguished
group. Brown narrowed the possibilities to twelve: Professor
James Angell, University of Chicago; Dr. George Fellows, ex-
President of the University of Maine; President James McLean,
University of Idaho; Dr. Frank Graves, Ohio State University;
President Kendric C. Babcock, University of Arizona; and seven
others.[22]

Wheeler studied the list of finalists and opined that "of all
those mentioned probably President Babcock is the one who
would give you the most real assistance. He is a very satisfactory
man; I have seen him lately and recognize that he has grown. He
was always, however, satisfactory in carrying out details of work
he had undertaken." [23] Hadley was in substantial agreement:
"Babcock I know but slightly, but my impressions of him are
very favorable indeed. All things considered, he seems to me the
best man on your list." [24]

Agreement was not unanimous. Lowell favored a man from an
Eastern university. His choice was President Sanford of Clark.[25]

On October 6, 1910, Brown offered Sanford his nomination for
the position, explaining that the Commissioner could only nominate and the Secretary of the Interior would make the appointment. Sanford had almost certainly made up his mind to reject
the position before the offer had been made. His letter declining
it was dated October 7 and the following day Commissioner Brown
offered the nomination to Babcock.[26]

Dear Doctor Babcock:
At its session of this year Congress has provided for the
employment in the Bureau of Education of a Specialist in
Higher Education at an annual salary of three thousand dollars. This is a notable step in more ways than one. The salary,

---

[21] These letters from Brown are from Babcock's Personnel Folder, St. Louis
Records Center, St. Louis, Missouri: Russell, June 13, 1910; Schurman,
September 15, 1910; Lowell, September 14, 1910; Hadley, September 15,
1910; and Sanford, October 6, 1910.

[22] *Ibid.*, Ltr. Babcock to Schurman, September 15, 1910.

[23] *Ibid.*, Ltr. Wheeler to Brown, September 29, 1910.

[24] *Ibid.*, Ltr., Hadley to Brown, September 16, 1910.

[25] *Ibid.*, Ltr., Lowell to Brown, September 20, 1910.

[26] *Ibid.*, Ltrs., Brown to Sanford, October 6, 1910; Sanford to Brown,
October 7, 1910.

while modest enough, is higher than has ever before been provided for any member of the staff of this Office excepting the Commissioner. It marks, moreover, the beginning of the new movement for building up in the Bureau a corps of competent experts in different Branches of American education. It will enable the Office to take up the rather fragmentary and amateurish information service which it has been rendering to institutions of higher education, and put it upon something like a scientific basis. I am now looking for a man for the place. The $3,000 salary calls imperatively for a $10,000 man. My only hope of success in such a venture lies in the fact that the position offers something more than a salary. It presents an opportunity of doing work of national importance.

The position is to be filled irrespective of civil service regulations, by appointment of the Secretary of the Interior on the nomination of the Commissioner of Education. I am writing now to ask you directly if I may nominate you for the position.

My reasons for offering the place to you, aside from our warm personal relations, are, first, that I believe you are especially well fitted by training and experience to fill it creditably and usefully; secondly, that although the salary is relatively small I believe the position would afford you an opportunity for doing such work as you might like to do next in the making of your career in life; and, thirdly, that some of my advisers have also spoken of you warmly in connection with the position, particularly Presidents Hadley and Wheeler.

 *  *  *  *  *  *  *

. . . If you are disposed to consider it, I should be glad to know how soon your definite answer might reasonably be expected.
  With cordial greeting,
   I am, believe me,
     Very sincerely yours,
     (signed) Elmer E. Brown [27]

A week later Babcock accepted and announced he would leave Arizona in December. He spoke of the "very high honor" the Commissioner had conferred on him and said the "chance to justify your judgment of me, your confidence in me, will be a real and abiding inspiration." [28]

Babcock was able to get away from Arizona earlier than planned and was sworn in as the first specialist in higher education on November 9, 1910.[29] This completed "a definite step toward organization of the Bureau on a professional basis." [30]

[27] *Ibid.*, Ltr., Brown to Babcock, October 8, 1910.

[28] *Ibid.*, Ltr., Babcock to Brown, October 15, 1910; Telegram, Chief Clerk Kalbach to Brown, October 15, 1910. Quotation from letter.

[29] *Ibid.*, Oath of Office, November 9, 1910, sworn November 12, 1910.

[30] Charles H. Judd, *Research in the United States Office of Education* (Washington, 1939), p. 47. A biographical sketch of Babcock will be found in Appendix I, *infra*. At this point it should be observed that brief biographi-

A second step came within three months. On February 3, 1911, the Division of Higher Education was created by an Office order. The specialist was made chief of the division. The role that the division was to play was briefly described by Dr. Philander P. Claxton who succeeded Brown as Commissioner in the summer of 1911.

> This division was created by an order of February 3, 1911, and the specialist in higher education who entered upon duty in November, 1910, was appointed chief of the division which has "charge of all matters, including statistical work, relating to higher education, agricultural and mechanical colleges, professional schools, and normal schools, and such other duties as may be formally assigned to it from time to time, or which would naturally fall to it in the ordinary course of the work of this office." To this division were assigned those persons who have hitherto had charge of the routine work upon the reports, catalogues, and publications of these institutions, and also the specialist in charge of land-grant college statistics.[31]

Numerically, the new division was not impressive. It consisted of but two professionals, the specialist in higher education, and the specialist in land-grant college statistics, with such clerical assistance as they required.[32]

The appointment of the specialist in higher education and the establishment of the division may well have been Brown's crowning achievement. Certainly, these events were among the last to occur in his administration. In early 1911 he received an offer to become Chancellor of New York University. He resigned the Washington position effective June 30. The new career was to be longer and even more successful for he was to serve as Chancellor of New York University for 22 years during which time that institution grew in physical and academic stature. He retired in 1933 and died on November 3, 1934.[33]

---

cal sketches of all professional personnel who have been determined to have had any significant association with the Division of Higher Education from 1911 to 1953, and sketches of others who played a part in higher education activities prior to 1911, are in this appendix. The arrangement of names is alphabetical except for those seven men who served as chief of the division during the period under consideration and who are listed first.

[31] Philander P. Claxton, *Statement of the Commissioner of Education to the Secretary of the Interior for the Fiscal Year Ended June 30, 1911* (Washington, 1911), p. 3; and Smith, *op. cit.*, p. 31.

[32] Claxton, *op. cit.*, p. 3.

[33] *Elmer Ellsworth Brown, August 28, 1861–November 3, 1934* (New York, 1935); Theodore F. Jones, "Elmer Ellsworth Brown," in *Dictionary of American Biography* (New York, 1928 et seq.), XXI, pp. 124–125; and H. R. Evans, and E. A. Wright, "The United States Office of Education" (Washington, 1939, typewritten ms.), p. 55.

## The Development of an Active Program

During the years from 1911 to 1916 the pattern of divisional activities was determined. This six year span saw the development of nearly all the important functions it was eventually to perform. This was possible because of the vigorous support given by the Commissioner of Education, the hard work of the professional staff, and the demand for help and advice in many institutions of higher education across the Nation.

The sixth Commissioner of Education was Philander Priestley Claxton (1862–1957). He was born in Bedford County, Tennessee, on September 28, 1862, and received his B.A. degree from the University of Tennessee in 1882. This period of formal education was followed by two years of teaching and school administrative work in North Carolina.

In 1884 Claxton entered John Hopkins Graduate School. His intention had been to study electrical engineering but he abandoned this to study education under Dr. G. Stanley Hall. In 1885, and again in 1896, he went abroad to study foreign educational systems. From 1886 to 1893 he served as a school superintendent in North Carolina and in the latter year was appointed professor of pedagogy at the newly established State Normal and Industrial College, Greensboro, North Carolina. In 1902 Claxton was made professor of education, and head of the Department of Education, at the University of Tennessee, Knoxville. Honorary degrees of Litt. D. and LL. D. were conferred on him by Bates College and Western Reserve University in 1906 and 1912. Claxton was at Tennessee when President Taft appointed him Commissioner. He entered on duty July 8, 1911.[34]

The new Commissioner was primarily interested in the promotion of elementary and secondary school education, particularly in rural communities, when he took office. But he did not let this interest divert his attention from the need for expanded activity in many areas. He planned a reorganization for the improvement of all services of the Office.

It was . . . during the administration of Dr. P. P. Claxton (1911–21) that real expansion took place, resulting in a permanent professional staff attached to the Washington office which

---

[34] C. L. Lewis, *Philander Priestley Claxton, Crusader for Public Education* (Knoxville, Tenn., 1948); Evans and Wright, *op. cit.*, pp. 58–66; Wright, *op. cit.*, pp. 70–72; *Who's Who in America*, XVI, p. 528; T. B. Ford, "The Educational Contributions of the U.S. Commissioners of Education, 1867–1928" (Washington, 1933, typewritten ms.), pp. 77–78; and "Office of Education and the Commissioners of Education," File of material in Education library, Department of Health, Education, and Welfare Library.

represented education in its varied fields. Dr. Claxton conceived of the Bureau of Education as a center of educational leadership, Nation-wide in extent, and encompassing all of the varied aspects which make up a comprehensive program of education.[35]

During the time Dr. Claxton was in office the number of professional staff members of the Division of Higher Education increased to three. This does not constitute a crowd but the growth was significant of Claxton's interest in higher educational studies and work.[36] One student who made a study of the administrative development of the Office of Education said of Claxton: "With the possible exception of Studebaker, no commissioner since John Eaton has tried so hard to build up the Office of Education. From the beginning to the end of his ten-year term he worked to enlarge and expand the Bureau." [37]

Claxton repeatedly made requests for additional specialists of nearly all kinds and requested higher salaries for his people.[38] Appropriations for the operation of the Office rose from $122,200 in 1910 to $307,629 in 1920.[39] Although the First World War stimulated appropriations, Claxton's efforts were an important contribution to the struggle for funds. Larger appropriations made possible better salaries, more travel, a richer publications program, and a larger staff.

In his first *Report* Claxton showed his awareness of the need for increased activity in higher education.

Much remains to be done in higher education also. Of the four or five millions of young men and women of college age in the country, only about 200,000, or about 5 per cent, are doing college work in standard institutions. Less than 2 per cent do the full four years' work and take a degree. The best interests of the civic and industrial life of the country demand that a

[35] cf. Lewis, *op. cit.*, p. 172; Evans and Wright, *op. cit.*, p. 65; and Judd, *op. cit.*, pp. 47–48. Quotation from Judd, p. 47.

[36] Table 10, Chapter VI, *infra.*, shows the number of professional employees in the Division of Higher Education for the period from fiscal year 1911 to fiscal year 1953.

[37] J. N. Rodeheaver, Jr., "The Relation of the Federal Government to Civic Education" (Cambridge, Mass., 1951, typewritten ms.), p. 119.

[38] See, for example, Philander P. Claxton, *Statement of the Commissioner of Education to the Secretary of the Interior for the Fiscal Year Ended June 30, 1912* (Washington, 1912), pp. 17–18; and Philander P. Claxton, *Statement of the Commissioner of Education to the Secretary of the Interior for the Fiscal Year Ended June 30, 1913* (Washington, 1913), p. 19.

[39] Appropriation figures supplied by Mrs. Genevieve Dane, Assistant Budget Management Officer, Office of Education, from material in Budget Management Office files, Office of Education. See Table 8, Chapter VI, *infra.*, for other appropriation figures.

larger per cent of its citizens should have the preparation for
leadership and direction of affairs which the colleges are supposed to give.[40]

What, specifically, remained to be done? In 1914 he pubished
an article in the *Colorado School Journal* which listed the things
the Office of Education was to do to further educational progress.
Among them were the following: serve as a clearing house of
information on education; make careful studies of educational
systems; give expert advice and opinion on education at all levels;
serve as a meeting ground for all educational agencies; serve as a
point of contact between the United States and other countries;
and cooperate with other educational groups in working out better
and higher ideals of education. The most immediate demand in
higher education was to work out "a more effective correlation
between the units of the systems of higher education in the several
states." [41] This was to be accomplished in a variety of ways;
through reports, studies, surveys, statistical publications, meetings, and consultative visits.

During the formative years the Division of Higher Education
began the performance of those duties which were to be the heart
of its routine operations throughout the next four decades. Since
these duties set the pattern for, or developed into, recurring
operations a discussion of them at this place will prevent needless
repetition. They may be classified in four categories much as
Claxton arranged them in his 1912 *Statement.*[42]

First were the routine statistical operations. The Division of
Higher Education was deeply involved in collection of statistical
information. The compilation of recurring statistical information
was the responsibility of the Statistical Division but special
statistical studies, and the utilization of statistics for special reports and studies, was the task of the Division of Higher Education. It helped the Statistical Division gather data relating to
colleges, universities, theological schools, professional schools, and
normal schools. These data were used for the annual reports and
statements and after 1917 they became chapters in the *Biennial
Survey of Education.* They were also utilized by the Division of
Higher Education in preparing special studies.

Gathering this information presented problems to both divisions
throughout the thirty year period following 1910. These problems

---

[40] Philander P. Claxton, *Report of the Commissioner of Education for the
Year Ended June 30, 1911* (Washington, 1912), I, p. xv.

[41] Philander P. Claxton, "The National Bureau of Education," *Colorado
School Journal*, XXIX, No. 7, March 1914, pp. 18–20.

[42] Claxton, *Statement . . . 1912*, pp. 3–4.

were largely the result of a lack of cooperation by many college administrators in supplying data. This lack of cooperation existed on other educational levels as well but to a lesser degree. It was not until the latter part of the 1930's that this resistance disappeared in higher education, long after it had completely disappeared from the ranks of elementary and secondary educators.[43]

---

[43] Lester B. Herlihy, "For Mr. Lykes' Use in Connection with the Historical Record . . ." (handwritten document on statistical development), December 1959. Mr. Herlihy has prepared a capsule history of the problem of statistical compilation and has also captured a story in his paper, part of which is reproduced here.

". . . Under Dr. William John Cooper, U. S. Commissioner of Education from 1929 to 1933, the first step was taken to achieve a practical working basis for implementing the efforts thus far made by the Office in conjunction with other outside national organizations, e. g., such as the U. S. Census Bureau, the National Education Association, the National Association of Public School Business Officials, and Committees composed of Professional Personnel from State Departments of Education, when this U. S. Commissioner of Education prevailed upon Congress to grant funds, specifically, for this promotional field work.

"As a result of the granting of these funds personnel with experience in educational teaching and administration and specially qualified in financial accounting and educational statistics were employed through Civil Service Com'n Examinations for this type of promotional work, as well as to prepare the data collected for publication as Chapters in the Biennial Survey of Education, and for special current data studies." [These persons were part of the Statistical Division, not of the Division of Higher Education].

"The writer was appointed by Dr. Cooper to the position of Assistant Educationist (Statistician in Education) in May of 1931. The work of promoting uniformity in the recording, reporting, and accounting of educational statistics had been initiated some years earlier, and he was the successor to numerous personnel who had filled the position for brief periods . . .

"The writer was allocated as his territory the States of New England, the North Atlantic section, Maryland, Delaware, and the District of Columbia. The start was made on this field work early in October, 1932, and extended to June, 1933. The questionnaires which we had prepared for the use by schools in reporting data on all levels of education covered the 1931–32 school year. The data were for publication as chapters of the *Biennial Survey of Education, 1930–32*."

\*　　\*　　\*　　\*　　\*　　\*　　\*

"Thus charged with this responsibility the writer reached Boston, Mass., as the starting point from which to radiate in covering the multiplicity of schools in and about the 'Hub of Culture.' As this field work was a new venture for the writer, he decided to test it out on the oldest, and admittedly most important institution of higher learning in the United States, if not the Universe, viz., Harvard University. To this end, and in line with standard procedure approved by the U. S. Office of Education, a post card signed by the U. S. Commissioner giving my name and the time I would visit the school was addressed to the school's president. The card of course also stated in brief the purpose of the intended visit with the request that as a repre-

Second of the recurring operations was the preparation and publication of special bulletins, circulars, and other materials. Claxton planned an annual bulletin giving segregated statistics of State universities and other institutions of higher education partially supported by the State. Work on this bulletin was begun

---

sentative of the U. S. Office, I should be accorded the cooperation necessary to fill my mission.

"I presented myself at the Administrative Offices of Harvard University according to schedule, and the Assistant to the President, Mr. Honeywell to whom I submitted credentials, told me that I was expected and that the President, Dr. Lawrence Lowell, had instructed him to have me wait until he (Dr. Lowell) ended his meeting with the Deans of Colleges. He wished to speak to me personally regarding the requested Harvard report. In fact, the instructions left by Dr. Lowell for Mr. Honeywell precluded any other course than my remaining on the campus until the Doctor had spoken with me. My schedule for visiting the Boston area schools was a tight one since the schools were many, the allotted time short, the terrain strange, and the transportation facilities not too good.

"So as 10—15—-20 minutes ticked away while I cooled my heels in Mr. Honeywell's office I became impatient and expressed the same in explaining that I was on a time schedule, and accountable to the Federal Gov't for all time consumed on my trip, etc. Could I return for the interview at the President's pleasure? No! I was to wait, if you please.

"So another 20 minutes elapsed when I rose and stated I would be back and take my chances in meeting the President later in the day, for I was scheduled at another school as of that moment. There was general consternation among the President's Personnel, particularly Mr. Honeywell, who in much stress appealed to Lowell's personal secretary, an elderly peppering lady, to take him 'off the hook' by communicating to the Doctor my intention to leave unless seen at once. The good lady went into the faculty hall where Dr. Lowell was conducting his meeting with Deans of Colleges, and immediately thereafter, these dignitaries came filing out of the hall. Thereupon I was conducted into The Presence.

"Dr. Lowell, a rather superannuated physical specimen (he was I believe, in his eighties then) immediately launched into a lengthy lecture on the uselessness of the Federal Bureaucracy, the extravagance of government, the inefficiency of its operation, the effrontery of an agency like the U.S. Office of Education in requesting an institution such as Harvard to prepare a report for submission for any purpose whatever.

"During this diatribe I stood at respectful attention, although for the greater part of the time of this lecture, I believe the old man was oblivious of my presence. I represented, if anything at all, an object to which he could direct his indignation, scorn, and the resentment he so keenly felt and expressed toward the policy of any Federal agency in demanding and requesting his cooperation.

"Finally after some thirty minutes of this peripatetic scolding—for he strutted (not too vigorously) back and forth while delivering his harrangue —he stopped abruptly, faced me, and almost in a shout—tho' it was a feeble, pathetic effort, ordered that I go back to Washington and tell the U. S. Office of Education administrators and professional personnel to pack up their effects and go back to wherever they originated for the country did not need

and it became an annual affair. Claxton also planned several other publications, among them a pamphlet on "Federal laws, regulations, and rulings affecting the land-grant colleges of agriculture and mechanic arts," and a circular classifying universities and colleges with reference to the bachelor's degree. The former was greeted with approbation when it appeared; but the latter had a mixed reception as will be shown later.[44]

The publication program in higher education upon which the Office of Education embarked was more varied and more comprehensive than that of the previous years. This reflects no discredit on the accomplishments of the staff prior to 1911 but it does clearly show that with full-time professional personnel available to prepare and edit studies of higher education a better program became possible. In the forty-four years from 1867 through 1910, 218 publications appeared relating to higher education; during the forty-three years from 1911 through 1953 there were 576. This represents an increase of more than 160 per cent. The changes which occurred in the publication program after the establishment of the Division of Higher Education will be noted in Chapter VI.[45] Not all were the work of members of the division but most of them owe something to the professional staff in the way of stimulation, editing, or general supervision.

Third recurring activity was the supervision of finances and administration of land-grant colleges as they related to Federal funds, i. e. the acts of 1862, 1890 and 1907 (and the later Bankhead-Jones Act of 1935). During fiscal year 1912 forty institutions were visited. Some of them were inspected for the first time. A few irregularities in the application of Federal grants were discovered and steps taken to correct them. This procedure

---

nor desire what they were offering as a service to higher education. He then extended his hand, thanked me for waiting, and very graciously dismissed me from his presence. His personal secretary subsequently was most profuse in her thanks to me for listening so patiently and courteously while her 'Boss' blasted the U. S. Government and its Agencies. I told her it was an experience to be treasured and cherished; one I'd be proud to relate to whomever of my children and grandchildren would be willing to listen.

"The above incident while an extreme example of the resistance to the efforts of the Office program in promoting the acceptance of a system of compatible reporting among institutions of higher education, was in a way quite typical of the attitude either latent, or openly expressed with which field men such as ourselves . . . had to contend as the reaction from an older generation of schoolmen such as Dr. Lowell."

[44] Claxton, *op. cit.*, pp. 3–4. The Babcock report, *A Classification of Universities and Colleges with Reference to Bachelor's Degrees*, is discussed under the accreditation movement, *infra*.

[45] See also Table 11, Chapter VI, *infra*.

of visitation and careful scrutiny was made possible through the establishment of the division. The land-grant specialist had visited colleges and universities in the past but the appointment of a specialist in higher education, and his assignment as head of the division, made for a better distribution of the workload and freed the land-grant specialist from other duties he had been performing.[46]

Fourth recurring activity was the field work of the division members in areas other than inspection of land-grant colleges. At first the chief of the Division of Higher Education traveled as extensively as the land-grant specialist. This condition prevailed up until the 1930's when a larger staff and increased administrative workload made it advisable for the chief to curtail travel considerably.

Claxton was gratified with the field work of the specialists during the early years. He wrote warmly of the work. Babcock visited sixteen State universities during his first full fiscal year in office. He inspected the facilities, organization, and activities of those institutions and prepared a report on each. Nine privately endowed colleges and universities were inspected at their request and suggestions made for improvement. The specialist in land-grant college statistics visited forty institutions and made reports on their use of Federal funds.[47]

Brown had been justified in stressing the need for a specialist in higher education and he had also been a reliable prophet of the activities of this specialist.[48] It is doubtful if Brown, for all his perspicacity and breadth of vision, could have predicted the program would be so quickly established. But determined it was and, in essence, the work of the Division of Higher Education would continue around these four activities: collection and dissemination of statistical information; preparation and distribution of publications relating to higher education; supervision of land-grant colleges; and field work which eventually included the college survey movement and the services of professional specialists as advisors and consultants.

The relationship of the Federal Government to higher institutions, however, was something not clearly determined in 1911 nor, for that matter, was it determined for several years to follow. It

---

[46] Claxton, *op. cit.*, pp. 3–4. For figures on appropriations to land-grant colleges see Table 5, Chapter IV, *infra.*

[47] *Ibid.*, pp. 3–4.

[48] cf. (U.S. Office of Education), *Commissioner of Education . . . 1887–1907*, Brown, "Statement," 1907, p. 17; Brown, *Statement . . . 1910*, p. 3; and Wright, *op. cit.*, p. 66.

stood ready to assist in an advisory capacity, and occasionally with substantial financial aid, but colleges and universities were usually not a part of an organized system of administration and operation like the public schools. Privately supported institutions were, and are still, proud of their independence and there was no over-all planning or advisory agency to tell them what to do. Also, because of the advanced and specialized nature of studies and research projects in many of these institutions, specialized interests in State and Federal Government became involved in their activities. National interests in such matters as defense training, development of patriotism, and scientific progress can be promoted through colleges and universities. This naturally stimulated specialized interests to promote their ideas and activities in colleges. In short, the relatonship of the Federal Government to institutions of higher education was fragmented and lacking in central organization.[49]

The Office of Education was dependent upon what the college and university was willing to supply in the form of statistics or other information and the specialist in higher education could serve as a consultant only when asked. Exceptions to this rule were the land-grant institutions. In all others, no matter how sincere the intentions of the representative of the division, nor how sound his advice, he was only a guest tolerated at the pleasure of his host. As time went on more and more institutions inclined toward the "honored guest" rather than "poor relation" treatment of him, but at first the going was difficult.

Obviously, the relationship between the Office and the institution was delicate. Occasionally, an Office representative met with outright hostility.[50] But more often the relationship had to be developed through slow, tedious, and sometimes painful, trial and error. It was still in the process of being "worked out" in some areas by 1953. Occasionally the efforts of the Office to be helpful resulted in the singeing of an academic beard or two. Babcock learned this to his regret for his was the first to be singed.

The trouble developed because of the interest of the Office of Education in college classification and accreditation. From the first days of its life, this interest had existed. When the Office of Education was established in 1867 "there was much confusion in such matters as entrance requirements of collegiate institutions, curriculums leading to collegiate degrees, and the resources an

---

[49] Hollis P. Allen, *The Federal Government and Education* (New York, 1950), p. 247.

[50] See fn. 43, *supra*.

institution should have before calling itself a 'college'." [51] First
Barnard, and later Eaton, Harris, and Brown wrote of the need
for some sort of procedure to be developed.[52]

Claxton and Babcock shared this interest in the accreditation
movement. In his chapter in the 1911 *Report*, a chapter entitled
"Higher Education in the United States," Babcock spoke out for
standards of classification.[53] The following year he wrote, "Not-
withstanding innumerable efforts to give a definition of a college,
the word still remains almost as hard to define as 'gentleman'." [54]
Claxton in the same publication observed that "We are beginning
to look with suspicion on colleges which, with very small incomes,
attempt to support large numbers of professional schools or departments; and professional schools established and maintained
for personal profit do not flourish as they once did." There were
564 professional schools reporting in fiscal year 1912 but many of
this impressive number were operating on an inadequate foundation. "It is not so important that we have a large number of
professional schools as it is that those we do have shall be adequately supported and do genuine work." [55]

It seems quite natural that, soon after taking office, Babcock
should turn his attention to the problem of classification. One of
his first official functions was to attend the meeting of the Association of American Universities in Charlottesville, Virginia,
in November, 1910. At the suggestion of the deans of graduate
schools attending, Babcock undertook a preliminary classification
of colleges and universities according to the manner of acceptance
of their bachelor's degrees by graduate schools and the amount
of work holders of these degrees would need to advance to the
next higher degree.

For the next ten months Babcock spent as much time as he
could spare from other duties studying catalogues, registers, reports, and statistical statements of nearly 350 institutions. During
part of this period he traveled to graduate schools to study ad-

[51] Lloyd E. Blauch, (ed), *Accreditation in Higher Education* (Washington,
1959), p. 15.

[52] cf. Henry Barnard, *First Report of the Commissioner of Education
(1867–68) with Circulars and Documents Accompanying the Same* . . .
(Washington, 1868), pp. xvii–xviii; John Eaton, Jr., *Report of the Commissioner of Education made to the Secretary of the Interior for the Year 1870,
with Accompanying Papers* (Washington, 1870), pp. 506–517; and Lloyd E.
Blauch (ed), *op. cit.*, pp. 15–17.

[53] Philander P. Claxton, *Report* . . . *1911*, pp. 39–50.

[54] Philander P. Claxton, *Report of the Commissioner of Education for the
Year Ended June 30, 1912* (Washington, 1913), I, p. 97.

[55] *Ibid.*, I, p. xvii.

mission requirements, handling of students, and other aspects of graduate education. He apparently checked all the available sources he could uncover in that short space of time.[56]

By the Autumn of 1911 he had completed a "preliminary" survey of 344 institutions. He arranged them in four arbitrary classes:

"Class I" consisted of those institutions whose graduates would ordinarily be able to take a master's degree in one year of work;

"Class II" were those institutions whose graduates would usually require more than one year of work, although several institutions placed in "Class II" were on the border between this class and the highest class and were indicated by a star;

"Class III" were those institutions whose graduates would probably require two years of work for the master's degree; and

"Class IV" institutions were those "whose bachelor's degrees would be approximately two years short of equivalency with the standard bachelor's degree of a standard college as described above." [57]

There were 59 institutions in Class I; 161 in Class II, 84 in Class III, and 40 in Class IV. These 344 institutions number far less than half the more than 950 institutions in operation in 1910.

Page proofs of the preliminary report were prepared and distributed to a limited number of institutions for comment and criticism. This was in November, 1911. Somehow, by means unknown, the report came to the attention of the press, perhaps the last thing Babcock would have wanted to happen. Parts of the report were then printed along with comments from members of the fourth estate.[58]

The opposition flame kindled by the "leaking" of the report was crackling and hot. Several clippings filed in the National Archives attest to the protest that flared in 1912. Chancellor James R. Day, Syracuse University, wrote a letter to the Boston *Evening Transcript* on September 25, 1912, which made no attempt to conceal his anger. It reads in part as follows:

---

[56] Kendric C. Babcock, *A Classification of Universities and Colleges with Reference to Bachelor's Degrees* (Washington, 1911), p. 3; Fred J. Kelley, *et al.*, *Collegiate Accreditation by Agencies within States* (Washington, 1940), pp. 16–18; Blauch, *op. cit.*, pp. 17–18; and George F. Zook, "The Bureau of Education and Higher Education," *School Life*, IX, No. 9, May 1924, pp. 199–201.

[57] Babcock, *op. cit.*, p. 5. This document is reproduced in full in Appendix II, *infra*.

[58] Blauch, *op. cit.*, p. 17; Zook, *op. cit.*, p. 199; and Archives File 204–a, "Certification of Chartering and Authority to Confer Degrees in Colleges and Universities," (National Archives, Labor and Transportation Branch).

Syracuse University, and I am told that the same was true of Boston University, New York University, the University of North Carolina and many other prominent universities, received no notice of this standardizing proposition and had no opportunity to defend itself against this one-sided procedure. We knew nothing about what had been done until a secret circular that had been sent confidentially to a few favored colleges was handed to us by a friend.

No man had come here from the Department at Washington, no questions had been asked by letter or circular, no hint had been received that our work was not satisfactory. Our own State department of education was ranking us in the first class. No university where our students had gone for graduate work had ever intimated that their preparation was not satisfactory. The scholars and teachers of our city had given us their confidence. Of 131 students of our central high school going to college this year, 119 came to us. We had placed three times more teachers in the public schools of New York State than any other university of the State and they had passed rigid examinations. Our Law and Medicine schools had passed a larger per cent of graduates through State examinations than any other such schools in the State.

In the face of these facts, without a question being raised by any man from Washington, we learn that an obscure man by the name of Babcock had sent out a tentative, confidential circular, placing us with 160 other universities and colleges which he had assumed to rank in the second class, as he called it.

By what authority? Not by law, for no such authority is given the Department at Washington. Not by justice, for we had been granted no hearing. Not by competency of the classifier for he is unknown to the educational world and is without experience or expert ability and knowledge. He had been president for a short time of the little State University of Arizona, where he was catalogued as filling at the same time the presidency and two professorships!

After I had made a vigorous protest to Commissioner Claxton against this rating on us, Dr. Babcock, the specialist in higher education came to look into our standards! He came after he rated us! He was here three days. He came in an offensive manner evidently to make out a case. But after he had made an examination of the college in which our students are preparing for graduate work, he declared himself satisfied. He asserted his regret at what had been done. He even complemented us in comparison with the best colleges . . .

\*        \*        \*        \*        \*        \*        \*

"The whole thing is a farce and no institution should be disturbed by it. Nothing could be more preposterous than the assumption of this man Babcock. Can anyone imagine anything more ridiculous than for one man to set himself up as the standardizer of American colleges and universities and to make himself the arbitrary dictator of these institutions, over-riding

State departments of education and declaring that he "may change his views and decisions," perhaps; that it is for him to say what is first and second and third and fourth.

\* \* \* \* \* \* \*

Because of the harm that will be done to colleges that will have to defend themselves and that cannot afford to be held up in their communities as third and fourth rate, we protest that standardizing should not be done by faddists or by incompetent tools of "other men." Such a work if it could be done helpfully at all, which we doubt, should be performed by a committee of eminent and indisputably fair men of the largest educational ability and experience, who would carry the confidence of the institutions standardized and of the public.

James R. Day [59]

In part this indictment was unjust. Aside from calling the Office of Education, then a Bureau, a "Department," Chancellor Day appeared to have misunderstood the purpose of the classification and he cast some unreasoned doubts on the motives and abilities of Dr. Babcock. But the anger he expressed was, in large measure, justified. Babcock had "led with his chin" by acting hastily and alone. His action could do great harm to institutions placed in the lower classes.

In the Boston *Evening Transcript* of September 24, 1912, there appeared a long article by Mr. Harry T. Claus. It was entitled "Judgment Day for Our Colleges: A Startling Government Classification." Claus contended that the document should be given wide distribution if of any value, or suppressed:

And now a word or two regarding the dissemination of all the information heretofore given. It would seem on the face of things that the classification of American colleges was important business. It certainly is important to a good many people. If fifty-nine colleges are maintaining higher standards than all others, the country ought to know about it: if 285 other colleges are not quite "up to snuff" that fact ought to be proclaimed. And yet the Government has printed only two hundred of the reports containing the results of Dr. Babcock's investigations. Indeed it is not even certain that all of the institutions investigated were favored with copies. A survey of this sort, if it is worth anything at all or even semi-authoritative, deserves the very widest public notice. If it isn't sufficiently accurate or good enough to receive the Federal indorsement, it should be shelved entirely. Why two hundred copies should be settled upon as the size is surely a mystery. What good is it to Harvard or Yale to be quietly informed in a Government paper that they are standard colleges. They have always known it. The ones to be told of this fact are the laymen, the persons who are not in

---

[59] Archives File 204–a.

intimate touch with educational affairs, but who are, nevertheless, interested to know how their favorite college stands in
relation to other institutions . . . Then why all this secrecy
about the public's business? There may be a suitable explanation and if there is many of us would be more than pleased to
hear it.[60]

Another clipping from an unidentified source, probably a Cin-
cinnati paper, expressed the resentment of Dean Joseph Harry,
Graduate School of the University of Cincinnati, over the "Class
II" rating of his school.[61]

President J. M. C. Hardy, Mississippi Agricultural and Mechanical College, acted as spokesman for his own and nine other
agricultural and mechanical institutions in a letter to Claxton:

> We are thoroughly in sympathy with the great work of the
> U. S. Department of Education, but we enter our earnest pro-
> test against publications of the kind under discussion as being
> only harmful and undesirable, and earnestly request that our
> institutions be omitted from any similar publications in the
> future.[62]

These are only a sampling of the protests. On the other hand,
there were several letters received from graduate institutions
praising the document for its pioneering spirit and usefulness.
Among those commenting favorably were Dean Haskins of Harvard University, Dean Angell of the University of Chicago, Associate Dean William Carpenter of Columbia University, Dean
David Kinley of the University of Illinois, and Dean Thomas
Holgate of Northwestern University. Most of them agreed that
this was one of the more valuable publications ever prepared by
the Office of Education and hoped the work would continue.[63]

But the voices of protest were too strong. Even an apologetic
paper prepared by Claxton in 1912, *An Explanatory Statement*,
failed to stop protests from the injured deans and other educators.[64] The immediate problem the Commissioner faced was
whether to make broad distribution of the document or to with-
hold it from further distribution. If the latter course were fol-

---

[60] *Ibid.*

[61] *Ibid.*

[62] *Ibid.*, Ltr. J. C. Hardy to Claxton, December 13, 1911. See also Ltrs. from
President Charles Dabney, University of Cincinnati, to Claxton, January 30,
1912, February 6, 1912, and September 12, 1912.

[63] *Ibid.*, Ltrs., Haskins to Claxton, November 1, 1911; Angell to Claxton,
January 8, 1912; Carpenter to Claxton, October 2, 1911; Kinley to Claxton,
September 25, 1911; and Holgate to Claxton, October 10, 1911.

[64] This document is reproduced in full in Appendix II, *infra*.

lowed it would mean the temporary, and possibly permanent, end of this classification type of activity in the Office.

No decision was made until the problem had reached the highest desk in the government, that of President Taft. On February 19, 1913, the publication and distribution of the list was stopped by Executive Order.[65] Perhaps because of the fact that this was Taft's last month in office, Secretary of the Interior Warren Fisher left the door ajar: "It is his [Taft's] opinion that this matter should be permitted to go over to the next administration, when it can be discussed with the new President, who is especially qualified to determine a matter of this sort." [66]

The incoming President, Woodrow Wilson, had been a college president and professor for many years, far more in point of fact than he had been in politics. But he was no more amenable to permitting the report to go out than Taft had been.[67]

Thus ended the attempt of the Office of Education to classify institutions of higher education. It became Office policy to avoid such activity from that time on.[68]

There is no record of Babcock's feelings. No account of his opinion seems to exist for he apparently make no written justification or defense against the attacks made on him. It is reasonable to assume that he resented remarks such as those written by Chancellor Day. It is also fairly safe to assume that the furor helped stimulate his early resignation from the position as head of the division and specialist in May 1913.

Although the Office of Education made no further attempts to classify institutions in the manner used by Babcock, this groundbreaking report had a considerable influence. In 1914–15 the Office of Education organized a committee of the principal associations dealing with higher education to discuss the advisability of preparing a classification. If found desirable, methods of procedure would be discussed. Included on the committee were representatives of the Association of American Universities, the National Association of State Universities, the American Medical Association, the Society for the Promotion of Engineering Education, The Association of American Colleges, and the Office of Education.

---

[65] Zook, *op. cit.*, p. 199; and Blauch, *op. cit.*, pp. 17–18.

[66] Archives File 204–a, Ltr., Secretary Fisher to Claxton, February 19, 1913.

[67] Kelly *et al.*, *op. cit.*, pp. 16–18; George F. Zook and M. E. Haggerty, *Principles of Accrediting Higher Institutions* (Chicago, 1936), p. 19.

[68] J. Harold Goldthorpe, "Office of Education Relationships to Educational Accreditation," *Higher Education*, XI, No. 4, December 1954, pp. 51–54.

On May 3, 1915, the Committee reported that it was not desirable to classify colleges although the status of institutions might be indicated by statistical comparisons of resources, equipment, and other items. Then universities could make their own evaluation. The committee organized itself into a permanent committee on higher education statistics to cooperate with the Office of Education in studying standards. Babcock's successor, Dr. Samuel Paul Capen, acting as the committee's secretary prepared a report using material collected by it. This report, *Resources and Standards of Colleges of Arts and Sciences*, listed ten categories of collegiate standards and set up thirteen "suggested requirements for a successful college of arts and sciences." The First World War ended further study by the Office and the independent committee and the Office did not return to it after hostilities had ceased.[69]

In 1913, after leaving Washington, Babcock served as chairman of a committee appointed by the Association of American Universities to grade institutions whose graduates apply for admission to graduate schools. He, and his two co-committeemen, prepared such a classification using his 1911 report as the basis.[70] Babcock's work also influenced the classification system adopted by the American Association of University Women.[71] Even though it injured feelings and forced the Office of Education away from the classification field, the suppressed report was an important, perhaps essential, step in overcoming a perplexing problem. It was a contribution to the accreditation movement.[72]

A problem nearly as serious as classification and accreditation was that of "degree mills." Degree mills are institutions working under legally granted charters authorizing them to award degrees of various sorts for "academic achievement" which in no way approximates the requirements of regular academic institutions. Several of these unscrupulous institutions were flourishing at the time the Division was established. They were nurtured by lax

---

[69] See Samuel P. Capen, *Resources and Standards of Colleges of Arts and Sciences* (Washington, 1918), esp. pp. 7–8, 15–17. Kelly *et al.*, *op. cit.*, pp. 18-19; Blauch, *op. cit.*, pp. 18–19; and *School Life*, II, No. 6, March 16, 1919, pp. 3–4.

[70] Capen writing in Philander P. Claxton, *Report of the Commissioner of Education for the Year Ended June 30, 1915* (Washington, 1915), I, pp. 151–152.

[71] Lewis, *op. cit.*, p. 173.

[72] Fred J. Kelly, writing in *Journal of Proceedings and Addresses of the Forty-first Annual Conference Held at the University of Missouri, October 30–31 and November 1, 1939* (Chicago, 1939), p. 95. See also Blauch, *op. cit.*, pp. 18–19; and Zook; "The Bureau of Education," pp. 199–200.

incorporation laws in several States and the District of Columbia. Their tills were filled by a large number of men and women who wanted to buy college degrees for prestige and career advancement. Nearly all of the "work" of the students was by correspondence.

Babcock was bombarded with letters requesting information on several institutions. Some of them were legitimate residence or correspondence schools, while others were degree mills. He had to sift the good from the bad. This was no easy matter in a day when there was no accreditation system. Then, upon making a determination, he had to prepare a reply which would make his position clear without opening the Office of Education to indefensible attack.

One of the most active and prolonged examples of the degree mills operated in the District of Coumbia almost directly under the noses of the Office of Education staff which was forced to sit and watch with pained frustration. This institution was "Potomac University." It had been incorporated on August 1, 1904, for the purpose of granting "all such degrees as are customary in other colleges and universities, and to give diplomas or certificates of the same . . . in the following branches or departments of knowledge: Liberal Arts, Fine Arts, Sciences, Literature, Philosophy, Mathematics, Pedagogy, Commerce, Theology, and Law."

The certificate was signed by five "trustees" and attested by a Notary Public. Potomac University was then in business ready to grant degrees of virtually any sort to anyone who had sufficient funds to finance his "education." [73] This organization was to operate until 1930 and was not formally dissolved until April 11, 1958.[74] During the 26 active years it awarded an unknown number of degrees, probably numbering in the thousands. Among the degrees it is known to have granted were Bachelor of Arts, Bachelor of Science, Bachelor of Philosophy, Bachelor of Laws, Bachelor of Divinity, Master of Arts, Doctor of Philosophy, Doctor of Letters, Doctor of Law, and Doctor of Sacred Theology.[75]

---

[73] "Bogus Institutions," Acc. No. 57–A–681, RG 12, Federal Records Center, Alexandria, Virginia, "Certificate of Inspection."

[74] Information supplied by Boise L. Bristor, Statistician, D. C. Public Schools, and James Sherier, Lawyer, Washington, D. C. U. S. District Court Order No. 3265–57, filed April 11, 1958. Operation of the institution stopped in 1930 as a result of 45 Stat. 1504, Ch. 523, March 2, 1929, which amended subchapter 1 of Chapter 18 of the Code of Laws for the District of Columbia relating to degree-conferring institutions.

[75] "Bogus Institutions," Ltr., President E. W. Porter, Potomac University, to Rev. Kayhoe, Nashville, Tennessee, August 4, 1910. See also Claxton, *Report of the Commissioner . . . 1911*, I, pp. 50–54.

The Division of Higher Education was powerless to suppress Potomac University or any other degree mill. All it could do was warn those requesting information that degrees from the institution would not be recognized by standard established colleges and universities.

Replies to requests for information varied but two samples extracted from Office correspondence show the general type of reply issued in the 1910's and 1920's:

> Your statement regarding recognition of degrees granted by these institutions, especially Potomac University, led me to re-read a letter received from Reverend F. J. Barwell-Walker under date of July 12th, which contained some four or five questions from letters from State universities and others, not one of which offered any positive assurance of recognition of the degrees in question. Since Columbia is one of those which you have been told recognizes the Potomac degrees, I am glad to be able to quote to you from an official letter from the acting dean of the faculties of Political Science, Philosophy, and Pure Science of Columbia University, under date of July 30, 1911:
>
> "The present list of 'approved institutions' upon the basis of which we accept graduates of acceptable colleges and universities as candidates for our higher degrees does *not* contain the name of Potomac University, nor do I find upon investigation that Coumbia ever has recognized the degrees of this institution."
>
> The Bureau of Education has not yet been able to obtain any positive information indicating that any standard university has given recognition to the degrees of either Potomac or Oriental University.[76]

*    *    *    *    *    *    *

> I quote from the last official communication sent from this Office regarding Potomac University: "Potomac University . . . is legally chartered under the liberal incorporation laws of the District of Columbia and authorized to grant degrees. Its principal course is in law, though other degree courses are offered. Most of its work is done by the correspondence method. It is doubtful whether its degrees would be recognized by any of the standard institutions of the country."
>
> In addition I might say that the sole requirement for becoming a college or university in the District of Columbia is that any five persons sign a document stating it to be their intention so to incorporate. In 1912 the Carnegie Foundation for the Advancement of Teaching reported on the Potomac University as follows: "The Potomac University, which is established in a dwelling-house in Washington, certified in 1908 that its assets, including bills receivable, amounted to $450. It also had a

---

[76] *Ibid.*, Ltr., Babcock to Thomas Walker, Ontonagon, Michigan, September 23, 1911.

library of 5,000 books, office furniture—desks, chairs, and type-writers." [77]

Since positive action could not be taken against degree mills, they continued to thrive. Especially throughout the 1910's and 1920's the Office of Education was plagued by their activities. In addition to Potomac University there were an unknown number of others, perhaps as many as a hundred operating in the first half of the 20th Century at various times. Among some of those with whom the Office of Education encountered difficulties were Teacher's Professional College, Washington, D.C.; The International University of Illinois (which specialized in granting degrees in Asian countries); Oriental University, Washington, D.C.; The Odessa University, Odessa, Washington; Oskaloosa College, Oskaloosa, Iowa; Research University, Washington, D.C.; Lincoln-Jefferson University, Chicago, Illinois; and Peoples National University, Atlanta, Georgia.[78]

The 1930's and 1940's witnessed a decline in the number of requests for information about degree mills. This was possibly due to the diverting of attention to other matters by the depression and the Second World War. Another factor was a more stringent regulation for the licensing of degree-granting institutions in the District of Columbia. This was accomplished in 1929 largely through the activity of the District of Columbia Board of Education with the cooperation of the Office of Education.[79]

Babcock found other things to do which occupied what little time he had left from his daily routine. In 1912 the *Educational Directory* first appeared as a separate document. About one-third was devoted to higher educational information compiled and checked by the Division of Higher Education.[80] Originally one volume in size the *Educational Directory* later became a three-part

---

[77] *Ibid.*, Ltr., Capen to Elliot Mayhew, Chilmark, Massachusetts, September 3, 1914.

[78] *Ibid.*, This file contains information on a large number of institutions. In addition see Claxton, *Report to the Commissioner . . . 1911*, pp. 50–54; and Robert H. Reid, *American Degree Mills* (Washington, 1959). The activities of some of these institutions were audacious if not impertinent. In the *Complete Register of Oriental University, January 1, 1920*, Dr. William T. Harris, ex-Commissioner of Education, was listed as a "patron." Dr. Harris had died in 1909. In a later *Bulletin*, dated November 1921, the President of the University, Helmuth P. Holler, (Ph.D., S.T.D., D. Ps. T.), stated that he had not been appointed Commissioner of Education in 1921 by President Harding because he had voted for Eugene Debs!

[79] William J. Cooper, *Annual Report of the Commissioner of Education for the Year Ended June 30, 1929* (Washington, 1929), p. 30.

[80] Henry G. Badger, "Higher Education Directory for 1947-48," *Higher Education*, IV, No. 9, January 1, 1948, pp. 105–106.

and then four-part annual publication. Babcock also prepared the first list of accredited high schools which was published as a bulletin in 1913. This list was revised regularly and republished from time to time.[81] In addition, there were letters to answer, special studies to prepare or edit, and several routine functions to perform.[82]

The specialist in higher education and his land-grant specialist assistant had more things to do than time to do them. Claxton held to the belief that a larger staff was needed. In 1911 he recommended the addition to the division of a specialist in normal school education, a specialist in agricultural education to work with Negro land-grant colleges in the South, and an additional specialist in agricultural education to supervise expenditure of land-grant funds. He further recommended an increase in salary for the chief of the division and three clerks to help with office routine.[83]

In 1913 Claxton noted the work of the Office had increased more than three-fold over a three year period. Meanwhile the appropriation had increased only 20 per cent. More money was needed in order to provide additional services, including help in higher education.[84] Other recommendations were made for an increased staff but it was not until 1927 that the Division of Higher Education could boast of four professional employees.

Early in 1913 Babcock was offered the deanship of the College of Literature, Arts, and Science of the University of Illinois. His resignation from the Office of Education was accepted effective May 2, 1913.[85] He did not completely sever his connection with the Office of Education at that time. The next day he was appointed a "Special Collaborator" at $1.00 per annum and continued to serve, without a pay increase, until the end of fiscal year 1921.[86]

From May, 1913, until February, 1914, the Office was without

---

[81] Kendric C. Babcock, *Accredited Secondary Schools in the United States* (Washington, 1913), Ltr., Claxton to Secretary of the Interior F. K. Lane, May 1, 1913, p. 5; Samuel P. Capen, *Accredited Secondary Schools in the United States* (Washington, 1915), p. 5.

[82] See Claxton, *Statement . . . 1913*, pp. 5, 17–29.

[83] Claxton, *Statement . . . 1911*, p. 11. cf. P. P. Claxton, *Statement . . . 1912*, p. 17.

[84] Claxton, *Statement . . . 1913*, pp. 18–19

[85] Babcock's Personnel Folder, St. Louis Records Center, St. Louis, Missouri: Ltrs. Babcock to Secretary of the Interior F. K. Lane, April 21, 1913, Lane to Babcock, April 23, 1913.

[86] For additional information on Babcock see Appendix I, *infra*.

a permanent specialist or division head. Dr. George E. MacLean, former President of the State University of Iowa, was given a temporary appointment as a specialist to make a study of higher education in England, Scotland, and Ireland. He was abroad working on this study from 1913 to 1916. Also in 1913, Dr. Charles Judd of the School of Education, University of Chicago, was given a temporary appointment. He made a study of the preparation of secondary school teachers in Germany, France, and England. The following year another temporary appointment was given to Dr. Otis Caldwell, also of the University of Chicago, to make an inspection of the teaching of science in several Southern States.[87]

The search for a permanent successor to Babcock went on through the summer and fall of 1913. It was not until January of the next year that Dr. Samuel Paul Capen, Professor of German and foreign languages in Clark University, was appointed. Interestingly enough, Capen's name first appeared in October, 1910, when Brown was seeking his first specialist in higher education. President Sanford, himself a leading candidate, proposed Capen as "the man . . . most likely to do that sort of work with interest and success." Several others recommended Capen highly to Claxton. Professor Capen was possibly his own most enthusiastic promoter, actively campaigning for the position. His campaign was successful and he began service as chief of the Division of Higher Education on February 1, 1914.[88]

The most important development under Capen, and one of the most significant activities of the Division of Higher Education prior to the Second World War, was the college survey movement. Surveys of educational institutions began prior to 1914. Capen cannot take credit as the originator although a later chief credited

---

[87] Philander P. Claxton, *Report of the Commissioner of Education for the Year Ended June 30, 1913* (Washington, 1914), I, p. xxi; Philander P. Claxton, *Report of the Commissioner of Education for the Year Ended June 30, 1914* (Washington, 1915), I, pp, xv–xvi; Claxton, *Statement . . . 1913*, p. 5; and Philander P. Claxton, *Statement of the Commissioner of Education to the Secretary of the Interior for the Fiscal Year Ended June 30, 1914* (Washington, 1914), pp. 3–4. See Appendix I, *infra*.

[88] Capen's Personnel Folder, St. Louis Records Center, St. Louis, Missouri, contains the following documents of special interest relative to his appointment: Ltrs., Sanford to Brown, October 7, 1910, and October 17–19, 1910; Sanford to Claxton, May 23, 1913; Representative Samuel E. Winslow, House of Representatives, to Claxton, September 4, 1913; and Capen to Claxton, August 29, 1913, and September 10, 1913; Telegrams Claxton to Capen, January 5, 1914; and Capen to Claxton, January 5, 1914, January 10, 1914, and January 24, 1914; Oath of Office, February 1, 1914.

Capen "for having laid a sound basis of surveys of higher educational institutions." [89] In 1911 the Board of Education of Baltimore, Maryland, made a request for a survey of its schools system.[90] This launched the survey movement. There had been a few surveys in past years but they were too widely scattered in time and space to constitute a "movement."

The Baltimore survey did not draw upon the resources of the Division of Higher Education but the next year it entered the field with gusto: ". . . in the first year surveys and reports [were] made upon sixteen state universities and nine privately supported institutions. Reports were also made upon standardization of the institutions of higher learning in Oregon and of five institutions in Virginia." [91]

In 1912 the educational survey was a relatively new device in the field of education. A State or local school system, or an educational institution, would request an outside group to study its operation and make recommendations for improvement. The Office of Education was in a unique position to serve since it was a National organization and possessed an unusually wide knowledge of conditions throughout the United States and abroad. It could also act without bias. Finally, its services were free; a consideration of no small importance.[92]

Claxton was delighted to take an active part in surveys. They gave the Office an unparalleled opportunity to raise educational standards and help in the shaping of policy.[93]

Under Babcock surveys were usually made in conjunction with other organizations. They were not as complete nor thorough as they were later to become. When Capen came into office he assumed a position of importance in the survey of higher educational activities which his predecessor was unable to do because of the press of other duties and lack of funds. Frequently, Capen pre-

---

[89] Zook, *op. cit.*, p. 200. On contribution of Capen see Ltr., Edward C. Elliott, President Emeritus, Purdue University, to author, December 10, 1959, and Edward C. Elliott, "A Tribute to Samuel Paul Capen," *The Educational Record* XXXVIII, No. 1, January 1957, pp. 18–19. See also Ford, *op. cit.*, p. 84.

[90] Charles H. Judd, "Contributions of School Surveys," *Thirty-Seventh Yearbook, National Society for the Study of Education, Part 2* (Bloomington, Indiana, 1937), pp. 12–13.

[91] Smith, *op. cit.*, p. 32; Rodeheaver, *op. cit.*, pp. 126–127; and Philander P. Claxton, *Report of the Commissioner of Education for the Year Ended June 30, 1916* (Washington, 1916), I, pp. xvii–xxv.

[92] L. E. Hartley, "A Critical Study of the United States Office of Education Since 1933," (Boulder, Colorado, 1941, typewritten ms.), pp. 34–35.

[93] See Samuel P. Capen, *The Bureau of Education and the Educational Survey Movement* (Washington, 1918).

pared the entire survey report himself. Ably supported by Claxton, Capen became a recognized leader in the survey movement.[94]

The first complete survey organized and conducted by the Office of Education in the field of higher education was made at the University of Oregon. The report was published by the State in 1915. It was followed in the same year by a survey of institutions of Iowa although that report was not published until 1916.[95]

Throughout his six years in office Capen worked incessantly to perfect survey operations. He had ample opportunity to develop his techniques for the Iowa survey was followed by surveys of institutions in Washington, North Dakota, and other States. By 1916, according to Capen, the survey had "undoubtedly occupied the forefront of attention in the field of higher education during the academic year just completed." [96]

Capen's contributions to the survey movement were threefold:

First, he developed the principle of "major" and "service" lines in his effort to eliminate duplication in institutions within the same State. In a university "major" lines would be such subjects as literature, history, philosophy, medicine, and others traditionally associated with higher education. These would be "service" lines at an agricultural and mechanical institution where the "major" lines would be such subjects as agriculture, home economics, and others of a technical nature. These of course, would be "service" lines at standard universities.[97]

Second, Capen forced attention on the over-all State program of higher education. His surveys, and those of others who followed, reduced duplication of curriculums, lessened administrative inefficiency, and in general improved the State system of higher education.

Third, he insisted that prophetic vision was the major gift of any surveyor. The survey was not to be short-ranged but was to make suggestions for the inevitable expansion that was to occur in higher education.[98] Surveys should establish guidelines for new ideas and concepts.

In 1916 the first survey of an area larger than a single State was completed. This was a survey of Negro schools and institutions prepared with the assistance of the Phelps-Stokes fund. It

---

[94] Walter C. Eells, *Surveys of American Higher Education* (New York, 1937), pp. 33–35; Claxton, *Report . . . 1914*, I, pp. xxx–xxxviii; and Claxton, *Report . . . 1916*, I, pp. xvii–xviii.

[95] Eells, *op. cit.*, pp. 34–35.

[96] Claxton, *Report . . . 1916*, I, pp. xviii–xx, 121–129.

[97] Capen, *op. cit.*, p. 5.

[98] *Ibid.*

utilized the services of a large group of educators headed by Dr. Thomas Jesse Jones. Capen and other Office of Education officials assisted in the survey which was published as a two-volume Bullétin (1916, No. 37, No. 38).[99]

Professor Walter Eells of Stanford University found that up to 1936 there had been 230 surveys of higher education published by various agencies. The most active surveying agency had been the Office of Education with 35 completed by it, or under its direction, from 1910 to 1936. The list of surveys is here arranged chronologically according to the number series of the Bulletin if a government publication or according to year of publication if by another agency.[100]

*University of Oregon* (1915, published by the State of Oregon from a report prepared by the Office of Education).

*Problems Involved in Standardizing State Normal Schools* (1916).

*Negro Education* (1916).

*Educational Survey of Wyoming* (1916).

*State Higher Educational Institutions of Iowa* (1916).

*Survey of Educational Institutions of the State of Washington* (1916).

*State Higher Educational Institutions of North Dakota* (1916).

*Educational Conditions in Arizona* (1917).

*Report of a Survey of the University of Nevada* (1917).

*A Survey of Education in the Province of Saskatchawan, Canada* (1918, published by the Province of Saskatchawan).

*The Educational System of South Dakota* (1918).

*An Educational Study of Alabama* (1919).

*A Survey of Education in Hawaii* (1920).

*Educational Survey of the University of Arkansas* (1921).

*Report on the Higher Educational Institutions of Arkansas* (1922).

*Report of a Survey of the State Institutions of Higher Learning in Kansas* (1923).

*Report of the Commission for an Investigation Relative to Opportunities and Methods for Technical and Higher Education in the Commonwealth* (1923, published by the State of Massachusetts).

---

[99] Published as *Negro Education: a Study of the Private and Higher Schools for Colored People in the United States* (Washington, 1917, 1916 Bulletin series), II Vols. See Eells, *op. cit.*, p. 39.

[100] Eells, *op. cit.*, pp. 293 ff. Eells lists 36 but included in this figure is the survey of District of Columbia schools prepared by Barnard in 1868–70 and published in 1871.

*Report on a Survey of the University of Arizona* (1923).

*Report on a Survey of the North Carolina State College of Agriculture and Engineering* (1923).

*Hampton Normal and Agricultural Institute* (1923).

*The Public School System of Arkansas* (1923).

*Public Education in Oklahoma* (1922, 1923).

*Land-grant Education, 1910–20* (1924, 1925).

*Survey of Higher Education in Cleveland* (1925).

*A Survey of Higher Education in Tennessee* (1926, published by Tennessee College Association).

*Survey of Education in Utah* (1926).

*Survey of Rutgers University* (1927, published by Rutgers University).

*Survey of Negro Colleges and Universities* (1928).

*Survey of Land-grant Colleges and Universities* (1930).

*Survey of State-supported Institutions of Higher Learning in Arkansas* (1931).

*Survey of Public Higher Education in Oregon* (1931).

*A Study of the Educational Value of Military Instruction in Universities and Colleges* (1932).

*National Survey of Secondary Education* (Bulletin, 1932).

*National Survey of School Finance* (1932–33, published by the American Council on Education).

*National Survey of the Education of Teachers* (Bulletin, 1933).

In addition to the published surveys there were a large number which never appeared in print. By the time Claxton left office in 1921 it is estimated that more than 120 surveys involving all levels of education had been completed. The movement continued through the 1920's and into the mid–1930's.[101] The higher educational survey movement which Capen did so much to promote and develop, and in which his staff assisted, was successful in helping institutions to plan more effective programs and to operate more efficiently.[102]

In order to implement his small staff Claxton started the "dollar-a-year man" system in the Office of Education around 1913. The object was to get virtually unlimited expert help within a very limited budget. The payment of one dollar a year gave the payee an official relationship to the Office, entitled him to franking privileges, and made it possible for him to be reimbursed for certain expenses.

---

[101] Figures on the number of surveys are conflicting. cf. Rodeheaver, *op. cit.*, pp. 126–127; and Judd, *op. cit.*, p. 30. Brief discussion of national surveys will be found in Chapter III, *infra.*

[102] Eells, *op. cit.*, Chapter VII, pp. 179–217.

The "dollar-a-year men" belong to one of two groups. One group comprised those expert consultants who formed part of, or headed, a staff in the Office of Education for a special project of limited duration. The second group consisted of consultants who worked outside Washington and seldom, if ever, came into the Office. Included in this were people working on studies to be published by the Federal Government, and people who were advising in special educational areas.[103]

There were "dollar-a-year men" at all levels from elementary through higher education. Among those in higher education were Judd of the University of Chicago, McLean of Iowa, T. J. Jones who supervised the Negro education survey of 1916, and Babcock.[104] By fiscal year 1916 Claxton had 137 collaborators in his "dollar-a-year man" ranks.[105]

The practice had died out by the 1930's but while it lasted it made possible several studies which could not otherwise have been made and gave the Office of Education access to academic talent of a high order.

The most immediate and pressing need of the Division of Higher Education, indeed of the whole Office, was portrayed by this consultant program. More full-time employees were needed. Repeatedly the Commissioner requested additional specialists in higher education and other educational areas. Not until fiscal year 1918 was a permanent increase made in the Division bringing the number to three. It did not increase again for nine years.[106] By then demand for higher educational assistance had grown so much that the additional staff did not fill the gap.

---

[103] Interview of author with Dr. W. Carson Ryan, Professor of Education Emeritus, University of North Carolina, November 27, 1959.

[104] *Ibid.* At least one consultant was anxious to get his salary, perhaps to keep as a souvenir. In a handwritten postscript to a letter to Chief Clerk L. A. Kalbach, July 12, 1921, Dr. Babcock wrote: "I have just received notice of the termination of my appointment as special collaborator, June 30, 1921. Please see that I get my $1.00 (or is it $2.00 by this time?)." Babcock's Personnel Folder, St. Louis Records Center, St. Louis, Missouri.

[105] Philander P. Claxton, *Statement of the Commissioner of Education to the Secretary of the Interior for the Fiscal Year Ended* June 30, 1915 (Washington, 1915), p. 39; and Philander P. Claxton, *Statement of the Commissioner of Education to the Secretary of the Interior for the Fiscal Year Ended June 30, 1916* (Washington, 1916), p. 33.

[106] See Claxton, *Report . . . 1914*, pp. xxvi ff; Claxton, *Statement . . . 1914*, pp. 28–30; Claxton, *Statement . . . 1915*, p. 41; and Claxton, *Statement . . . 1916*, pp. 36, 41. Requests for additional help in higher education may be found in his *Statements* for 1917 (p. 22), 1918 (p. 30), 1919 (pp. 56,58), and 1920 (pp. 50-51).

The size of the Office of Education was far from impressive in the period

The formative years ended with the coming of the First World War. The first six years were among the most hectic it was to know. Much has been accomplished and a way of life established. The Division of Higher Education had retreated from the field of accreditation but it was giving vigorous battle against degree mills and was in the vanguard of the survey movement. In addition, routine activities had been established and were being performed regularly and successfully. Among these were consultation, formal visitation, research, writing, and advising. The Division was making itself an agreeable and useful adjunct to higher education throughout the Nation.[107]

---

prior to the First World War. This description by a 1915 visitor, Isaac Miles Wright, was written in 1915 or 1916; "The Bureau was unknown to the several employees of the Government I happened to meet, the telephone directory did not contain the address and I found it necessary to call the Bureau on the telephone for directions to find the office . . . The quarters for the Library are so small that it was necessary to remove a large pile of books in order that I might have one corner of a desk to use in consulting the material that was not available in the libraries of New York." (Wright, *op. cit.*, pp. I–II).

For the number of professionals assigned see Table 10, Chapter VI, *infra*. The following served as professional staff members during the period from 1911 to 1916 (dates of service with the division shown in parentheses): Dr. Kendric C. Babcock (1910–13); Mr. Floyd B. Jenks (1911–13); Dr. George E. MacLean (1913–16); Dr. Samuel P. Capen (1914–19); Dr. Charles H. Judd (1913); Mr. Benjamin F. Andrews (1914–18); Dr. Otis W. Caldwell (1914); Dr. Chester D. Jarvis (1915–21); Mr. John H. Higson (1914); and Dr. Arthur C. Monahan (1911–18). See Appendix I for biographical sketches.

[107] The *Reports* and *Statements* of Claxton from 1912 to 1920 contain summaries of routine operations including formal visits to institutions of higher education and attendance at academic functions. For routine land-grant functions an additional source is Archives File 26, "Office of Education, Commissioner's Office, Land-Grant College Correspondence, Research on Education Correspondence, 1921–26" (National Archives, Labor and Transportation Branch). The contents of this file cover a somewhat wider period than the label would indicate.

CHAPTER III

# From World War I
# Through the Years of Prosperity
# (1917–1928)

*The First World War*

President Wilson's war message to the Congress on April 2, 1917, ended more than two years of a strange twilight period when we hovered between a wistful neutrality and a practical, albeit half-hearted, preparedness.

The Office of Education, like many other Federal agencies, had continued its activities up to 1917 much as though things were "as usual." This was not so much due to an unrealistic attitude, although such an attitude would have been understandable since it was shared by so many Americans, as it was to the insufficient resources and understaffing from which the Office suffered. Normal peacetime operation took all the slender resources of the staff. There was no expansion prior to the actual declaration of war. Consequently there was little time to prepare.[1]

The declaration of war, following Wilson's message by four days, had the effect of diverting nearly all activity to national defense. Peacetime educational activities came to a virtual standstill in the Office as it was caught in the whirlwind of war.

The war activities of the Office of Education were concentrated in three broad general areas. One was stimulation of patriotism through preparation of school programs, and the writing, editing, and publishing of materials. A second area was the development of better international educational relations with allied nations and neutrals. Some of the ways in which the Office promoted inter-

---

[1] Parke R. Kolbe, "War Work of the United States Bureau of Education," *School and Society*, VII, No. 178, May 25, 1918, pp. 606–609; and L. E. Hartley, "A Critical Study of the United States Office of Education Since 1933" (Boulder, Colorado, 1941, typewritten ms.), pp. 38–39.

national good-will were preparation of materials on educational programs for foreign consumption, arranging to bring foreign students to America for study, and keeping in touch with institutions and educators abroad. A third area was constant study and evaluation of the effect of the war on American schools at all levels. The withdrawal of students to enter military service or defense work was studied and remedies proposed to prevent unreasonable dropout. The contribution of schools to the war effort, actual and potential, was also studied.[2]

It is doubtful if any level of education was affected so immediately or so profoundly by the coming of the war as the colleges and universities of the Nation. Students in college were of the age most suitable for military service. The inflated wages of war workers were powerful incentives for leaving school in the case of those not drafted for service.

> Immediately after our entrance into the war in April, 1917, young men in college began to volunteer for service in the Army, and the exodus was large. During the summer, fall, winter, and spring the demand for men and women of higher education and training for service in the Army, both at home and abroad, in the departments at Washington, and in the war industries, continued to increase and became so large that both students and instructors left the colleges, universities, and technical schools in large numbers. Before the end of the school year the attendance at these institutions was reduced 25 per cent or more.[3]

Commissioner Claxton and Capen, chief of the Division of Higher Education, considered that the declaration of war brought an end to an epoch in the history of higher education. The "broad and liberal system of elective studies has reached the limits of its evolution" and a new trend of more rigidly controlled curricula and program study system was setting in. The war would mean a stricter regimentation of higher education in the national welfare.[4]

On May 22, 1917, less than seven weeks after our entrance into the war, the Office of Education published a pamphlet entitled *Suggestions for the Conduct of Educational Institutions during the Continuance of the War.* One suggestion was that all young

---

[2] Kolbe, *op. cit.* For more details on general war activities of the Office of Education see *School Life* (Washington, 1918 *et seq.*), I, August 1918, through II, 1919.

[3] Philander P. Claxton, *Report of the Commissioner of Education for the Year Ended June 30, 1918* (Washington, 1918), p. 6.

[4] *Ibid.*, pp. 9–15. Quotation from p. 9. See also S. P. Capen, and W. C. John, *Survey of Higher Education, 1916–18* (Washington, 1919), p. 3.

men in college remain there until called to military service or special war duty. Education was essential for all "to the end that they may be able to render the most effective service in the later years of the war and the times of need that will follow."

The Office urged institutions to reduce the cost of living as far as they could so more students would remain in college. Calendars should be modified, i.e., speeded up, so that school plants could be more fully utilized. A school year of four 12 week quarters was recommended. Every effort should be made to use all facilities to the maximum extent, and as much as possible. Technical and scientific knowledge was more important to victory than unskilled or semi-skilled labor, no matter how zealous and hard-working the laborer might be. So students and college officials should unite their efforts to produce the scientists and technicians needed for victory over the Central Powers.[5]

The Division of Higher Education was extremely active in helping to marshal the resources of colleges and universities so they could contribute to the Allied cause.[6] "It devoted its attention to aid in regimenting college graduates for specialized or technical patriotic service. Members of the divison served in numerous advisory bodies and took active part in the supervision of the education of civilians for mechanical and other technical war service and of the Student Army Training Corps."[7]

The most direct way in which the Division aided in regimenting higher educational resources was through its contact with institutions. Immediately after the declaration of hostilities, blanks were sent to colleges, universities, and other institutions of learning asking them to catalogue and report on their manpower resources: faculty, students, and alumni. The blanks had been developed by Columbia University in order to catalogue the resources represented by its faculty, graduates, and students. This enabled colleges and universities, when applied across the Nation by the

---

[5] "Suggestions for the Conduct of Educational Institutions during the Continuance of the War" as reprinted in Philander P. Claxton, *Report of the Commissioner of Education for the Year Ended June 30, 1917* (Washington, 1917), p. 13.

[6] Throughout the war the Division of Higher Education had but three professional staff members. Capen remained chief throughout the period. Mr. Benjamin F. Andrews served as specialist in land-grant college statistics until January 27, 1918, when he transferred to the Bureau of Internal Revenue. He was succeeded by Dr. Walton C. John who took office on March 11, 1918. Dr. Chester Jarvis joined in October, 1917, as specialist in agricultural education. See Appendix I, *infra*.

[7] D. H. Smith, *The Bureau of Education. Its History, Activities and Organization* (Baltimore, Maryland, 1923), pp. 45–46.

Office, to make a personnel index of the entire university body, to perfect internal organization into larger and smaller subdivisions, and to establish cooperative relations with other groups.[8]

When possible, representatives of the Division visited institutions, and arranged conferences with institutional representatives in Washington or in the field.

Personal contacts were impossible with the vast majority of institutions. There were too many of them and not enough people in the Division. Publications and correspondence had to serve as a substitute for personal contact in most cases. The routine publication program was much curtailed early in the war period because of other demands on the Government Printing Office. Virtually all of the materials published under the Office of Education appropriation during fiscal years 1918 and 1919 bore directly on the war effort.[9] In the last half of fiscal year 1917 and throughout the following fiscal year seven Higher Education Circulars on the work of American colleges and universities during the war were published. A "Higher Education Letter" was written, printed, and distributed on the four-quarter system. Another was prepared on the "Canadian Soldiers' College." Other publications relating to patriotism were likewise prepared and distributed. In fiscal year 1919 three more Higher Education Circulars on the war effort of colleges and universities appeared. Another circular dealt with the educational opportunities for returning soldiers, and a multi-lithed pamphlet entitled "Suggestions to Colleges Concerning the Admission of Returning Soldiers" was reproduced and distributed.[10]

The direct contacts with higher educational institutions, and the publications program, were not the only contributions the Division of Higher Education made to the war effort. Capen took

---

[8] H. R. Evans, and E. A. Wright, "The United States Office of Education" (Washington, 1939, typewritten ms.), pp. 61–62; and Philander P. Claxton, *Statement of the Commissioner of Education to the Secretary of the Interior for the Fiscal Year Ended June 30, 1917* (Washington, 1917), pp. 12–13.

[9] Smith, *op. cit.*, pp. 28–29.

[10] Philander P. Claxton, *Statement of the Commissioner of Education to the Secretary of the Interior for the Fiscal Year Ended June 30, 1919* (Washington, 1918), p. 19; and Philander P. Claxton, *Statement of the Commissioner of Education to the Secretary of the Interior for the Fiscal Year Ended June 30, 1919* (Washington, 1919), p. 14. There were 34 Higher Education Circulars published in all. The first appeared in May 1917, and the last in February 1928. More than half were published prior to the end of calendar year 1919, and ten of these were in the series on the work of American colleges and universities during the war. The complete list is in Appendix III, *infra*.

an active role in planning war programs through his membership on various committees and advisory groups. The three most important of these were his services as a member of a committee subordinate to the Advisory Commission of the Council of National Defense, as a member of the Committee on the Relation of Engineering Schools to the Government, and as a member of the advisory board to the Committee on Education and Special Training of the War Department.

In the Autumn of 1916 the Congress created a Council of National Defense consisting of the Secretaries of War, Navy, Interior, Agriculture, Commerce, and Labor. On October 11, 1916, this Council, in turn, appointed an Advisory Commission. This consisted of seven nationally-known members:

Mr. Daniel Willard, Chairman;
Mr. Howard E. Coffin, commissioner for munitions, manufacturing, and industrial relations;
Mr. Julius Rosenwald, commissioner for supplies;
Mr. Barnard M. Baruch, commissioner for raw materials, minerals, and metals;
Dr. Hollis Godfrey, commissioner for engineering and education;
Mr. Samuel Gompers, commissioner for labor; and
Dr. Franklin Martin, commissioner for medicine and sanitation.[11]

The Advisory Commission was able to perform its advisory function largely through the activities of permanent committees which each commissioner headed in his special field. The appointing officer of the committee related to higher education activities, known officially as the Committee on Science, Engineering, and Education, and unofficially as the "university committee," was Hollis Godfrey, president of Drexel Institute of Technology, Philadelphia, Pennsylvania. Its objectives were enumerated by Claxton in his 1917 *Statement:*

> With the entrance of the United States into the war it became desirable to establish a common policy of cooperation between the higher institutions and the Government, a policy which would result in the fullest utilization of higher educational resources of the country for national defense and service. A committee of the Advisory Commission of the Council of National Defense undertook to bring representatives of higher education together for this purpose, and, concurrently, to act as a medium of communication between the institutions and the

[11] The National Archives, *Preliminary Inventory of the Council of National Defense Records, 1916–1921* (Washington, 1942, typeset), pp. 1–7 (World War I Branch); and The National Archives, *Handbook of Federal World War Agencies and Their Records, 1917–1921* (Washington, 1942), p. 159.

Government and among the institutions themselves. The specialist in higher education has served as executive officer of this committee since its formation.[12]

In early May, 1917, Godfrey called a meeting of representatives of the principal associations of colleges and universities in Washington to aid him in the selection of the permanent committee.[13] Among those present were official representatives of the National Association of State Universities, the Association of American Agricultural Colleges and Experiment Stations, the Association of American Universities, the Association of American Colleges, and the Society for the Promotion of Engineering Education. In addition, there were 187 higher institutions represented.[14]

This group of college and university officials proceeded to formulate a program of cooperation between the higher institutions and the government as well as advise in the selection of a committee. They were unanimous in their willingness to cooperate; many were enthusiastic about the effort to be made. But no program existed and they were not clear about what was needed. Capen recalled the confusion that existed in a paper he wrote a quarter-century later:

> In their dealings with the government, university officers suffered from the existence of a state of confusion such as I hope they will never have to encounter again. I was then stationed in Washington at the point where university officers converged, from whence they radiated, and to which they returned utterly confused by the things which they did and did not find out from the various departments. Commonly they went home without receiving any assistance in the solution of their local problems, baffled and frustrated.[15]

Two items of paramount importance came from this May meeting. They were among the most important actions taken in the establishment of a working relationship between colleges and Federal Government during the war years. They were unquestionably the most positive. The first was the drafting and adoption of

---

[12] Claxton, *Statement . . . 1917*, pp. 12–13. cf. Samuel P. Capen, "The Colleges in a Nationalized Educational Scheme," *School and Society*, IX, No. 230, May 24, 1919, pp. 613–618.

[13] "War Department Committee on Education and Special Advisory Board, 1918–1919 (C. R. Mann), Miscellaneous Papers," Box 3 of 3, World War I Branch, National Archives, Washington, D. C. According to Claxton this meeting was held on May 3 (*Report . . . 1917*, p. 1) while Capen reported that it was held on May 5 (Capen and John, *op. cit.*, p. 39).

[14] Capen and John, *op. cit.*, pp. 39–40.

[15] S. P. Capen, "The Experiences of Higher Education in 1917–18," in C. S. Marsh (ed), *Higher Education and the War* (Washington, 1942), pp. 16–23. Quotation from p. 18. Also Evans and Wright, *op. cit.*, p. 61.

a "Statement of Principles," and the second was the appointment of a permanent Committee on Science, Engineering, and Education.[16]

Because it was the most concise statement of the role of higher education in the war effort, the "Statement of Principles" is recorded in full:

### STATEMENT OF PRINCIPLES

It is our judgment that our colleges and universities should so organize their work that in all directions they may be of the greatest possible usefulness to the country in its present crisis.

We therefore believe, first, that all young men below the age of liability to the selective draft and those not recommended for special service, who can avail themselves of the opportunities offered by our colleges, should be urged so to do in order that they may be able to render the most effective service, both during the full period of the war and in the trying times which will follow its close.

We believe, second, that all colleges and universities should so modify their calendars and curricula as will most fully subserve the present needs of the Nation and utilize most profitably the time of the students and the institutional plant, force, and equipment. With this end in view, we suggest that, as an emergency measure, the colleges consider the advisability of dividing the college year into four quarters of approximately 12 weeks each, and that, where necessary, courses be repeated at least once a year so that the college course may be best adapted to the needs of food production.

We believe, third, that in view of the supreme importance of applied science in the present war, students pursuing technical courses, such as medicine, agriculture, and engineering are rendering, or are to render, through the continuance of their training, services more valuable and efficient than if they were to enroll in military or naval service at once.

We believe, fourth, that the Government should provide or encourage military training for all young men in college by retired officers of the Army and National Guard or by other persons competent to give military instruction, and that the colleges should include as a part of their course of study teaching in military science, in accordance with the provisions of the national defense act of June, 1916.

We believe, fifth, that the Bureau of Education of the Department of the Interior and the State Relations Service of the Department of Agriculture, with the cooperation of the committee on science, engineering, and education of the advisory commission of the Council of National Defense, should be the medium of communication between the Federal departments and the higher educational institutions of the country.

---

[16] Capen and John, *op. cit.*, pp. 39–40; "War Department Committee . . . Miscellaneous Papers," Box 3.

Finally, we believe that an educational responsibility rests on the institutions of higher learning to disseminate correct information concerning the issues involved in the war and to interpret its meaning.[17]

The permanent committee of twenty-four members, the Committee on Science, Engineering, and Education, was headed by Godfrey as chairman and Capen as executive secretary. With minor changes the committee remained as originally constituted. Capen served as executive secretary throughout.[18]

But if the colleges and universities expected comprehensive and authoritative direction from this group, Capen wrote two years later,

. . . their expectations were only in part fulfilled. The Council of National Defense [which the committee advised] is not an executive, but purely an advisory body . . . However, through the agency of the university committee and the committee on the relation of engineering schools to the Govern-

---

[17] Capen and John, *op. cit.*, pp. 40–41.

[18] *Ibid.*, pp. 41–42. The complete list of members of the permanent committee, often referred to as the "university committee," as found on those pages:

"Hollis Godfrey, Sc.D., member of the advisory commission of the Council of National Defense, president, Drexel Institute, chairman.

Henry E. Crampton, Ph.D., professor, Columbia University, vice chairman.

Frederick C. Ferry, Ph.D., dean, Williams College, secretary.

Samuel P. Capen, Ph.D., specialist in higher education in the United States Bureau of Education, executive secretary.

Edwin A. Alderman, LL.D., president, University of Virginia.

Guy Potter Benton, LL.D., president, University of Vermont.

Kenyon L. Butterfield, L.D., president, Massachusetts Agricultural College.

Augustus S. Downing, LL.D., assistant commissioner for higher education, University of the State of New York.

Wilson Farrand, M.A., headmaster, Newark Academy.

Guy S. Ford, Ph.D., direction of the division on Civic and educational co-operation of the Committee on Public Information.

Frank J. Goodnow, LL.D., president, Johns Hopkins University.

Edward K. Graham, LL.D., president, University of North Carolina.

Charles S. Howe, Ph.D., president, Case School of Applied Science.

Harry Pratt Judson, LL.D., president, University of Chicago.

A. Lawrence Lowell, LL.D., president, Harvard University.

Frank L. McVey, LL.D., president, State University of North Dakota.

Alexander Meikeljohn, LL.D., president, Amherst College.

Joseph A. Mulry, Ph.D., president, Fordham University.

John S. Nollen, LL.D., president, Lake Forest College.

Raymond A. Pearson, LL.D., president, Iowa State College of Agriculture and Mechanic Arts.

Winthrop E. Stone, LL.D., president, Purdue University.

Henry Suzzallo, Ph.D., president, University of Washington.

William O. Thompson, LL.D., president, Ohio State University.

Robert E. Vinson, LL.D., president, University of Texas."

ment . . . it was able to bring to the attention of the operating departments some of the major problems of the colleges and to assist in the development of an effective national policy for the utilization of these training facilities.[19]

The National policy of which he spoke was determined largely through the Committee on the Relation of Engineering Schools to the Government. Godfrey appointed this group in July 1917. It was composed of Dean F. L. Bishop, Engineering School, University of Pittsburgh (chairman); Dr. Capen (secretary); President C. S. Howe, Case School of Applied Science; Dean M. S. Ketchum, College of Engineering, University of Colorado; and Dr. C. R. Mann, special investigator for the Carnegie Foundation for the Advancement of Teaching.[20]

This group worked closely with War Department representatives in determining need for men with technical training, and with colleges and universities in making these needs known. But the activity of both this and the larger "university committee" resembled piecemeal attacks on a huge problem in comparison with the Engineering, Science, and Management War Training program of World War II. In the final analysis, the education of engineers and other much needed technicians and scientists was a hit-and-miss affair. The supply did not approximate the demand at the time of the Armistice in November 1918. If the war had continued longer it is possible a comprehensive program would have evolved. But the committees were advisory only and lacked the strength to execute comprehensive programs, and the Office of Education was a reporting and advisory body without power.[21]

The third committee with which Capen was associated was related to these two subsidiaries of the Council of National Defense. On February 10, 1918, the Secretary of War, Newton D. Baker, created a Committee on Education and Special Training. It was composed of three Army officers and charged with these functions:

To study the needs of the various branches of the service for

[19] *Ibid.*, p. 42.

[20] *Ibid.*, pp. 49–50; "War Department Committee . . . Miscellaneous Papers," Box 3.

[21] For additional comments on the activities of these committees see Claxton, *Report . . . 1917*, pp. 1–3; Claxton, *Statement . . . 1918*, p. 10; Claxton, *Report . . . 1918*, pp. 122–123; and Capen, "The Experiences of Higher Education in 1917–18," pp. 16–23. In the Archives file referred to in fn. 13, *supra*, there is an undated document evidently prepared by Capen and entitled "Summary of the Activities of S. P. Capen in Connection with the Council of National Defense Since May 1, 1917." This outlines his activities in detail.

skilled men and technicians; to determine how such needs shall be met, whether by selective draft, special training in educational institutions, or otherwise; to secure the cooperation of the educational institutions of the country and to represent the War Department in its relations with such institutions; to administer such plan of special training in colleges and schools as may be adopted.[22]

Associated with this committee was to be an "advisory civilian board" appointed by the Secretary of War. He initially appointed five men to the board, later adding the last two names listed below:

Dr. C. R. Mann, Carnegie Foundation for the Advancement of teaching, representing engineering education (chairman);

Dean James R. Angell, University of Chicago, representing university education;

Mr. J. W. Dietz, educational manager of the Western Electric Company, representing vocational education;

Mr. J. P. Monroe, member of the Federal Board for Vocational Education (when he resigned he was replaced by Dean Herman Schneider of the Engineering School, University of Cincinnati);

Dr. Capen (who was later appointed secretary);

President R. A. Pearson, Iowa State College, representing agricultural education; and

Mr. Hugh Frayne, representing labor interests.[23]

Immediately after its formation in February it took over the work of the committees subsidiary to the Council of National Defense. The Committee on the Relation of Engineering Schools to the Government ceased to exist and the "university committee," which was to be dissolved in September 1918, turned its recommendations over to the War Department group for its consideration and possible implementation.[24]

The War Department Committee on Education and Special Training thus became the official Governmental body in dealing with colleges and universities. It alone, of all Government or semi-Government representative bodies dealing with education during the war, had status and power.

One of its two major accomplishments was the establishment of National Army Training Detachments in colleges and universities. Through these detachments a total of 130,000 men were trained in seven months. The program covered 47 Army occupa-

---

[22] Capen and John, *op. cit.*, p. 53.

[23] *Ibid.*, pp. 52–53; Claxton, *Statement . . . 1918*, p. 10; Claxton, *Statement . . . 1919*, p. 13, and "War Department Committee . . . Miscellaneous Papers," 3 boxes.

[24] The National Archives, *Handbook*, p. 159.

tional fields. Men were trained in such prosaic, but essential, trades as auto mechanics, plumbing, cement laying, and railroad engineering. There were 147 training centers in operation at the time of the Armistice, 123 of them at engineering schools. An interesting development, rich in implication for the next war, was the weekly discussion of American war aims as part of the training program. This was a forerunner of the orientation programs of World War II. From the point of numbers trained and quality of training, the National Army Training Detachment program was the most successful educational operation of the war.[25]

The second accomplishment was in no way as successful but was noteworthy more for what it failed to accomplish than for what it achieved. "Having inaugurated the units of the National Army Training Detachments, the committee and its advisory board proceeded to study the more complicated question of the proper development of the potential officer material contained in colleges and universities.[26] From this study came the short-lived Students' Army Training Corps.

On August 24, 1918, War Department General Order No. 79 created the Corps. Institutions volunteering to participate in the Corps program made contracts for the housing, feeding, and instructing of student soldiers who were to be, at all times, under military authority. The student-soldiers were volunteers. The original plan said that all men over the age of 18 were to be encouraged to enlist while younger men, who could not legally enlist, could "enroll" for training. None of the men in the program were to be called to service until the age of 21.[27]

Before this far-sighted plan could become operative the military situation changed for the worse. This was in the Summer of 1918, shortly before the issuance of General Order No. 79. So the plan was modified before any action on it could be taken. A call for more officers and enlisted men went out and the authorities considered it impractical, if not impossible, to allow men to stay in college until they were 21 years old. Under the modification, 18 year-old volunteers were to receive a nine month training program in the Corps before being called to service; 19 year-olds were to receive six months; and 20 year-olds were to receive three months. Training in academic subjects virtually disappeared under this

---

[25] Capen and John, *op. cit.*, pp. 54–57; and Capen, "The Experiences of Higher Education in 1917–18," pp. 16–23.

[26] Capen and John, *op. cit.*, p. 57.

[27] Ltr., Secretary of War to presidents of colleges, dtd. May 6, 1918, as reproduced in Philander P. Claxton, *Report of the Commissioner of Education for the Year Ended June 30, 1919* (Washington, 1919), pp. 5–6.

pressure program and the Corps became a purely military training device.[28]

The Students' Army Training Corps was dissolved on December 21, 1918, having been rendered unnecessary because of the Armistice. Part of the time it was virtually inoperative because of the terrible influenza epidemic of October-November 1918. However, there were approximately 142,000 young men from 517 colleges and universities enrolled in its programs. It "ran just long enough to develop all the possible centers of friction and to expose all its serious defects."[29] Although unsuccessful in its attempt to combine military and academic education, largely because of circumstances beyond its control, the Corps provided some valuable lessons in officer training for World War II. It indicated interest on the part of students and college administrators and showed the necessity for retaining academic subjects. The Corps stimulated officer training at educational institutions. It was an incentive for the establishment in 1920 of a Reserve Officers' Training Corps in land-grant colleges and universities through which persons completing four years of study in military training could receive commissions in the Army Reserve.[30]

The War Department Committee on Education and Special Training continued operation on a limited basis for nearly a year after the end of the war. On September 5, 1919, it was dissolved and ten days later the functions it had performed were transferred to the War Plans Division of the General Staff.[31]

These committees were the most important but by no means the only groups with which Capen was associated during the war years. He was a member of the War Council of the Office of Education, assisting in formulating policy for the furtherance of the war effort of the Government. He was a member of the advisory committee of the educational bureau of the Young Men's Christian Association, and participated in conferences of the

---

[28] Capen expressed his disappointment in Students' Army Training Corps in "The Experiences of Higher Education in 1917–18," pp. 16–23.

[29] Claxton, *Report . . . 1919*, p. 7. Claxton stated "The Students' Army Training Corps had a brief 10 weeks of life." (*Ibid.*, p. 7). Capen and John, *op. cit.*, p. 59, say "The Students' Army Training Corps had a brief six weeks of life." Actually it lasted about four months, from August 24 to December 21, 1918. See Claxton, *op. cit.*, pp. 5–11; Capen and John, *op. cit.*, pp. 57–63; and *School Life*, I, No. 1, August 1918, p. 6.

[30] Claxton, *Report . . . 1919*, pp. 11–12; and Lloyd Blauch, "Higher Education and the Federal Government," (mimeographed paper, 1956), p. 3.

[31] War Department General Order No. 107, September 5, 1919, and War Department General Order No. 109, September 15, 1919, in The National Archives, *Handbook*, p. 144.

YMCA Overseas Educational Commission. He also served as a member of the committee on educational relations of the National Research Council.[32]

In January 1918, an event occurred not directly related to the Division of Higher Education but which would soon claim the full attention of its chief. This was the establishment of an "Emergency Council on Education" at a meeting held in Washington. Present, in addition to members of the Office of Education, were representatives of the Association of American Colleges, the National Association of State Universities, the Association of Urban Universities, the Catholic Educational Association, the American Association of University Professors, the Society for the Promotion of Engineering Education, the Association of American Medical Colleges, and various branches of the National Education Association. Dr. Capen presided at this meeting which resulted in the formation of the Emergency Council whose purpose was:

> To place the educational resources of the country more completely at the service of the National Government and its departments, to the end that through an understanding cooperation:
> The patriotic services of the public schools, professional schools, and colleges and universities may be augmented;
> A continuous supply of educated men may be maintained; and
> Greater effectiveness in meeting educational problems arising during and following the war may be secured.[33]

An executive council of six members was elected and the first president, Dr. Donald J. Cowling, President of Carleton College, took office. The Office of Education had no representatives on this initial council. After the first meeting the organization changed its name to the American Council on Education.

The American Council on Education was particularly active in the field of international educational relations. One of the most publicized of its responsibilities was making arrangements for, and planning the itinerary of, seven British educators representing an equal number of leading British universities. The group visited the United States in the fall of 1918. Capen took a major part in both the planning phase and the visit of the educators. Also in the international field and related to the British educational mission, Dr. Capen prepared a report on fellowships and

[32] Claxton, *Statement* . . . *1918*, p. 10; Claxton, *Statement* . . . *1919*, pp. 13–16; Claxton, *Report* . . . *1919*, pp. 209–211; and typewritten ms, in "War Department Committee . . . Miscellaneous Papers," Box 3 of 3.
[33] Capen and John, *op. cit.*, p. 52.

scholarships available to British students in American universities.[34]

In December 1918, at a meeting in Cambridge, Massachusetts, it was decided that the American Council should make itself into a permanent organization which would be the agent for the unification of higher educational interests. Plans were developed for the establishment in Washington of an organization to represent "higher institutions of the United States in dealing with educational institutions of foreign countries, the representation of the opinions of educational interests before Congress and the Government departments, and the study of important problems in educational organization and practice." [35] The plans were approved by the members in May 1919, and on December 1, Capen resigned as chief of the Division of Higher Education to become the first permanent Director of the American Council on Education. He was to remain there for three years at which time he left to become Chancellor of the University of Buffalo.[36]

Despite the good work accomplished by the Committee on the Relation of Engineering Schools to the Government and the War Department's Committee on Education and Special Training, the Federal Government's effort to channel the work of higher educational institutions into those areas where they could most effectively contribute was far from successful. There was too much confusion, a plethora of conflicting suggestions and directives, and no clear-cut statement of objectives. In place of a concise goal toward which to work, colleges were given inspiring, but nebulous, ideals toward which to strive.

There were two major contributors to this inefficiency in marshalling higher educational resources. The first was that the war did not last long enough to permit any comprehensive programs to be organized and put into operation. The second, and far more important, was the failure of both governmental and university officials, considered as a group, to appreciate the need for a program of controlled production of skilled and educated manpower. This may have been due to the newness of the concept

---

[34] On the British educational mission see C. L. Lewis, *Philander Priestley Claxton, Crusader for Public Education* (Knoxville, Tennessee, 1948), pp. 217, 233; Claxton, *Statement . . . 1919*, p. 16; and *School Life*, I, No. 6, October 16, 1918, p. 2.

[35] Claxton, *Report . . . 1919*, p. 18.

[36] *Ibid.*, p. 18; Capen's Personnel Folder, St. Louis Records Center, St. Louis, Missouri; and Edward C. Elliott, "A Tribute to Samuel Paul Capen," *The Educational Record*, XXXVIII, No. 1, January 1957, pp. 18–19.

of total war, the reluctance of Federal educational leaders to interfere in college affairs, the deep-rooted tradition of academic freedom, or all three. But whatever was behind it, colleges and universities did not contribute more than a fraction of what they were able, and willing, to contribute.

This is not to say that the role of the college, and its relationship to the Office of Education, must be charged off as total failure. On the contrary, some of the accomplishments were noteworthy while those which were not successful provided clues for the future. The war showed that there was a definite need for a strengthened Office of Education to supervise and operate it. Perhaps most important of all, the war showed that higher education was vital to national defense.

## *"Normalcy," 1919–1928*

In 1919 the Office of Education had the largest number of employees in its fifty-three-year history. In Washington it had a force of 91 officers and specialists, 133 clerks and office workers, and 11 messengers, for a total of 235. There were also 380 collaborators of various types, including the "dollar-a-year men." The work of the Office was divided among 22 divisions, one of which was the Division of Higher Education.[37]

The end of the war and the change of administration which followed soon after helped stimulate agitation for an increase in the size of the Office of Education and a corresponding expansion of responsibilities. Claxton, like earlier Commissioners, had pushed for higher salaries and more help, stressing repeatedly the need for additional specialists.[38] His efforts had met with only partial success so far as the Division of Higher Education was concerned for it had increased by only one staff member and was still below a desirable strength.[39]

The small size of the Division did not keep Capen from big ideas. In the months following the end of the war, late in 1918

---

[37] *School Life*, III, No. 1, July 1, 1919, p. 9.

[38] His *Statements* invariably recommended an increase in both staff and salaries. His list of recommendations kept growing. In the 1911 *Statement*, his first, the section on "Recommendations" covered 3-1/2 pages; in his 1920 *Statement*, his last, they filled 11 pages. See also *School Life*, I, No. 9, December 1, 1918, pp. 1–2.

[39] In 1919, the first year of peace, the staff consisted of Dr. Capen as chief; Dr. Chester D. Jarvis, specialist in agricultural education; and Dr. Walton C. John, specialist in land-grant college statistics. See Appendix I, *infra*.

or in the early weeks of 1919, he wrote an article for *School and Society* in which he came out strongly for a more active Federal role in higher education. The Students' Army Training Corps in which more than 500 colleges and universities had willingly participated represented a form of nationalization. Although not successful, this program showed that Washington could perform a larger role in higher education. "The federal government should participate in the direction of education more largely than it now does, but should not control it." [40]

He proposed this should be through subsidies to institutions meeting rigid predetermined standards, or through intellectual leadership from the Federal level. This was more than desirable; it was inevitable if our institutions were to keep pace with the world.

This meant the Office had to be expanded if it were to be "a coordinating, planning and investigating body, under mandate to draw into its councils the representatives of every educational interest, commissioned to tap the ultimate sources of national wisdom in framing the educational policies of the nation." [41] Perhaps, if the Office were to do this job well, it should be made a Department.

There was a lot of talk about a "Department of Education" in 1919 and 1920. A Mr. C. L. Staples, clerk in the Research Division of the Bureau of Foreign and Domestic Commerce, Washington, prepared an article which showed the lowly position occupied by the Office in 1919. According to appropriations made, it was 45th in standing of the Government, and the Commissioner of Education was 750th in rank. While the Interstate Commerce Commission was handsomely housed in an eleven-story building of its own, the Office of Education had only a few rooms in a corner of the Pension Building. [42] This article may have been motivated by a bill then before the Congress which would have established a Department of Education. This was the "Towner Bill" introduced in the House of Representatives on January 30, 1919. [43] The Towner plan, and similar plans for a Department of Education, received the support of National organizations such as the Na-

---

[40] Capen, "The Colleges in a Nationalized Educational Scheme," pp. 613–618. Quotation from p. 614.

[41] *Ibid.*, p. 618.

[42] C. L. Staples, "A Critique of the U. S. Bureau of Education," *Education*, XL, No. 2, October 1919, pp. 78–97.

[43] "The Education Bill," *School and Society*, IX, No. 218, March 1, 1919, pp. 272–277. The bill was later known as the "Towner-Stirling Bill."

tional Education Association, the American Federation of Labor, the Daughters of the American Revolution, and the League of Women Voters.[44]

The struggle over the proposed Department need not concern us except to note that it continued for five years after the war, well into the Harding administration, and it was the major factor in the resignation of Claxton in 1921. But before the event took place, the Division of Higher Education had experienced a change in leadership. Capen resigned in December 1919, to become the first permanent Director of the American Council on Education.[45] When he left, the Division lost, in the words of the Commissioner, "a strong man, conservatively aggressive, with a broad knowledge of higher education throughout the United States, deliberate in making up his judgment but strong in holding to it when once it is made. He thinks keenly and acts promptly." [46] President Emeritus Edward C. Elliott of Purdue University, a life-long friend of Capen, has called him "a driving force in the Bureau of Education and the American Council on Education, and as Chancellor of the University of Buffalo." [47]

[44] Hugh S. Magill, "Education and the Federal Government," *School and Society*, XIV, No. 354, October 8, 1921, pp. 259–263. See also "Enlargement of the Bureau of Education," *The School Review*, XXXI, No. 10, December 1923, pp. 721–722; and William T. Bawden, *The National Crisis in Education* (Washington, 1920), pp. 131–141, for comments on the need for an expanded activity in education.

[45] Ltrs., Capen to the Secretary of the Interior (Franklin K. Lane), November 29, 1919; Secretary of the Interior to Capen, December 1, 1919; in Capen's Personnel Folder, St. Louis Records Center, St. Louis, Missouri. There is a letter of comment on the relationship of the American Council on Education to the Office of Education written by Claxton to President William J. Kerr, Oregon Agricultural College, Corvallis, Oregon, July 7, 1919. In this letter Commissioner Claxton expressed his approval of a permanent Council "with the feeling that until the Bureau of Education or another agency has sufficient funds to do the work in the name of the Government, that the Council may do much valuable work which the Bureau cannot."

See also Philander P. Claxton, *Report of the Commissioner of Education for the Year Ended June 30, 1920* (Washington, 1920), pp. 16–17.

[46] Ltr., Claxton to Mr. R. L. Burger, Trustee, Ohio University, Athens, Ohio, December 15, 1920, in Capen's Personnel Folder, St. Louis Records Center, St. Louis, Missouri. Capen was being considered for the presidency of that institution in 1920.

[47] Ltr., Dr. Elliott to author, December 10, 1959. In "A Resolution of Tribute to Samuel Paul Capen" prepared by Dr. Elliott in 1956, a copy of which was sent to the author, the President Emeritus of Purdue University wrote:

"By heritage, by thorough intellectual preparation in leading institutions of learning of the United States and Europe; by quality of mind and personality; by innate character and integrity; by tested and successful ap-

It did not take long for a successor to be appointed. The possibility that Capen would resign if the American Council position were offered to him was open knowledge in higher education circles. As early as August 21, 1919, Dr. George F. Zook, the 34-year-old head of the Department of History, Political Science, and Economics at Pennsylvania State College, made application for the impending vacancy. The Commissioner offered it to him in December. Zook was at first reluctant to accept because the $3,000 salary was insufficient. But on January 2, 1920, he gave a "conditional acceptance on the understanding that my salary will be very considerably increased as soon as it becomes financially and legally possible for the Bureau to do so." [48] He entered on duty on February 1, 1920, at the salary which he justifiably protested. Incidentally, it took more than four years before he got the salary boost that he expected in 1920. On July 1, 1924, Zook received an increase to $5,200 per annum under the provisions of the Classification Act of March 4, 1923.[49]

During Claxton's last years in office, from the end of World War I to the middle of 1921, several actions relating to higher education were taken. Some were instrumental in the development of long-range programs or in establishing a rapprochement with higher education; others were not so successful. Among the latter was the abortive attempt in fiscal year 1919 to have State Departments of Education collect educational statistics at all levels within their geographical areas for the Federal Government. The idea may have been sound but few States had resources adequate for the task.[50] A loss to the Division, and to the Office of Educa-

---

prenticeship in the fine art of teaching; by varied experience in the constructive leadership of country-wide educational and social enterprises; and, above all, by his clear vision of things to come, Dr. Capen was a 'natural' for the courageous acceptance of the challenge presented by the conception of the American Council on Education in 1918. The activating nucleus of this conception was the creation of an agency to bring about common understanding and cooperative effort, especially by the institutions of higher and professional education, for rendering the most effective service to the national well-being . . .

. . . We remember him as a scholar, as a gentleman and as a civilized man. Most of all, as a friend with whom it was a delight to work, dream and do."

[48] Ltrs., Zook to Claxton, August 21, 1919; Claxton to Zook, December 20, 1919; and Zook to Claxton, January 2, 1920; and telegram, Zook to Claxton, December 23, 1919; in Zook's Personnel Folder, St. Louis Records Center, St. Louis, Missouri.

[49] Oath of Commission, January 10, 1920; and formal notification of change of grade and service title, June 30, 1924; in *Ibid.* For biographical information on Zook see Appendix I. *infra.*

[50] Smith, *op. cit.,* pp. 21–23; and Claxton, *Statement . . . 1919,* pp. 5–6.

tion, came with the resignation of Chester Jarvis, specialist in agricultural education. He resigned in March 1921, and the space was not filled. However, the Division was able to retain its strength when John was promoted from specialist in land-grant college statistics to specialist in rural and technical education, and Mr. Lloyd C. Blauch joined the staff in August 1921, as specialist in land-grant college statistics.[51]

One of the more successful programs, considered from the long-range view, was the meeting called by the Commissioner on educational research problems. It was held in St. Louis, Missouri, on January 2–3, 1920. Representatives from seven large State universities, representing various sections of the country, were present.[52] As a result sixteen research stations were established at an equal number of universities throughout the Nation. The Office of Education was assigned the task of coordinating their activities and publishing certain of their research reports. This was a forerunner of the cooperative research program which developed in the mid-1950's.[53]

One of Zook's major interests was the junior college movement. He demonstrated this soon after taking office by arranging a conference of junior college officials in St. Louis. The conference was held on June 30 and July 1, 1920. There were deans and presidents of thirty institutions present. From this meeting on the problems of the rapidly expanding junior college movement came the American Association of Junior Colleges.[54]

In 1919 the Office of Education was called upon to evaluate the

---

[51] Smith, *op. cit.*, pp. 32, 44; and George F. Zook, "The Bureau of Education and Higher Education," *School Life*, IX, No. 9, May 1924, pp. 199–201. For further information see Appendix I, *infra*.

[52] One of the delegates, representing the University of Kansas, was Dr. Frederick J. Kelly who was to serve as specialist in higher education and director of the Division of Higher Education from 1931 to 1946.

[53] "The Federal Bureau and Educational Research," *Journal of Educational Research*, I, No. 1, January 1920, pp. 156–157; and Philander P. Claxton, *Statement of the Commissioner of Education to the Secreary of the Interior for the Fiscal Year Ended June 30, 1920* (Washington, 1920), pp. 38–39.

[54] Archives File 205, "Junior Colleges, Historical" (National Archives, Labor and Transportation Branch); Archives File 905, "Exclusion of Foreign Education in Annual Reports, etc." *(Ibid.)*; Claxton, *Statement . . . 1920*, p. 18; Claxton, *Report . . . 1920*, pp. 10–11; Zook, *op. cit.*, p. 201; and "George F. Zook," *Higher Education*, VIII, No. 2, September 15, 1951, pp. 22–23. This last noted article states that the meeting was held "June 30 and July 1, 1925," an obvious error. In his 1921 *Report* Commissioner John J. Tigert noted that the Office of Education was about to publish a Circular on the junior college conference held at St. Louis on "June 30–July 1, 1921." See Tigert, *Report of the Commissioner of Education for the Year Ended June 30, 1921* (Washington, 1921), p. 15.

academic credentials of foreign students seeking admission to higher institutions in the United States.[55] This work was the responsibility of the Foreign Educational System Division (sometimes known as the Comparative Education Division) with advisory functions performed by the Division of Higher Education. In February, 1951, there was an administrative reorganization of the Office of Education and at that time there was a Foreign Educational Systems Branch established in the Division of Higher Education. This gave the division complete responsibility for evaluation of foreign student credentials. This responsibility was not retained by the division very long for by September, 1952, the evaluation activity was turned over to the new Division of International Education, which continued the work of the former Comparative Education Division.[56]

The evaluation program began in a small way, so small in fact that it was not noted in annual reports for several years. After the war several foreign students applied for admission to American colleges and some of these institutions asked the Office to check their credentials. There is no record of how many institutions or students were involved during the first five or six years but it was probably less than 100 each year. As the service became more widely known and the tide of foreign students rose, the demands on the Office increased. In fiscal year 1928 credentials of 307 students from 53 countries were evaluated; the following year 481 from 57 countries. In 1951, when the Division of Higher Education had full responsibility, Dr. Marjorie Johnston of the Office staff reported, "During the past few years approximately 450 colleges and universities have requested this service." [57]

Routine activities of the Division which had been disturbed or curtailed by the war effort were quickly renewed. The specialist in higher education and others on his staff were called upon to attend conferences which they did as frequently as possible. Both

---

[55] Marjorie C. Johnston, "Evaluation of Foreign Student Credentials: A Preliminary Report," *Higher Education*, VIII, No. 10, January 15, 1952, pp. 115–116.

[56] On administrative reorganization of the Office of Education see Earl J. McGrath, *Annual Report of the Federal Security Agency 1951. Office of Education* (Washington, 1952), pp. 12–15; and Public Administration Service, *A Report on an Administrative Survey of the United States Office of Education of the Federal Security Agency* (Washington, 1950). Additional information supplied by Miss Lora Brookley, Educational Reference Librarian, Department of Health, Education, and Welfare Library.

[57] John J. Tigert, *Report of the Commissioner of Education for the Year Ended June 30, 1928* (Washington, 1928); p. 30; William John Cooper, *Annual Report of the Commissioner of Education for the Year Ended June 30, 1929* (Washington, 1929), p. 31; and Marjorie C. Johnston, *op. cit.*, p. 115.

Capen and Zook were in demand as speakers to educational and lay groups, as were their successors in office. The publications program returned to peacetime topics and there was an increase in the number and variety of publications relating to higher education.[58]

In noting the struggle for a "Department of Education" which occurred in the post-war years, reference was made to the resignation of Claxton. President Harding had stated during his campaign that he favored the establishment of a Department of Education and Welfare. When elected to office he asked Claxton to prepare the bill for the new Department with the understanding the Commissioner would become the first Secretary. Claxton did as requested but let it be known he favored a reorganization of the Office along different lines. The plan he wanted would have a nine-member "National Board of Education" as the top policy formulating group. This "opposition to the President's plan evidently led to Harding's request for his resignation, which was submitted May 12, 1921, to take effect June 1." There is some irony in Claxton's career with the Office of Education. He had been appointed by a Republican (Taft), had served with distinction through two terms of a Democratic President (Wilson), only to be removed by another Republican.[59]

The seventh Commissioner of Education, Dr. John James Tigert (1882–1965) took office on June 2, 1921. Tigert was another Tennessean, the third from that State, having been born in Nashville on February 11, 1882. He graduated from Vanderbilt University, Nashville, in 1904. His record there as a student and athlete won him a Rhodes scholarship, the first to be awarded in Tennessee. He received a master's degree at Oxford University and returned to the United States in 1907 to become a professor of philosophy

---

[58] For example, in the three years preceeding our entrance into World War I (1914–1916) there were 46 publications relating to higher education. The three years following (1919–1921) there were 62. A list of conferences attended, and speaking commitments filled, can be found in the annual reports for the period.

[59] The full story of the resignation of Claxton is told in J. N. Rodeheaver, Jr., "The Relation of the Federal Government to Civic Education," (Cambridge, Mass., 1951, typewritten ms.), pp. 130–131. See also Lewis, op. cit., p. 335. Quotation from Rodeheaver, op. cit., p. 131. Claxton devoted the rest of his life to education in the South. He became Provost of the University of Alabama in 1921. From 1923 to 1930 he was superintendent of schools in Tulsa, Oklahoma. In 1930 he became President of Austin Peay State College, Clarksville, Tennessee. He retired in 1945 and died in Knoxville, Tennessee, on January 12, 1957. Lewis, op. cit.; Evans and Wright, op. cit., pp. 65–66; and "Office of Education and the Commissioners of Education," File of material in Education Library, Department of Health, Education, and Welfare Library.

and psychology at Central College, Fayette, Missouri. In 1909 he became President of Kentucky Wesleyan College, Winchester, Kentucky, and in 1911 went to the University of Kentucky as professor of philosophy and psychology, the position he held at the time of his appointment. Tigert held doctorates from several schools including an LL.D. from Kentucky (1921) and an Ed.D. from Rhode Island College of Education (1923).[60]

Tigert undertook an extensive reorganization of the Office almost immediately upon coming to Washington. In place of the large number of semi-independent divisions which had existed under Claxton, he reorganized by grouping the work of the office into two major types of activities. The first he called "general service activities" and he placed at the head the chief clerk of the Office, Mr. Lewis Kalbach. This group had seven divisions: Editorial; Library; Statistics; Alaskan Affairs; Stenographic; Mail and Files; and Messenger. These divisions constituted the routine administrative functions of the Office. The second Tigert called "technical activities" and it was headed by an Assistant to the Commissioner, Dr. William T. Bawden. It had four Divisions: Higher Education; Rural Schools; City Schools; and Services.[61] In 1924, Zook, then specialist in higher education, was promoted to the position of Assistant to the Commissioner, following Bawden to the position.[62]

This organization underwent some modification in the following years. As of July 1, 1927, the organization chart showed nine divisions and two sections reporting directly to the office of the Commissioner. This meant that the separation of activities in two major groupings had been abolished. The latter arrangement continued until the major reorganization which took place under Commissioner William J. Cooper in 1930.[63]

---

[60] *Who's Who in America*, XVI, p. 2192; "Office of Education and the Commissioners of Education," File of material in Education Library, Department of Health, Education, and Welfare Library; Rodeheaver, *op. cit.*, pp. 133–136; Evans and Wright, *op. cit.*, pp. 67–70; and T. J. Ford, "The Educational Contributions of the U.S. Commissioners of Education, 1867–1928" (Washington, 1933, typewritten ms.), pp. 88–89.

[61] cf. John J. Tigert, "The Organization of the Bureau of Education," *School Life*, VII, No. 1, September 21, 1921, pp. 6–7; Rodeheaver, *op. cit.*, pp. 136–138; Tigert, *Report . . . 1921*, p. 6; and John J. Tigert, *Report of the Commissioner of Education for the Year Ended June 30, 1923* (Washington, 1923). pp. 2–4.

[62] U. S. Office of Education, *Educational Directories, 1920–1925* (Washington, 1921 *et seq.*), 1924, pp. 1–2; and *School Life*, IX, No. 9, May 1924, p. 197.

[63] William John Cooper, *Annual Report of the Commissioner of Education for the Year Ended June 30, 1930* (Washington, 1930), Figure 1 following p. 2. This reorganization is noted in Chapter IV, *infra*.

Under Commissioners Tigert and Cooper the survey movement reached its peak. The higher education survey, which owed so much to Capen, experienced a revival in the post-war years. Tigert indicated the extent of the increase in the survey movement at all levels in his 1922 *Report:*

One of the most important types of service rendered by the bureau, and probably most far-reaching in effect, is in its conduct of educational surveys. Shortly after I took office I caused a summary to be made of the activities of the bureau in this matter, and found that an aggregate of 156 surveys have been made by it, in 42 States and the District of Columbia, also Hawaii, Porto Rico, and one of the Provinces of Canada. These surveys may be classified as follows:

 (a) State public-school systems _____ 9
 (b) State systems for higher education _____ 7
 (c) Higher educational institutions _____ 88
 (d) Public school systems of cities _____ 17
 (e) School buildings in cities _____ 10
 (f) Public-school systems of counties _____ 9
 (g) Negro education in the United States (26
   States and District of Columbia) _____ 1
 (h) Unclassified _____ 15

    Total _____156

\*  \*  \*  \*  \*  \*  \*

During the fiscal year 1921–22 the following surveys were made:

 (a) State system of public schools, Arkansas _____ 1
 (b) State system of higher education, Kansas _____ 1
 (c) Higher educational institutions _____ 31
   Arkansas, 13 colleges and universities
   Arizona, State University
   Oregon, 12 colleges and universities
   Tennessee, 4 colleges
   State College for Women, Greensboro, N.C.
 (d) Public school systems of cities _____ 4
   Trenton, N. J. (administration)
   Washington, D. C. (administration)
   Shreveport, La.
   Sparta, Wis.
 (e) School buildings in cities _____ 3
   Parkersburg, W. Va.
   Washington, N. C.
   Greenfield, Ohio
 (f) County system of public schools _____ 1
   Washington County, Va.

    Total _____ 41

The surveys made during the past fiscal year are therefore almost a third of the total number of surveys made by the bureau in the 54 years of its previous existence.[64]

By the end of fiscal year 1927, Tigert was able to report that the number had increased to more than 200:

Educational surveys constitute a most important phase of the

---

[64] John J. Tigert, *Report of the Commissioner of Education for the Year Ended June 30, 1922* (Washington, 1922), pp. 5–6.

service of the Bureau of Education. This service has been increasing in quantity in recent years. From the establishment of the bureau in 1867 a total of 203 educational surveys has been made under its auspices, of which number 88 have been made since 1921. These surveys covered the whole of continental United States, as well as Hawaii and Puerto Rico. They may be classified as follows:

| | |
|---|---:|
| National (study of negro education) | 1 |
| State systems of education | 11 |
| State systems of higher education | 10 |
| County systems | 22 |
| City systems | 26 |
| Building programs in city systems | 15 |
| Higher educational institutions | 98 |
| Miscellaneous | 20 |
| Total | 203 [65] |

Zook proved a worthy successor to Capen in the higher educational survey movement. Not only was the rate of production increased under his direction but he also succeeded in maintaining a thoroughness similar to that which existed under his predecessor. Among the most comprehensive surveys he directed were those of the University of Arkansas, North Carolina College of Agriculture and Engineering, higher education in the city of Cleveland, and in the States of Tennessee, Kansas, Oklahoma, and Massachusetts.[66]

Dr. Arthur J. Klein, successor to Zook in 1925, considered the educational surveys made between 1922 and 1926 the most varied in the history of the Office. They ranged from surveys of privately-controlled institutions through city systems to entire State systems.[67]

The successors to Zook and Tigert carried on the movement but starting in 1926 there was a pronounced change in the type of survey and the manner of conducting it.[68] In that year Klein began

---

[65] John J. Tigert, *Report of the Commissioner of Education for the Year Ended June 30, 1927* (Washington, 1927), p. 20. In both the 1922 and 1927 listings of surveys Commissioner Tigert has counted each institution of higher education included in a State or other type survey as a separate survey. This accounts for the large number of surveys of higher educational institutions in his list. Dr. Walter C. Eells, *Survey of American Higher Education* (New York, 1937), did not break the surveys down in this manner which accounts in part for the much smaller listing found in Chapter II, *supra*. Another factor involved was Tigert's counting of unpublished surveys which Eells did not do.

[66] "George F. Zook," p. 22. See Chapter II, *supra*, for list of Office surveys of higher education to 1936.

[67] Eells, *op. cit.*, pp. 41–42.

[68] *Ibid.*, p. 42. For information on surveys and some remarks on the changing pattern of higher educational surveys see Archives File 206, "Teacher Training—Historical" (National Archives, Labor and Transportation

the survey of land-grant colleges which marked the start of the emphasis on national surveys.[69] Prior to 1926 there had been two higher education surveys which crossed State boundaries: the Negro education survey completed in 1916, and the study of land-grant education from 1910 to 1920. These had been exceptions to the general type of survey. After 1926 the large national survey became far more common. This kind required a large number of specialists and consultants so the Office of Education usually served as a coordinator and director of the survey. In many of the smaller, earlier surveys Office personnel had performed a large part of the field work.

There were seven national surveys involving higher education and in which the Office of Education participated extensively between 1926 and 1942:

1. The land-grand college survey. This had been requested by the Association of Land-grant Colleges and Universities. It lasted from fiscal year 1926 to fiscal year 1930 and was financed by a special appropriation of $117,000 from the Congress. Data were drawn from the returns on 20 lengthy questionnaires from 69 institutions located in 51 States and territories. These returns, which provided the basic source of information, totaled about 500,000 pages. There were 85 people on the survey staff, 13 from the regular Office of Education staff and the remainder temporary employees paid from the special appropriation. The survey was directed by Klein. Results were published in the 1930 series of Office of Education Bulletins in two volumes adding up to more than 1,900 pages.[70]

2. Negro college survey. This was undertaken in 1927 at the request of Negro colleges and universities. The survey was financed with a $5,000 fund established by 79 Negro institutions of higher education, a grant of $5,000 from the Phelps-Stokes Fund, and the remainder from the Office of Education. Work was completed in 1929 under the direction of Dr. Klein. Personnel from the 79 institutions involved in the survey assisted, along with members of State departments of education in the 19 States in which the institutions were located, members of

---

Branch); and the article by Walton C. John entitled "National Surveys of the Office of Education" in *Biennial Survey of Education, 1928–1930* (Washington, 1931), pp. 695–726.

[69] Ltr., Chief Clerk Kalbach to F. B. Jenks, Burlington, Vermont, April 4, 1927, in Jenks' Personnel Folder, St. Louis Records Center, St. Louis, Missouri.

[70] Charles H. Judd, *Research in the United States Office of Education* (Washington, 1939), pp. 25–26, 29; Eells, *op. cit.*, p. 381; Cooper, *Report . . . 1930*, pp. 19–20; and Arthur J. Klein, "Land-Grant Colleges are Participating in Work of Survey," *School Life*, XIII, No. 9, May 1928, p. 180. The survey report was *Survey of Land-grant Colleges and Universites*, Bulletin, 1930, No. 9 (2 Vols.).

the Association of Colleges for Negro Youth, and the educational boards of seven church bodies. The survey was published in a volume of approximately 1,000 pages in the 1928 series of Office of Education Bulletins.[71]

3. National survey of secondary education. In March, 1928, the North Central Association of Colleges and Secondary Schools requested a survey of secondary education. The Congress appropriated a fund of $225,000 for the survey which ran from fiscal year 1930 to fiscal year 1932. It was directed by Commissioner Cooper who was assisted by a nine member board of consultants, a professional advisory committee of 30 members, and a lay advisory committee of 56 members. More than 60 consultants were employed during the investigation. There were over 200,000 inquiries sent out in connection with the survey and more than 850 visits to schools were made. Higher education was involved through studies made of junior colleges and the connection of secondary schools with higher education through admission standards and requirements. The survey results were published in the 1932 series of Office of Education Bulletins as a group of twenty-eight monographs totaling approximately 4,400 pages. Five of the monographs were concerned in whole or part with higher education.[72]

4. National survey of the education of teachers. This was requested by the National Council of State Superintendents and Commissioners of Education, the American Association of Teachers Colleges, and the Association of Deans of Education. The Congress appropriated $180,000 extending through fiscal years 1930–1933. During the survey approximately 500,000 public school and college administrators and teachers contributed information and data, and more than 800 teacher education institutions supplied information. Commissioner Cooper was director with Dr. E. S. Evenden, professor of education, Teachers College, Columbia University, as associate director. Dr. Benjamin Frazier, senior specialist in teacher training, Office of Education, was coordinator of the survey. There were, in addition, 15 survey staff members, 5 special advisors, 7 research

[71] Judd, *op. cit.*, pp. 25–26; and Eells, *op. cit.*, pp. 42–43, 382. Judd stated that this was the first national survey of the Office of Education (p. 25) but Eells, who made a more detailed study of the higher education survey movement, wrote: "In 1926 the Bureau began its rather extensive survey . . . of the 69 land-grant colleges and universities, which was completed in 1930 and published in two large volumes. In 1927 was initiated the survey of 79 Negro colleges and universities in 18 states . . ., completed in 1929." (p. 42). The survey report was entitled *Survey of Negro Colleges and Universities*, Bulletin, 1928, No. 7.

[72] Judd, *op. cit.*, pp. 26–27, 29; and Eells, *op. cit.*, pp. 42–43, 413. The report was published as *National Survey of Secondary Education*, Bulletin, 1932, No. 17. The five monographs of the twenty-eight in the series relating to higher education are: I. Summary, 1934; V. The Reorganization of Secondary Education, 1933; VIII. District Organization and Secondary Education, 1933; IX. Legal and Regulatory Provisions Affecting Secondary Education, 1933; and X. Articulation of High School and College, 1933.

assistants, and 17 associate members on the project. They were advised by a 12 member consultant board and a 47 member advisory committee. The survey results were published as Bulletin, 1933, No. 10, in six volumes totaling nearly 1,800 pages.[73]

5. National survey of school finance. This had been requested by the Council of State Superintendents and Commissioners of Education. The initial appropriation of $50,000 for the project was made by the Congress in fiscal year 1932. There was to be $300,000 appropriated over the following three fiscal years but the Congress did not authorize the additions so the survey did not extend past fiscal year 1932. The survey itself did not get beyond an analysis of the literature on school finance and inquiries to State departments regarding plans for school support. Cooper served as director of the survey assisted by a 17 member board of consultants, a 6 member research staff, and 10 special consultants. The findings which had been reached before the sudden and premature termination of the survey were published in two volumes by the American Council on Education, and a 1932 series Bulletin by the Office of Education.[74]

6. Study of the educational value of military instruction in universities and colleges. This was a relatively low-budget survey with a total cost of less than $2,700 financed by the Mershon Fund (administered by the New York Community Trust). However, it was one of the most extensive of the voluntary questionnaire studies conducted during the survey movement period, based on 10,166 replies from 16,416 inquiries to students in 54 institutions in 39 States and the District of Columbia. Major Ralph C. Bishop was in charge of the study which was published by the Office of Education as Pamphlet No. 28 in 1932 (24 pages).[75]

---

[73] Judd, *op. cit.*, pp. 27–30; Eells, *op. cit.*, pp. 42-43, 413–414; Interview of author with Mr. John H. Lloyd, Chief, Reports Section, Publications Service, Office of Education, October 28, 1959; and Archives File 206, "Teacher Training—Historical."

The survey report was published as *National Survey of the Education of Teachers*, Bulletin, 1933, No. 10. The six volumes were: I. Selected Bibliography; II. Teacher Personnel in the United States; III. Teacher Education Curricula; IV. Education of Negro Teachers; V. Special Survey Studies; and VI. Summary and Interpretation.

[74] Judd, *op. cit.*, pp. 28–29; Eells, *op. cit.*, p. 415; and John H. Lloyd, "A Study of the School Tax Dollar," *School Life*, XVI, No. 8, April 1931, pp. 141-142.

The Office of Education publication on the survey was *Bibliography on Educational Finance, 1923–1931*, Bulletin, 1932, No. 15. The American Council on Education's publications were *Research Problems in School Finance*, and *State Support for Public Education*.

[75] Eells, *op. cit.*, pp. 116, 313, 390. The report was published as a pamphlet: *Study of the Educational Value of Military Instruction in Universities and Colleges*, No. 28, 1932.

In a study of the results of surveys, Dr. Eells classifies several of them as "very successful," "moderately successful," "somewhat successful," "little

7. National survey of higher education of Negroes. Following the completion, or termination, of the six surveys described above there was a lapse of six years before the Office of Education participated in another, and final, national survey touching on higher education. The Association of Colleges and Secondary Schools for Negroes requested this study in 1939, and the Congress appropriated $40,000 for the project. It was directed by Frederick J. Kelly, then chief of the Division of Higher Education, with Dr. Ambrose Caliver, senior specialist in the education of Negroes, as associate director. A temporary survey staff of 7 members served until completion of the project in 1942, and 8 regular Office staff members contributed to special projects. Among the latter were Dr. Lloyd E. Blauch, Dr. Benjamin Frazier, and Miss Ella Ratcliffe of the Division of Higher Education professional staff. An advisory committee of fourteen nationally recognized leaders in Negro education also contributed their talents to the project. The findings of the survey were published as "Miscellaneous No. 6" in four over-size volumes, totaling more than 450 pages, in 1942 and 1943. In the latter year Commissioner John W. Studebaker wrote that the study "marks the close of one of the most extensive and thorough studies ever made of the higher education of Negroes." In addition to its thoroughness the survey was significant for being the first one in which a "respectable amount" of time and money was devoted to the socio-economic aspects of education. About one-third was devoted to a thorough study of the interplay and influence of social and economic factors on higher education of Negroes. Volume I, "Socio-Economic Approach to Educational Problems," consisted of 166 pages of text and figures bearing on this subject.[76]

In fiscal year 1930 Cooper reorganized the Office of Education.[77]

---

or no success," "harmful—more harm than good," or "not evaluated." He classified the Negro college survey and the land-grant college survey as "moderately successful," and the study of the educational value of military instruction as "somewhat successful." The remainder of the national surveys were not classified. *Ibid.*, pp. 205–207.

[76] John W. Studebaker, *Annual Report of the United States Commissioner of Education for the Fiscal Year Ended June 30, 1941* (Washington, 1942), pp. 45–46; John W. Studebaker, *Annual Reports of the United States Office of Education for the Fiscal Years 1941–42, 1942–43* (Washington, 1943), p. 52; John W. Studebaker, "Foreword," *National Survey of the Higher Education of Negroes* (Washington, 1942, Vol. I), p. VII; and Interview of author with Dr. Ambrose Caliver, Chief, Adult Education Section, Division of State and Local School Systems, Office of Education, November 2, 1959. The Studebaker quotation is from his 1941–42, 1942–43 *Report;* the other quotation on socio-economic aspects is from interview with Dr. Caliver.

The titles of the four volumes in the *National Survey of the Higher Education of Negroes:* I. Socio-Economic Approach to Economic Problems; II. General Studies of Colleges for Negroes; III. Intensive Study of Selected Colleges for Negroes; and IV. A Summary.

[77] This will be further described in Chapter IV, *infra.*

At that time he established a Division of Major Surveys under his immediate direction. This division lasted only through the period of the large national surveys in the 1930's but its existence was symbolic of the importance placed on them by the Office of Education.[78]

The practice of conducting, or participating in, higher education surveys of less than national scope ended with a survey of public higher education in Oregon in 1931. National surveys involving the Division of Higher Education, except for the 1939–1942 Negro higher education survey, ended in 1934. The withdrawal of the Division of Higher Education from the field, except as an advisor, was acknowledged by Commissioner Studebaker in his *Report* for 1939:

> A new plan of state surveys of higher education was tried in 1939. In general, requests to the Office of Education to make surveys of higher education in a given State have either not been possible due to lack of facilities or have been accepted and staff members assigned to devote a considerable amount of time to them. The survey in 1939 of higher education in the State of Nebraska, however, has been conducted largely with the help of Nebraska educators working with a staff member in the Division of Higher Education acting as adviser.[79]

In his 1937 study of higher education surveys, Eells listed the names of 41 men most experienced in that work. The first three names on the list were those of men who have served as chiefs of the Division of Higher Education. Zook led having served as director of 13, and staff member of 8, printed surveys, and participant in one mimeographed survey. Capen was second with 10, 7, and 5 respectively. Third was Klein with 8, 2, and 3. The ninth man on the list was Frederick J. Kelly, Division chief from 1931 to 1946; the thirty-sixth man was Lloyd Blauch, then a comparative beginner in survey work, who served as Division head from 1955 to 1959, and thirty-seventh was John Dale Russell, head from 1946 to 1952. Cooper was sixteenth, and John was twenty-second.[80]

Routine activities under Zook continued as they had developed under Capen. There was no change in the numerical strength of the Division and the professional staff of three made an effort to

---

[78] Cooper, *Annual Report . . . 1930*, pp. 7–12; Figure II following p. 2, and Rodeheaver, *op. cit.*, pp. 153–154.

[79] John W. Studebaker, "Office of Education" in *Annual Report of the Secretary of the Interior for the Fiscal Year Ending June 30, 1939* (Washington, 1939), p. 73.

[80] Eells, *op. cit.*, pp. 85–86.

attend as many conferences as possible.[81] Throughout most of the
1920's the specialist in rural and technical education, Walton John,
helped organize and participated in the annual national conferences on Negro education held at various places throughout the
South. He also helped plan the agenda for an international conference on highway engineering which was held in Buenos Aires,
Argentina, in May, 1925.[82] From 1920 to 1925 more than 100
publications relating to higher education appeared, a figure
slightly above normal. Members of the Division prepared, or
assisted in the preparation of nearly all of these.[83]

In 1925, Zook was offered the presidency of the University of
Akron, Ohio, which was then in a period of change and development. He resigned his Office position effective August 31 and was
appointed a special Collaborator, at $1.00 per year, on September
17.[84]

The fourth specialist in higher education and chief of the
Division was Dr. Arthur Jay Klein who took office on December
10, 1925.[85] He continued Zook's policies in routine office operation,
school visitation, and attendance at conferences. The record indi-

---

[81] During the period when Zook headed the Division of Higher Education
(1920–25) the following persons served as members of the professional staff
(dates of service with the division shown in parenthesis) : Dr. Walton C. John
(1918–42) ; Dr. Chester Jarvis (1917–21) ; Dr. Lloyd C. Blauch (1921–23) ;
and Dr. Walter J. Greenleaf (1924–47). The sections of the annual reports
dealing with higher education list the important conferences attended and
the addresses given each fiscal year.

[82] Tigert, *Report . . . 1923*, pp. 9–10; John J. Tigert, *Report of the Commissioner of Education for the Year Ended June 30, 1924* (Washington, 1924),
pp. 7–8; and John J. Tigert, *Report of the Commissioner of Education for
the Year Ended June 30, 1925* (Washington, 1925), pp. 6–7.

[83] See Table 11, Chapter VI, *infra*.

[84] Ltr. Zook to Secretary of the Interior, Hubert Work, August 25, 1925,
in Zook's Personnel Folder, St. Louis Records Center, St. Louis, Missouri.
Zook had been subjected to some criticism in 1921, and possibly later, because
of his service on the Committee on Public Information ("the Creel Committee") in 1918. He was accused in 1921 of being a bitter spokesman against the
Harding administration. This criticism seems to have had no influence on
his resignation in 1925 nor did it hamper his efficiency. (Memorandum from
"Brock," Department of the Interior, to Mr. Safford—probably Dr. William
Edwin Safford—Department of Agriculture, August 24, 1921.)

Dr. Walter Gaumnitz of the Office of Education recalled that Zook had
been noted for his teaching ability while in Washington. Zook had taught
a men's class in the Petwork Methodist Church where "the men of the church
testified to his effectiveness as a teacher long after his years as a teacher
there." (Walter H. Gaumnitz, "Reminiscences Concerning Chiefs of the Division of Higher Education," typewritten ms. prepared for the author in 1959.)

[85] Klein's Personnel Folder, St. Louis Records Center, St. Louis, Missouri.
See Appendix I, *infra*, for biographical information.

cates he did more traveling than any of his predecessors or the two division heads who were to follow him. His crowded schedule in the latter half of one year, 1927, included visits to the Universities of Minnesota and Wisconsin in July; New England States, Middle Atlantic States, and West Virginia in October; Missouri, Illinois, and Michigan in November; and Ohio and New York City in December.[86]

There were three significant developments while Klein was in office which bore on higher education and were in addition to the previously noted national survey movement. These were the start of the annual inspections of Howard University, the inauguration of a research service, and the improvement of procedures for gathering statistical information.

Howard University, Washington, D.C., had been privately controlled and operated from the time of its establishment in 1867 but starting in 1879 the Congress had, from time to time, contributed sums of money for its operation.[87] A regular program of Federal financial assistance was begun in 1928 which, in turn, brought about an annual inspection. An act of Congress dated December 13, 1928, read in part:

> ... annual appropriations are hereby authorized to aid in the construction, development, improvement, and maintenance of the university, no part of which shall be used for religious instruction. The university shall at all times be open to inspection by the Bureau of Education and shall be inspected by the said bureau at least once each year. An annual report making a full exhibit of the affairs of the university shall be presented to Congress each year in the report of the Bureau of Education.[88]

Secretary of the Interior Roy O. West called a meeting in his office which was attended by Klein, President Mordecai W. Johnson of Howard University, and other interested officials. It was decided at that time that

> an initial report be made which would outline a plan for the development of Howard University extending over a period of from 15 to 20 years. It was indicated that this plan should, first, suggest the needs of the negro people for a university of the highest type; second, estimate the probable growth in attendance in the various fields of work offered; third, provide for a plant adequate to care for the program suggested and the

---

[86] Klein's Personnel Folder, St. Louis Records Center, St. Louis, Missouri.

[87] Hartley, *op. cit.*, pp. 46–47; and Charles A. Quattlebaum, *Federal Education Activities and Educational Issues Before Congress* (Washington, 1952), pp. 58, 276.

[88] "Congress Assigns Another Function to the Bureau of Education," *School Life*, XIV, No. 7, March 1929, p. 127.

student growth estimated; and fourth, suggest a plan for the division of the financial burden involved between Congress and the private board of trustees of the university.[89]

The initial study, in effect a program of long-range development, was not completed until the end of fiscal year 1930. It was a lengthy report which became a basis for the development of Howard University. Starting in fiscal year 1930 annual reports were made of the inspections of Howard University by members of the Division of Higher Education. A shortage of professional staff members brought about a system whereby one or two of the ten schools which form the university were inspected annually. Under this procedure a thorough inspection, or survey, of all facilities of the institution was accomplished each five years.[90]

The research service activity of the Office of Education began in 1927. Requests were sent to all known agencies of educational research in State and local educational groups, institutions of higher education, educational boards, foundations, and associations requesting abstracts or copies of studies recently completed. Information on studies in progress was also requested. The purpose of the program was to establish the Office of Education as a clearing house for information on research at all educational levels.[91]

By March, 1928, approximately 800 replies on research in progress had been completed and a mimeographed report issued. This was followed by an additional report in May and a printed *Bibliography of Research Studies in Education, 1926–1927*, pre-

---

[89] Cooper, *Annual Report . . . 1929*, pp. 39–42. Quotation from p. 39. Also, interviews of author with Dr. Ambrose Caliver, Chief, Audit Adult Education section, Instruction, Organization, and Services Branch, Division of State and Local School Systems, Office of Education, November 2, 1959; and Mr. Ralph C. M. Flynt, Assistant Commissioner and Director, Legislative and Program Development Branch, Office of Education, November 4, 1959.

[90] Cooper, *Annual Report . . . 1930*, p. 15; and interview of author with Dr. Ernest V. Hollis, Director, College and University Administration Branch, Division of Higher Education, Office of Education, October 27, 1959.
The expansion of Howard University from 1929 to 1953 is shown to some extent by its enrollment figures:
    1929–30—2,872 total enrollment—326 graduates
    1952–53—5,378 total enrollment—616 graduates
Figures from William John Cooper, *Annual Report of the Commissioner of Education for the Year Ended June 30, 1931* (Washington, 1931), p. 14; and Oveta Culp Hobby, *Annual Report of the U.S. Department of Health, Education, and Welfare, 1953* (Washington, 1954), "Howard University," pp. 269–275. The first report and subsequent reports to 1942 were in large part the work of Dr. John.

[91] John D. Wolcott, "Clearing House of Educational Research," *School Life*, XIII, No. 3, November 1927, p. 46.

pared by John Wolcott. This bibliography contained more than 1,500 titles representing 225 institutions and organizations. It was the first of a series of research listings of educational studies to be prepared by the Office in the following years. The Division of Higher Education assisted in the work of preparing the listings, concentrating its attention on research programs conducted in institutions of higher education, or related to education of collegiate and graduate levels.[92]

In 1929 the problem of gathering statistical information from institutions of higher education was far from solved. It was particularly difficult to obtain meaningful financial data.[93] Dr. Klein called a meeting of a group of college business officers to work out a system for improving this situation. From this came a committee the following year which represented the three regional associations of university and college business officers, the Association of American Colleges and the Council of Church Boards of Education, the American Association of Collegiate Registrars, and the American Association of Teachers Colleges. The body that was formed was the National Committee on Standard Reports for Institutions of Higher Education. It formulated principles to be followed in the organization and arrangement of financial and statistical reports of colleges and universities. Although statistical problems were not solved completely, this action did much to alleviate the situation.[94]

Klein was an affable man who possessed two traits which seemed contradictory to each other. One was a certain disdain for Federal service despite his conscientious attention to duty. A member of the Office of Education professional staff recalled this incident: "At lunch one day he [Dr. Klein] complimented me upon my effectiveness, stating that he had a high regard for me and my work, but that if he found me still in the government employ after three more years, he would lose all respect for me." [95]

The second trait was his ambition to become Commissioner. In August 1928, when Tigert resigned the Secretary of the Interior received a large number of letters requesting that Klein be con-

[92] Edith A. Wright, "Bureau Inaugurates Research Information Service," *School Life*, XIV, No. 5, January 1929, p. 89. The Wolcott study was Bulletin, 1928, No. 22. For additional titles see U.S. Office of Education, *List of Publications of the Office of Education, 1910–1936* (Washington, 1937).

[93] Some of the difficulties involved in the gathering of statistics have been noted in Chapter II.

[94] Emery M. Foster, "Contributions of Arthur J. Klein," (typewritten ms. prepared for the author) ; and Cooper, *Annual Report . . . 1930*, p. 21.

[95] Gaumnitz, "Reminiscences . . ". Gaumnitz was awarded a 30-year service pin by the United States Government at a date long after this lunch.

sidered to succeed to that office. Among those writing were the Dean of the School of Agriculture, Texas Agricultural and Mechanical College; the Secretary of Ohio State University; the Dean of the Division of Home Economics, Kansas State Agricultural College; the President of the University of Minnesota; the Dean of Iowa State University; and the Director of Extension Work of Indiana University. Senator Wesley Jones of Washington wrote a recommendation to President Coolidge stating that Klein "has an attractive personality and wins the good will of people everywhere he goes." Senator James E. Watson of Indiana also wrote the President on Klein's behalf.[96]

There is no conclusive evidence that Klein worked directly for the appointment but it is difficult to believe that letters from so many different sources were entirely spontaneous. It is reasonable to assume that he did some prompting of the correspondence campaign. It is also curious that a man who had once expressed so little regard for Government service should exert himself to stay in it. Apparently he had no rancor about not being appointed Commissioner. When Cooper was appointed he remained for a time as head of the Division of Higher Education.

The last of the golden years of prosperity drew to a close with the Division of Higher Education larger than it had ever been with a staff of four full-time professionals.[97] It was also busier than ever, for combined with the regular activities there were the large national surveys to supervise and assist. Respect for the work of the Federal Government in higher education, and specifically for the Division was stronger than it had ever been and still growing.

---

[96] There is a large collection of letters relating to this matter in Klein's Personal Folder, St. Louis Records Center, St. Louis, Missouri. Most of them were written in August 1928, althought a few of them are dated in September or October.

[97] The professional staff in 1928 (dates of service with the division shown in parentheses): Dr. Klein (1925–30); Dr. John (1918–42); Dr. Greenleaf (1924–47); and Dr. (then Mr.) Benjamin W. Frazier (1927–48).

# CHAPTER IV

# From the Depression Through the Second World War (1929–1945)

## The Depression Years

A different period in the history of the Division of Higher Education began with a change in the Commissioner of Education. In 1928 Tigert was offered the presidency of the University of Florida in Gainesville. He accepted the offer leaving the Office of Education on August 31.[1] A successor was not appointed for several months and while the search was on for the eighth Commissioner, Lewis Kalbach, Chief Clerk of the Office, served as Acting Commissioner.[2] By January of 1929 the successor had been found, and the new man, William John Cooper, took office on the 11th of the following month.

Dr. Cooper (1882–1935) was born in Sacramento, California, on November 24, 1882. He received the A.B. degree from the University of California in 1906 and his M.A. from the same institution in 1917. Following graduation in 1906 he taught history and Latin in the Stockton High School, California. In 1910 he became head of the history department in the junior and senior high schools of Berkeley. Five years later he took a similar position in Oakland. In 1918 Cooper began his career in the field of school superintendency, serving successively as superintendent in Piedmont, Fresno, and San Diego, California, and in 1927 he was made State Super-

---

[1] J. N. Rodeheaver, Jr., "The Relation of the Federal Government to Civic Education" (Cambridge, Mass., 1951, typewritten ms.), p. 147.

Dr. Tigert remained on duty as President of the University of Florida, Gainesville, until the mid-1950's. He continued living in Gainesville following his retirement. *Who Was Who in America*, II (Chicago, 1950), p. 533, incorrectly carries Tigert as "deceased". He died in 1965.

[2] William John Cooper, *Annual Report of the Commissioner of Education for the Year Ended June 30, 1929* (Washington, 1929), p. 1.

intendent of Public Instruction. During the First World War he obtained a leave of absence from his Oakland position to serve as business manager of the Committee on Education and Special Training in the Western States. In 1928 the University of Southern California conferred an honorary doctorate of education on him. He was serving as State Superintendent at the time of his appointment as Commissioner of Education by President Coolidge.[3]

Cooper's arrival in 1929 was followed by several important changes. During the next fiscal year the Commissioner of Education was reclassified in rank and salary which raised him to a position equal to the chiefs of other bureaus in the Department of the Interior. Provision was made for an Assistant Commissioner who would be equal in rank and salary to that formerly held by the Commissioner, and the name "Office of Education" became official by order of Secretary of the Interior Ray Lyman Wilbur.[4] These changes were accompained by an extensive reorganization of the Office. Cooper reduced the number of divisions from nine to six and removed the two independent sections which had existed under Tigert. The six divisions, which he called "major divisions," were Administration (headed by the Chief Clerk); Editorial; Library; Service; Major Surveys (under the Commissioner's immediate direction); and Research and Investigation (under the Assistant Commissioner).[5]

After this reorganization the Division of Higher Education no longer reported directly to the Commissioner. It also underwent a change in name for the only time in its history. It became, simply, "Colleges and Professional Schools," a branch of the Research and Investigation Division. Thus, Klein became, in everything but name, a branch chief under Assistant Commissioner Goody-

---

[3] H. R. Evans and E. A. Wright, "The United States Office of Education," (Washington, 1939, typewritten ms.), pp. 71–72A; *Who's Who in America*, XVI, p. 576; *Who Was Who in America*, I (Chicago, 1942), p. 259; Rodeheaver, *op. cit.*, p. 147; and "Office of Education and the Commissioners of Education," File of material in Education Library, Department of Health, Education, and Welfare Library.

[4] William John Cooper, *Annual Report of the Commissioner of Education for the Year Ended June 30, 1930* (Washington, 1930), pp. 2–4; Evans and Wright, *op. cit.*, p. 72A; and Rodeheaver, *op. cit.*, pp. 148–152. The first Assistant Commissioner of Education was Miss Bess Goodykoontz, formerly assistant professor of education at the University of Pittsburgh. She joined the Office of Education on October 1, 1929. The salary of the Commissioner at that time was $7,500 and the Assistant Commissioner $6,500. (Kardex, Office of Education Personnel Office, and information supplied by Legislative and Program Development Branch, Office of the Commissioner, Office of Education).

[5] Cooper, *Annual Report . . . 1930*, pp. 2–4; figures 1 and 2 following p. 2.

koontz.[6] Although Cooper called the higher education activity the "Division of Colleges and Professional Schools" from time to time, it was a part of the "major division" of Research and Investigation.[7] Administratively, from the time of the reorganization in fiscal year 1930 to fiscal year 1934 it was a branch.

The reorganization did not mean any loss of status for Klein nor did it lessen his responsibilities. The reorganization was undertaken for administrative improvement although it is difficult to say whether this worthy objective was achieved by it.[8] The fact that Cooper thought highly of the work of the Division of Higher Education, to use its former name, and intended no discredit by the reorganization is shown in a statement he prepared for the use of *School and Society* magazine:

> Every position in the Office of Education is important. Some positions, however, are of such a key character that the carrying on of the responsibilities connected with them should not depend upon the health, tenure or life of any human being. Positions of this character are: the chief clerk, the editor-in-chief, the librarian, the chief of the division of higher education. In the past but one of these, the editor-in-chief, has had an assistant. It is my recommendation that there be assistant chiefs for all of these offices.[9]

The organizational changes of 1929–1930 were retained by Cooper throughout his tenure of office which lasted until the middle of 1933. The Division of Higher Education did not regain its lost name until fiscal year 1934.

The most important contribution Cooper made to the Office of Education was his work in strengthening its research activities. His purpose in requesting that the name be changed from "Bureau" to "Office" was to show that it was something more than an administrative unit. It was a creative force in educational scholarship.[10] Under his guidance the national survey movement reached its height.[11] If the depression had not ended the national surveys, except for the survey of the higher education of Negroes,

---

[6] *Ibid.* On reorganization see also Evans and Wright, *op. cit.*, p. 81; *School Life*, XV, No. 4, December 1929, p. 70; U. S. Bureau of Education, *Educational Directories, 1926–1930* (Washington, 1926 *et seq.*), Directory for 1930, p. 1; and "United States Office of Education," *The Journal of the National Education Association*, XVIII, No. 8, November 1929, pp. 241–242.

[7] Cooper, *Annual Report . . . 1930*, p. 2.

[8] Rodeheaver, *op. cit.*, p. 152.

[9] "The Reorganization of the Bureau of Education," *School and Society*, XXX, No. 774, October 26, 1929, p. 565.

[10] Rodeheaver, *op. cit.*, pp. 159–160.

[11] See Chapter III.

by diverting funds to other needs, it is possible that Cooper's short period in office would be remembered as one of the most significant in the history of the Office of Education. Even though the national survey movement was short-lived, Cooper's contributions were substantial because of the stress he placed upon organization of the Office for greater efficiency in research (the Division of Major Surveys), and because he was able to recruit outstanding research men like Frederick J. Kelly for service with the Office.

When Klein resigned from the Division of Higher Education in July, 1930, to become professor of education at Ohio State University, the position of chief of "Colleges and Professional Schools" was left vacant for nearly a year.[12] During this period Benjamin Frazier served as acting chief.[13] In the Spring of 1931, after careful investigation of several possibilities, Cooper decided on Dr. Kelly, survey specialist and professor of higher education at the University of Chicago as the permanent successor to Klein.[14]

Fred Kelly, as he preferred to be called, was chief of the Division of Higher Education longer than any other man. He served just over 15 years, retiring on June 30, 1945, shortly before his 65th birthday. He returned to Federal service in November 1948, and continued until ten days prior to the close of fiscal year 1952, and later came on duty as a consultant. Not only did Kelly devote many years of service to the Division, but he was also the first to serve in it as Assistant Commissioner and Director. When that position was established by Commissioner John W. Studebaker on September 9, 1945, Kelly received it.[15]

Members of the Office of Education professional staff who worked with Dr. Kelly remember him for many different qualities although most agree on his interest and ability in research. He possessed the open-minded flexibility essential to the first-rate research specialist. Research was unquestionably his first interest, and administration was second.[16]

---

[12] Klein's Personnel Folder, St. Louis Records Center, St. Louis, Missouri.

[13] Cooper, *Annual Report . . . 1930*, p. 19.

[14] Kelly's Personnel Folder, St. Louis Records Center, St. Louis, Missouri; and *School Life*, XVI, No. 8, April 1931, p. 158.

[15] *Ibid.* See also The Division of Higher Education, "Fred J. Kelly Retires from the Office of Education," *Higher Education*, III, No. 2, September 16, 1946, pp. 2–3. On various titles given to Division of Higher Education chiefs in the period prior to 1937 see Walter S. Eells, *Surveys of American Higher Education* (New York, 1937), p. 39, fn. Biographical information on Kelly in Appendix I, *infra*. On Dr. Kelly's promotion to Assistant Commissioner see Chapter V, fn. 14.

[16] Interviews of author with Mr. H. H. Armsby, Chief of Engineering Education, Division of Higher Education, October 27, 1959; Dr. Ambrose

Kelly possessed, in addition to acknowledged research talent, a sense of loyalty to his co-workers, and the respect of his colleagues in higher education. He gave wide latitude to those who worked under him in the division, and he was open-minded and willing to be convinced by new ideas and suggestions.[17] An intense interest in the liberal arts did not prohibit him from doing all he could to promote interest in engineering education and studies both within the Office of Education and outside it.[18] At the time of his retirement in 1946, a tribute appeared in *Higher Education* which listed his outstanding qualities:

> Among Dr. Kelly's characteristics which have most deeply impressed his close associates are: A quiet and dignified manner; kindly dealing with his fellowmen; great adaptability; a wide range of intellectual interests; clear logical thinking; an objective approach to educational questions; a lively imagination in dealing with problems; lucid expression; extraordinary ability for incisive statement after the careful analysis of a problem; skill and tact in presenting ideas; unusual organizing ability and continuing intellectual growth.[19]

On the other hand, one of his colleagues was struck by Kelly's "Mid-West attitude" toward higher education. By this he meant that Kelly was more familiar with, and concerned over, the problems of the large State university than the smaller private institution.[20] Another felt he was a little inclined to look outside for assistance rather than to draw upon the professional resources available in the Office. This was probably due in large part to the fact that he joined the Office at the height of the national survey movement when great emphasis was placed on consultive services by groups not directly affiliated with the Office.[21] This tendency decreased as time passed and the number of professional members of the Division increased from five in 1931 to eight in 1940, on the eve of the World War II expansion.[22]

---

Caliver, Chief, Adult Education Section, Division of State and Local School Systems, October 28, 1959; Mr. Ralph C. M. Flynt, Assistant Commissioner and Director of Legislative Services Branch, November 4, 1959; and Mr. Kendric N. Marshall, Finance Aid Officer, Division of Higher Education, October 13, 1959; all of the Office of Education.

[17] Interviews of author with Dr. Caliver, October 28, 1959; Mr. Flynt, October 7, 1959; and Mr. Marshall, November 3, 1959; and Walter H. Gaumnitz, "Reminiscences Concerning Chiefs of the Division of Higher Education," (typewritten ms. prepared for the author in 1959).

[18] Interview of author with Mr. Armsby, October 27, 1959.

[19] Division of Higher Education, "Fred J. Kelly Retires," p. 3.

[20] Interview of author with Mr. Flynt, October 7, 1959.

[21] Interview of author with Dr. Caliver, October 28, 1959.

[22] The following professional persons served in the Division of Higher Education under Dr. Kelly from 1931 to 1940 (dates of service with the Division

Shortly after Kelly took office the report of the National Advisory Committee on Education appeared. This Committee had been organized in May 1929, by Secretary of the Interior Ray L. Wilbur, acting for President Hoover. Its purpose was to determine the policies of the Federal Government in relation to education. The Committee, as finally constituted, consisted of 52 citizens "engaged or interested in education." [23] Chairman was Dr. C. R. Mann, Director of the American Council on Education. Capen and Zook were members along with Charles Judd who had served briefly with the Division of Higher Education in 1913. All three were on a Conference Committee of fifteen elected from the larger Committee, and it was this Conference Committee which did the bulk of the work.[24]

The Committee report which appeared in 1931 pointed out the complete lack of unity or cohesion in Government operations to help education. It emphasized disjointed control and incoherent policy making. It recommended the establishment of a "Department of Education with a Secretary of Education at its head . . ." and stressed the research and information role that such a department should play in educational leadership:

### RECOMMENDATIONS

1. *Develop the services.* Develop the Federal Government's research and information services with increasing emphasis on comprehensive research and on the diffusion of information that is pertinent to the decision of critical national issues.

2. *Expand in education.* Continue to expand the federal research and information service in the field of education until it meets adequately the needs of the American people for intellectual assistance in all phases of education, including the

---

shown in parentheses) : Dr. John (1918–42) ; Dr. Greenleaf (1924–47) ; Dr. Frazier (1927–48) ; Miss Ella Ratchliffe (1930–46, prior service in clerical position) ; Dr. Kline Koon (1931–37) ; Mr. John McNeely (1936–40) ; Dr. John Lund (1940–43, 1947–51) ; Dr. Andrey Potter (1940–45) ; Dr. Lloyd Blauch (1921–23, 1940–59) ; Dr. John C. Patterson (1940–42) ; Dr. Roy A. Seaton (1940–42), and Mr. George W. Case (1940–46). The dates do not include the months when these people came to, or left, the Division which accounts for the fact that in 1940 there were actually more than eight names of people associated with it. For additional information, see Appendix I, *infra.*

[23] National Advisory Committee on Education, *Federal Relations to Education* (Washington, 1931), Part I, p. 1.

[24] See *Ibid.*, pp. 424–426 for complete list of members. George Zook is the only person to serve on the three national Presidential committees appointed between 1929 and 1946. He was a member of the National Advisory Committee on Education and the Conference Committee (1929–1931) ; Vice-Chairman of the Advisory Committee on Education (1936–1938) ; and Chairman of the President's Commission on Higher Education (1946–1947).

educational aspects of health, recreation, and other community activities that vitally affect physical, mental and moral growth.[25]

The report of the National Advisory Committee on Education had a direct effect on the organization of the Office of Education. This was the incorporation of the Federal Board for Vocational Education into the Office.[26] In addition, the Committee strengthened the case for more educational research sponsored by the Office of Education. It is possible that if the Nation had not then been sliding into the lowest depths of the depression, and was not soon to enter an administration radically different from that which was in power in 1931, the recommendations would have been followed. As it was, the Committee did succeed in impressing educators with the need for research controlled or directed from the national level.

By fiscal year 1932 the depression had taken a heavy toll of Office of Education programs. The requested appropriation was cut 11 per cent by the House of Representatives, and the Senate reduced the House figure by 26 per cent. The total cut for fiscal year 1933 was 34 per cent when the President signed the appropriation act. Later, the appropriation for printing was cut an additional 15 per cent. Cooper observed that under these conditions all employees would have to be furloughed for a half month or from 10 to 15 would have to be discharged. He observed that research activities would have to be curtailed and the publications program, and the distribution of publications seriously reduced.[27] Total fiscal year appropriations for salaries, general expenses, and

[25] *Ibid.,* p. 76. See also pp. 95–99; and Dawson Hales, *Federal Control of Public Education: A Critical Appraisal* (New York, 1954), p. 67. Rodeheaver, *op. cit.,* pp. 157–58, discusses the Committee report and points out that the vote for the "Department of Education" plan was 43 for and 8 opposed. Those opposed "were strong in influence and were supported by the Secretary of the Interior and others." (p. 158). There were only 51 votes cast because one member had died during the period when the Committee was in session.

[26] The Federal Board for Vocational Education had been created by the Congress in 1917. On June 10, 1933, it was transferred to the Department of the Interior by Executive Order 6166. The Secretary of the Interior, Harold L. Ickes, in turn assigned it to the Office of Education on October 10, 1933. In time this became the Division of Vocational Education. See Charles H. Judd, *Research in the United States Office of Education* (Washington, 1939), p. 9; *Annual Report of the Secretary of the Interior for the Fiscal Year Ended June 30, 1933* ("Federal Board for Vocational Education, 1933"), p. 264; and Rodeheaver, *op. cit.,* p. 158. Also Interview of author with Mr. Lane C. Ash, Division of Vocational Education, Office of Education, December 16, 1959.

[27] Bess Goodykoontz, *Annual Report of the Commissioner of Education for the Fiscal Year Ended June 30, 1932* (Washington, 1932), pp. 2–3.

printing were $367,000 in 1932, $304,314 in 1933, and $252,500 in 1934. These figures show a drop of 31.2 per cent from 1932 to 1934.[28] The regular staff in June, 1932, was 100. One position was closed out in February, 1933; seven more in April; and one at the end of June. All temporary survey employees were removed and the rest of the regular staff, now numbering 91, was required to take a short furlough.[29] The Division did not lose any staff members but it did suffer, along with the rest of the Office, from curtailment of survey program.

Most immediate of the effects on higher educational programs were the increasing efforts of some States to consolidate their institutions of higher education for economic reasons, and a newly revived interest in financial problems. The *Report* for 1932 shows the changing emphasis in higher educational studies:

> Higher education is just now entering upon a period of applying the scientific method to the solution of its educational problems. Criticism of higher education is widespread today. Changes are being made in both methods of teaching and in curricula of colleges to an unpredented extent. That these changes should be made wisely is the most important interest of higher education to-day. This calls for a program of research.
>
> *The study of questions in higher education which arise primarily from the economic depression.*—While the movement originated earlier, the economic depression has hastened the urge to coordinate or consolidate the public institutions of higher education within a given State so as to avoid duplication and competition. To be in position to respond to the States calling upon the Office of Education for assistance, a series of three studies was planned and carried half way to completion: First, the assembling of data which reveal variations among the States in their financing of higher education and in the percentages of their young people who attend college; second, a study of the governing authority and curriculum offerings in institutions of higher education State by State, choosing those States first which maintain separate State universities and land-grant colleges; third, the investigation of the historical development of higher education in a few typical States where the movement for consolidation has made the greatest headway. It is believed that such a study would shed light upon the problems confronting the various States which are contemplating steps in coordination or consolidation.
>
> Two other studies were prompted largely by the economic difficulties of higher education: First, a study of the salaries in land-grant colleges and universities seems to be particularly

---

[28] George F. Zook, "Office of Education" in *Annual Report of the Secretary of the Interior for the Fiscal Year Ended June 30, 1933* (Washington, 1933), p. 258.

[29] *Ibid.*, pp. 258–259.

timely in view of the lack of reliable data as to the variations in salaries paid in different academic divisions and academic ranks; second, a study of 147 small colleges, including accredited and nonaccredited types which have enrollments of 500 students or less, shows the changes in growth and support during the past 10 years. This study will shed light on the financial problems which confront so many small colleges to-day.[30]

It was in the midst of this lowest period of the depression that Cooper resigned. There was no reason for the resignation. One student of the history of the Office was convinced that the resignation was given reluctantly and for other than political reasons since his successor was George F. Zook.[31] This is questionable since Cooper had been appointed by a Republican, Calvin Coolidge, and his successor had been active during World War I as a member of the Committee on Public Information, a fact pointed out in the letter of nomination which Secretary Ickes sent to the Senate Committee on Education and Labor. Furthermore, Zook had been criticized as early as 1921 for being a critic of the Republican administration of Harding, and a Democratic president had taken office in March, 1933, at about the time when Cooper resigned. No other reason for the change of commissioners has been found.[32]

Dr George Zook (1885–1951) was the first and, up to 1953, only Commissioner of Education to have had prior service with the Office of Education, having been chief of the Division of Higher Education from February, 1920, to August, 1925. He was destined to serve as Commissioner for less than a year (July 11, 1933, to June 30, 1934), too short a period of time to markedly influence

---

[30] Goodykoontz, *Annual Report . . . 1932*, pp. 12–13. The reports for fiscal years 1933 through 1937 show this emphasis on financial studies and related matters: student drop-out; unit costs; annuity programs; financial aid; and so forth. There was not as much emphasis on curriculum studies as in the 1920's except for one year, 1933, when a large number of mimeographed circulars on curriculum matters was released. See also L. E. Hartley, "A Critical Study of the United States Office of Education Since 1933," (Boulder, Colorado, 1941, typewritten ms.), pp. 54–56.

[31] Rodeheaver, *op. cit.*, p. 159.

[32] Ltr., Secretary of the Interior Harold L. Ickes to Senator David T. Walsh, Chairman of Committee on Education and Labor, U.S. Senate, May 31, 1933, in Zook's Personnel Folder, St. Louis Records Center, St. Louis, Missouri. On the 1921 criticism of Zook see Chapter III, fn. 84.

Cooper became professor of education at George Washington University, Washington, D. C. in 1933. According to Evans and Wright, *op. cit.*, p. 73, he had resigned from George Washington University in 1935 and died on September 19, 1935, at Kearney, Nebraska, enroute to California.

Biographical information on Zook may be found in Appendix I, *infra*.

the Division of Higher Education.[33] He did restore the old name so it was once again the "Division of Higher Education," and no longer simply "Colleges and Professional Schools." However, it did remain under the direction of the Assistant Commissioner.[34]

The new Commissioner did much to set the policy for the activities of the Office of Education at the start of Franklin D. Roosevelt's New Deal. This is the way an unidentified writer in an article in *Higher Education* described Zook's impact on the Office of Education:

> It was recognized everywhere that the depression was having its most devastating effect upon young people. Boys were lined up on the tops of moving freight trains. Street corners were crowded with young people with nothing to do and no place to go. Many young people were forced to leave high school because they lacked suitable clothes. Many others had insufficient funds to go to college.
>
> Just when these problems were most acute Dr. Zook came to Washington as Commissioner of Education. What policies were to be adopted with reference to Federal participation in activities for young people? The answer would affect not only the emergency years of the depression but the future as well.
>
> The Civilian Conservation Corps had been launched the year before, but there was no education program associated with it. Should there be? If so, what sort? By whom administered?
>
> The Federal Emergency Relief Administration had been set up, but there was no recognition of its relation to schools and colleges. Should work opportunities or scholarships, or both, be made available to college youth? Should these compete with jobs for family breadwinners? Should funds for these relief jobs be made available to privately controlled colleges as well as to public ones? What should be the relation with State agencies in the management of the program?
>
> These were the types of policy questions confronting Dr. Zook in 1933. His approach to their solution was through calling conferences of the leaders most concerned. The technique itself was a contribution to Federal procedures. He called upon the best minds he could summon and formulated policy on the basis of their deliberations.
>
> The outcomes are well known. There came into being an educational program of the CCC, and it was administered by the Office. There came into being a college-student-aid section

---

[33] Rodeheaver, *op. cit.*, p. 160. Rodeheaver writes that "George Zook did not serve as Commissioner of Education long enough to make any noticeable impression on the work of the office." This is not entirely correct for, although he did not greatly influence the Division of Higher Education, he did help to establish Office policy in relief activities.

[34] U.S. Office of Education, *Educational Directories, 1931–1935* (Washington, 1931 *et seq.*), Directory for 1934, Part I, pp. 1–2; and *School Life*, XIX, No. 6, February 1934, rear cover.

of the FERA administered in the FERA by a director assigned
from the staff of the Office. From this beginning grew the
college-student-aid program of the NYA.

These were new concepts in education. They called for forth-
right leadership of a Commissioner not hampered by tradition.
That is what Dr. Zook possessed. One cannot know what a vast
difference it might have made in education in this country if
the Office had been under the direction of a less able man during
those crucial 12 months.[35]

The inception of these programs owed much to Zook but their
implementation was the work of his successor, John Studebaker,
and the rest of the Office including Kelly and his staff in the
Division of Higher Education.

In May, 1934, Zook resigned his position with the Office, the
resignation to take effect at the end of the fiscal year, so he could
become Director of the American Council on Education. He held
this position for the next sixteen years. Bess Goodykoontz served
as Acting Commissioner until the arrival of the tenth Commissioner of Education who took office on October 23, 1934.

John Ward Studebaker (1887-     ) was born in McGregor,
Iowa, on June 10, 1887, and graduated from Leander Clark College, Toledo, Iowa, in 1910. Most of his life was spent in educational work in Iowa. He served successively as principal of the
Guthrie Center high school; principal of the elementary and
junior high school in Mason City; and Assistant Superintendent
and Superintendent of the Des Moines schools. He received an
A.M. from Columbia University in 1917 and an honorary LL.D.
from Drake University in 1934. During World War I he was
National Director of the Junior Red Cross with headquarters in
Washington. At the time of his appointment as Commissioner he
was Superintendent of Schools in Des Moines. It is interesting to
recall that this man who was to serve nearly fourteen years considered the appointment to be a "temporary affair" and took
leave of absence from his position in Des Moines. In fact he did
not resign the Iowa position until 1937.[36]

When Studebaker arrived in Washington the regular staff of
the Office of Education was down to 73 and the appropriation for

---

[35] "George F. Zook," *Higher Education*, VIII, No. 2, September 15, 1951,
pp. 22–23. The article is in error in stating that the CCC "had been launched
the year before." The CCC was established by an act dated March 31, 1933,
and Zook took office on July 11 of the same year.

[36] Evans and Wright, *op. cit.*, p. 75; Rodeheaver, *op. cit.*, pp. 161–163;
*Who's Who in America*, XXX, p. 2692; and "Studebaker Resigns: Grigsby
Acting Commissioner," *Higher Education*, V, No. 1, September 1, 1948, pp.
1–3. Studebaker also received honorary degrees from Muhlenberg College, the
University of Maryland, and Boston University.

salaries for fiscal year 1935 was only $231,022. Low as this amount was in comparison with the $280,000 appropriated for salaries in fiscal year 1932, it represented an increase of more than $15,000 over the preceding year. From the time he took office both the staff and appropriation increased.[37] More important than regular appropriations when it came to meeting depression emergencies were certain emergency relief funds. These made it possible for the Office of Education to carry out programs which had been developed by Zook and Studebaker himself, with the assistance of other staff members.[38]

Five special projects were financed by these relief funds. One was the educational forum program, a favorite with Studebaker, which was designed to encourage discussion of economic, social, and intellectual problems of the period. The other four were the educational radio project, a survey of local school administrative units, the vocational education and guidance of Negroes, and the program of research in educational problems conducted at universities.[39] In addition, the Office of Education helped direct and coordinate the miscellaneous educational activities of the Federal Emergency Relief Administration, the Civilian Conservation Corps, the Works Progress Administration, and the National Youth Administration.[40] The Division of Higher Education played

---

[37] John W. Studebaker, "Office of Education" in *Annual Report of the Secretary of the Interior for the Fiscal Year Ended June 30, 1935* (Washington, 1935), p. 307; and Rodeheaver, *op. cit.,* p. 164. The figure of 73 regular staff members does not include vocational education, temporary survey employees, or other employees working on emergency programs. This accounts for the difference between 73 and 170 as shown in Table 9, Chapter VI, *infra.*

[38] John W. Studebaker, "Office of Education" in *Annual Report of the Secretary of the Interior for the Fscal Year Ended June 30, 1936* (Washington, 1936), p. 238. In fiscal year 1932 there were no emergency funds available for education, in 1934 there was approximately 1.4 million dollars available, and in 1936, 15.9 million. See Clarence Heer, *Federal Aid and the Tax Problem* (Washington, 1939), Table 1.

[39] Studebaker, "Office of Education" in *Annual Report . . . 1936,* p. 238; and Hartley, *op. cit.,* pp. 168–194. See also *School Life,* XXIII, No. 6, February 1938, p. 232. There is an excellent brief account of the public affairs forums and the educational radio projects of the Office of Education in Doak S. Campbell, Frederick H. Blair, and Oswald L. Harvey, *Educational Activities of the Works Progress Administration* (Washington, 1939), pp. 45–49.

[40] Bess, Goodykoontz, "Office of Education" in *Annual Report of the Department of the Interior, 1934* (Washington, 1934), p. 254; and Federal Security Agency and War Manpower Commission, *Final Report of the National Youth Administration, Fiscal Years 1936–1943* (Washington, 1944), pp. 23–24.

a major part in only one of the special projects—the university research project. Before discussing this, some mention should be made of the role taken by the Division in the work of the National Youth Administration and the Civilian Conservation Corps.

Shortly after its establishment in May 1933, the Federal Emergency Relief Administration called together committees representing various college associations which conferred with specialists in higher education in the Office and with Administration officials. They discussed programs of part-time jobs for needy college students so they could stay in school. Authorization was provided for 100,000 such jobs "open to all colleges and universities organized on a non-profit basis." [41] Students entitled to participate were to be paid at least 30¢ per hour but were limited to maximum earnings of $20 per month. They could not work more than 30 hours a week or eight hours in any one day.[42] Specialists in the Division of Higher Education advised the Federal Emergency Relief Administration on programs involving institutions of higher education. On June 26, 1935, the National Youth Administration was established within the Works Progress Administration and at that time it took over the student aid program of the Federal Emergency Relief Administration. The National Youth Administration was considerably broader in scope and purpose than the earlier program. It had four objectives which took it far beyond a program of jobs for needy students in college:

1. To provide funds for part-time employment of needy school, college, and graduate students so they could continue their education;

2. To provide funds for part-time employment in work projects of young persons, not only to give them valuable experience but to help youth in local communities;

3. To establish and encourage establishment of job training, counseling, and placement services for youth; and

4. To encourage development and extension of constructive educational and job-qualifying leisure-time activities.[43]

From time of establishment in 1935 until the program was abolished in 1943, Office of Education officials served as advisors to the National Youth Administration Program. One of the most active was Fred Kelly, Chief of the Division of Higher Education.

---

[41] Goodykoontz, "Office of Education" in *Annual Report . . . 1934*, pp. 260–262.

[42] Fred J. Kelly, and John H. McNeely, *Federal Student Aid Program* (Washington, 1935), pp. 1–3, Appendix A.

[43] Federal Security Agency, *op. cit.*, pp. 23–24.

He had served as a member of the group that had proposed the National Youth Administration and he remained a major advisor from start to finish.[44]

In 1939 the National Youth Administration became part of the new Federal Security Agency, as did the Office of Education. Three years later it was made a part of the War Manpower Commission. "By 1936, some 600,000 persons were engaged in NYA activities, with a peak in 1939–40 when about 750,000 students in 1,700 colleges and universities and more than 28,000 secondary schools received NYA benefits . . . During 1941–43 it trained workers for national defense activities at an average rate of 30,000 a month." [45]

The educational program of the Civilian Conservation Corps involved the Division of Higher Education to a lesser extent than the National Youth Administration program. The Civilian Conservation Corps was established at the end of March, 1933, one of the first emergency measures taken by Roosevelt. In 1935 it was made a part of the Works Progress Administration. More than 2,000,000 youth had been employed in its camps by the time it was phased out during fiscal year 1942.[46] Starting in 1934 the Office of Education contacted colleges and universities on behalf of enrollees desiring a college education. Approximately 15 percent of the enrollees had graduated from high school and were eligible for either collegiate study or some sort of post-secondary school work. Kelly and his staff helped find institutions which would admit qualified enrollees and provide them with some kind of financial assistance. In 1937 for example, largely through the work of the Division, 39 colleges and universities offered scholarships to enrollees, 35 offered National Youth Administration assistance, and 18 agreed to make loan funds and jobs available.[47] But the educational programs at the college level, as well as other educational programs conducted in the Civilian Conservation Corps camps, were not controlled or directed by the Office of Education. It acted solely as an advisor and then only when requested. In fiscal year 1936 the Division of Higher Education advised colleges and universities offering college work to approxi-

[44] Interviews of author with Dr. Caliver, October 28, 1959, and Mr. Flynt, October 7, 1959. For additional information on the general relationship of Office of Education with the NYA program see "Forums, Correspondence, etc. (1931–1947)" Acc. No. 56-A-506, RG 12, Federal Records Center, Alexandria, Virginia.

[45] Richard B. Morris, (ed), *Encyclopedia of American History* (New York, 1953), p. 350.

[46] *Ibid.*, p. 342; and Federal Security Agency, *op. cit.*, pp. 22–23.

[47] Howard W. Oxley, "CCC Enrollees Go to College," *School Life*, XXIV, No. 1, October 1938, pp. 25–26.

mately eight thousand young men. The number of students assisted through advisory work to institutions remained as high or higher until our entrance in World War II.[48]

Most important of the relief projects directly involving the Division was the program of emergency research.[49] The idea behind this was to use trained white collar workers on relief to conduct important research projects. These embraced several levels of education: occupational problems of the deaf and hard-of-hearing and what education could do to help; organization of local school units; vocational education and guidance of Negroes; and some 200 smaller studies of various types in colleges and universities throughout the Nation.[50] These studies were supervised by members of the Division with Frazier in general charge of the work.[51]

The emergency research project started in fiscal year 1934 in three institutions: Columbia University; New York University; and the University of Chicago. More than 1,700 persons were employed for periods ranging from a few weeks to more than six months in these first studies.[52] The projects were expanded the following year and before it was ended on June 30, 1937, a total of $411,695 had been appropriated from emergency funds. The result was a series of studies which, along with the research stations established in the 1920's, contributed greatly to the development of the cooperative research program of the Office of Education in the mid-1950's.[53] Studebaker summarized the significance of the program in his report of office activities for fiscal year 1937:

. . . Sixty universities located in 32 States, the District of Columbia, and Hawaii joined the Office of Education in this activity. More than 165 separate study reports for 40 studies were made by the universities, and the major findings were

[48] Studebaker, "Office of Education" in *Annual Report . . . 1936*, pp. 233–237. Kelly assisted in planning the educational program of the CCC according to Flynt in an interview with the author, October 7, 1959. The annual reports of the mid-1930's discuss the development of educational programs but do not mention Kelly. This is not unusual since he participated in many meetings and conferences which were not mentioned in reports.

[49] See John H. Lloyd, "Expanding the Office of Education," *The American Teacher*, XXIV, No. 8, April 1940, pp. 46–50.

[50] Hartley, *op. cit.*, pp. 187–188; and *School Life*, XXI, No. 9, May 1936, p. 253.

[51] "Office of Education to Head New Projects," *The Journal of the National Education Association*, XXV, No. 2, February 1936, p. 42.

[52] Goodykoontz, "Office of Education" in *Annual Report . . . 1934*, p. 266.

[53] Judd, *op. cit.*, pp. 90–92. The establishment of "research stations" came as the result of a meeting on educational research problems held in St. Louis, Missouri, January 2–3, 1920. This has been noted in Chapter III.

assembled and coordinated by the Office. Findings are being made available in 11 bulletins and 4 pamphlets. Many of the universities are also publishing material growing out of this research.

More than 60,000 individuals and hundreds of institutions of higher education assisted in providing data for the several studies. A number of the institutions continued work on the former project studies on their own funds after the project closed. It is believed that the success of this undertaking will encourage future research programs involving cooperative activities of the Office of Education and of higher educational institutions.[54]

It cannot be shown that the Division of Higher Education profited from the depression through expanded size or increased activity to the same extent as many other Federal agencies. It increased by only one member prior to 1940 and, aside from advising when requested, assumed only one responsibility directly related to emergency relief, the university research project. Taken as a whole, the role of the Division as an instrument for the promotion of New Deal programs was negligible.

The Bankhead-Jones Act of June 29, 1935, was prompted to a slight extent by the total recovery program, as were most of the other legislative acts of the mid-1930's. But it was more a long-range development program to provide additional assistance to land-grant colleges. This act was a supplement to the Second Morrill Act of 1890 and the Nelson Amendment of 1907, both of which provided for financial grants to land-grant colleges stemming from the Morrill Act of 1862.[55]

The Bankhead-Jones Act provided for the appropriation of $20,000 to each State and territory for the operation of qualified institutions with payments starting in fiscal year 1936. It differed from the earlier acts in one important respect. They provided for continuing appropriations requiring no further congressional action. The Act authorized appropriations on which the Congress was required to act each year.[56] As a result of the 1935 legislation $980,000 was appropriated the first year of operation and dis-

---

[54] John W. Studebaker, "Office of Education" in *Annual Report of the Secretary of the Interior for the Fiscal Year Ending June 30, 1937* (Washington, 1937), p. 273. For additional information on the research program see Judd, *op. cit.*, pp. 90–92; Malone M. Willey, *Depression, Recovery, and Higher Education* (New York, 1937), pp. 383–384; "New Appropriations for the Federal Office of Education," *School and Society*, XLII, No. 1096, December 28, 1935, p. 886; and "The University Research Project on the Office of Education, *School and Society*, XLV, No. 1172, June 12, 1937, pp. 807–808.

[55] See Chapter I, footnote 60.

[56] Fred J. Kelly, *Land-Grant Colleges and Universities: A Federal-State Partnership* (Washington, 1952), pp. 4–6.

tributed to the 48 States and the Territory of Hawaii. Alaska and Puerto Rico did not participate. The Act further provided that $500,000 more be appropriated in fiscal year 1937, $1,000,000 in 1938, and $1,500,000 in 1939 and annually thereafter. These increases were to be apportioned according to the ratio that the total population of each State and the Territory of Hawaii bore to the total population of the States and Hawaii.[57]

The funds for campus instruction at the 69 land-grant institutions which were authorized under the 1890, 1907, and 1935 acts were administered by the Office of Education. From 1939 on through the following years the sums distributed to land-grant colleges and universities amounted to more than $5,000,000 annually.[58] The Division of Higher Education continued the administration of the funds, and receiving and reviewing reports from land-grant institutions, which it had taken over in 1911. The title "specialist in land-grant college statistics" was not used for several years after 1931 when Walter Greenleaf was redesignated from that to "specialist in higher education." [59] The title "specialist in land-grant colleges and universities" was used following World War II when Lloyd E. Blauch was administering the land-grant funds for the Division of Higher Education.[60]

Although the Division of Higher Education did not expand or

---

[57] George A. Works and Barton Morgan, *The Land-Grant Colleges* (Washington, 1939), pp. 15–17, text of act on pp. 125–128; and J. W. Studebaker, "Office of Education" in *Annual Report . . . 1935*, pp. 309–310. The Bankhead-Jones Act was amended in June, 1952, and Alaska was included at that time. Puerto Rico still was not participating under it. See Kelly, *op. cit.*, p. 6.

[58] Annual figures are given in Table 5, *infra*.

[59] Greenleaf's Personnel Folder, St. Louis Records Center, St. Louis, Missouri. For additional information on the Federal relationship to land-grant institutions and experiment stations (funds administered by the Department of Agriculture) see V. O. Key, Jr., *The Administration of Federal Grants to States* (Chicago, 1937); H. J. Bitterman, *State and Federal Grants-in-Aid* (New York, 1938); Jane Perry Clark, *The Rise of a New Federalism: Federal-State Cooperation in the United States* (New York, 1938); and Lloyd E. Blauch, "Federal Relations to Education" in Walter S. Monroe (ed), *Encyclopedia of Educational Research* (New York, 1950), pp. 435–448. The first three items listed discuss several aspects of land-grant education and of problems arising from the administration of funds. Some of the records are available in Archives File 26, "Office of Education, Commissioner's Office, Land-Grant College Correspondence, Research on Education Correspondence, 1921–26," (National Archives, Labor and Transportation Branch); and "Report of Treasurer—A M Colleges (Morrill-Nelson)," Acc. No. 56–A–506, RG 12, Federal Records Center, Alexandria, Virginia.

[60] "New Assistant Commissioner for Higher Education," *Higher Education*, XII, No. 2. October 1955, pp. 17–18; and John Dale Russell, "The Role of the Division of Higher Education of the United States Office of Education," *American Association of University Professors, Bulletin*, XXXIII, No. 3, Autumn 1947, p. 441.

TABLE 5.—*Funds Appropriated to the Office of Education for Colleges of Agriculture and the Mechanics Arts*

| Fiscal year | Second Morrill Act of 1890 and Nelson Amendment of 1907 | Bankhead-Jones Act of 1935 (Amended 1952) |
|---|---|---|
| 1890 | $ 660,000 | $ — |
| 1891 | 704,000 | — |
| 1892 | 782,000 | — |
| 1893 | 864,000 | — |
| 1894 | 912,000 | — |
| 1895 | 960,000 | — |
| 1896 | 1,008,000 | — |
| 1897 | 1,056,000 | — |
| 1898 | 1,104,000 | — |
| 1899 | 1,152,000 | — |
| 1900 through 1907 [1] | 1,200,000 | — |
| 1908 | 1,500,000 | — |
| 1909 | 1,750,000 | — |
| 1910 | 2,000,000 | — |
| 1911 | 2,250,000 | — |
| 1912 through 1922 [1] | 2,500,000 | — |
| 1923 through 1935 [1] | 2,550,000 | — |
| 1936 | 2,550,000 | 980,000 |
| 1937 | $2,550,000 | $1,480,000 |
| 1938 | 2,550,000 | 1,980,000 |
| 1939 through 1953 [1] | 2,550,000 | 2,480,000 |

(Figures supplied by Mrs. Genevieve Dane, Assistant Budget Management Officer, Office of Education, from material in Budget Management Office Files.)
[1] Annually.

take on a workload comparable to other Federal activities more closely allied to relief, education was not outside the consideration of the Federal Government. There was a growth of interest in education as shown by the appointment of the Advisory Committee on Education by President Roosevelt. This should not be confused with the National Advisory Committee on Education appointed by Hoover in 1929. On September 19, 1936, Roosevelt appointed a committee of 24 distinguished citizens

> . . . to study the experience under the existing program of Federal aid for vocational education, the relation of such training to general education and to prevailing economic and social conditions, and the extent of the need for an expanded program; and to develop recommendations that would be available to the Congress and the Executive.[61]

Two members of the Advisory Committee had been with the Division of Higher Education. They were Zook, Vice-Chairman,

---

[61] The Advisory Committee on Education, *Report of the Committee* (Washington, 1938), p. III. See p. II for membership.

and Judd. Although the latter had been with the Division for a short period of time, both were familiar with the work it did and knew its members.

On April 19, 1937, the President broadened the Committee's field of study. He requested it to "give more extended consideration to the whole subject of Federal relationship to State and local conduct of education." [62] The Committee reported on February 18, 1938, that the Federal Government should expand its activities and responsibilities in the field of education. The Office of Education should have a large share of responsibility in the administration of the laws which the Committee proposed. Recommendations were made for increased activity by the Government in nine specific educational areas which would be administered by the Office of Education:

   1.  Establishment of a Federal equalization fund to provide equal educational opportunity to all citizens;
   2.  Procedures for improvement of teacher training;
   3.  Stimulation of school building programs to enable communities to bring about an efficient scheme of district organizations;
   4.  Assistance to State departments of education;
   5.  Helping bridge the gap between school and vocation;
   6.  Stimulation of adult educational programs;
   7.  Improvement of rural library services;
   8.  Provisions for education of children living on Government property; and
   9.  More activity in educational research, planning, and leadership. [63]

Two of the recommendations had direct application to colleges and universities. If they had been implemented, the proposals to improve teacher training and to expand Office activity in educational research would have affected the Division. The Committee recommended that grants of $2,000,000 in fiscal year 1940, $4,000,000 in 1941, and $6,000,000 in each of the following fiscal years be made to the States for their use in improving teachers and other educational personnel. The plans for programs financed by these grants would be "jointly agreed upon for each State by the respective State agency and the United States Office of Educa-

---

[62] *Ibid.*, p. III.
[63] *Ibid.*, pp. 142–157, 180–221. See also Hartley, *op. cit.*, pp. 208–209; Hales, *op. cit.*, pp. 67–68; and John W. Studebaker, "Office of Education" in *Annual Report of the Secretary of the Interior for the Fiscal Year Ended June 30, 1938* (Washington, 1938), pp. 346–348. Studebaker stated that the Committee reported in March 1938 (*Ibid.*, p. 346) but the published report contains a letter of transmittal to the President dated February 18, 1938.

tion." [64] The obvious place within the Office for formulating these plans would be the Division of Higher Education.

Concerning educational research, planning, and leadership, the Committee stated:

> The United States Office of Education should remain predomi-
> nantly an agency for research and leadership; its administrative
> duties should be confined primarily to the administration of
> grants. Provision should be made for an adequate staff of
> highly competent leaders in the various educational fields who
> can cooperate effectively with the States on an advisory basis
> in the planning of programs.
>
> *        *        *        *        *        *        *
>
> A special Federal fund should be established for cooperative
> educational research, demonstrations, and planning, to be ad-
> ministered by the United States Office of Education. The
> amounts recommended are $1,250,000 during the fiscal year
> 1938–39; $2,000,000 during the fiscal year 1939–40; and
> $3,000,000 during each of the succeeding fiscal years through
> 1944–45.[65]

The outbreak of the Second World War made certain that the recommendations of the Committee would not be acted upon for some time, if at all. Nothing concrete had been established by the time the Nazis invaded Poland in September 1939. When the war ended in 1945, there were other, more urgent, problems of recon-struction and conversion from war to peace. The Committee's recommendations gathered dust on library shelves. Although it cannot be shown that any recommendations were acted upon as submitted in 1938, the group was successful in outlining the possi-bilities of Federal aid to education. As far as the Division was involved, the Committee recommendations made a strong case for a thorough study of teaching qualifications and preparation pro-cedures, and an even stronger plea for a comprehensive, continu-ing program of educational research.[66]

---

[64] Advisory Committee, *op. cit.*, pp. 201–202. Quotation from p. 201.

[65] *Ibid.*, pp. 219–221. Quotation from p. 219.

[66] Although the Committee's recommendations were not acted upon imme-diately or directly it is interesting to see how many of them have since be-come established policy of the Federal Government. Twenty years after the Committee report was prepared, in 1958, the National Defense Education Act became operative. It contained titles which fulfilled, in varying degrees, recommendations 1, 2, 4, 5, and 9 as stated in the text, *supra*. The coopera-tive research program of the Office of Education established in 1954 also assists in the fulfillment of recommendation 9. The George-Barden Act (1946) and amendments thereto applied to recommendation 5. Public Laws 815 and 874 (1950) help recommendations 3 and 8. There are a large num-ber of schools operated on Federal reservations and at installations through-

The economic upheaval of the 1930's did not interfere to any appreciable extent with established routine.[67] A large number of visits to institutions were made. Now the trips could be shared by a half dozen people rather than divided between the division chief and one other person as before. The professional staff continued to serve as consultants and advisors to institutions, educational groups, and lay groups when requested.

Three activities in which the Division of Higher Education participated, and which involved groups outside the Office of Education, deserve special mention.[68] One was the study of accreditation of post-secondary institutions made in 1938–1939 at the request of the National Council of Chief State School Officers. An advisory committee of chief State school officers from California, Connecticut, Michigan, Missouri, and Virginia was appointed to work with Kelly, Frazier, McNeely, and Ratcliffe in recommending standards that might be used by State departments of education in accrediting post-secondary institutions. The findings of the group were published in 1940. They concluded "accreditation of higher education was a State responsibility, and that the function of private educational organizations should be the improvement, but not the accreditation, of education." [69]

A second activity was educational relationship with Latin America. Kelly served as an alternate for Commissioner Stude-

---

out the world and these relate to recommendation 8. The Library Service Act of 1956 relates to recommendation 7. These are only a few of the activities, although the most prominent, which bore a relationship to the Committee's 1938 recommendations within 20 years of the date of their appearance.

In addition to its recommendations the Advisory Committee published 19 Staff Studies on various educational problems. The studies appeared in 1938 and 1939. Lloyd Blauch, later to serve as Director of the Division of Higher Education, was the author of three of these studies and the co-author of two others; John Dale Russell, also to serve as Director at a later date, was the co-author of one; and Judd, formerly with the Division for a brief period, was the author of one. The list of titles may be found in Judd, *op. cit.*, p. 133.

[67] A good brief statement on recurring services and activities of the Division of Higher Education in the mid-1930's appeared in a paper prepared for a "Conference on Higher Education, May 22–23, 1936" in Archives File 209–a, "Professional Education, etc." (National Archives, Labor and Transportation Branch).

[68] The national survey of the higher education of Negroes came in the late 1930's and should be noted as one of the most important cooperative activities. This has been discussed in Chapter III.

[69] Jennings B. Sanders, "The United States Office of Education and Accreditation" in Lloyd E. Blauch (ed), *Accreditation in Higher Education* (Washington, 1959), p. 19. The study published in 1940 was Fred J. Kelly *et al.*, *College Accreditation by Agencies Within States* (Washington, 1940).

baker on the Interdepartmental Committee on Cooperation with the American Republics. This group was created in 1938 and continued to function throughout World War II. John Patterson attended meetings as an advisor.[70] Discussions of this Interdepartmental Committee led to the assignment of responsibility to the Division for selection of nominees for exchange with Latin American Nations agreeing to the Convention for the Promotion of Inter-American Cultural Relations, signed December 23, 1936. According to the Convention one professor and two graduate students or teachers were to be exchanged between the United States and each ratifying power. The Division was to select those to go to Latin America and place those coming here from abroad.[71] This was the start of a highly successful teacher and student exchange program. Perhaps one could call it the precursor of the famous Fulbright international education programs starting after World War II.

The study of the objectives of graduate education in the American democracy was the third of these activities. This was begun in 1937 under the leadership of Dr. Isaiah Bowman, President of Johns Hopkins University. The study was stimulated, and directed, by the Office of Education and Bowman. When it was published by the Office of Education in 1939 it was a clear and timely statement of the role of the graduate school in the preservation and promotion of democracy.[72]

Publications and studies, as has been noted, tended to emphasize financial problems although a glance at Table 11 shows that there was variety in the material published and distributed.[73] There was a sharp drop in the number of publications relating to higher education. In the decade from 1921 to 1930 there were 158, and in the succeeding decade 123; a decline in number of nearly 25

---

[70] "Commissioners Office, Interdepartmental Committee on Cooperation with American Republics, 1938–1944," in "Forums, Correspondence, etc. (1931–1947)," Acc. No. 56–A–506, RG 12, Federal Records Center, Alexandria, Virginia.

[71] John W. Studebaker, *Annual Report of the United States Commissioner of Education for the Fiscal Year Ended June 30, 1940* (Washington, 1941), p. 12. See also John W. Studebaker, *Annual Report of the United States Commissioner of Education for the Fiscal Year Ended June 30, 1941* (Washington, 1942), pp. 44–45.

[72] John W. Studebaker, "Office of Education" in *Annual Report of the Secretary of the Interior for the Fiscal Year Ending June 30, 1939* (Washington, 1939), pp. 73, 91. The study published as a result of the work on graduate schools was Isaiah Bowman, *The Graduate School in American Democracy* (Washington, 1939).

[73] See Chapter VI.

percent. The reduction was caused in part by smaller appropriations for printing during the early 1930's but other factors, such as rising production costs and more comprehensive and better illustrated publications, contributed. The improvement in quality of the publications more than balanced the loss in quantity.

In 1939, one of the most crucial years in the history of man and at which one can look and say "Here one era ended and another began," Kelly appeared before the 41st Annual Conference of the Association of American Universities to explain the contributions of his Division of Higher Education to the Nation. The paper he presented summarized so well the overall contribution of the Federal Government, as well as the Division, that it can serve as a valedictory to the 1930's. Kelly wrote that the Federal Government aided higher education in three ways: grants of land; appropriations of funds through such devices as the Second Morrill Act, the National Youth Administration, and so forth; and the services of the Office of Education. These services, all performed in whole or part by the Division of Higher Education, were five:

1. Educational relations with foreign countries such as credential verification, exchange of students, and exchange of professional licenses;
2. Services rendered to the States such as survey advising, and State accreditation of colleges and universities;
3. Services rendered to groups of colleges and universities such as the land-grant survey of 1926–1930 and similar surveys,[74] studies of alumni in 31 colleges, dropouts from 25 colleges, and so forth;
4. Services rendered to individual colleges and universities such as the assistance rendered to five State universities; one State agricultural and mechanical college, and one Negro college in the first half of 1939, assistance in collecting statistics, graduate school studies, publication of special studies, and so forth; and
5. Services rendered through facilitation of conferences among leaders in higher education such as the conference on graduate study let by Bowman.[75]

It was a comprehensive and balanced program of services which the Office of Education offered higher education through its Di-

---

[74] For a list of the national surveys of the 1930's see Chapter III.

[75] *Journal of Proceedings and Addresses of the Forty-first Conference Held at the University of Missouri, October 30–31 and November 1, 1939* (published for the Association of American Universities at Chicago ,1939), paper by Kelly on pp. 92–101. Another summary statement of value relating to the activities of the Office of Education in the late 1930's is in Educational Policies Commission, *Federal Activities in Education* (Washington, 1939), pp. 111–123.

vision of Higher Education.[76] But this well organized program was thrust more and more into the background as the Second World War absorbed increasing amounts of America's energies. The war would leave its mark on all it touched. The Division would not be the same when peace returned for, as any student of history knows, no matter how many times history repeats its themes they are always played with variations.

## The Second World War

The general attitude of the American people toward war changes almost as much as the way it is fought. The Spanish-American War, in the words of Mr. Dooley, was a "grand moonlight an' picnic excursion." That is the way a large segment of the public seemed to regard it. The First World War was a moral crusade to "make the world safe for democracy." But the Second World War was a scientific, business-like affair fought, by the United States at least, with methodical detachment bolstered by a sober devotion to democracy seldom equaled in our history. There were far fewer illusions in 1942 than in 1917, and many more well-laid plans.[77]

This business-like attitude was reflected in educational planning such as in the emergency training program for defense workers which began a year and a half before our entrance into the war:

Between April 1939 and May 1940 officials of the U.S. Office of Education and representatives of the Army and Navy had carried forward careful inventory of the training facilities of the public schools of the Nation, with special attention to the potentialities of the Federal-State cooperative program of vocational education with its billion dollar plant, its 35,000 skilled teachers and supervisors, its 75,000 training stations in public trade schools. Consequently, it was not a surprise when the schools were called upon to use these facilities in an emergency training program for defense workers.[78]

[76] On July 1, 1939, the Office of Education was transferred from the Department of the Interior where it had been for seventy years to the new Federal Security Agency. (53 Stat. L., pt. 2, Reorganization Plan No. 1 of Reorganization Act of 1939, approved April 3, 1939.)

[77] When dealing with a large number of people, statements of this type are dangerous. But regarded as generalizations and not infallible laws, these contain much truth. Songs coming from the three conflicts tend to bear them out. The most enduring song to come from the Spanish-American War was the roistering "Hot Time in the Old Town Tonight." World War I's great hit was "Over There," a thumping, crusade-like song. World War II failed to produce a single song that possessed the staying power and universal popularity of these.

[78] Studebaker, *Annual Report . . . 1941*, p. 1.

This inventory was followed in June, 1940, by Public Law 668 which appropriated $15,000,000 for emergency training of defense workers. Courses in this program were to be of less than college grade. Four months later, Public Law 812 appropriated $60,500,000 to expand the program and include "short engineering courses of college grade, provided by engineering schools or by universities of which the engineering school is a part, pursuant to plans submitted by them and approved by the Commissioner. . . ." [79] Nine million dollars was authorized for these short engineering courses. This was the start of the Engineering, Science, and Management War Training program which will be discussed in more detail later.

Obviously the abrupt entrance into World War II did not find the total lack of defense educational programs which had existed 24 years earlier. Programs of vocational defense training for adults and youths, and college level courses in engineering were already operating. In fiscal year 1941 more than $75,000,000 had been made available for national defense work and this money was to be administered by the Office of Education.[80]

Within a few days after the attack on Pearl Harbor, Studebaker and his staff had developed a comprehensive list of the services which the Office of Education could offer to further the war effort. There were three major categories of services:

1.  Administering cooperative action programs of education and training in the States which would enable them to make a maximum contribution to the war effort;

2.  Providing leadership, advice, and information to the schools, colleges, and libraries of the Nation concerning special educational problems of the wartime situation; and

3.  Establishing effective liaison between organized education on the one hand and the war agencies of the Federal Government on the other.[81]

The Division of Higher Education was involved in varying degrees in each of these broad categories of activity. The Engineering, Science, and Management War Training and Student War Loans Programs were important cooperative enterprises it administered. In the second category the Division participated in an information exchange program involving institutions and organizations at all educational levels, and prepared and issued, through the Office of Education, various publications relating to

---

[79] *Ibid.*, pp. 1–3. Quotation from P.L. 812, 76th Congress, 3d sess.

[80] See Table 6, *infra.*

[81] John W. Studebaker, "The United States Office of Education and the War," *The Educational Record*, XXIII, No. 3, July 1942, pp. 453–463.

TABLE 6.—*Appropriations Made Available for National Defense, Office of Education, FY 1941–1946*

| Program | FY 1941 | FY 1942 | FY 1943 | FY 1944 | FY 1945 | FY 1946 | Program |
|---|---|---|---|---|---|---|---|
| Salaries and expenses of office of education for national defense | $ — | $ 1,222,000 | $ 1,264,000 | $ 1,200,000 | $ 866,700 | $384,900 | $ 4,937,600 |
| Vocational education of defense workers | 15,000,000 | — | — | — | — | — | 15,000,000 |
| Vocational courses of less than college grade | 26,000,000 | 61,900,000 | 104,000,000 | 90,000,000 | — | — | 281,900,000 |
| Equipment | 8,000,000 | 22,000,000 | — | — | — | — | 30,000,000 |
| Engineering, science, and management war training | 9,000,000 | 20,500,000 | 30,000,000 | 25,000,000 | 4,000,000 | — | 88,500,000 |
| Out of school rural youth | 10,000,000 | 15,000,000 | 15,000,000 | 12,500,000 | 10,500,000 | — | 63,000,000 |
| NYA projects | 7,500,000 | 10,000,000 | — | — | — | — | 17,500,000 |
| Loans to students | — | — | 5,000,000 | 900 | — | — | 5,000,900 |
| Salaries and expense (loans to students) | — | — | 100,000 | — | — | — | 100,000 |
| Visual aids for war training | — | — | 1,000,000 | 2,000,000 | 175,000 | — | 3,175,000 |
| Totals | $75,500,000 | $130,622,000 | $156,364,000 | $130,700,900 | $15,541,700 | $384,900 | $509,113,500 |

(Figures supplied by Mrs. Genevieve Dane, Assistant Budget Management Officer, Office of Education, from material in Budget Management Office files.)

the war. In the third category were the services of Kelly and other members of the Division on, or for, emergency war bodies, most important of which was the Office of Education Wartime Commission.

Less than a month after the opening Japanese attack on the United States, a National Conference of College and University Presidents convened in Baltimore, Maryland. This meeting was sponsored jointly by the National Committee on Education and Defense and the Office of Education.[82] It lasted from January 3 to 4, 1942, and was attended by approximately 1,000 delegates, making it the "largest meeting of college and university executives ever held in the United States." [83] It was also an enthusiastic meeting at which the conferees pledged "the total strength of our colleges and universities—our faculties, our students, our administrative organizations, and our physical facilities. The institutions of higher education of the United States are organized for action, and they offer their united power for decisive military victory, and for the ultimate and even more difficult task of establishing a just and lasting peace." [84]

Kelly addressed this group using as his subject the U.S. Office of Education Wartime Commission which had just been organized. The National Conference resolved that the Commission should be a major agency in preparing reports on needs and requirements in higher education. The resolution was propitious and the timing right; the Wartime Commission served throughout the first and darkest year of the war as the main liaison between the Office of Education and the colleges and universities and other institutions of higher education throughout the Nation. Although it lasted only one year its influence continued to be felt throughout the war.[85]

This Wartime Commission had been established in December 1941, at the request of the Federal Security Administrator, Paul V. McNutt. He explained its purpose in these words:

> The object is (1) to facilitate the adjustment of educational agencies to war needs, and (2) to inform the government agencies directly responsible for the war effort concerning the

[82] The National Committee on Education and Defense was organized in August 1940. It represented sixty national educational associations and was sponsored and supported by the American Council on Education and the National Education Association. For membership see Clarence Stephen Marsh (ed), *Higher Education and the War* (Washington, 1942), pp. 159–163.

[83] *Ibid.*, p. iv.

[84] *Ibid.*, "preamble" to the resolutions and recommendations of the Conference, p. 154.

[85] *Ibid.*, pp. 72–81, 153–158.

services schools and colleges can render, and (3) to determine
the possible effects upon schools and colleges of proposed policies
and programs of these government agencies.[86]

At the first meeting of the Wartime Commission in Washington,
December 23, 1941, Studebaker issued a statement which read in
part:

> To be the largest possible service to the Government in gen-
> eral, to a number of agencies of the Government in particular,
> and to organized education throughout the Nation, the Office
> of Education now needs and requests the united assistance of a
> workable group of key officials in or near Washington engaged
> in different fields of education. Acting upon Administrator Mc-
> Nutt's request, I am, therefore, establishing the Office of Edu-
> cation Wartime Commission.[87]

Studebaker served as Chairman and Goodykoontz as Vice Chairman, with Kelly as Executive Director. Administrator McNutt was
an ex officio member. The total membership at the start was thirty-
eight. In order to facilitate the work of the Commission several
of its members were organized into two Divisional Committees:
State and Local School Administration; and Higher Education.
The latter contained sixteen Commission members and had the
ubiquitous George Zook as Chairman and Kelly as a member. Dr.
John Lund, Specialist in School administration in the Division of
Higher Education, was Executive Director.[88] In addition to the
regular members of the Wartime Commission, there were several
members of the Office of Education staff, including nine from
Higher Education, who served as consultants and advisors. The
numerical strength of the Commission apparently varied from
thirty-four to sixty.[89]

One of the most important missions of the Commission was "to

---

[86] *Ibid.*, p. 76.

[87] "U.S. Office of Education Wartime Commission," *Education for Victory*,
I, No. 1, March 3, 1942, pp. 3–4. Quotation from p. 4.

[88] Dr. Fred Kelly served as a member of the Divisional Committee on State
and Local School Administration as well as on this Committee. (*Ibid.*, p. 5).

[89] There is some confusion in the available information on the size of the
Commission. The article in *Education for Victory* (see fn. 87) lists 38 members with McNutt as one of them. It also lists 10 "additional persons" who
served on the two divisional committees but were not on the Commission
itself. Other figures on the Commission do not list McNutt but total 58 members, 33 members and 1 alternate, and 58 members and 2 alternates. cf. John
W. Studebaker, *Annual Reports of the United States Office of Education for
the Fiscal Years 1941–1942, 1942–43* (Washington, 1943), p. 47; Marsh (ed),
*op. cit.*, pp. 164–166; and *Handbook on Education and the War . . .* (Washington, 1943), pp. X–XII. The last-named volume has a Foreword by Studebaker
which states that the Wartime Commission "is made up of 53 educational
leaders." (P. IX).

facilitate the wartime contacts of the Government agencies with schools and colleges and to make such contacts more effective." [90] It issued several reports, many of which were influential in determining the policies of the Government and of educational institutions and organizations. Probably the most effective of these reports grew out of a meeting sponsored by the Commission in the Summer of 1942. This report was entitled *Handbook on Education and the War,* the published proceedings of a National Institute on Education and the War which was held on the campus of The American University, August 28–31, 1942. More than 700 leading educators attended the four-day session which was addressed by a number of leading Government and wartime figures, among them Lt. General Brehon Somervell, McNutt, Secretary of Agriculture Claude Wickard, Senator Thomas of Utah, and Elmer Davis, Director of the Office of War Information. The influence of a document of the nature of this report cannot be measured accurately, but it was widely distributed and its suggestions for accelerated school and college programs, adaptation of curricula to meet defense needs, and additional Federal action to educational services were adopted by the colleges and universities of the Nation as well as by elementary and secondary schools.[91] This volume and *Higher Education and the War,* which resulted from the January, 1942, National Conference of College and University Presidents, were far better guides than any which appeared in the First Word War.

The Wartime Commission continued regular meetings until the Fall of 1942 when it ceased functioning believing the task of organizing and planning had been accomplished and the actual operation of programs should be left to such agencies as the War Manpower Commission and to the individual educational institutions. Members of the Commission, however, "continued to assist the Office of Education and other Federal agencies . . . as individuals, or in small groups called together for consultation and work on special problems." [92]

---

[90] Studebaker, *Annual Reports . . . 1941–1942, 1942–43,* p. 47. For additional commentary on mission and on the Commission in general see "The Wartime Commission of the United States Office of Education," *The Elementary School Journal,* XLII, No. 8, April 1942, p. 569. McNutt's three objectives for the Commission are there listed as: First, to facilitate adjustment of educational agencies to war needs; Second, to inform Government agencies directly responsible for the war effort the services that schools and colleges can perform; and Third, to determine possible effects on schools and colleges of the programs and policies of these war agencies.

[91] *Handbook,* pp. IX, 133–137, 173–192, 260–275, and 322–344.

[92] Studebaker, *Annual Reports . . . 1941–42, 1942–43,* p. 47. The War Man-

There were "five essential wartime programs administered by the U.S. Office of Education." Two were the responsibility of the Division of Vocational Education: Vocational Training for War Production Workers; and Food Production War Training. A third was the responsibility of a special emergency division, Visual Aids for War Training. The remaining two were the responsibility of the Division of Higher Education and, as it proved, they were the major contributions it made to the war effort: Engineering, Science, and Management War Training; and the Student War Loans Program.[93]

McNutt, in a statement made early in the war, considered Engineering, Science, and Management War Training one of the two most important contributions of the entire Office of Education.[94] It continued to be of primary significance until the war had virtually ended. More than $88,000,000 was spent in training the nearly 1,800,000 students enrolled in the courses it sponsored.[95]

Engineering, Science, and Management War Training extended from October 9, 1940 to June 30, 1945. It underwent two changes of name in this period. In the first fiscal year of operation, 1941, it was officially Engineering Defense Training (EDT) since science and management courses were not yet involved and it was not a wartime program. The next fiscal year it was expanded to become Engineering, Science, and Management Defense Training (ESMDT); then in fiscal year 1943 the "Defense" in the title became "War." For brevity it is usually identified as ESMWT throughout the entire period.

On October 9, 1940, the President signed the basic ESMWT law:

Public Law 812 of the Seventy-sixth Congress, 3rd Session, was approved by the President on October 9, 1940. This act

---

power Commission was established on April 18, 1942, with McNutt as chairman of the nine member board. See Morris, (ed), *op. cit.*, p. 379. Kelly represented Studebaker at several meetings of the War Manpower Commission. Interview of author with Hollis, October 27, 1959.

[93] Roy W. Bixler, "The Student War Loans Program," *Higher Education*, II, No. 2, September 5, 1945, pp. 3–5. Appropriations for these and other programs are shown in Table 6, *supra*.

[94] Paul V. McNutt, "Mobilizing Education for Victory" in Marsh, (ed), *op. cit.*, pp. 3–8. The second important contribution he noted was Civilian Morale Service in Schools and Colleges. The Division of Higher Education helped in this program to some extent by publication of material relating to the war, and by advising on programs. The Student War Loans Program had not yet started when McNutt made his statement.

[95] For costs see Table 6, *supra;* for enrollment see Table 7, *infra*.

appropriated $9,000,000 to cover the cost for the remainder of the fiscal year ending June 30, 1941, of "short engineering courses of college grade, provided by engineering schools or by universities of which the engineering school is a part, pursuant to plans submitted by them and approved by the Commissioner, which plans shall be for courses designed to meet the shortage of engineers with specialized training in fields essential to the national defense—*Provided*, That only engineering schools which operate under charters which exempt their educational property from taxation shall be eligible to receive these funds: *Provided further;* That not to exceed 20 per centum of the amount allotted to any school shall be allotted to it for expenditure for purchase or rental of additional equipment and leasing of additional space found by the Commissioner necessary for carrying out its approved plan." [96]

During the following four years of its life the program underwent few modifications:

The principal changes were: (1) the addition of courses for chemists, physicists, and production supervisors to the objectives of the program; (2) the provision that courses must be of types approved by the Chairman of the War Manpower Commission; (3) the reduction of the percentage of funds which might be allotted for equipment and space from 20 per centum to 12½ per centum; and (4) the provision that approved equipment purchased with ESMWT funds should become the property of the institutions.[97]

The size and scope of the ESMWT program made it impossible for the small permanent professional staff to handle.[98] The Office

---

[96] An excellent detailed history of the ESMWT program has been written. The account in the text is based primarily on this history which was prepared by a professional staff member who was active in ESMWT from the early days. For complete details see H. H. Armsby, *Engineering, Science, and Management War Training—Final Report* (Washington, 1946). Quotation from pp. 14–15.

[97] *Ibid.*, p. 15.

[98] Table 10, Chapter VI, *infra*, shows the size of the Division. The regular staff, in which are included the chief figures of the ESMWT program, never numbered more than 14 during the war years although, in an interview with the author, October 27, 1959, Armsby stated that the total staff, including temporary clerical and professional people, reached about 80 at the height of the war.

The following professional persons served with the Division of Higher Education under Kelly during the period from 1941 through 1945 (dates of service with the Division shown in parentheses and only ESMWT people listed are the Directors and Field Coordinators): Dr. John (1918–42); Dr. Greenleaf (1924–47); Dr. Frazier (1927–48); Miss Ratcliffe (1930–46, prior service in clerical position); Dr. Lund (1940–43, 1947–51); Dr. Potter (1940–45); Dr. Blauch (1921–23, 1940–59); Dr. Patterson (1940–42); Dr. Seaton (1940–42); Mr. Case (1940–46); Mr. Guy Butler (1941); Mr. Henry

of Education was fortunate in obtaining the services of a group of highly qualified people. The first to be appointed was Dr. Andrey A. Potter, Dean of the School of Engineering, Purdue University, who served as an expert consultant from July to November 1940, assisting in organizing the program and served as a consultant until the program ended in 1945.[99] Mr. Allan W. Horton, Jr., joined the staff as a specialist in engineering education in the Summer of 1940 to assist Dean Potter.[100] Dean Roy A. Seaton, School of Engineering and Architecture, Kansas State College, served as Director of ESMWT from November 1940 to June 1942. He was followed by Dean George W. Case, College of Technology, University of New Hampshire. Dean Case remained with ESMWT until January 1945, by which time action had begun to close out the program by the end of the fiscal year.

---

Armsby (1941–    ); Mr. Ralph C. M. Flynt (1942–1946, 1951–    ); Mr. Kendric Marshall (1942–45); Dr. Frederic Hamilton (1942–43); and Dr. Ernest V. Hollis (1944–    ). Armsby, Flynt and Hollis were still with the Division in 1960.

[99] Armsby, op. cit., p. 10

[100] Potter, Seaton, and Case are included in the biographical section (Appendix I) because they served as heads of the ESMWT program. Armsby is also included because he remained with the Division after the war and also played a major role in ESMWT. Other important figures in the program, but not included in Appendix I, were:

Allan W. Horton, Jr. (formerly assistant to President Karl T. Compton of M.I.T., secretary to the Committee on Engineering Schools of the Engineers' Council for Professional Development, and currently engineer for Standard Oil Company of California);

H. M. Crothers, principal specialist in engineering education and later deputy director (Dean of Division of Engineering, South Dakota State College);

A. M. Patterson, principal specialist in chemical education (formerly vice president and professor of chemistry at Antioch College);

I. H. Solt, senior specialist in physics;

L. W. Hunt, associate specialist in engineering education and later principal specialist in chemical education;

G. T. Schwenning, principal specialist in management education (professor of business administration, University of North Carolina);

Theodore H. Morgan, assistant director and later deputy director (head of Department of Electrical Engineering, Worchester Polytechnic Institute);

F. W. Marquis, principal specialist in engineering education (chairman of the Department of Mechanical Engineering, Ohio State University);

A. C. Jewett, principal specialist in engineering education (formerly director of the College of Industries, Carnegie Institute of Technology);

E. T. Donovan, principal specialist in engineering education (assistant professor of mechanical engineering, University of New Hampshire); and

R. L. Peurifoy, principal specialist in engineering education (director of division of engineering, Texas College of Arts and Industries). Ibid., pp. 10, 78–79.

The main objective of ESMWT was "to aid the defense program and war effort by training people for specific defense tasks, giving them only such instruction as was directly and immediately needed in the limited tasks to be performed." [101] A fundamental policy of ESMWT was "that it should be a program of the institutions in which the Office of Education assisted, rather than a program of the Office in which the institutions assisted; that it should be administered by the colleges and universities themselves so far as possible. . . ." [102] The Office of Education was thus an administrator and not an operator of ESMWT. Each participating institution of the total of 227 involved before the program closed appointed a member of its staff to serve as representative. It then proceeded to determine local training needs and develop courses to meet them. The institution applied through its regional adviser to the Office of Education for funds to cover the costs of these courses. Determination of course need was the responsibility of the War Manpower Commission. The institution was to realize no profit from the course; monetary allowance was only to cover the costs.[103]

The Office of Education appointed 22 of these regional advisers throughout the Nation. They served as coordinators of the college programs with industrial and military needs, and as liaison between the Office of Education and the field. They met regularly in Washington to advise Kelly and the ESMWT Washington Staff. In addition, each of them served as chairman of a regional committee in the field.[104]

Courses were offered in four general fields after fiscal year 1941 when they had been offered in only the first listed: engineering, chemistry, physics, and production supervision. Engineering courses enrolled the largest number of students; nearly 75 percent. Production supervision was second with an enrollment of more than 21 percent. The remaining 4 percent was almost evenly divided

---

[101] *Ibid.*, p. 4.

[102] *Ibid.*, p. 4.

[103] Interview of author with Armsby, October 27, 1959. The institutions had to show a need for the course before it could be approved by the War Manpower Commission and the Office of Education could act. One proposal from an institution gave as a need the fact that the physics professor wanted "very badly" to teach. This was rejected, of course, since it was not related to the defense program. In addition to need, the proposal had to show content of the course, cost, length, and certain other pertinent information.

[104] Armsby, *op. cit.*, pp. 16, 95–98. The National Advisory Committee on Engineering Defense Training (1940–45) also advised the ESMWT program. This group consisted of 11, later expanded to 20, leaders in engineering, science, and management education. Horton, and later Armsby, served as secretary of the Committee. For more information see *Ibid.*, pp. 12, 93–95.

TABLE 7.—*Summary of EDT, ESMDT, ESMWT–I, ESMWT–II, and ESMWT–III (October 9, 1940– June 30, 1945)*

| Item | EDT 1940–41 | ESMDT 1941–42 | ESMWT–I 1942–43 | ESMWT–II 1943–44 | ESMWT–III 1944–45 | All programs 1940–45 |
|---|---|---|---|---|---|---|
| Number of participating institutions | 143 | 194 | 214 | 195 | 172 | 227 |
| Courses: * | | | | | | |
| All fields | 2,182 | 7,598 | 12,740 | 11,547 | 8,501 | 42,568 |
| Engineering | 2,182 | 6,174 | 9,527 | 7,859 | 5,723 | 31,465 |
| Chemistry | 0 | 220 | 480 | 437 | 296 | 1,433 |
| Physics | 0 | 132 | 231 | 270 | 238 | 871 |
| Production supervision | 0 | 1,072 | 2,502 | 2,981 | 2,244 | 8,799 |
| Enrollment: | | | | | | |
| All fields | 120,802 | 438,503 | 596,134 | 402,684 | 237,593 | 1,795,716 |
| Engineering | 120,802 | 350,564 | 443,938 | 265,366 | 156,555 | 1,337,225 |
| Chemistry | 0 | 7,914 | 13,929 | 10,664 | 6,331 | 38,838 |
| Physics | 0 | 5,813 | 11,998 | 8,620 | 5,984 | 32,415 |
| Production supervision | 0 | 74,212 | 126,269 | 118,034 | 68,723 | 387,238 |
| Number of full-time courses | 18,607 | 22,021 | 47,305 | 14,379 | 3,942 | 106,254 |
| Enrollment of: | | | | | | |
| Females | 811 | 38,341 | 130,245 | 79,612 | 33,226 | 282,235 |
| Negroes | 849 | 3,265 | 10,539 | 7,574 | 2,931 | 25,158 |
| Armed forces | 1,554 | 7,970 | 12,967 | 15,325 | 0 | 37,816 |
| Veterans | 0 | 0 | 0 | 6,094 | 8,221 | 14,315 |

* "Course" as used in the ESMWT program included all training conducted by one institution under one approved course proposal. This might be limited to one section or it might include as many as 100 sections in different locations.

(From Armsby, H. H., *Engineering, Science, and Management War Training—Final Report*, Bulletin 1946, No. 9 (Washington, 1946), p. 45.)

between chemistry and physics. The minimum requirement for most courses was a high school diploma while several required first-level degrees and there was at least one course that required a doctor's degree for admission. Few of them carried college credit since they were essentially training to meet emergency needs of the Armed Forces or industry and were not part of a degree program. Generally, the courses were for people already at work, or about to go to work, and not for regularly enrolled full-time students although there was a radar course taught at some 40 institutions which enrolled college students. Since a large percentage of the students were employed during the day, most classes met in the evening.[105]

There is no question but that this program run by the institutions and administered by the Division of Higher Education was a valuable contribution to the war effort.

> ESMWT made available to war industries thousands of men and women with specialized training and abilities, who were able to perform important technical and supervisory tasks vital to the war effort, and which they could not have performed without the training given them by ESMWT courses. It served to increase the efficiency of other thousands of employees and to expedite war production in hundreds of plants in all parts of the country. In fact without the aid furnished by ESMWT many industrial plants would have been unable to make the valuable contributions which they did make to the war effort.[106]

In addition, the ESMWT program had long-range benefits that reached beyond immediate war-time need:

> ESMWT set a pattern for relationships between the Federal Government and the colleges in a federally sponsored educational program, which many observers feel has important implications for the future. ESMWT was based on the fundamental policy of institutional autonomy and administrative responsibility to the greatest possible extent consistent with the responsibility placed on the U.S. Office of Education by Congress. The colleges planned and conducted courses to meet training needs uncovered largely by themselves, and the Office exercised a minimum of controls, adopting only such as were necessary to insure that the will of Congress should be carried out.[107]

---

[105] Ibid., pp. 44–51; and interview of author with Armsby, October 27, 1959. More detailed statistical information is shown on Table 7, infra.

[106] Ibid., pp. 59–60. A spot check of six labor market areas, made in early 1945, showed nearly all the trainees were going into, or already in, war work. The breakdown on trainees and graduates from courses was as follows: 97.5 percent in war work; 1.2 percent assured of employment in war work after training was completed; and 1.3 percent in "other work." Ibid., pp. 140–142.

[107] Ibid., pp. 64–65. For additional information on ESMWT see William T.

There was an attempt to revive the ESMWT program, or one similar to it, in the Korean War period. The new program was tentatively named "National Defense College Training." The move for it reached its height in 1951. The National Defense College Training program was to be a joint undertaking of the Divisions of Higher Education and Vocational Education, Office of Education, and the Department of Labor which would replace the War Manpower Commission of World War II. But the program was never started since it was opposed by officials high in the Federal service.[108]

The second major program involving the Division of Higher Education was the Student War Loans Program.[109] This was not as long-lasting nor did it involve as many people as ESMWT but it was important in helping to provide well-trained manpower for the war effort.[110]

The Baltimore Conference of January 3–4, 1942, was a major factor in the development of the program. It had come out strongly in favor of an accelerated college calendar. Higher educational institutions had been almost unanimous in adopting such a schedule. Holidays were curtailed and summer recesses eliminated. As a result of the wartime policy and the rising costs of living, college costs went up while, at the same time, students had less opportunity to earn money to pay expenses. Scholarship and fellowship

---

Clark, "College Level War Training Completes Four Years of Activity," *Higher Education*, I, No. 1, January 1, 1945, pp. 5–6; "College-Level Courses in ESMWT," *Education for Victory*, I, No. 20, December 16, 1942, pp. 17–18; Roy A. Seaton, "Engineering, Science ,and Management Defense Training," in Marsh (ed), *op. cit.*, pp. 63–67; Studebaker, *Annual Report . . . 1941*, pp. 18–33; Studebaker, *Annual Reports . . . 1941–42, 1942–1943*, pp. 11–16; John W. Studebaker, *Annual Report of the United States Office of Education for the Fiscal Year 1944* (Washington, 1945), pp. 27–31; John W. Studebaker, *Annual Report of the Federal Security Agency, Section Two. U.S. Office of Education for the Fiscal Year 1945* (Washington, 1945), pp. 7–11; and the bibliography in Armsby, *op. cit.*, pp. 144–149

[108] Interview of author with Armsby, October 27, 1959; and "National Defense College Training." Miscellaneous Forms and Regulations in personal file of Armsby.

[109] This is properly entitled "Loans to Students in Technical and Professional Fields (National Defense) of the Labor-Federal Security Appropriation Act 1943," P.L. 647, 77th Congress 2d Session, approved July 2, 1942. See Ralph C. M. Flynt, *Student War Loans Program—Final Report* (Washington, 1946), p. 11. This is a succinct account of the program by one of its chief administrators.

[110] The program was active from July 2, 1942, to June 30, 1944, less than half as long as ESMWT. Figures on participation are given in the text and fn. 115, *infra*. Table 6, *supra*, shows the total appropriation for loans although the actual amount of money loaned was considerably less.

programs were not, in most cases, flexible enough to permit the student to meet increasing costs. Consequently, additional help was needed if the accelerated program were not to defeat its own purposes of providing more skilled manpower by forcing the financially handicapped to leave college.[111] Suggestions from educational leaders led to the adoption of a program of financial assistance to students in certain subject fields. The program was adopted as a part of Public Law 647, approved July 2, 1942, and contained the following provisions:

> . . . (1) assistance was to be in the form of a loan; (2) only degree-granting institutions maintaining an accelerated program were authorized to participate; (3) loans were to be made to students in the fields of engineering, physics, chemistry, medicine (including veterinary), dentistry, and pharmacy; (4) students receiving loans were required to be within 2 years of graduation; (5) loans were not to exceed $500 to a student in any 12-month period; (6) interest was to be charged at 2½ percent per annum; (7) the borrower was required to agree in writing to remain in the accelerated program and after graduation accept employment as directed by the Chairman of the War Manpower Commission; (8) loans were to be cancelled upon induction of the borrower into the armed forces under the Selective Training and Service Act of 1940 before the completion of his course, or upon death or permanent disability; (9) sums repaid were to be covered into the miscellaneous receipts of the Treasury Department.[112]

The program was obviously intended to be of a temporary emergency nature. Also, it was to be available only to those students who were well along in their education, usually juniors or seniors. With the Act as a guide the Office of Education prepared detailed regulations which were approved by the Chairman of the War Manpower Commission. Administration was given to the Division of Higher Education and a small staff was assembled, headed by Kendric N. Marshall, former president of Chevy Chase Junior College, Washington, D.C. Assisting Marshall were an associate director, four field representatives, and a specialist in student personnel problems. This small group administered the Student War Loans Program through its active operation.[113]

---

[111] *Ibid.*, pp. 1–2. On Office of Education activity in the accelerated curriculums see "Adjustment of the College Curriculum to Wartime Conditions and Needs," *Education for Victory*, II, No. 21, May 3, 1944, p. 21.

[112] Flynt, *op. cit.*, p. 2.

[113] Roy W. Bixler, "The Student War Loans Program," *Higher Education*, II, No. 2, September 15, 1945, pp. 3–5; and "Three New Office of Education Programs," *Education for Victory*, I, No. 16, October 15, 1942, p. 2.

This period of activity was scheued to be quite brief as Studebaker explained in his 1944 *Report:*

However, as a result of factors arising subsequent to the inauguration of the loan program—such as the lowering of the draft age and the establishment of college training programs by the Army and Navy—the Congress decided in 1943 that the usefulness of the loans had been too seriously curtailed to warrant continuation of the program after June 30, 1944.[114]

During the two year period when loans were arranged and granted more than 11,000 students were assisted by the program. These were enrolled in nearly 300 institutions and the total amount of financial assistance they received was approximately three and one-third million dollars.[115]

The contribution of the program was stated by Flynt, the staff member who prepared its official history:

The men who were aided by this program, more than 11,000 of them, were in a position where the amount of time saved by the acceleration of their educational programs sent them into the service of their country earlier and better prepared, and with a quality of morale that is generated by the satisfaction of having a job completed without interruption. Furthermore, these men, by virtue of their completed training, were saved for postwar civilian services in the fields for which they had begun preparation.[116]

---

[114] Studebaker, *Annual Report . . . 1944,* p. 31. See also Studebaker, *Annual Report . . . 1945,* pp. 12–13; and John W. Studebaker, *Annual Report of the Federal Security Agency, Section Two. U.S. Office of Education for the Fiscal Year 1946* (Washington, 1947), pp. 132–133.

[115] The exact figures on the number of borrowers, participating colleges, and amount loaned vary in three important sources. Flynt, *op. cit.,* in summarizing data for fiscal year 1943 states that 11,081 students received loans (p. 6). He uses the figure 11,081 again on pp. 7, 8, and 9. But in Appendix IX, "Cumulative report of student war loans program for fiscal years 1942–43 and 1943–44," the total number of students is given as 11,044 (pp. 33–39). This is the figure used in Appendix X, also (p. 40). Studebaker, *Annual Report . . . 1946,* pp. 132–133, uses 11,081. In an article written in 1949 (George E. Van Dyke, "Government Experience with the Student War Loan Program," *Higher Education,* VI, No. 6, November 15, 1949, pp. 61–63) the figure 11,044 is given. Flynt lists 287 particpating colleges in Appendix IX, pp. 33–39; Studebaker states there were 286 colleges and universities (p. 132); and Van Dyke states there were 287 (p. 62). Flynt and Studebaker agree on the total amount loaned as being $3,327,838.32; while Van Dyke uses a total figure of $3,335,521.14.

[116] Flynt, *op. cit.,* p. 10. For additional information see Van Dyke, *op. cit.,* pp. 61–63, and Kendric N. Marshall, "Federal Loans for Students." Manuscript prepared for publication in an educational journal in early 1943 (Mr. Marshall's personal file).

The other contributions of the Division to the war effort were of a more routine nature. Specialists contributed regularly to the Office wartime journal, *Education for Victory*. In addition to publishing several articles on higher education in it, the Division maintained a regular column entitled "Higher Education and the War" (originally "Higher Educational Institutions and the War"), and contributed to a feature on "School and College Civilian Morale Service." The Division attempted to keep readers abreast of affairs beyond the immediate scope of the war effort although, as was to be expected, virtually everything appearing in the magazine related to it.[117]

During the five year period starting in 1941 and ending in 1945, the Office of Education issued 43 publications relating to higher education. This was a drop from an average of approximately 12 per year during the preceding decade to about 8½ per year during the war period. Nine of these publications were directly related to the war and national defense but the remainder covered a surprisingly wide range of subject matter considering the fact that so much of the national effort was concentrated on the war.[118]

One of the most sensitive and trying problems faced by higher education was that of speeding up the curricula without suffering a loss in the quality of education. In 1942 Studebaker appointed a committee of five people, headed by Lloyd Blauch, to prepare a series of reports on how this could be accomplished. Only Blauch was a member of the Division of Higher Education; the others came from positions outside the Office.[119] This committee immediately "requested the national association of college teachers in each of the principal fields of study in the arts and sciences to appoint a committee to prepare the report for that field."[120] In this manner reports in 21 subject areas were compiled in 1943 and early 1944, and were then distributed to the heads of departments concerned in the institutions of higher education throughout the Nation. Limited publication facilities made it impossible to make

---

[117] *Education for Victory* began publication on March 3, 1942 (Vol. 1, No. 1) and was published biweekly until June 20, 1945 (Vol. III, No. 24). It replaced the regular journal of the Office of Education, *School Life*, which resumed regular publication in October 1945.

[118] See Chapter VI, Table 11, *infra*. For titles of publications see Appendix III.

[119] Committee members in addition to Blauch were Dean Levin B. Broughton, College of Arts and Sciences, University of Maryland; Dr. Walter C. Eells, executive secretary, American Association of Junior Colleges; Dr. Kathryn McHale, general director, American Association of University women; and Dr. Levering Tyson, president, Muhlenberg College. See "Adjustment of the College Curriculum. . . .," *op. cit.*, p. 21.

[120] *Ibid.*, p. 21.

distribution of the studies to each faculty member but apparently each institution was reached.[121]

The phenomenal growth of educational facilities at all levels in the Twentieth Century greatly increased the demand for well-trained teachers. The Division of Higher Education had perennially been concerned with raising the standards of the teaching profession and increasing the supply of well-qualified people. The war aggravated this concern. Studebaker, early in the conflict, reported "that 7,500 classrooms were closed in October 1942 and that the number was increasing rapidly." [122] The primary cause was the drain of the draft and defense industry on the teaching profession. In 1943 the Division, in cooperation with consultants from national educational organizations, prepared a series of proposals which were approved by the Office of Education and the War Manpower Commission. These were submitted to the Bureau of the Budget. They called for short courses of college grade, including part-time refresher courses, for teacher preparation at various colleges and universities. The total cost of the program was set at $3,700,000.

The following year additional studies of teacher shortages were made and disseminated. It was found, among other things, that 7,700 classrooms were closed in fiscal year 1944 because of the inability of school systems to find qualified teachers.[123] Apparently, the Bureau of the Budget was not greatly impressed by this, or it found other matters more demanding, for the emergency teacher training program was never instituted.

Three events in the history of the Division during the Second World War exerted their influence beyond the temporary emergency. In fiscal year 1943 it was transferred from the office of the Assistant Commissioner, where it had been administratively assigned since Cooper's 1929–1930 reorganization, to a separate position which made the chief of the Division responsible directly to the Commissioner.[124]

The second event was the establishment of *Higher Education* magazine on January 1, 1945. In an open letter which served as a preface to the first issue, Studebaker wrote:

---

[121] *Ibid.*, p. 21; Studebaker, *Annual Reports . . . 1941–42, 1942–43*, pp. 44–45; and Studebaker, *Annual Report . . . 1944*, pp. 25–26.

[122] Studebaker, *Annual Reports . . . 1941–42, 1942–43*, pp. 45–46. Quotation from p. 45.

[123] Studebaker, *Annual Report . . . 1944*, pp. 23–24.

[124] U.S. Office of Education, *Educational Directories, 1942–43, 1944–45* (Washington, 1943 *et seq.*). Directory for 1942–43, pp. 1–4. Cooper's reorganization is discussed earlier in this chapter.

For years the U.S. Office of Education has felt a need for a suitable medium of communication with American colleges and universities. To meet this need it is now establishing a new periodical, HIGHER EDUCATION, which this year will be published semimonthly except in July and August.

\*    \*    \*    \*    \*    \*    \*

The Division of Higher Education of the Office will be responsible for the new periodical. In this undertaking it will be assisted by representatives of other divisions. The publication will, therefore, represent all the higher education interests of the Office.[125]

The periodical thus established became the major medium of communication between the Office of Education and individuals and institutions in higher education. It continued bimonthly from January 1, 1945, until May 15, 1953, thereafter becoming a monthly publication. Except for Volume I which ran until June 15, 1945, publication was suspended annually during the months of June, July, and August.[126]

Third, postwar planning absorbed more and more of the attention of the Division of Higher Education as victory approached. Beginning in the Fall of 1943 groups of college officials began to study problems higher education would have to face. These groups were assembled and their work directed and coordinated by the Division.

The regular staff, supplemented by a temporary specialist employed for the purpose, published a *Workbook* in early 1944 which was based on the study of this staff and the findings of field groups. The *Workbook* was distributed to colleges and universities across the land and was widely used in post-war planning.[127] In January 1944, a full-time professional member was added to the staff "to give direction to State-wide and similar conferences on post-war planning." [128] This new member was Ernest V. Hollis who came over to the Office from the American Council on Education. Prior to that he had been a college professor and administrator.[129] Within a year from the time of his appointment, Hollis

---

[125] J. W. Studebaker, "To College and University Officials," *Higher Education*, I, No. 1, January 1, 1945, p. 1.

[126] In addition to the file of members of *Higher Education* in the Department of Health, Education, and Welfare Library see Studebaker, *Annual Report . . . 1945*, pp. 1–2.

[127] Studebaker, *Annual Report . . . 1944*, p. 26. The workbook was U.S. Office of Education, *Conference Workbook on Problems of Post-War Higher Education* (Washington, 1944).

[128] Studebaker, *Annual Report . . . 1944*, p. 26.

[129] For biographical information see Appendix I.

had assembled a volume of data on post-war planning which contained information on age and education of veterans. With Flynt, also of the Division of Higher Education, he prepared a "round-up of information secured from the colleges and from professional and lay associations on what they are doing to readjust program and procedure to meet postwar educational needs, especially those of returning veterans and young war workers whose education has been interrupted." [130]

When the war ended in 1945 the Division of Higher Education could look back with a sense of accomplishment and forward with assurance. It had made substantial contributions to the defense of the Nation, particularly through ESMWT and the Student War Loans Program. Its efforts had been better organized and far more beneficial than those of World War I primarily because the total national effort was itself better organized. But the greater appreciation among Government officials and educators of the contribution to be made by higher education was also important.

On V–J Day the Division was not totally unprepared for the trying transition from war to peace. It had some plans for conversion on which reliance could be placed since they had been made with the help of educators throughout the Nation.

---

[130] Studebaker, *Annual Report . . . 1945*, pp. 6–7. Quotation from p. 7. Titles of these publications: E. V. Hollis, *Data for State-wide planning of Veteran's Education* (Washington, 1945); and E. V. Hollis, and Ralph C. M. Flynt, *Higher Education Looks Ahead* (Washington, 1945).

CHAPTER V

# The Post-War Years
# (1946–1953)

In a sense the post-war years began long before the war had ended. As early as November 1942, when victory was far from sight of even the most optimistic, President Roosevelt appointed a committee of educators to study the problem of veteran education after the war.[1] For two years this committee worked on plans and recommendations. The results were far reaching as the President indicated in his letter discharging the group:

> I am happy to state that the Committee has, indeed, done its work well and that many of its recommendations have already been largely realized—through the enactment of Public Law 346, popularly known as the G.I. Bill of Rights, and through policies established by the Veterans Administration, the Armed Forces educational programs, civilian educational institutions, and various other agencies.[2]

Thus, the post-war planning of this committee was a vital factor in the unprecedented expansion of colleges and universities. "Higher education in the United States experienced the greatest

---

[1] Ltrs. from the President of the United States to Studebaker, December 14, 1942; and Studebaker to President, January 13, 1943. The date when Roosevelt appointed the first members of the committee was November 13, 1942. See "Post-War Educational Opportunities for Service Personnel," Message from the President of the United States, HR Document No. 344, 78th Congress, 1st Session, October 27, 1943. Material from "Forums, Correspondence, etc. (1931–1947)," Acc. No. 56–A–506, RG 12, Federal Records Center, Alexandria, Virginia.

Members of the committee were Brig. Gen. Frederick H. Osborn, USA, Chairman; Capt. Cortlandt C. Baughman, USN, Co-Chairman; Dr. R. C. Harris, President, Tulane University; Dr. D. M. Keezer, Office of Price Administration; Mr. Y. B. Smith, Dean, Columbia Law School; Commissioner Studebaker; Lt. Col. Ralph Sentman, alternate; and Col. Francis T. Spaulding, Secretary. (Ltr., Gen. Osborn to Commissioner Studebaker, January 16, 1945).

[2] Ltr., Roosevelt to Osborn, Dec. 2, 1944, from *Ibid.*

growth in enrollments during 1946–47 that has ever been recorded in any one year in any country. The 2,078,095 students estimated to be in attendance at some 1,700 colleges and universities in the autumn of 1946 represented a 100 percent increase over the enrollment of the preceding year, and a 50 percent increase over the peak enrollment of the prewar years." [3]

The Division of Higher Education had anticipated some expansion following the war although it probably did not expect an increase of such proportions. It did, however, prepare for the problems that would result from the flow of veterans to college campuses as best it could. The steps taken included preparation and publication of the *Conference Workbook*, the appointment of a full-time professional staff member to deal with the problem of planning, and the publication of bulletins on postwar planning which have been noted earlier.[4] In addition, Kelly led his staff in cooperating with other groups attacking the problem. He observed in 1946 that "One of the major interests of the Higher Education Division of the U.S. Office of Education for many months has been to cooperate with national groups, regional groups, statewide groups, and individual institutions in planning for the years ahead. The entire staff has participated in this cooperative effort." [5]

Typical of these cooperative meetings was one held in the Office of Education on December 12–13, 1944. The topic was the post-war education of Negroes, with special reference to returning veterans and war workers. Dr. Ambrose Caliver, senior specialist in the education of Negroes, was the director of the meeting at which four national organizations in higher education were present.[6] As the war drew to a close the number of conferences increased and the tempo of planning stepped up. Furthermore, "These postwar plans did not call for a mere reconversion to prewar college practices; they were calculated to meet the life needs of the much larger number and greater variety of our population that was expected to be in college through the provisions of the Servicemen's Readjustment Act." [7]

---

[3] John W. Studebaker, *Annual Report of the Federal Security Agency, Section Two. U.S. Office of Education for the Fiscal Year 1947* (Washington, 1948), p. 205.

[4] See chapter IV, for more discussion on post-war planning. On the *Workbook* see also "Conference Workbook on Problems of Post-war Higher Education" *Education for Victory*, II, No. 22, May 20, 1944, p. 14.

[5] Fred J. Kelly, "Foreword," in E. V. Hollis ,and Ralph C. M. Flynt, *Higher Education Looks Ahead* (Washington, 1945), p. v.

[6] "Conference on the Education of Negroes," *Higher Education*, I, No. 2, January 15, 1945, pp. 9–10.

[7] John W. Studebaker, *Annual Report of the Federal Security Agency,*

Postwar planning touched every level of education and even the Office of Education itself. In the 1944 *Annual Report* Commissioner Studebaker announced a comprehensive program of reorganization developed that year. It did not contemplate any "innovations in the types of activities which the Office of Education would carry on, but rather an expansion of staff and improvement of organization within the Office by which to accomplish more efficiently the purpose for which the Office of Education was established. . . ." [8] His plan, developed with the cooperation of Federal Security Agency and Bureau of the Budget staff members, called for an expansion from 209 empoyees (105 professional and 104 clerical) to 1,353 employees (643 professional and 710 clerical). In place of the fifteen divisions and smaller units which then existed there were to be only eight divisions: Elementary Education, Secondary Education, Vocational Education, Higher Education, International Educational Relations, School Administration, Auxiliary Services, and Central Services. [9]

The Division of Higher Education would expand from a strength of 11 (7 professional) to 156 (91 professional) under the reorganization. It would have four sections: Organization, Administration and Finance; General and Semi-Professional Programs; Professional Schools; and Colleges of Arts and Sciences. The Division would remain responsible for the same activities as before which were research and development of plans, collection and dissemination of information and consulting and advising institutions, individuals, and groups. [10]

The expansion proposal was favorably received throughout the educational world. *The American School Board Journal* observed

---

Section Two. *U.S. Office of Education for the Fiscal Year 1946* (Washington, 1947), pp. 124–125. Quotation from p. 124. See also John W. Studebaker, *Annual Report of the Federal Security Agency, Section Two. U.S. Office of Education for the Fiscal Year 1945* (Washington, 1945), pp. 6–7.

[8] Studebaker, *Annual Report . . . 1945*, p. iv.

[9] John W. Studebaker, *Annual Report of the United States Office of Education for the Fiscal Year 1944* (Washington, 1945), pp. 63–138. See also John W. Studebaker, "Development of the United States Office of Education," *Higher Education*, II, No. 12, February 15, 1946, pp. 1–4. Prior to reorganization the Office had the following divisions and administrative units: Higher Education; Vocational Education; School Administration; General Instructional Services; Physical Education and Health Activities; Inter-American Educational Relations; Special Programs and Projects; Services for the Blind; Visual Aids for War Training; Educational Uses of Radio; and Publications. (Studebaker, *Annual Report . . . 1945*, p. II). The reorganization plan was also prepared in mimeograph form: John W. Studebaker, "Plan of Organization to Improve the Service of the U.S. Office of Education, A Three Year Program of Development," (Washington, 1944).

[10] Studebaker, *Annual Report . . . 1944*, pp. 84–86, Chart I, opp. p. 138.

that if the Office got only a part of what it wanted it would "build in Washington some respect for education which the other governmental agencies have never shown." [11] The National Education Association was certain that the plan would permit the Office to provide a "much needed" service to education.[12] *The School Executive* felt the plan was far from unreasonable even though it would expand the Office more than 600 percent. Even then the Office would be smaller than the New York State Department of Education.[13] The only apparent opposition of importance, was that of the Congress which was unwilling to vote the appropriation required for the total expansion program to take effect.

Consequently, there was a lot of discussion but not much action in fiscal year 1945, but the following year the appropriation did permit some reorganization. The eight divisions were established as planned. In addition, a temporary Division of Surplus Property Utilization was established. The Division of Higher Education did not follow the original plan of organization in four sections as noted earlier. Instead, it was organized in three permanent sections (Organization and Administration, Professional Education, and Arts and Sciences), and a temporary section (Veterans' Educational Facilities Program) which lasted until fiscal year 1949. Kelly was promoted from Chief to Assistant Commissioner and Director of the Division of Higher Education in September 1946.[14]

The Office of Education, however, did not expand to the extent desired by Studebaker. The total personnel strength in 1950 was 314, an increase of 77 over 1940, and a far cry from the more than 1,300 called for in the plan. Appropriations in 1950 totaled $2,178,600, an increase of more than 150 percent over 1940 but

---

[11] "For a Better Office of Education," *The American School Board Journal*, CX, No. 4, April 1945, p. 50. cf. National Education Association of the United States, *et al.*, *Federal-State Relations in Education* (Washington, 1945).

[12] "Toward a Stronger Office of Education," *The Journal of the National Education Association*, XXXIV, No. 3, March 1945, pp. 53–54.

[13] "Reorganization of the U.S. Office of Education, "*The School Executive*, LXIV, No. 7, March 1945, p. 31

[14] Studebaker, *Annual Report . . . 1946*, p. 69; and U.S. Office of Education, *Educational Directories, 1945–46; 1947–48* (Washington, 1945 *et seq.*), Directory for 1945–46, pp. 1–6. The appointment of Kelly as Assistant Commissioner is not noted in the Directory nor *Higher Education* but in Kelly's Personnel Folder, St. Louis Records Center, St. Louis, Missouri, there is a "Notice of Personnel Action" dated September 6, 1945, effective September 9, 1945, which promotes Kelly from "Specialist in Higher Education," to "Assistant Commissioner (Director, Division of Higher Education)." This is an official action of the Office of Education and proves that the head of the Division of Higher Education was made Assistant Commissioner at that time.

For Division organization see Part I of *Educational Directories* published during the period, especially 1947–48, pp. 2–3, and 1949–50, p. 3.

not sufficient to meet the planned expansion. The Division had grown faster than the Office as a whole. It expanded from 12 professional members in 1946 to 26 by 1953.[15]

On June 30, 1946, Kelly retired from office after 15 years of "distinguished service." [16] He was succeeded on September 3, by Dr. John Dale Russell of the University of Chicago. Russell had an extensive background in higher education and at the time of his appointment he was "widely known for his work in conducting surveys of institutions of higher education and for advisory service he has given to a large number of colleges and universities." [17] During his half-decade of service with the Division he earned the respect and admiration of his colleagues within, and outside, the Office of Education and added to the stature gained under Kelly. One of the men in the Division later wrote that "Under the leadership of John Dale Russell . . . I felt that the Division was making significant impact on higher education in the United States . . . It was a source of great regret to most of the members of the

---

[15] See Tables 8, 9, and 10, chapter VI, *infra*. The figure for the Division of Higher Education for 1953 includes the professional staff of the Division of International Education which was then temporarily assigned. The following comment on the effect of the reorganization, one of the very few that appeared in print from a source outside the Office, is from Hollis P. Allen, *The Federal Government and Education* (New York, 1950), p. 193:

"Soon the plan for reorganization was placed in effect [1945], although most divisions are still staffed in only skeleton form. In this connection, some criticism has been leveled at the office for having too many top-flight specialists and administrators in proportion to individuals in lower positions. The Office has believed that, if it is to develop more status in leadership and service to the schools of the nation, it must have capable men and women on its staff. To this end, if only a few positions could be filled in the divisions of the Office, as has often been the case, an effort has been made to bring strong personnel to top positions. It is argued that to fill subordinate positions first would deny competent professional leadership and service to the states and unduly complicate personnel problems if more competent individuals were added at the top later. A tradition of relative incompetency, started early in the reorganization, would jeopardize the whole program. The Divisions of Secondary Education and of Higher Education are cases in point. The high type individuals recently brought to leadership in these divisions, even though the subordinate staffs therein are as yet very small, have already demonstrated a degree of leadership and service to the schools of the country out of proportion to the size of these divisions. Within limits, it is believed that the Office has been justified in its policy of giving priority to the filling of top positions when its appropriations are insufficient to fill all positions which are encompassed in its long-range plans."

[16] Studebaker, *Annual Report . . . 1946*, p. 119. Kelly's service within the Division of Higher Education did not end in 1946. He served as a full-time member from late 1948 to mid-1952, and later as a consultant. See Appendix I.

[17] "New Director of the Higher Education Division," *Higher Education*, III, No. 2, September 16, 1946, p. 1.

Division that a person of John Dale Russell's stature in the field of higher education saw fit to resign for another position." Like Kelly, Russell was interested in research and adept at handling people but he was more interested in the financial problems of higher education and was a better administrator, more analytical in his approach to problems, and somewhat less imaginative.[18]

The hundreds of thousands of veterans who returned to college campuses in 1946 brought with them problems which were of concern to the highest circles in the Federal Government. They caused the appointment of the third presidential educational advisory group in 17 years.[19] This was the President's Commission on Higher Education appointed July 13, 1946, by President Truman.[20] The primary purpose for the Commission was to investigate and report on the ability of higher education to play its full role in American Democracy. This included discussion of expanding educational opportunity to all able young people, the need for technical institutes, and the adequacy of the financial structure of institutions.[21]

The Commission studied higher educational problems and development for eighteen months before issuing its report in December, 1947. Of most immediate concern to the Office of Education were these recommendations:

> This Commission recommends a fundamental change in the position given to the central educational agency in the Government organization. First, the financial support given to the United States Office of Education must be commensurate with the great tasks confronting that agency. Second, the status of the agency within the framework of the Government must be raised.[22]

\*          \*          \*          \*          \*          \*          \*

To aid in improving the program carried on in the institu-

---

[18] Interviews of author with Mr. H. H. Armsby, Chief of Engineering Education, Division of Higher Education, October 27, 1959; Dr. George C. Decker, Chief, Loans to Schools Section, Division of State and Local Systems, October 29, 1959; and Mr. Ralph C. M. Flynt, Assistant Commissioner and Director of Legislative Services Branch, November 4, 1959; all of Office of Education. The quotation is from a biographical Résumé prepared by Dr. Claude Hawley for the author in the Fall of 1959.

[19] The first two of these groups were the National Advisory Committee on Education (1929–31) and the Advisory Committee on Education (1936–38). They were discussed in Chapter IV.

[20] See President's Commission on *Higher Education, Higher Education for American Democracy: Report of the Commission* (Washington, 1947), Vol. I of VI, p. iv, for list of members.

[21] George F. Zook, "President's Commission on Higher Education," *Higher Education*, III, No. 1, September 2, 1946, pp. 1–3.

[22] President's Commission, *op cit.*, Vol. III, p. 41.

tions of higher education throughout the country, there is need of a Federal agency staffed with personnel of such high quality as to enable them to exercise effective leadership without authority. This requires a high place in the Government for the agency representing education. The position now occupied by the United States Office of Education does not give the necessary status and recognition to education to enable the Office to function effectively. *The Commission recommends legislation aimed to raise the status of this office.*[23]

The President's Commission proved itself to be the strongest advocate of Federal aid to education in American history to that time. If its recommendations had been implemented, the Division would have expanded tremendously, perhaps even beyond the 156 total strength Studebaker envisioned. But the Commission's findings were to suffer a fate similar to those of earlier groups. That is, only a few of its recommendations were to be followed and these over a period of years. The Congress and Executive were involved in other matters and obviously felt that the vast Veteran's Readjustment Program made further activity of the kind recommended by the Commission unnecessary. Instead of concentrating its educational activities in one agency, the United States Government continued a policy of scattering its educational help through a large number of agencies. In fiscal year 1947, for example, Federal aid to higher education including all programs amounted to $1,772 million and less than $11 million of this was administered through the Office of Education.[24] Major Federal agencies involved in higher educational activities that year, and throughout most of the following years, were:

Department of State
Department of the Treasury
Department of War and Department of the Navy
    (Later Department of Defense)
Department of Justice

---

[23] *Ibid.*, pp. 72–73. See also George F. Zook, "The President's Commission on Higher Education Reports," *Higher Education*, IV, No. 12, February 15, 1948, pp. 133–136; Francis J. Brown, "President's Commission on Higher Education Reports Further," *Higher Education*, IV, No. 13, March 1, 1948, pp. 145–148; Rall I. Grigsby, *Annual Report of the Federal Security Agency, 1948. Office of Education* (Washington, 1948), pp. 454–457; and "National Commission on Coordination in Secondary Education, etc. (Including President's Commission on Higher Education, 1946–48)," Acc. No. 57–A–681, RG 12, Federal Records Center, Alexandria, Virginia.

[24] President's Commission, *op. cit.*, Vol. III, p. 39 (Chart 1); and James Earl Russell, *Federal Activities in Higher Education After the Second World War* (New York, 1951), pp. 3, 178. The Veteran's Administration charged with administration of the "G.I. Bill of Rights" expended $1,595 million that same year, which was 145 times more than the amount administered by the Office of Education. (*Ibid.*, p. 210.)

Department of Agriculture
Department of Commerce
Federal Security Agency
Federal Works Agency
National Housing Agency
U.S. Maritime Commission
Civil Service Commission
The Library of Congress
Bureau of Indian Affairs (Department of the Interior)
The District of Columbia.[25]

The results of each fragmentation, and of the "marked tendency of the federal government [sic] to by-pass existing educational coordinating agencies such as the U.S. Office of Education," were confusion, inequities, and duplication of effort.[26] But the activities remained scattered, none-the-less, and the Division played only a minor advisory role in the huge Veteran's Readjustment Program.

Two somewhat smaller programs of the post-war period did utilize the services of members of the Division. One was helping to implement the Surplus Property Act of 1944.[27] This provided for the sale or gift of certain types of property surplus to the needs of the Nation to tax-supported and non-profit educational institutions. The Office of Education determined the educational need for such property and advised the three-member Surplus Property Board which administered the Act. This assistance to the Board was rendered through an Office of Education Advisory Committee with Armsby of the Division of Higher Education as the only full-time member of the Office on the committee. The size of the program is shown by a two-year period ending May 1948, when "property surplus to the needs of the government initially valued at $646,663,358 was made available" under this program. The Act was amended and liberalized in 1948 and the two following years. Although the Korean conflict brought sharp curtailment it continued to operate past 1953.[28]

The other was the Veteran's Educational Facilities Program.

---

[25] *Ibid*, pp. viii–x. cf. Charles A. Quattlebaum, *Federal Education Activities and Education Issues Before Congress* (Washington, 1952), esp. "Part 3, Survey of Federal Education Activities," pp. 133–349; and "Federal Educational Activities," *Higher Education*, VIII, No. 5, November 1, 1951, pp. 49–55.

[26] Russell, *op. cit.*, pp. 59–69. Quotation from p. 61.

[27] P.L. 457, 78th Congress, approved by the President on October 3, 1944.

[28] Hollis P. Allen, *The Federal Government and Education* (New York, 1950), p. 57. See also Quattlebaum, *op. cit.*, pp. 280–281; Henry H. Armsby, "Federal Surplus War Property and Educational Institutions," *Higher Education*, I, No. 6, March 15, 1945, pp. 1–3; Henry H. Armsby, "Federal Surplus Property and Educational Institutions," *Higher Education*, II, No. 1, September 1, 1945, pp. 3–4; and Grigsby, *op. cit.*, p. 512.

The increase in enrollment in higher educational institutions caused a severe shortage of classroom and other instructional facilities as early as 1946. To combat this shortage, the Congress enacted Public Law 697 in the summer of that year authorizing Federal appropriations so educational institutions enrolling veterans could obtain surplus property.[29] The program was under the administration of the Federal Works Agency but the Commissioner of Education had to certify that the institution needed the facilities because of the increased number of veterans. Determination of need was made under the direction of Hollis who supervised, at the height of the program, a staff of more than twenty people working in regional offices throughout the Nation. When the Office had certified need, buildings were taken from Federal installations where they were surplus and transported to the campuses of the receiving educational institutions. The cost of erecting the buildings was borne by the institutions. In addition to buildings, items of equipment were transferred to qualified institutions. By the end of fiscal year 1948 more than 100 million items and buildings providing 17 million square feet of instructional floor space had been transferred to schools and colleges.[30] The program slowed down in 1949 but continued to operate until the impact of the Korean War brought it to a halt.[31]

These activities, important though they were, remained at best temporary in nature and directed at emergency situations. Russell was intent on developing an expanded Division to provide continuing and diversified programs in higher education. Accordingly he worked out a plan which would enable the Division to help institutions of higher education to:

1. Improve instruction in the social sciences in order to develop the fullest appreciation of democracy;

2. Improve instruction in the natural sciences to maintain a constant supply of scientists; and

3. Improve services in health and physical education so young people could enjoy better lives and make more worth-while contributions to the Nation.[32]

According to Russell this would require "an associate chief for

[29] P.L. 697, 79th Congress, approved by the President on August 8, 1946.

[30] Interview of author with Ernest V. Hollis, Director, College and University Administration Branch, Division of Higher Education, Office of Education, October 27, 1959. Figures from Grigsby, *op. cit.*, p. 513.

[31] Interview of author with Hollis, October 27, 1959. See also Allen, *op. cit.*, pp. 57–58; Russell, *op. cit.*, p. 171; Quattlebaum, *op. cit.*, pp. 280–281; and E. V. Hollis, "College and University Building Needs," *Higher Education*, IV, No. 18, May 15, 1948, pp. 205–209.

[32] John Dale Russell, "Plans for Development of Federal Services in Higher Education," *Higher Education*, IV, No. 2, September 15, 1947, pp. 13–14.

biological sciences, an associate chief for physical sciences and mathematics, an associate chief for social sciences, and specialists for history, economics, geography, and psychology." Also "an associate chief for education in the health professions" was to be added.[33]

An increased salary appropriation for fiscal year 1948 made it possible for a large part of the plan to be put into effect. Russell was able to increase his professional staff from 11 to 18. He took on a specialist in each of five subject areas: junior colleges and lower divisions; social sciences; land-grant colleges and universities; economics; and history. In addition he assigned specialized areas in college and university administration, the health professions, and the higher education of Negroes to staff members already in the Division.[34]

The two most characteristic developments in the post-war history of the Division were its involvement in veteran educational problems, and the growth in the number of specialists. There had been specialists before. Most of its history it had retained the services of a man who worked as a specialist in land-grant college statistics. Dr. Benjamin Frazier had served as specialist in teacher training in the late 1920's, Dr. Chester Jarvis had been specialist in agricultural education in the post-World War I years, and Dr. Kline Koon had served as specialist in radio education in the early 1930's. But the majority of the professional staff had carried broader titles such as "specialist in higher education" or "senior specialist." In the post-World War II years, particularly after 1947, the number and kind of specialists multiplied. From 1948 through 1953 the list of specialists, and persons serving for all or part of the period, includes:

College and University Administration (Dr. Ernest V. Hollis);
College Business Management (Mr. George E. Van Dyke, Mr.
  Granville Keith Thompson);
Junior Colleges and Lower Divisions (Dr. William Conley, Dr.
  William Wood);
Student Personnel Services (Dr. Willard Blaesser);
Health Professions (Dr. Lloyd E. Blauch);
Higher Education of Negroes (Dr. Ambrose Caliver; Dr. Walter Daniel);
Teacher Education (Dr. Wesley Armstrong);
Engineering Education (Mr. Henry Armsby);
Physics (Dr. Bernard Watson);
Social Sciences (Dr. Claude Hawley, Dr. Howard Anderson);

---

[33] *Ibid.*, p. 14.
[34] "Staff of the Higher Education Division," *Higher Education*, V, No. 7, December 1, 1948, pp. 81–83.

Geography (Dr. Otis Freeman) ;
History (Dr. Jennings Sanders) ;
Economics (Dr. John Phalan) ; and
International Education (temporarily assigned when the Division of International Education, then the Division of International Educational Relations, was merged with the Division of Higher Education in 1951–52. Dr. Marjorie Johnston, Dr. Alina Lindegren, Dr. Helen Reid ,and Dr. Abul Sassani).

In addition to these, there were specialists working in temporary or emergency programs for part of the period. Among these were the Veteran's Educational Facilities Program (Dr. Hollis, Mr. Robert Iffert) ; the College Housing Loan Program (Dr. George Decker, Mr. Ralph Moor, Mr. John Rork, and Dr. James Van Zwoll) ; and the Controlled Materials Plan (Dr. Robert Wilson, Mr. John Thomas, Mr. John Rork, and Mr. Julius Nelson).[35]

This expansion enabled the Division to increase and improve its services to the colleges and universities of the Nation. It was able to provide consultative services to a larger number of institutions, groups, and individuals, and there was a sharp increase in

---

[35] This list is based on *Ibid.*; "Social Science Unit Organized in Office of Education," *Higher Education*, V, No. 1, September 1, 1948, pp. 5–6; Earl J. McGrath, *Annual Report of the Federal Security Agency, 1949. Office of Education* (Washington, 1950), pp. 55, 65; *Educational Directories* of the period; and information found in Appendix I.

The complete list of professional staff members of the Division from the time Dr. Russell took office until the end of fiscal year 1953 (dates of service with the Division shown in parentheses) : Dr. Frederick J. Kelly (1931–46, 1948–52) ; Dr. Walter Greenleaf (1924–47) ; Dr. Benjamin Frazier (1927–48) ; Miss Ella Ratcliffe (1930–46, prior service in clerical position) ; Dr. John Lund (1940–43, 1947–51) ; Dr. Lloyd Blauch (1921–23, 1940–59) ; Mr. Henry Armsby (1941–   ) ; Mr. Ralph C. M. Flynt (1942–46, 1951–58) ; Dr. Ernest V. Hollis, (1944–   ) ; Mr. Robert Iffert (1946–   ) ; Dr. Ambrose Caliver (1946–50) ; Dr. John H. Goldthorpe (1947–48, 1953–   ) ; Dr. John Phalan (1947–50) ; Dr. Jennings Sanders (1948–59) ; Dr. Otis Freeman (1948) ; Mrs. Theresa Wilkins (1948–   , prior service in clerical position) ; Dr. William Conley (1948–49) ; Mrs. Elizabeth Layton (1948–54, prior service in clerical position) ; Dr. Claude Hawley (1948–51) ; Dr. Wesley Armstrong (1949–56) ; Mr. George Van Dyke, Jr. (1949–51) ; Dr. Willard Blaesser (1949–53) ; Dr. Bernard Watson (1949–52) ; Dr. William Wood (1950–54) ; Dr. George Decker (1950–   ) ; Dr. Howard Anderson (1951–54) ; Mr. Samuel Greene (1951) ; Mr. Julius Nelson (1951) ; Dr. Robert Wilson (1951–52) ; Mr. William Jaracz (1951) ; Dr. Walter Daniel (1951–53) ; Mr. John Rork (1951–   ) ; Mr. John Thomas (1951–52) ; Mr. Granville Thompson (1951–55) ; Dr. James Van Zwoll (1951–52) ; Mr. Ralph Moor (1951–52) ; Dr. Buell Gallagher (1952) ; and Mr. Rall Grigsby (1952).

In addition the following became members of the professional staff from early 1951 until mid-1952 when the Division of International Education was temporarily merged with the Division of Higher Education: Dr. Marjorie Johnston; Dr. Alina Lindegren; Dr. Helen Reid; and Dr. Abul Sassani.

the number of field trips over the pre-war period. One or more representatives of the staff were now able to attend virtually every important national conference in higher education after World War II. The Division continued to prepare and distribute a magazine which was the voice of higher education in the Office; advised, and helped administer, several veteran's programs; and carried on several research projects of national significance to higher education in the areas of curriculums, finance, administrative practices, and teacher training.[36]

The addition of the social sciences and history specialists enabled the Division to take an active role in the "Zeal for American Democracy" project which the Office of Education launched in 1948 and continued until the Korean conflict. "Zeal for American Democracy" had as its purpose the affirmation of faith in American democracy, the exposure of the threat of totalitarianism, and the definition of responsibility of schools and colleges to teach democracy.[37]

In 1947 an event took place which was destined to affect the Office of Education considerably although it appeared at the time to bear no direct relationship to it. This event was the appointment of Oscar Ewing to succeed Watson Miller as Federal Security Administrator. Since the Office of Education was a part of the Federal Security Agency, the Administrator was the immediate superior of the Commissioner. Ewing "took a more active interest in the Office" than had either Miller or McNutt who had preceded Miller. He had the Office of Education library merged with the Agency library and curtailed the "Zeal for American Democracy" program far below the level desired by Commissioner Studebaker. These, and other actions, motivated Studebaker to submit his resignation effective on July 15, 1948. Until a successor was appointed Mr. Rall I. Grigsby, Director of Auxillary Service, took over as Acting Commissioner.[38]

---

[36] The increasing activity of the Division is shown in the Commissioner's reports for the period. Listings of duties and projects may be found in John Dale Russell, "The Role of the Division of Higher Education of the United States Office of Education," *American Association of University Professors. Bulletin* XXXIII, No. 3, Autumn 1947, pp. 432–442; and "Educational Planning (The U.S. Office of Education)," *The School Executive*, LXVI, No. 10, June 1947, p. 57.

[37] See special issue of *Higher Education*, IV, No. 17, May 1, 1948; Grigsby, *op. cit.*, pp. 485–487; and J. N. Rodeheaver, Jr., "The Relation of the Federal Government to Civic Education," (Cambridge, Mass., 1951, typewritten ms.), pp. 298–313.

[38] Rodeheaver, *op. cit.*, pp. 193–194. Quotation from p. 193. Studebaker became vice-president and chairman of the editorial board of *Scholastic* magazines in New York City.

The eleventh Commissioner of Education, Earl James McGrath (1902–    ), took office on March 16, 1949. McGrath was born in Buffalo, New York, on November 16, 1902, and had received his B.A. and M.A. degrees at the University of Buffalo in 1928 and 1930 respectively. He was awarded the degree of Doctor of Philosophy at the University of Chicago in 1936 and ten years later Coe College conferred an honorary L.H.D. on him. Nearly all of McGrath's background was in higher education. He was a lecturer in psychology and a professor of education at the University of Buffalo from 1929 to 1949, and Dean of Admissions for part of that period of time; Dean of the College of Liberal Arts at the University of Iowa, 1945–1948; and professor of education at the University of Chicago at the time of his appointment. Mc-Grath had served on the President's Commission on Higher Education, 1946–1948, and was well known for his activities in administration, teaching, and writing.[39]

McGrath had been in office only a few weeks when he decided there was a "need for an evaluation of the purposes and the program of the United States Office of Education." Accordingly, he requested and received $15,000 from a special Presidential fund on manpower improvement to pay the Public Administration Service of Chicago, a private consulting, research, and publishing organization, for a survey of office administration.[40] The survey was conducted under the direction of Dr. Francis S. Chase, professor of educational administration at the University of Chicago. He submitted a report on October 31, 1950. The report found that the energies of the Office had been dissipated by what McGrath himself termed a "scatter-gun approach . . . the result of the Office's organization and staffing pattern." [41] To eliminate this, the report recommended that activities be consolidated in three di-

---

[39] "Earl James McGrath Appointed Commissioner of Education," *Higher Education*, V, No. 15, April 1, 1949, pp. 169–170; "Earl James McGrath— 11th Commissioner of Education," *School Life*, XXXI, No. 8, May 1949, pp. 1–3, 14; and Rodeheaver, *op. cit.*, pp. 194–195.

Since McGrath remained as Commissioner until April 22, 1953, the approximate time when this account ends, some comment on his later career may be made here. From 1953 to 1956 he was President and Chancellor of the University of Kansas City, and in 1956 he was made Executive Officer and professor of higher education at Teacher's College, Columbia University. *Who's Who in America*, XXX, p. 1852.

[40] Open letter to educational colleagues from McGrath, March 7, 1951, inserted in Public Administration Service, *A Report on an Administrative Survey of the U.S. Office of Education of the Federal Security Agency* (Washington, 1950).

[41] Earl J. McGrath, *Annual Report of the Federal Security Agency, 1951. Office of Education* (Washington, 1952), pp. 12–15. Quotation from p. 13.

visions: State and Local School Systems; Higher Education; and Vocational Education.

In February, 1951, McGrath reorganized along the lines suggested in the report with three major operating divisions. The most immediate effect on the Division of Higher Education was the consolidation of the Division of International Educational Relations with it. Aside from the tacit recognition of its importance and the temporary role assigned in international education, the 1951 reorganization appeared to have had no other effect on the activities and responsibilities of the Division.[42]

In the fall of 1949 the Division, in conjunction with the American Council on Education, completed plans for a conference which was to stimulate as much discussion as any held in the field of education from 1946 to 1953. This was the Conference on the Preparation of College Teachers which met in Chicago from December 8 to 10, 1949. Fred Kelly, who had returned to the Division in the fall of 1948, was a major figure in planning this Conference which was attended by 175 representatives of all phases in the preparation of college teachers.[43]

---

[42] *Ibid.*, p. 14; and Public Administration Service, *op. cit.*, pp. 68 ff. and Chart II. The Division of International Education was established in the late summer of 1952 taking over the same personnel as the former Division of International Educational Relations. For additional comment on McGrath's reorganization see "Reorganization of the Office of Education," *The School Review*, LIX, No. 5, May 1951, pp. 255–257; and "To Strengthen and Improve Office of Education Administration," *School Life*, XXXIII, No. 7, April 1951, pp. 97–101, 106–109. There was some opposition to the reorganization within the Office of Education. *The Nation's Schools* published an article after the reorganization had begun which stated that "Nobody, but nobody, in Washington was happy about the reorganization of the U.S. Office .of Education. Tempers were hot. Feelings were ruffled." (p. 86). The major cause of ill-will appeared to be the feeling among some personnel of the divisions scheduled for elimination that the reorganization indicated a lack of interest in their work and a loss of stature to them personally. See "Tangled Office of Education," *The Nation's Schools*, XLVII, No. 4, April 1951, pp. 86, 88; and "Office of Education Reorganization Completed," *The Nation's Schools*, LXVII, No. 6, June 1951, p. 92.

Some comment on the discussion of a strengthened Office of Education, or a separate Department, is germane to this discussion of McGrath's reorganization. The major writings on this matter in the post-war period were stimulated by the "Hoover Commission" *Task Force Report on Public Welfare* (1949). c.f. Allen, *op. cit.*, pp. 298–310; Russell, *op. cit.*, pp. 69–77; Hollis P. Allen, "The Place of the Office of Education in the Federal Government," *The School Executive*, LXX, No. 1, September 1950, pp. 47–50; and Hollis P. Allen, and Franklin K. Patterson, "Federal Policy and Organization for Education," *Higher Education*, VI, No. 13, March 1, 1950, pp. 149–155.

[43] Fred J. Kelly, "The Preparation of College Teachers: Report of a Conference," *Higher Education*, VI, No. 11, February 1, 1950, pp. 125–131; and No. 12, February 15, 1950, pp. 143–147.

The Conference had been motivated by the increasing need for college teachers. Commissioner McGrath had summarized the problem in a few sentences in his 1950 *Report:*

Before World War II, the common assumption in colleges and universities was that a ratio of 1 teacher to 10 students was "satisfactory." Under the pressures of post-war enrollments, that ratio has been generally disregarded. Furthermore, all estimates of future college enrollments over a period of years indicate a continuing upward trend. These estimated increases are to be welcomed in the national interest and need encouragement if the "national loss of the able" is to be corrected.

Assuming merely normal enrollment for higher education in the decade ahead, the colleges will need approximately 20,000 new full-time teachers annually for the next 10 years. Over against this need is the tragically inadequate supply of well-qualified personnel. The number of doctorates awarded to persons entering or continuing in college teaching in any one year has never exceeded 2,116. That was less than half of the normal number of retirements and deaths in the profession. While the doctorate may not necessarily be a prerequisite for *all* college teaching, the maintenance of educational standards in the face of facts such as these has become a major difficulty for American higher education.[44]

At its final session the Conference adopted a resolution to appoint a committee "including representation from the United States Office of Education" to negotiate with the American Council on Education for establishment of a commission on teacher preparation.[45] The following December this commission, working with the American Council, called a second conference in Chicago to discuss the improvement of college faculties. The results of this second conference, along with the summarized work of the commission, were published in a volume edited by Kelly and financed by the American Council. In addition to this work, several special studies were made in specialized fields of teaching such as dentistry, engineering, political science, and the teaching of college introductory courses in United States history.[46]

The 1949 and 1950 Chicago meetings were significant in focusing national attention on a problem growing more acute each

[44] Earl J. McGrath, *Annual Report of the Federal Security Agency, 1950. Office of Education* (Washington, 1951), p. 13.

[45] Kelly, *op. cit.*, p. 147.

[46] McGrath, *Annual Report . . . 1951*, pp. 38–39. The volume published by the American Council on Education was by Fred J. Kelly, (ed), *Improving College Instruction* (Washington, 1951). Professional staff members active in the work of improving college instruction, in addition to Kelly, were: Henry Armsby, Claude Hawley, William Wood, Wesley Armstrong, Lloyd E. Blauch, John Dale Russell, and Bernard Watson. Dr. Buell Gallagher, later Director of the Division, was also active. *Ibid.*, pp. 1–8, 186–189.

academic year. The conferees pointed out two disturbing facts. One was, very simply, the supply of qualified college teachers was not meeting the demand and the situation was likely to grow worse. The second was that some re-evaluation of the processes of preparing people to teach in college would be appropriate. But, as has happened so often before in history, the orderly process of improvement was interrupted by a powerful outside force. This time it was the Korean crisis of 1950–1953. Even with this interference, the questioning of the conferees left an irritating residue of doubt about the supply of college teachers among those in higher education.

On June 25, 1950, the North Korean military forces invaded South Korea. For the third time in its brief history of forty years the Division of Higher Education found its attention concentrated on emergency defense programs. This time, however, these programs would not be as demanding as those of World War I and World War II.

The invasion of South Korea, followed by the prompt action of the United Nations against unprovoked aggression, had three effects on higher education which began to be felt within a matter of weeks. The first was the loss of students because of increased draft quotas and the drain of war-stimulated industry. As early as the fall of 1950 there was a decline of about 200,000 from the preceding years. This was due largely to the smaller number of students entering college under the "GI Bill" but the situation in Korea stimulated the decline and as the conflict continued it exerted a greater effect.[47] Second, there was a loss of teachers who left the profession "in increasing numbers to take better paid jobs elsewhere." [48] Third, short supply critical materials had had to be diverted from school construction, maintenance, and operation and applied to defense needs.

The Division could do little about the loss of college students or teachers beyond those functions it had aways exercised: advising, consulting, researching, and distributing information. For example, in the spring of 1951 it assembled information on the number of college teachers who were likely to lose their appointments because of the anticipated decline in enrollment caused by Selective Service. Throughout the conflict the Division prepared

---

[47] cf. McGrath, *Annual Report . . . 1950*, p. 7; and McGrath, *Annual Report . . . 1951*, p. 2. Approximate figures for 1949–50 were 2,700,000; for 1950–51 2,500,000.

[48] McGrath, *Annual Report . . . 1951*, p. 2. For a longer discussion of the teacher shortage see Earl J. McGrath, *Annual Report of the Federal Security Agency, 1952. Office of Education* (Washington, 1953), pp. 9–12.

defense information of interest to higher education and distributed it in various ways including through the columns of *Higher Education* and *School Life*. It made a survey of needs for personnel workers in the armed forces, prepared studies on teaching in specialized subject areas, and helped work out a plan for a revised form of World War II's Engineering, Science, and Management War Training.[49] In these and other ways, the Division did what it legally could to hold students and teachers in college. It is not possible to give an exact measurement of its contributions but, considering the wide distribution of the Office of Education publications, it is probable they were substantial.

During the Korean War years control over the human resources for defense rested in the hands of the National Security Resources Board, a part of the Executive Office of the President of the United States. Robert L. Clark, Director of the Manpower Office of that Board, announced the role the Office of Education was expected to play shortly after the United Nations entered Korea:

> In the field of education, the National Security Resources Board and the President are looking to the Federal Security Agency and the Office of Education as the focal point within the Federal Government where we will attempt to bring together all the information we can gather to provide assistance to the schools and colleges and universities of this country in making their contribution to the total national effort.[50]

The Office of Education interpreted this statement to mean that they were to investigate the educational resources of the Nation, and to work toward safeguarding and improving educational standards.[51] McGrath assigned 27 professional staff members within the Office of Education to work in individual areas of responsibility where they could seek various courses of action. These people were also the Office channels between Government

---

[49] McGrath, *Annual Report . . . 1951*, pp. 3, 38–39. The plan for the revival of ESMWT has been noted in chapter IV in the discussion of the World War II period. It will be recalled that the plan was not put into effect although prepared in some detail. There was one large conference of note early in the Korean War period. The Office of Education helped the American Council on Education organize and run the Conference on Higher Education in the National Service which was held in Washington on October 6–7, 1950. There were 974 persons in attendance of which approximately 600 represented specific institutions of higher education, 400 of them being presidents of their institutions. For information on the Conference see Francis J. Brown, "Conference on Higher Education in the National Service," *Higher Education*, VII, No. 6, November 15, 1950, pp. 67–69.

[50] Robert L. Clark, "Planning for Defense Mobilization," *Higher Education*, VII, No. 5, November 1, 1950, pp. 49–50. Quotation from p. 50.

[51] McGrath, *Annual Report . . . 1951*, p. 3.

departments and agencies, and individuals and institutions concerned with defense problems. Twelve men who were, at some
time or other, to serve as members of the Division of Higher Education were among the 27 given these "defense mobilization assignments." They covered a variety of subjects including teacher
recruitment, acceleration of programs, education for the health
professions, and legislation on student loans and fellowships.[52]
Unlike World Wars I and II, there was an effort made to provide
specialized sources within the Office for every important problem
the schools and colleges of the Nation would be likely to meet in
the defense situation. While this was made possible because of a
larger professional staff, it would not have been done unless there
had been the recognition of the need for highly specialized attack
on a variety of problems.

But the most direct services the Division was to provide were
those involving physical facilities for institutions of higher education such as the Controlled Materials Plan and the College Housing Loan Program.

The Controlled Materials Plan was essentially a system for
the control of materials critical to defense needs. Under this Plan,
established by the Defense Production Act of 1950, certain designated Federal agencies were to appear before the Defense Production Authority as claimants for civilian activities. The Federal
agencies were authorized to request quantities of those materials
on the critical list which were essential to the civilian authorities
they represented. The Federal Security Administration was the
designated claimant for materials used in school and hospital
construction and for supplies and equipment relating to health,
education, and welfare. The Federal Security Administrator,
Oscar Ewing, in turn appointed the Commissioner of Education
to perform claimant functions relating to schools, colleges, and
libraries.[53]

In order to comply with this directive the Division assigned
five regular staff members to full-time or part-time work and
took on four others as temporary members to assist.[54] By March
1, 1951, the Office of Education had completed a survey of anticipated needs of education at all levels through calendar year 1952.

---

[52] "Defense Mobilization Assignments in the Office of Education," *Higher
Education*, VII, No. 6, November 15, 1950, p. 69. The twelve were: Russell,
Marshall, Hollis, Flynt, Blauch, Armsby, Caliver, Gallagher, Watson, Hawley,
Wood, and Armstrong.

[53] Earl James McGrath, "Civilian Education Requirements Program,"
*Higher Education*, VIII, No. 6, November 15, 1951, pp. 61–66.

[54] "New Appointments in the Division of Higher Education," *Higher Education*, VIII, No. 1, September 1, 1951, p. 10.

When the Controlled Material Plan went into effect in July, 1951, the Division was prepared to present a detailed list of needed materials, and the quantities needed, in higher education.[55] From the time the Plan began functioning until the end of fiscal year 1953 when it was discontinued the Office of Education was the claimant for materials used in construction of schools, colleges, libraries, and eventually, museums. Within the Office the official title for this work was the Civilian Education Requirements Program of the Controlled Materials Plan. After September 1, 1951, it was administered through a temporary Division of Civilian Education Requirements with the other divisions advising and assisting in the work.[56]

The College Housing Loan Program, unlike the Controlled Materials Plan, was not inspired by the international situation although it was soon affected by defense needs. The College Housing Loan Program was motivated by the rapid increase in enrollments far in excess of the construction of housing facilities for students and faculty. From 1940 to 1949 enrollments nearly doubled in institutions of higher education while housing construction remained at a virtual standstill. To alleviate this situation the Housing Act of 1950 contained a title (Title IV) which permitted low interest-bearing loans to colleges and universities for periods up to 40 years.[57]

The Korean War intervened before the College Housing Loan Program could get started. On July 19, 1950, less than three months after the passage of the Housing Act, Title IV was suspended. On January 15 of the following year, however, an executive order released $40 million of the $300 million which the Congress had authorized for college housing loans under the Act. It stipulated that "the funds thus released were to be used for college or university housing which contributed to defense activities." [58] So the College Housing Loan Program was quickly integrated into the defense policies of the Nation. During the following years as construction materials became available, additional sums were released for loan purposes.

The Division became involved in this program in a consultative capacity. Institutions of higher education desiring loans made

---

[55] McGrath, *Annual Report . . . 1951*, pp. 3–6.

[56] S. M. Brownell, "Office of Education" in Oveta Culp Hobby, *Annual Report of the U.S. Department of Health, Education, and Welfare, 1953* (Washington, 1954), pp. 197–198.

[57] P.L. 475, 81st Congress, approved by the President on April 20, 1950.

[58] George C. Decker, "College Housing Loan Program," *Higher Education*, VIII, No. 6, November 15, 1951, pp. 69–71. Quotation from p. 70.

application to the Housing and Home Finance Agency, the administrator of the Housing Act. This agency submitted the application to the Office of Education for investigation. Within the Division in 1951 there was established a "Housing Loan Program" section headed by Dr. George C. Decker.[59] This section conducted the required investigation and recommended on the loan request relative to:

1. Whether the applicant was an educational institution as defined by law;

2. Whether the statement of need for housing was justified; and

3. Other pertinent professional factors relative to the statement of need.[60]

The College Housing Loan Program filled an urgent need in higher education. Colleges and universities plagued with cramped dormitories and housing facilities and lacking the financial resources to alleviate the situation found it was a way out of what appeared to be an otherwise insoluble problem. The acceptance of the program shows the need it filled. By the end of fiscal year 1953 there had been $80.5 million committed. This sum of money was to provide housing for 600 student and faculty families and 25,661 single students.[61] The program continued beyond fiscal year 1953 and gained even greater acceptance as the defense situation eased. It was the most significant long-range physical facilities program in which the Division participated after World War II.[62]

Fiscal year 1951 had been "a year of armed conflict in Korea. It began a week or so after the invasion of South Korea; it ended a week or so after the United Nations broadcast by the Soviet delegate, Jacob Malik, which set in motion the truce negotiations between the United Nations command and that of Communist

[59] Others in the program were Dr. James A. Van Zwoll, Mr. John Rork, and Mr. Ralph C. Moor.

[60] Interview of author with Decker, October 29, 1959; and College Housing Loan Program material in possession of Dr. Decker.

[61] Brownell, *op. cit.*, p. 183.

[62] After the Korean situation had settled down enough to allow a more normal resumption of building, the College Housing Loan Program had a wide acceptance. In fiscal year 1954 loans nearly doubled from $86.5 million to a total of $150 million and applications on file were in excess of $350 million. By August 1956, 327 institutions had received loans totaling more than $280 million. See S. M. Brownell, "Office of Education" in Oveta Culp Hobby, *Annual Report of the U.S. Department of Health, Education, and Welfare, 1954* (Washington, 1955), pp. 187–188; and Lloyd E. Blauch, "Higher Education and the Federal Government" (mimeographed, 1956), p. 6.

China in North Korea." [63] Following the year of "hot war" in which the attention of the Division, and of virtually the entire Office, had been concentrated on defense activities, the tedious period of truce negotiations began. It continued to drag on until the middle of 1953. There was one advantage to this as far as the Division was concerned. It was now possible to devote more time to peacetime pursuits.

Russell was not destined to remain in office much beyond the "hot war" period. On January 15, 1952, he resigned as Assistant Commissioner and Director of the Division to become Executive Secretary of the New Mexico Board of Educational Finance. Three months later the position he vacated was filled by Dr. Buell Gordon Gallagher who had been Assistant Commissioner and head of the Program Development and Coordination Branch. Gallagher was to serve less than four months, the shortest period of time that anyone had held that position, before he resigned effective August 1, 1952, to accept the presidency of the College of the City of New York. His incumbency was to have little, if any, lasting effect on the Division.[64] After Gallagher left, the position was filled by "acting heads" and it was not until September 1955, that a permanent Assistant Commissioner was appointed.[65]

In fiscal year 1953 the Division of Higher Education was organized as follows:

College and University Administration Branch
 Administrative Section
 Educational Advisory Services on College
  Housing Loan Program Section
General and Liberal Education Branch
 General Education Section
Professional Education Branch.[66]

---

[63] McGrath, *Annual Report . . . 1951*, p. 1.

[64] Gallagher apparently did not particularly desire the position. He stated in a letter to the author, dated October 20, 1959: "Frankly, I took the position at the earnest personal request of the Commissioner who had been attempting for some time to find an incumbent from the outside and had been unsuccessful." Gallagher further stated in the letter that he felt he had had no lasting effect on the Division. One of the Office of Education staff members regarded Gallagher as "one of the most brilliant men to have occupied that position." (Walter H. Gaumnitz, "Reminiscences Concerning Chiefs of the Division of Higher Education," typewritten ms. prepared for author in 1959.)

[65] Following the resignation of Gallagher on August 1, 1952, Rall I. Grigsby served as "Acting Head" until September 15. He was succeeded by Wesley E. Armstrong but the position was not permanently filled until the appointment of Lloyd E. Blauch on September 11, 1955. See Appendix I.

[66] U.S. Office of Education, *Educational Directory, 1951–52* (Washington, 1952), Part 1; and U. S. Office of Education, *Educational Directory, 1952–53* (Washington, 1953), Part 1.

In that year of administrative transition the Division was engaged in three types of activity:

1. Routine or continuing responsibilities such as contributing to the annual *Educational Directory* and to *Higher Education* and other periodicals, investigating college housing loan applications, administering land-grant college funds, collecting and disseminating statistics, advising and consulting, and visiting institutions of higher education;

2. Major projects not directly related to national defense such as studies of ways to improve college teaching, promoting teacher education, furthering the cause of engineering education, studying causes for student withdrawal from college, and other studies on scholarship and fellowships, costs of attending college, community college programs, college accreditation, promoting international understanding; and

3. Defense-related projects such as college-level training for defense industry, assisting in the Controlled Materials Plan, and liaison with other Government agencies.[67]

This was its organization, and these its functions, at the time of the creation of the Department of Health, Education and Welfare on April 11, 1953, one of the first acts of President Dwight David Eisenhower.[68] For the first time in American history education was a part of the title of a member on the President's cabinet.[69] This achievement was symbolic of a growing sense of awareness of the role of the Federal Government in the education of its citizens. The Office of Education, and its Division of Higher Education stood on the threshold of a new period of responsibility, expansion, and service.

---

[67] S. M. Brownell, "Office of Education" in Hobby, *Annual Report . . . 1953,* pp. 182–189. Also valuable for a brief discussion of Division duties although written prior to fiscal year 1953 is E. J. McGrath, "Program of the Division of Higher Education in the Office of Education," *Higher Education,* VIII, No. 15, April 1, 1952, pp. 169–172.

[68] P.L. 13, 83rd Congress, approved by the President April 11, 1953.

[69] S. M. Brownell, "Office of Education" in Hobby, *Annual Report . . . 1953,* p. 159.

CHAPTER VI

# Conclusion

---

The years from 1910 to 1950, roughly the period covered by this account of the Division of Higher Education, were marked by dynamic growth and change in higher education. The number of institutions reporting to the Office of Education nearly doubled; growing from 951 in 1910 to 1,851 in 1950. Total enrollment increased nearly 700 percent and earned doctorates went up by 1,500 percent.[1] The variety of courses open to undergraduates and graduates alike increased to a bewildering extent. An undergraduate in 1950 could find a fully developed program of study available to prepare him for virtually any imaginable profession. Those wishing to enter a profession lacking a program could usually locate some obliging college or university ready and able to develop a course of study to follow.

These indicate the two outstanding characteristics of American higher education at mid-century. One was the opportunity to attend college available to an extent never realized by any people before. The other was a variety of programs almost beyond imagining.

Through all this period of change and growth, the Division of Higher Education was the Federal conscience in regard to the post-secondary education of the American people. Like other forms of conscience it could not be ignored and yet it was not fully heeded. Paradoxically, the Division was a recognition that the government of a democracy should do something to foster and promote higher education while, at the same time, this government should not go all out to provide strong and forceful leadership.

The three tables that follow show that the Federal Government expanded its facilities in the Office of Education to meet the needs of education at all levels. For example, Table 8 shows that

---

[1] See Table 4, Chapter II, *supra.*

appropriations for the Office of Education, excluding certain special appropriations and transfers of funds, amounted to $122,200 in 1910. By 1950 they had increased about 18 times over. This is impressive unless one remembers that a large part of this increase in appropriations was nullified by a very substantial growth in operating costs due to the shrinking value of the dollar. Even more significant, the total Federal expenditures in 1950 were about 57 times greater than in 1910. So the appropriation increase for the Office did not come close to keeping up with the average for the Federal Government as a whole.[2]

Similarly, Tables 9 and 10 show there were substantial increases in the number of employees in the Office of Education generally, and in the Division of Higher Education, but they were not equal to the gains made throughout the Executive Branch of the Federal Government, of which the Office was a part.[3]

Figures are, in themselves, no final measurement of trends and developments in education. Sometimes they are actually misleading. But these few statistics do support the conclusion that the Federal Government recognized the need for helping education while refusing to give it the support extended to many other activities of the American people.

The Division of Higher Education was not the only organization through which the Federal Government aided higher education, as the Office of Education was not the only agency through which it aided education as a whole. As the Twentieth Century progressed the Federal Government, realizing at first that more help was desirable and later that it was essential, gave more and more assistance to higher education. But this was not done through the logical coordinating agency, the Office of Education. It was done through a variety of departments, agencies, and offices. So diversified were its activities that by 1950 the Office of Education was handling only about 1 percent of the Federal expenditures for educational purposes.[4]

---

[2] Expenditures, rounded to the nearest million, were $694 million in 1910, and $39,617 million in 1950. (Information supplied by the Treasury Department and published in Harry Hansen (ed), *The World Almanac and Book of Facts, 1960* (New York, 1960), p. 749).

[3] Total civilian employment in the Executive Branch of the Federal Government in 1910 was approximately 384,000, and in 1953 the average monthly employment figure was 2,278,800. (Based on Bureau of Labor Statistics in *Ibid.*, p. 767; and Bureau of the Census, *Historical Statistics of the United States. 1789–1945* (Washington, 1949), p. 294.) Civilian employment in the Executive Branch increased approximately 600 percent while increasing only about 400 percent in the Office of Education as a whole.

[4] Charles A. Quattlebaum, *Federal Educational Activities and Educational Issues Before Congress* (Washington, 1952), pp. 140–141, 148.

TABLE 8.—*Appropriations and Operating Costs, Office of Education*

This Table does not include appropriations for work in Alaska nor transfers of funds from other agencies. Figures are rounded off to nearest dollar.

| Fiscal year | Appropriation | Operating costs |
|---|---|---|
| 1867–68 | 24,676 | (not available) |
| 1870 | 9,150 | 9,150 |
| 1875 | 43,825 | 43,825 |
| 1880 | 37,116 | 37,116 |
| 1885 | 76,239 | 76,239 |
| 1890 | 91,932 | 91,932 |
| 1895 | 112,914 | 112,914 |
| 1900 | 101,180 | 101,180 |
| 1905 | 99,941 | 99,941 |
| 1910 | 122,200 | 122,200 |
| 1915 | 175,500 | 175,500 |
| 1920 | 307,629 | 507,629* |
| 1925 | 274,303 | 549,303* |
| 1930 | 351,624 | 739,144* |
| 1935 | 520,398 | 587,520* |
| 1940 | 838,880 | 947,080* |
| 1945 | 983,100 | 2,098,885* |
| 1950 | 2,178,600 | (not available) |
| 1953 | 2,992,000 | (not available) |

* Figures for the years so indicated inculde cost of temporary programs (such as defense programs and relief programs) and other programs no longer performed by the Office of Education.

(Appropriation figures supplied by Mrs. Genevieve Dane, Assistant Budget Management Officer Office of Education, from material in Budget Management Office files; operating costs from Allen, Hollis P., *The Federal Government and Education* (New York, 1950), p. 191, based on Information supplied by the Office of Education in 1948.)

TABLE 9.—*Number of Employees, Office of Education*

This table shows the total number of employees for selected years. It includes those in the Alaska Division and those engaged in temporary assignments in survey work, or employed under VE, CWA, CCC, and ERA funds.

| Year | Number | Year | Number |
|---|---|---|---|
| 1868 | 4 | 1935 | 170 |
| 1888 | 60 | 1940 | 237 |
| 1908 | 127 | 1945 | 495 |
| 1928 | 298 | 1950 | 314 |
| 1933 | 136 | 1953 | 487 |

(Figures for 1868 to 1935, 1950, and 1953 supplied by Mrs. Genevieve Dane, Assistant Budget Management Officer, Office of Education, from material in Budget Management Office Files; figures for 1940 and 1945 from Allen, Hollis P., *The Federal Government and Education* (New York, 1950), p. 191, based on information supplied by the Office of Education in 1948.)

TABLE 10.—*Number of Professional Employees in the Division of Higher Education*

This table includes the specialists in land-grant college statistics. It also includes Miss Ella Ratcliffe after 1930 because she was given a sub-professional rating in September of that year, and Mrs. Elizabeth Layton from May 1948 when she was promoted to research assistant. It does not include field or regional representatives such as those involved in the World War II Engineering, Science, and Management War Training Program.

| Fiscal year | Number | Fiscal year | Number | Fiscal year | Number |
|---|---|---|---|---|---|
| 1911 | 2 | 1926 | 3 | 1941 | 14 |
| 1912 | 2 | 1927 | 4 | 1942 | 12 |
| 1913 | 2 | 1928 | 4 | 1943 | 13 |
| 1914 | 2 | 1929 | 4 | 1944 | 12 |
| 1915 | 2 | 1930 | 4 | 1945 | 11 |
| 1916 | 2 | 1931 | 5 | 1946 | 12 |
| 1917 | 2 | 1932 | 6 | 1947 | 11 |
| 1918 | 3 | 1933 | 6 | 1948 | 18 |
| 1919 | 3 | 1934 | 6 | 1949 | 21 |
| 1920 | 3 | 1935 | 6 | 1950 | 21 |
| 1921 | 3 | 1936 | 7 | 1951 | 27* |
| 1922 | 3 | 1937 | 7 | 1952 | 31* |
| 1923 | 3 | 1938 | 7 | 1953 | 26* |
| 1924 | 3 | 1939 | 6 | | |
| 1925 | 3 | 1940 | 8 | | |

* During part of this period the Division of International Education was merged with the Division of Higher Education.

(Compiled by author from U.S. Office of Education, *Educational Directory, 1894–1908, et. seq.;* Personnel Folders, St. Louis Records Center; Personnel Card File and Kardex, Office of Education Personnel Office; and the annual *Reports* and *Statements* of the Commissioners of Education.)

The Office of Education, and all of its component parts, operated under two handicaps that limited its effectiveness. It was not given enough money to pay the expenses necessary for it to keep pace with the demands for its services, and it was not permitted to become the central educational activity of the Federal Government. These were factors beyond the control of anyone in the Office but they were certainly not beyond the knowledge of any Commissioner. Almost every year the Commissioner of Education called attention to the fact that the Office of Education was understaffed and unable to meet demands for its services. Repeatedly, although not as often as he requested additional funds and personnel, the Commissioner would point out the inefficiency which resulted from scattering educational activities through a large number of departments and agencies.

The Division suffered from these Federal policies. Understaffing, lack of funds, and fragmentation of programming cut into the accomplishments of the Division.[5] But to look at this side of the picture only would be to completely ignore the positive accomplishments of the Division in the comparatively brief time it had been operating.

Most tangible of its achievements was the increase in publications relating to higher education, most of which were prepared by specialists in the Division and all of which were in some way or other affected by the Division acting as consultant and editor. In the first forty-four years of operation the Office of Education produced 218 publications relating to higher education. Nearly all of these were prepared by persons outside the Office and approximately one-third of the total amount were either studies of foreign institutions or nations, or were historical studies. There was only a scattered number of statistical studies, and there were no surveys, directories of colleges published separate from the *Annual Reports*, or studies of graduate programs. Publications relating to curriculum matters or teacher education were virtually unknown. In the forty-three years following 1910 publications relating to higher education increased by 160 percent. There were substantial declines in only two types of publications: reports on foreign institutions, and historial studies. These, incidentally, had amost invariably been prepared by persons outside the Office. Along with this increase in quantity there was a growth of both variety of material published and quality of publication.[6] The development of inexpensive and efficient methods of reproducing materials, such as the mimeograph machine, permitted a wide distribution of items prepared by the Division but not listed as official publications. Furthermore, members of the Division reached a large audience interested in higher education through

---

[5] In a letter to the author, dated November 19, 1959, Dr. Bernard Watson who served as a professional member of the Division of Higher Education from July 1949, to February 1952, wrote: "If its mission [Division of Higher Education's mission] were merely to collect and analyze facts concerning higher education then its staff might have been reasonably adequate for the task. If, on the other hand, it was expected to exercise leadership in the field of higher education, as some of us believed, then its staff was grossly inadequate and the almost complete absence of travel and printing funds made its inadequate staff entirely impotent."

This judgment is harsh but essentially true. There was not enough money to allow the publication of all the material that was prepared and travel funds were not adequate. However, there was enough money to allow attendance of one or more members at the most important conventions and conferences, and the material that was of the greatest national interest and importance was published.

[6] See Table 11, *infra*.

TABLE 11.—*Subject Matter of Publications Relating to Higher Education Prepared and Issued by the Office of Education, 1867–1953*

This table has been prepared after a study of the material listed in Appendix III. It includes chapters in the Annual Reports of the Commissioner of Education when those chapters are devoted to higher education. The "Miscellaneous" column is used for those publications which are devoted to more than one broad topic, or for certain subjects which are not recurring such as "College Extension Work," "Summer Sessions," "Scholarships and Fellowships," and so forth. There were no publications relating to higher education in 1867, 1869, or 1884.

| Calendar year | Statistical studies | Curriculum studies | Special types of schools | Teacher education | Foreign institutions | Specific institutions (by name) | Historical studies | Legislation studies | Surveys | Bibliographies | Educational directories | National defense and war effort | Graduate schools | Miscellaneous | Total for year |
|---|---|---|---|---|---|---|---|---|---|---|---|---|---|---|---|
| 1868 | | | 3 | | | | | | | | | | | | 3 |
| 1870 | | 1 | 1 | | | | | | | | | | | 1 | 3 |
| 1871 | 1 | 1 | | | | 1 | | | | | | | | | 3 |
| 1872 | 1 | 1 | | | 1 | | | | | | | | | | 3 |
| 1873 | | | | | | | | | | 1 | | | | 2 | 3 |
| 1874 | | | | | | | 1 | | | | | | | | 1 |
| 1875 | | | | | | | 1 | | | | | | | | 1 |
| 1876 | | | | | | | 2 | | | | | | | | 2 |
| 1877 | | | | | | | 1 | | | | | | | | 1 |
| 1878 | | | | | 1 | | | | | | | | | | 1 |
| 1879 | | | | | | | | | | | | | | 1 | 1 |
| 1880 | | 1 | | | | | | | | | | | | 2 | 3 |
| 1881 | | | 2 | | | | | | | | | | | | 2 |
| 1882 | 1 | | 1 | | 1 | 1 | | | | | | | | | 4 |
| 1883 | | | | | | | 1 | | | | | | | | 1 |
| 1885 | 1 | | | 1 | | | | | | | | | | | 2 |
| 1886 | | 1 | 1 | 1 | 1 | | | | | | | | | | 4 |
| 1887 | 1 | 1 | 4 | 1 | | | 1 | | | | | | | | 8 |
| 1888 | 1 | | 3 | 1 | | | 5 | | | | | | | 1 | 11 |
| 1889 | | | 2 | | | | 2 | | | | | | | 2 | 6 |
| 1890 | 1 | 2 | 1 | | 1 | | 1 | | | | | | | 4 | 10 |
| 1891 | 2 | 3 | 1 | 1 | 2 | | 4 | | | | 1 | | | | 14 |
| 1892 | 2 | | | | 2 | 2 | 2 | | | | | | | 3 | 11 |
| 1893 | | 2 | 1 | | 1 | | 3 | | | | | | | 2 | 9 |
| 1894 | 1 | 2 | 1 | 1 | | | 2 | | | | | | | 1 | 8 |
| 1895 | | 2 | 2 | | 2 | | | | | | | | | 2 | 8 |
| 1896 | | | 1 | | 1 | | | | | | | | | 1 | 3 |
| 1897 | | 3 | 1 | | 1 | | | | 1 | | | | | 3 | 9 |
| 1898 | | 3 | 2 | | 1 | | 3 | | | | | | | 3 | 12 |
| 1899 | | | | | 3 | 2 | 4 | | | | | | | | 9 |

TABLE 11.—*Subject Matter of Publications Relating to Higher Education Prepared and Issued by the Office of Education, 1867–1953*—continued

| Calendar year | Statistical studies | Curriculum studies | Special types of schools | Teacher education | Foreign institutions | Specific institutions (by name) | Historical studies | Legislation studies | Surveys | Bibliographies | Educational directories | National defense and war effort | Graduate schools | Miscellaneous | Total for year |
|---|---|---|---|---|---|---|---|---|---|---|---|---|---|---|---|
| 1900 |  | 1 |  |  |  |  | 4 | 1 |  |  |  |  |  | 1 | 7 |
| 1901 |  | 2 | 1 |  | 1 | 1 |  | 1 |  |  |  |  |  |  | 6 |
| 1902 | 1 | 1 |  |  |  | 2 | 4 | 1 |  |  |  |  |  | 2 | 11 |
| 1903 |  | 1 |  | 2 | 1 |  | 3 | 1 |  |  |  |  |  | 2 | 10 |
| 1904 |  |  |  |  | 3 |  | 1 |  |  |  |  |  |  | 1 | 5 |
| 1905 |  |  | 1 |  |  |  |  |  |  |  |  |  |  | 3 | 4 |
| 1906 |  |  | 1 |  | 1 |  |  | 1 |  |  |  |  |  | 1 | 4 |
| 1907 |  |  | 1 |  |  |  |  |  |  |  |  |  |  | 1 | 2 |
| 1908 | 1 |  | 1 |  | 2 |  |  | 1 |  |  |  |  |  |  | 5 |
| 1909 | 2 | 1 |  |  |  |  |  | 1 |  |  | 1 |  |  | 1 | 6 |
| 1910 | 1 |  |  |  |  |  |  | 1 |  |  |  |  |  |  | 2 |

(Division of Higher Education Established)

| Calendar year | Statistical studies | Curriculum studies | Special types of schools | Teacher education | Foreign institutions | Specific institutions (by name) | Historical studies | Legislation studies | Surveys | Bibliographies | Educational directories | National defense and war effort | Graduate schools | Miscellaneous | Total for year |
|---|---|---|---|---|---|---|---|---|---|---|---|---|---|---|---|
| 1911 | 2 | 3 |  | 1 | 2 |  | 1 |  |  |  |  |  | 2 | 1 | 12 |
| 1912 | 2 | 1 | 1 | 1 | 1 |  |  |  |  |  | 1 |  |  | 2 | 9 |
| 1913 | 1 |  | 2 | 2 |  | 1 |  |  |  | 1 | 1 |  |  | 4 | 12 |
| 1914 | 1 | 3 | 4 | 1 | 1 |  |  |  |  |  | 1 |  |  | 2 | 13 |
| 1915 | 1 |  | 2 | 1 | 2 |  |  |  | 1 |  | 1 |  |  | 5 | 13 |
| 1916 | 1 |  | 3 | 1 |  | 1 | 1 |  | 4 |  | 1 |  |  | 8 | 20 |
| 1917 | 2 |  |  | 1 | 4 |  |  |  | 2 |  | 1 | 8 |  | 2 | 21 |
| 1918 | 2 | 2 | 5 | 3 |  | 1 |  |  | 2 |  | 1 | 5 |  | 1 | 22 |
| 1919 | 2 | 2 | 3 | 4 |  |  |  |  |  |  | 1 |  |  | 13 | 25 |
| 1920 | 3 | 7 | 2 |  |  |  |  |  |  |  | 1 |  |  | 5 | 18 |
| 1921 | 2 | 9 | 1 | 1 |  |  |  |  | 1 |  | 1 |  | 2 | 2 | 19 |
| 1922 | 5 | 1 |  | 4 | 1 |  | 1 |  | 2 |  | 1 |  |  | 6 | 21 |
| 1923 | 3 | 3 | 1 |  |  | 1 | 1 |  | 1 |  | 1 |  |  | 2 | 13 |
| 1924 | 3 | 4 | 4 |  |  | 2 | 1 |  |  | 1 | 1 |  |  | 3 | 19 |
| 1925 | 5 | 4 | 2 | 2 |  |  | 1 |  |  |  | 1 |  |  | 1 | 16 |
| 1926 | 2 | 2 |  |  |  |  | 1 |  |  |  | 1 |  |  | 5 | 11 |
| 1927 | 4 | 1 | 1 | 2 |  |  |  |  |  | 1 | 1 |  |  | 3 | 13 |
| 1928 | 2 |  |  | 3 |  |  |  |  | 2 |  | 1 |  |  | 2 | 10 |
| 1929 | 4 | 1 | 1 | 2 |  |  |  |  |  |  | 1 |  |  | 3 | 12 |
| 1930 | 1 | 11 |  | 2 |  |  |  |  | 1 | 1 | 3 | 1 |  | 4 | 24 |
| 1931 |  | 2 |  | 1 |  |  |  |  | 2 | 1 | 1 |  |  | 3 | 10 |
| 1932 | 1 | 2 | 1 | 1 | 2 | 1 |  |  |  |  | 1 |  |  | 3 | 13 |
| 1933 | 1 | 17 |  | 2 | 1 |  |  |  |  |  | 1 |  | 1 | 3 | 26 |
| 1934 | 3 | 1 | 1 | 1 | 2 | 1 | 1 |  |  | 1 | 1 |  | 1 | 2 | 15 |
| 1935 | 1 |  |  |  |  |  | 1 |  |  | 2 | 1 |  |  | 2 | 7 |

TABLE 11.—*Subject Matter of Publications Relating to Higher Education Prepared and Issued by the Office of Education 1867–1953—continued*

| Calendar year | Statistical studies | Curriculum studies | Special types of schools | Teacher education | Foreign institutions | Specific institutions (by name) | Historical studies | Legislation studies | Surveys | Bibliographies | Educational directories | National defense and war effort | Graduate schools | Miscellaneous | Total for year |
|---|---|---|---|---|---|---|---|---|---|---|---|---|---|---|---|
| 1936 | 3 | 1 | | 1 | 1 | | | 1 | | 4 | 1 | | 1 | 2 | 15 |
| 1937 | 5 | 1 | | | | | | | | 1 | 1 | | | 4 | 12 |
| 1938 | 2 | | 1 | | | | | | | | 1 | | | 3 | 7 |
| 1939 | 2 | | | | | | | | | | 1 | | 1 | | 4 |
| 1940 | 5 | | | 1 | 1 | | | 2 | | 1 | 1 | | | 3 | 14 |
| 1941 | 3 | 1 | 2 | | | | | | | 1 | 1 | 1 | | 3 | 12 |
| 1942 | 2 | | 3 | | | | | | 1 | | 1 | 2 | | 1 | 10 |
| 1943 | 5 | | | | | | | | 1 | | 1 | 1 | | 1 | 9 |
| 1944 | 2 | | 1 | | | | | | | | 1 | 3 | | 1 | 8 |
| 1945 | 1 | | | | | | | | | | 1 | 2 | | | 4 |
| 1946 | 1 | 1 | | | | | | | | | 1 | 2 | | | 5 |
| 1947 | 4 | | | 1 | | | | | | | 1 | | 1 | | 7 |
| 1948 | 4 | | | | | 1 | | | | 1 | 1 | | 1 | | 8 |
| 1949 | 6 | 1 | | | | | | | | 2 | 1 | | | 1 | 11 |
| 1950 | 8 | 1 | | 1 | | 1 | | | | | 1 | | | | 12 |
| 1951 | 10 | 3 | 1 | | | | | | | | 1 | | | 1 | 16 |
| 1952 | 11 | 1 | 2 | 1 | | | | | | | 1 | 3 | | 1 | 20 |
| 1953 | 5 | 1 | 1 | | | | | | | | 1 | | | | 8 |
| Totals (to 1911) | 17 | 26 | 34 | 9 | 26 | 9 | 45 | 9 | 0 | 3 | 0 | 0 | 0 | 40 | 218 |
| Totals (from 1911) | 133 | 88 | 33 | 52 | 19 | 7 | 6 | 11 | 23 | 17 | 42 | 28 | 9 | 108 | 576 |
| Grand totals | 150 | 114 | 67 | 61 | 45 | 16 | 51 | 20 | 23 | 20 | 42 | 28 | 9 | 148 | 794 |

the pages of Office journals such as *Higher Education* and *School Life* and through outside publications.

Another important accomplishment was the contribution to the college survey movement. Capen, Zook, Klein, Kelly, Blauch, Russell, and John were among the most active and creative leaders in the surveys made prior to World War II. No single organization, within or outside the Federal Government, did more to further educational surveys than the Division of Higher Education.

With these surveys came more efficient and academically sound institutions in many States of the Nation.

Early in its history the Division interested itself in the maintenance of the highest levels of academic performance. Although its first attempt to serve as a classifying agency resulted in protests followed by suppression of a well-intentioned but rather tactless document, and although it could not take direct action to suppress degree mills and other questionable educational institutions, the Division did succeed in directing attention to those weak spots in the American postsecondary system of education. It pointed out the need for a stronger acceding system to people who had not been aware of it to that time. It also effectively warned of the damage degree mills could cause to all reputable educational institutions if they were permitted to operate. The fight for high academic standards, and against shoddy institutions, continues today but the progress which has been made owes much to the Division.

In national defense, it has helped organize colleges and universities for effective contribution to the cause of democracy. Even though the marshalling of American educational resources in World War I left much to be desired, much was learned from failure. In World War II such programs as Engineering, Science, and Management War Training and Student War Loans attest to the sound organization of higher education. The Division of Higher Education, working with organizations outside the Federal Government, and with official groups as well, provided the guidance and direction that institutions of higher education needed to make a maximum contribution to victory.

There are a large number of innovations in higher education that owe much to the Division. It helped to develop the American Council on Education and gave that body its first permanent Director, Dr. Capen. Since the early 1920's there has been a lively and mutually profitable exchange of ideas and personnel between it and the American Council. Meetings on problems of educational research called by the Commissioner and conducted by Division personnel helped stimulate the development of research throughout higher education and laid the foundation for the cooperative research program. The Division was instrumental in founding the American Association of Junior Colleges. Specialists in the Division led the movement to raise the standards of teacher preparation and of college teaching in general.

Other contributions were the development of a clearing house for educational research and higher education studies, suggestions for improvement in the collection of educational statistics in higher education, fostering of education through emergency relief projects such as the National Youth Administration and the university research project, and assisting with veterans' educational programs by administering and advising in such things as the Veteran's Educational Facilities Program and the College Housing Loan Program.

Above all else, and more important than any single contribution or any combination of them was the significance of the Division itself. The very fact that it existed and thrived throughout the years was its greatest contribution. The Division of Higher Education was an acknowledgment that higher education was not the right of a privileged few from a certain social or economic group. It was established and grew stronger as the century advanced because it represented an admission that higher education belonged to the Nation and was essential to the welfare and progress of that Nation. The Division was not as big or as strong in 1953 as it should have been to do all it needed to do, but it was larger and healthier than it had ever been before. It was an integral part of the educational structure of the Nation, firm in its accomplishments and confident of its future role.

# Appendices

# Biographical Sketches
## of Professional Staff Members of
## the Division of Higher Education

The following brief biographical sketches are concerned essentially with the professional qualifications of the various members of the Division of Higher Education from 1911 through 1953. I have tried to include the same basic kind of information on each. However, the length of each sketch depends upon the amount of biographical information which was available when they were compiled in 1960. Information on certain persons, particularly those who served on a consultant or temporary basis, is lacking.

This appendix is divided into two sections. Section A contains the biographical sketches of those men who served in the capacity of division chiefs to 1953. They are listed chronologically. Section B lists all others alphabetically.

Brief sketches are included in Section B of persons who were never members of the division but who filled positions relating to higher education prior to the establishment of a division (Wellford Addis, James E. McClintock, and Frederick E. Upton) or those who had positions which greatly influenced the division (Henry Badger, Rall I. Grigsby, Lewis Kalbach, and Harlan Updegraff).

Sources of information are listed immediately following each sketch. Office of Education publications written by these people are not listed although those publications relating to higher education may be found in Appendix III.

### Men Serving as Division Chiefs, 1911–1953

BABCOCK, KENDRIC CHARLES. Born September 8, 1864 in New York City; Litt. B., University of Minnesota, Minneapolis (1889); A.M. Ph.D., Harvard University, Cambridge, Massachusetts (1895, 1896) ; taught in country schools in New York, 1881–85; Instructor in history and English, University of Minnesota, 1890–94; Professor of American history and political science, University of California, Berkeley, 1896–1902; President and professor of history, University of Arizona, Tucson, 1903–1910.

Appointed as first Specialist in Higher Education, November 9, 1910. Resigned on May 2, 1913, to accept position as Dean of the College of Literature, Arts, and Science of the University of Illinois. Appointed "Special Collaborator in the Bureau of Education" at $1.00 per annum. Accepted this position on May 23, 1913; postdated to May 3, 1913. This appointment terminated on June 30, 1921 due to completion of work for which he was appointed.

Dean, University of Illinois, Urbana, 1913–20. Provost, University of Illinois, 1920–31. Died March 11, 1932.

(Sources: Personnel Folder, St. Louis Records Center; Claxton, P. P., *Statement . . . 1912*, pp. 3, 5; Ltr. Asst. Sec. of Interior F. M. Goodwin to K. C. Babcock, through Commissioner of Ed., June 30, 1921; Memo dtd. Oct. 21, 1910 prepared for Acting Commissioner of Ed.; *Who's Who in America*, 1930–31, XIV, p. 214).

CAPEN, SAMUEL PAUL. Born March 21, 1878 at Sommerville, Massachusetts; A.B., A.M., L.H.D., Tufts College, Medford, Massachusetts (1898, 1898, 1921) ; A.M., Harvard University, Cambridge Massachusetts (1900) ; Ph.D., LL.D., University of Pennsylvania, Philadelphia (1902, 1933) ; studied at University of Leipzig, Germany (1901–02) ; several honorary degrees; Instructor in modern languages, Clark University, Worchester, Massachusetts, 1902–03; Assistant Professor, Clark University, 1903–08; Professor, Clark University, 1908–14.

Appointed Specialist in Higher Education and assigned to Division as Chief on February 1, 1914. Resigned on December 1, 1919.

First permanent Director of the American Council on Education, Washington, D.C., 1919–22; Chancellor of the University of Buffalo, New York, 1922–1950; Chancellor Emeritus, 1950–1956. Died June 22, 1956.

(Sources, Personnel Folder, St. Louis Records Center; U.S. Office of Education, *Educational Directory, 1914–15; Ibid., 1918–19;* Claxton, P. P. *Statement . . . 1914*, pp. 3–4; Cattell and Ross (ed.), *Leaders in Education* (Lancaster, Pa., 1948), p. 167; Elliott, Edward C., "A Tribute to Samuel Paul Capen," *The Educational Record*, XXXVIII, No. 1, Jan. 1957, pp. 18–19).

ZOOK, GEORGE FREDERICK. Born April 22, 1885 at Fort Scott, Kansas; B.A., M.A., University of Kansas, Lawrence (1906, 1907) ; Ph.D., Cornell University, Ithaca, New York (1909) ; Instructor in European history, Pennsylvania State College, State

College, 1909–11; Travelling fellowship from Cornell for special investigation of modern European history in London, Oxford, The Hague, 1911–12, Assistant, Associate, and Professor of modern European history, Pennsylvania State College, 1912–20; Head of Department of History, Political Science, and Economics, Pennsylvania State College, 1914–1920; Committee on Public Information, United States Government, 1918; Educational Adviser, United States Treasury Department, 1919; Author of numerous historical studies and pamphlets on war savings programs.

Appointed Specialist in Higher Education on February 1, 1920. Also appointed as Chief of the Division. Resigned effective August 31, 1925. Served as alternate to the Federal Council of Citizenship Training. Appointed Special Collaborator at $1.00 per annum on September 17, 1925. Resigned on June 6, 1931.

President of the University of Akron, Ohio, 1925–33; United States Commissioner of Education, July 11, 1933–June 30, 1934; Director of the American Council on Education, 1933–1950. Died August 17, 1951.

(Sources: Evans and Wright, *The U.S. Office of Education* (unpublished, 1939), pp. 74a–74b; Personnel Folder, St. Louis Records Center; U.S. Office of Education, *Educational Directory, 1924;* "George F. Zook," *Higher Education,* VIII, 2, September 15, 1951, pp. 22–23.)

KLEIN, ARTHUR JAY. Born December 10, 1884, in Sturgis, Michigan; B.A. and Phi Beta Kappa, Wabash College, Crawfordsville, Indiana (1902); B.D. Magna cum laude, Union Theological Seminary, New York City (1909); M.A., Ph.D. Columbia University, New York (1909, 1916); Instructor in history, College of the City of New York, 1910–1915; Head of the Department of History and Economics, Wheaton College, Norton, Massachusetts, 1915–18; Assistant Director, Service Bureau, Committee on Public Information, Washington, D. C., 1918; Captain, U.S. Army, 1918; Associate Director of the Division of Educational Extension, Department of the Interior, in charge of University Extension Teaching Service, 1919; Executive Secretary of the National University Extension Association, Inc., 1919–20; Assistant Chief and Executive of Research and Development Service of the United States Army Education Service, 1920–24; Lt. Col., Education and Schools Section of the General Staff, U.S. Army, 1924–25.

Appointed Senior Educationist and Chief, Division of Higher Education, on December 10, 1925. When Dr. John Tigert resigned as Commissioner of Education in 1928 there was a strong effort made by several of Dr. Klein's friends to have him succeed to the office. However, Dr. W. J. Cooper was appointed in 1929. Dr. Klein resigned on June 10, 1930 effective July 15, 1930.

Professor of Education, Ohio State University, Columbus, Ohio, 1930–1937; Dean of the College of Education, Ohio State University, 1937–45; Retired, 1945; Author of numerous articles and *Intolerance in the Reign of Elizabeth, Queen of England* (1916).

(Sources: Personnel Folder, St. Louis Records Center; U.S. Office of Education, *Educational Directory, 1926, et seq.; Who's Who in America*, XXVI, p. 1503; Cattell and Ross (ed.) ; *Leaders in Education* (Lancaster, Pa., 1948), p. 599.)

KELLY, FREDERICK JAMES. Born September 7, 1880, in Wymore, Nebraska; A.B., University of Nebraska, Lincoln (1902) ; Ph.D. in Education, Teachers College, Columbia University, New York (1914) ; LL.D., University of Nebraska (1943) ; Teacher in public school systems, 1902–08; Superintendent of Training School, State Normal School, Spearfish, North Dakota, 1908–12, State Normal School, Emporia, Kansas, 1914–15; Dean, School of Education, University of Kansas, Lawrence, 1915–20; Research Professor and Dean of University Education, University of Kansas, 1920–23; Dean of Administration, University of Minnesota, Minneapolis, 1923–28; President, University of Idaho, Moscow, 1928–30; Survey Specialist and Professor of Higher Education at University of Chicago, Illinois, 1930–31.

Appointed Specialist in Higher Education on June 15, 1931. Appointed Assistant Commissioner and Director of the Division of Higher Education on September 9, 1945. Retired on June 30, 1946.

In 1948 Dr. Kelly expressed a desire to return to the United States Office of Education. Reemployed as Specialist for Land-Grant Colleges and Universities on November 8, 1948. Served as Acting Assistant Commissioner in interim period between resignation of Dr. Russell (January 19, 1952) and appointment of Dr. Gallagher (April 15, 1952). Retired on June 20, 1952. Reemployed as Consultant in Higher Education May 28, 1954 to May 27, 1955. Reemployed as Consultant to the President's Committee on Education Beyond the High School June 15–20, 1956. Died on August 1, 1959.

(Sources: Personnel Card File, Office of Education Personnel Office; U.S. Office of Education, *Educational Directory, 1932, et seq.;* Personnel Folder, St. Louis Records Center; *School Life*, XVI, 8, April 1931, p. 158; *Higher Education*, VIII, 12, February 15, 1952, p 143; *Who's Who in America*, XXVI, p. 1458; Division of Higher Education, "Fred J. Kelly Retires from the Office of Education," *Higher Education*, III, No. 2, Sept. 16, 1946, pp. 2–3.)

RUSSELL, JOHN DALE. Born November 8, 1895, in Bloomington, Indiana; A.B., A.M., Ph.D., Indiana University, Bloomington (1917, 1924, 1931); Graduate work at University of Kentucky, Lexington, and University of Chicago, Illinois; Ambulance Driver in United States Army, 1917–19; Farmer, Indiana, 1919–22; Assistant to the Dean of the School of Education and Assistant Director of Summer Session, Indiana University, 1922–25; Director of Research and Statistics, State Department of Public Instruction, Indiana, 1925–27; Assistant Professor of Education and Director of Research, Ball State Teachers College, Indiana, 1927; Associate Professor of Education, University of Kentucky, 1927–29; Assistant Director of Surveys, Board of Education of the Methodist Episcopal Church, 1929–31; Professor of Education, Associate Dean of Division of Social Sciences, Dean of Students, University of Chicago, 1931–1946; Dean and Academic Advisor, Biarritz American University, France, 1945–46.

Appointed Assistant Commissioner and Director of the Division of Higher Education on September 3, 1946. Resigned January 15, 1952 to accept position as Executive Secretary of the Board of Educational Finance of the State of New Mexico. Author of a large number of articles relating to many phases of higher education.

(Sources: U.S. Office of Education, *Educational Directory, 1946–47, et seq.*; Personnel Card File, Office of Education Personnel Office; Personnel Folder, St. Louis Records Center, *Who's Who in America*, XXVII, p. 2101; "New Director of the Higher Education Division," *Higher Education*, III, No. 2, Sept. 16, 1946, p. 1.)

GALLAGHER, BUELL GORDON. Born February 4, 1904, in Rankin, Illinois; B.A., Carleton College, Northfield, Minnesota (1925); B.D., Union Theological Seminary, New York (1929); Ph.D. in Education, Columbia University, New York (1938); Fogg Traveling Fellowship, London School of Economics (1929–30); Minister, Congregational Church, Passaic, New Jersey, 1931–33; President of Talladega College, Alabama, 1933–45; Professor of Christian Ethics, Pacific School of Religion, Berkeley, California, 1945–49; unsuccessful candidate for Congress, 7th District of California, 1948, although polling 49% of the vote in the general election; Consultant to Federal Security Administrator, 1949–50; Special Consultant on Technical and Professional Problems, Federal Security Administration, 1950–51; Assistant Commissioner, Office of Education, Program Development and Coordination Branch, February, 1951.

Appointed Assistant Commissioner for Higher Education, April

15, 1952. Resigned on August 1, 1952, to become President of the College of the City of New York.

Dr. Gallagher is the author of numerous articles and three studies of race relations: *American Caste and the Negro College* (1938) ; *Color and Conscience: The Irrepressible Conflict* (1946) ; and *Portrait of a Pilgrim: A Search for the Christian Way in Race Relations* (1946).

(Sources: Personnel Card File, Office of Education Personnel Office; Personnel Folder, St. Louis Records Center; Ltr., J. Donald Kingsley, Acting Administrator, FSA, to Dr. Gallagher, March 3, 1949; U.S. Office of Education, *Educational Directory, 1951–52; Who's Who in America*, XXX, p. 991; *Higher Education*, VIII, 18, May 15, 1952, p. 205.)

Following resignation of Dr. Gallagher, Mr. Rall I. Grigsby served as Acting Head, Division of Higher Education until September 15, 1952 when Dr. Wesley Earl Armstrong was made Acting Head of the Division. The position of Assistant Commissioner was not permanently filled again until the appointment of Dr. Lloyd E. Blauch on September 11, 1955.

(Sources: *Higher Education*, XII, 2, October 1955, p. 17; Personnel Card File, Office of Education Personnel Office, Interview, Dr. Blauch, November 5, 1959; U.S. Office of Education, *Educational Directory, 1952–53, et seq.;* Personnel Folder (Armstrong), St. Louis Records Center.)

## *Additional Professional Personnel*

ADDIS, WELLFORD. Addis served in the Office of Education (then a Bureau) from 1882 to 1902. Prior to his appointment in "proof reading and revising-editorial work" on August 17, 1882, he had served as an employee of Western Union in Washington, D.C. He served as a copyist and a clerk in the Bureau until April 30, 1895 when he resigned. On June 10, 1895, he was reappointed to the Bureau as "Clerk of Class 4" to work as a specialist in the Agricultural College area. His salary when accepting this appointment was $1,800, approximately $1,000 more per annum than he was making at the time of his resignation less than two months earlier. This position as Agricultural College Clerk was the first in the Bureau devoted full-time to the field of higher education. Addis resigned on June 30, 1902 and was succeeded by Frederick E. Upton.

(Sources: Official Record Card, St. Louis Records Center; Harris, W. T., *Statement . . . 1895, et seq.;* Ltr., Addis to Commissioner of Pensions, Nov. 20, 1884, in Personnel Folder.)

ANDERSON, HOWARD RICHMOND. Born October 1, 1898 in New York City; B.A., Augustana College, South Dakota (1922) ; M.A., University of Chicago, Illinois (1928) ; Ph.D. in history, University of Iowa, Iowa City (1930) ; World War I veteran; Head of social studies at Roosevelt High School, Wyandotte, Michigan, 1922–28; Instructor and Assistant Professor of History at the University of Iowa, 1928–37; Professor of Education, Cornell University, Ithaca, New York, and Director of Social Studies, Ithaca Public Schools New York, 1937–44; Director, School of Education and Summer Session, Cornell University, 1944–46.

Dr. Anderson joined the staff of the Office of Education as Specialist for Social Science and Geography in Secondary Education on February 15, 1946. Assigned to Division of Higher Education as Specialist on October 28, 1951. Resigned on January 29, 1954, to accept position as Dean, University School of Liberal and Applied Studies, University of Rochester, New York. Author and co-author of a large number of articles on education and the social studies. Co-author with Preston Slosson of a text on world history.

(Sources: U.S. Office of Education, *Educational Directory, 1951–52, et seq.;* Personnel Card File, Office of Education Personnel Office; Personnel Folder, St. Louis Records Center; *Who's Who in America,* XXX p. 67.)

ANDREWS, BENJAMIN FRANCIS. Born 1876; B.A., Wesleyan University, Connecticut (1898) ; attended Columbia Law School, New York (1898–99) ; in real estate and construction business which failed in 1908; elected to position as Secretary-Treasurer of the University of Puerto Rico, 1909. In 1914 Andrews was making $2,500 per annum in Puerto Rico but he desired a position in the United States where he could be with his wife and daughter who were unable to live in Puerto Rico.

Appointed Specialist in Charge of Land-Grant College Statistics at $1,800 per annum on temporary basis on April 2, 1914. Appointment made permanent on September 1, 1914. Transferred to Bureau of Internal Revenue on January 27, 1918. Andrews probably left Federal service in 1919 or 1920 because Commissioner Claxton wrote a strong recommendation for him on September 16, 1919, to the Guaranty Trust Company of New York.

(Sources: Claxton, P. P., *Statement . . . 1914,* pp. 3–4; U.S. Office of Education, *Educational Directory, 1914–15, et seq.;* Personnel Folder, St. Louis Records Center; Ltr., Claxton to Guaranty Trust Co., Sept. 16, 1919.)

ARMSBY, HENRY HORTON. Born March 12, 1891, in State College, Pennsylvania; B.S., C.E., Pennsylvania State University, State College (1911, 1916) ; D. Eng., Newark College of Engineering,

New Jersey (1955) ; D.Sc., Lowell Technical Institute, Massachusetts, (1956) ; Instructor in Civil Engineering, Pennsylvania State University, 1911; Engineer in Maintenance of Way Department, Pennsylvania Railroad, Altoona, Pennsylvania, 1912–14; Teacher of mathematics, drawing, and surveying, Wisconsin Mining School, Platteville, 1915–17; Instructor, Assistant Professor, Associate Professor of Civil Engineering, Missouri School of Mines, Rolla, 1917–22; Registrar and Student Adviser, Missouri School of Mines, 1922–41.

On March 7, 1941, Mr. Armsby joined the U.S. Office of Education as Field Coordinator of the Engineering, Science, and Management War Training Program. On May 20, 1946 he became the Specialist for Civil Engineering Education in the Division of Higher Education and on January 20, 1950, Assistant Chief for Engineering Education.

Mr. Armsby is the author of several articles and pamphlets dealing with engineering education. He is a member of two honor societies: Tau Beta Pi and Phi Kappa Phi. He has held national offices in the American Society for Engineering Education and served as a member of the Engineering Manpower Commission.

(Sources: Kardex, Office of Education Personnel Office; U.S. Office of Education, *Educational Directory, 1945–46, et seq.;* Biographical Résumé prepared by professional staff of the Division of Higher Education; *Who's Who in Engineering, 1954,* pp. 64–65.)

ARMSTRONG, WESLEY EARL. Born March 18, 1899, in Arkansas. A.B., East Central State College, Ada, Oklahoma (1927) ; M.S. in Education, Oklahoma A & M, Stillwater (1931) ; Ed. D., Stanford University, Palo Alto, California (1937) ; Supervisor of High School Teachers, Salt Lake City Public Schools, Utah, 1934–37; "Convenor," School of Education, Mills College, California, 1937–40; Field Coordinator, Committee on Teacher Education, American Council on Education, 1938–43; Dean of Ohio Wesleyan College, Delaware, Ohio, 1943–45; Dean, School of Education, University of Delaware, Newark, 1945–49.

Appointed as Associate Chief, Teacher Education, Division of Higher Education, on February 11, 1949. Detailed to position of Assistant Commissioner for Higher Education on September 15, 1952. On January 4, 1954 requested leave without pay for one year to serve as Executive Director of the National Council for Accreditation of Teacher Education. Resigned on May 4, 1956 from Office of Education to take position with the National Council.

In addition to several educational articles, Dr. Armstrong was the co-author of *The College and Teacher Education* (1944). He also has served as consultant in teacher education at George Washington University, D.C.

(Sources: Personnel Folder, St. Louis Records Center; U.S. Office of Education, *Educational Directory, 1948–49, et seq.*; Personnel Card File, Office of Education Personnel Office; Cattell and Ross (ed.), *Leaders in Education* (Lancaster, Pa., 1948), pp. 32–33.)

BADGER, HENRY GLENN. Born June 10, 1892; B.A., DePauw University, Indiana (1917) ; M.A., Indiana University, Bloomington (1925) ; graduate study at Indiana University and George Washington University, D.C.; Public School teacher, supervisor, principal, and superintendent in school systems in Illinois, Philippine Islands, and Indiana, 1912–15, 1917–27; Visiting professor of Education, Central Normal College (now defunct), Danville, Indiana, summer of 1927.

Mr. Badger joined the Office of Education as Principal Statistical Assistant on September 1, 1928. Served with the U.S. Civil Service Commission from July 20, 1930 to May 5, 1931. Specialist in education statistics from 1931 to present, specializing in higher education statistics from 1948 to present.

Mr. Badger is the author or co-author of approximately 80 statistical surveys and studies.

(Sources: U.S. Office of Education, *Educational Directory, 1946–47, et seq.*; Kardex, Office of Education Personnel Office; Memo, Henry Badger to author, October 22, 1959.)

BLAESSER, WILLARD WILLIAM. Born November 11, 1912, in Cedarburg, Wisconsin; B.A., M.A., work on Ph.D. in progress at time he was employed by the Office of Education, University of Wisconsin, Madison (1930, 1940) ; Teacher of social studies in Wisconsin high schools, 1934–36; Assistant Director, Division of Social Education and Instruction, University of Wisconsin, 1936–39; Assistant Dean of Men, Coordinator of Student Personnel, University of Wisconsin, 1939–45; Special Consultant, American Council on Education, Washington, for college training programs, 1943; Assistant Dean of Students and Director of Counseling Center, University of Chicago 1945–46; Director of Student Personnel and Associate Professor of Education, University of Montana, 1946–47; Dean of Students and Associate Professor of Education, Washington State College, Pullman, 1947–49.

Appointed Specialist for Student Personnel Services, Office of Education, on May 20, 1949. Resigned on June 8, 1953, to become Dean of Students at the University of Utah, Salt Lake City.

Most of his publications were in the field of guidance and personnel work. The majority were prepared for the American Council on Education. One volume published by the University of Wisconsin is *Educational Guidance and the War* (1944).

(Sources: Personnel Card File, Office of Education Personnel Office; Personnel Folder, St. Louis Records Center.)

BLAUCH, LLOYD E. Born May 26, 1889, in Myersdale, Pennsylvania; A.B., Goshen College, Indiana (1916); A.M., Ph.D., The University of Chicago, Illinois (1917, 1923); Teacher, principal, and superintendent of public schools, 1905–14; Statistician, Bureau of Education, February 15–June 30, 1919; Special Agent, U.S. Department of Labor, 1920–21; Specialist in charge of Land-Grant College Statistics, August 25, 1921–November 5, 1923; Professor of Education, North Carolina College for Women (now University of North Carolina at Greensboro, Greensboro, 1923–30; Member, Survey Staff, Methodist Board of Education, 1930–31; Secretary, Curriculum Survey Committee, American Association of Dental Schools, 1931–36; Principal Educational Specialist, National Advisory Committee on Education, 1936–39; Taught summer sessions at University of Maryland, Joliet Junior College, Loyola University (Chicago), and the University of Chicago.

Appointed Consultant to Division of Higher Education on October 4, 1939; Senior Specialist in Higher Education, August 1, 1940; Specialist in Land-Grant Colleges and Universities, May 20, 1946; Associate Chief for Education in the Health Professions, August 8, 1948. On September 11, 1955, Dr. Blauch became Assistant Commissioner and Director of the Division of Higher Education, a position which he held until his retirement on May 31, 1959. He remained on duty as a Special Consultant until September 11, 1959.

Dr. Blauch published a large number of articles on a variety of subjects and more than a dozen books and long reports on accreditation, curriculum, and the health profession. Received superior service award of Department of Health, Education, and Welfare in 1955 for outstanding service to American education.

(Sources: U.S. Office of Education, *Educational Directory, 1921–22, et seq.;* Personnel Card File, Office of Education Personnel Office; Biographical Résumé furnished the author by Dr. Blauch: *Higher Education,* XII, 2, October 1955, p. 17; *Who's Who in America,* XXX, p. 261; Lloyd, John H., "New Assistant Commissioner for Higher Education," *Higher Education,* XII, No. 2, Oct. 1955, pp. 17–18.)

BUTLER, GEORGE NORWOOD. Born November 26, 1912, in Pernambuco [Recife], Brazil; B.S., Wilson Teachers College, Washington, D.C. (1936); graduate study at Catholic University, D.C. and University of Maryland, College Park; employed as a teacher in D.C. public schools and with the General Electric Company, 1936–41.

Appointed as a Junior Educationist, Division of Higher Education on January 2, 1941; resigned on June 15, 1941.

(Sources: U.S. Office of Education, *Educational Directory, 1941*; Personnel Folder, St. Louis Records Center.)

CALDWELL, OTIS WILLIAM. Born December 18, 1869, in Lebanon, Indiana; graduated from Franklin College and received a Ph.D. from the University of Chicago, Illinois (dates not available); Assistant in Botany, University of Chicago, 1897–99; Professor of Botany, Eastern Illinois State Normal School, 1899–1907; Professor of Botany, University of Indiana summer session, 1904; Associate Professor of Botany, School of Education, University of Chicago, 1907–14.

Appointed to temporary position as Specialist in Higher Education for the purpose of making a personal inspection of the teaching of science in some of the more important schools in the Southern States on January 13, 1914. Appointment terminated on January 31, 1914.

Following his assignment with the Bureau of Education Dr. Caldwell served as a Dean at the University of Chicago until 1917; Professor of Education at Teachers College, Columbia University, 1917–27; and Director of the Institute of Educational Research, 1927–30. At the time of his death, July 5, 1947, he was General Secretary of the American Association for the Advancement of Science.

(Sources: Claxton, P. P., *Statement . . . 1914*, pp. 3–4; Personnel Folder, St. Louis Records Center; *Who's Who in America*, II, p. 97.)

CALIVER, AMBROSE. Born February 25, 1894, in Saltville, Virginia; B.A., Knoxville College, Knoxville, Tennessee (1915); M.A., University of Wisconsin, Madison (1920); Ph.D., Columbia University, New York (1930); Diploma in personnel management, Harvard University, Cambridge, Massachusetts (1918); principal of colored high school, Rockwood, Tennessee, 1916; instructor and assistant principal, Douglass High School, El Paso, Texas, 1917; teacher, director of summer school, and Dean, Fisk University, Nashville, Tennessee, 1917–30.

Dr. Caliver joined the professional staff of the Office of Education on September 2, 1930, as Senior Specialist in Negro Education. During this period of time he was engaged in activities involving all types of educational work with Negroes. On May 20, 1946, Dr. Caliver became Specialist for Negro Higher Education and on July 14, 1950, Assistant to the Commissioner in the Office of Education. He held this position until July, 1955, when he became Chief of the Adult Education Section.

Dr. Caliver has published nearly one hundred articles and studies, most of which relate to Negro education or adult education. Among his honors have been an honorary Doctor of Laws, Virginia State College, Ettrick (1951); honorary Doctor of Letters, Knoxville College, Tennessee (1953); honorary Doctor of Laws, Morgan State College, Baltimore, Maryland (1956); Superior Service Award, Department of Health, Education, and Welfare (1955); and winner of a national essay contest (1924). He has held several positions on national surveys and studies relating to education.

(Sources: Biographical Résumé prepared by the professional staff of the Division of Higher Education; Kardex, Office of Education personnel office; U.S. Office of Education, *Educational Directory, 1945–46, et seq.; Who's Who in America*, XXX, p. 428.)

CASE, GEORGE WILKINSON. Born March 2, 1880, in Fowler, Indiana; B.S. in C.E., Purdue University, Lafayette, Indiana (1905); Master of C.E., Cornell University, Ithaca, New York (1912); Assistant Instructor, Instructor, and Assistant Professor, Purdue University, 1905–13; Assistant Professor and Professor of Sanitary and Hydraulic Engineering, University of Pittsburgh, 1913–22; Chief Engineer and Executive Officer, American City Engineering Co., Pittsburgh, Pennsylvania, 1920–25; Dean, College of Technology, University of New Hampshire, Durham, 1925–49.

Dean Case entered duty as Principal Specialist in Engineering Education on November 4, 1940. The temporary appointment was extended in October of the next year. On June 24, 1942 Dean Case succeeded Dean Roy A. Seaton as Director of the Engineering, Science, and Management War Training Program. He remained as Director until January 31, 1946 when the Program was liquidated.

Dean Case returned to New Hampshire where he resumed his duties at the University. He retired in 1949 and became Emeritus Dean.

(Sources: Armsby, H. S., *Engineering, Science, and Management War Training. Final Report* (Washington, 1946), pp. ix, 10–14; Personnel Folder, St. Louis Records Center; U.S. Office of Education, *Educational Directory, 1942–43, et seq.; Who's Who in America*, XXVII, p. 441.)

CONLEY, WILLIAM HENRY. Born February 13, 1907, in Sharon, Wisconsin; B.S.C., M.A., Loyola University, Chicago (1930, 1935) ; M.B.A., Ph.D., Northwestern University, Evanston, Illinois (1932, 1947) ; Dean of Wright City Junior College, Chicago, Illinois, 1935–1946, with leave of absence from 1941 to 1946 for service with the Office of Price Administration, Chicago, and as an instructor and officer with the United States Navy; Dean, School of Commerce, Loyola University, Chicago, 1946–48.

Dr. Conley was appointed Specialist for Junior Colleges and Lower Divisions in the Division of Higher Education on March 26, 1948. He resigned on August 19, 1949, to return to Loyola University as Dean of the School of Education.

(Sources: Personnel Card File, Office of Education Personnel Office; Personnel Folder, St. Louis Records Center; U.S. Office of Education, *Educational Directory, 1948–49, et seq.;* Cattell and Ross (ed.), *Leaders in Education* (Lancaster, Pa., 1948), p. 215.)

DANIEL, WALTER GREEN. Born June 21, 1905, in Petersburg, Virginia; A.B., Virginia Union University, Richmond (1926) ; Ed. B., A.M., University of Cincinnati, Ohio (1927, 1928) ; Ph.D., Columbia University, New York (1941) ; Director of Practice Teaching, Winston-Salem State Teachers College, North Carolina, 1927–29; Assistant Professor, Associate Professor, and Professor of Education, Howard University, D.C., 1929–51.

Dr. Daniel was appointed Specialist for Higher Education (Negro Higher Education) on June 4, 1951. He resigned on September 11, 1953, to accept a position with Maryland State Teachers College at Bowie.

Prior to joining the Office of Education, and while in the Office, Dr. Daniel authored approximately forty articles relating to higher education and Negro education.

(Sources: U.S. Office of Education, *Educational Directory, 1950–51, et seq.;* Personnel Card File, Office of Education Personnel Office; Personnel Folder, St. Louis Records Center; Cattell and Ross (ed.), *Leaders in Education* (Lancaster, Pa., 1948), p. 253).

DECKER, GEORGE CLARE. Born May 5, 1900, in Menomonie, Wisconsin; B.S., Stout Institute, Menomonie, Wisconsin (1928) ; M.A., Ph.D., Ohio State University, Columbus (1932, 1942) ; secondary school teacher and supervisor in Kansas, California, and Ohio, 1921–35; teacher and supervisor in State colleges in North Dakota and New York, 1928–29, 1935–42; officer in United States Navy, 1942–46.

Dr. Decker joined the Office of Education on October 14, 1946, as a Regional Educational Officer with the Veterans Educational Facilities Program with headquarters at Fort Worth, Texas, and Atlanta, Georgia. On June 22, 1950, he came to Washington, D.C., as Program Representative, Housing for Institutions of Higher Education Programs. On October 23 of that year he was made Field Operations Advisor for school construction in the newly established program of School Assistance in Federally Affected Areas. On May 3, 1951, he was appointed Chief of the College Housing Loan Program, a position which he held throughout the remainder of the period.

(Sources: Kardex, Office of Education Personnel Office; Biographical Résumé prepared by Dr. Decker, February 24, 1956; U.S. Office of Education, *Educational Directory, 1950–51, et seq.*)

FLYNT, RALPH COMER MICHAEL. Born September 6, 1904, in Washington, Georgia; Mercer University, Macon, Georgia (1922–24); B.S., M.S., University of Virginia, Charlottesville (1928, 1931); M.A., Princeton University, New Jersey (1933); completed all but thesis for Ph.D. at Princeton; instructor and high school principal in Georgia public schools, 1925–26; instructor, Shenandoah Valley Academy, Winchester, Virginia, 1928–29; instructor in history, University of Virginia, 1929–31.

Mr. Flynt entered Federal Service on March 7, 1934, as a district educational advisor with the Civilian Conservation Corps in Anniston, Alabama. In August 1938, after serving in Columbus, Georgia, he came to the Office of Education in Washington, D.C. as Special Assistant to the Director of the CCC educational program. On April 20, 1942, he was made Corps Area Educational Advisor in Baltimore, Maryland. Two months later he returned to Washington as Senior Specialist in CCC camp education.

On August 24, 1942, Mr. Flynt began his service with the Division of Higher Education as a field representative of the Student War Loan Program. In May 1944 he was appointed a Senior Specialist in Higher Education serving as a consultant to State-wide groups of higher institutions in planning education of returning war veterans. On February 10, 1946, he was appointed Assistant Director of the Division of Central Services and in April 1948 he became Director and Executive Assistant to the Commissioner. On June 15, 1950, Mr. Flynt began serving as Director of the Division of Special Educational Services, and on May 11, 1951, Chief of Civilian Education Requirements Branch in the Office of the Assistant Commissioner.

Mr. Flynt returned to the Division of Higher Education when in October 1951 he was detailed as Associate Director. On

September 11, 1952, he was appointed Director of General and Liberal Education in the Division of Higher Education. He remained with the Division of Higher Education until 1958 when he became Director of the Laws and Legislation Branch under the Commissioner. Seven months later he was appointed to the rank of Assistant Commissioner.

In addition to being a Phi Beta Kappa Associate, Mr. Flynt has served as Chairman and Vice Chairman of the Atlantic Treaty Association, and Vice Chairman of the American Council on NATO.

(Sources: Biographical material loaned author by Mr. Flynt; Kardex, Office of Education Personnel Office; U.S. Office of Education, *Educational Directory, 1943–44, et seq.; Who's Who in America*, XXX, p. 932.)

FRAZIER, BENJAMIN WILLIAM. Born February 18, 1892, in Watauga Valley, Tennessee; A.B., University of Tennessee, Knoxville (1917); A.M., Columbia University, New York (1929); D. Ed., George Washington University, D.C. (1938); Principal of rural and junior high schools in Tennessee, 1910–15; high school teacher, Hartshorne, Oklahoma, 1917–18; U.S. Marine Corps, 1918–19; Superintendent of schools in Tennessee, 1919–21; Head of Department of Education and Director of Training, Alabama State Normal School, Jacksonville, Alabama, 1922–27.

Dr. (then Mr.) Frazier entered service with the Bureau of Education on June 16, 1927 as Specialist in Teacher Training. In 1930–31, during the interim period between the resignation of Dr. Klein and the appointment of Dr. Kelly, Dr. Frazier served as Acting Chief of the Division of College and Professional Schools (Division of Higher Education). He was Director of the University Research Project from 1935 to 1937. During his years of service, he prepared many articles and pamphlets on teacher training and teaching as a career.

Dr. Frazier died on September 15, 1948, while still in office with the Division of Higher Education.

(Sources: Personnel Folder, St. Louis Records Center; U.S. Office of Education, *Educational Directory, 1928, et seq.;* Cattell and Ross (ed.), *Leaders in Education* (Lancaster, Pa., 1948), p. 368; *Higher Education*, V, No. 9, January 1, 1949, p. 107.)

FREEMAN, OTIS WILLARD. Born April 13, 1889, in Otsego, Michigan; A.B., Albion College, Michigan (1910); M.S., University of Michigan, Ann Arbor (1913); Ph.D., Clark University, Worcester, Massachusetts (1929); teacher in high schools in Michigan, Montana, and California, 1910–23; Professor of Geography, San

Francisco State College, 1922–24; Head of the Department of Physical Sciences and Mathematics, and Professor of Geography, Eastern Washington College of Education, Cheney, Washington, 1924–47.

Dr. Freeman was appointed Specialist for Geography in the Division of Higher Education on January 5, 1948. He resigned on September 14, 1948, to become visiting Professor of Geography at the University of Hawaii and return to his position as Head of the Department of Physical Sciences and Mathematics at Eastern Washington College of Education. He served as President of that institution from 1951 until his retirement in 1953.

Dr. Freeman has published more than a hundred articles in geographical, scientific, and educational journals. He is the author of *The Pacific Northwest, Essentials of College Geography,* and *Economic Geography of Hawaii.*

(Sources: Personnel Folder, St. Louis Records Center; U.S. Office of Education, *Educational Directory, 1947–48, et seq.; Higher Education,* IV, 14, March 15, 1948, p. 161; *Ibid.,* VI, No. 5, November 1, 1959, p. 53; *Who's Who in America,* XXX, p. 967.)

GOLDTHORPE, JOHN HAROLD. Born in 1898, in Missoula, Montana; A.B., Hamline University, St. Paul, Minnesota (1920); M.A., Ph.D., University of Minnesota, Minneapolis (1923, 1928); teacher and superintendent, Minnesota, 1920–24; survey statistician, registrar and instructor, Northwestern University, Evanston, Illinois, 1924–26; teaching fellowship, University of Minnesota, 1926–28; Assistant Professor, Associate Professor, and Professor of Education, University of Rochester, New York, 1931–37; Field Studies Division, Teachers College, Columbia University, New York, 1937–39; Research Associate, American Council on Education, 1939–45; Administrative Analyst, Assistant Chief of Division of Exchange of Persons, Department of State, Washington, D.C., 1945–47.

Dr. Goldthorpe began his service with the Office of Education as a Specialist in Higher Education in 1947. The following year he entered a program for the exchange of teachers with foreign lands, returning to the Division of Higher Education in 1953.

Dr. Goldthorpe is the author of approximately 60 articles relating to higher education in various professional publications as well as five long studies of current higher education problems.

(Sources: Biographical Résumé prepared by professional staff of the Division of Higher Education; *Higher Education,* IV, 14, March 15, 1948, p. 157; Cattell and Ross (ed.), *Leaders in Education* (Lancaster, Pa., 1948), p. 405.)

GREENE, SAMUEL L. Born September 16, 1925; A.B., work on M.S. in progress, Indiana University, Bloomington (1950) ; U.S. Navy, 1943–46; Engineering Assistant to U.S. Department of Agriculture, Indiana, 1946–48; Head Resident Counselor, Indiana University, 1948–51.

Appointed March 13, 1951 as Research Assistant in the Division of Higher Education. Resigned August 28, 1951 to accept teaching position.

(Sources: Personnel Folder, St. Louis Records Center; Personnel Card File, Office of Education Personnel Office; U.S. Office of Education, *Educational Directory, 1950–51, et seq.*)

GREENLEAF, WALTER JAMES. Born March 23, 1889, in Norridgewock, Maine; A.B., Bowdoin College, Brunswick, Maine (1912) ; M.A., Princeton University, New Jersey (1918) ; Ph.D., George Washington University, D.C. (1922) ; additional study at Columbia University and Marine Biological Laboratory, Woods Hole, Massachusetts, Bailiff, U.S. Court, Portland, Maine, 1913; teacher of science in high schools in Maine and New Jersey, 1914–18; U.S. Army, 1918–19; supervisor of advisement and training, Veterans Bureau, 1919–24.

Dr. Greenleaf joined the Bureau of Education on July 16, 1924, as Associate Specialist in Land-Grant College Statistics. On January 1, 1931, he was appointed Specialist in Higher Education. He was transferred from the Division on September 5, 1947, when he was appointed Specialist for Educational and Occupational Information in the Vocational Education Division. Dr. Greenleaf remained with the Vocational Educational Division until his retirement on March 31, 1956. While in the Office of Education he published 19 guidance leaflets and more than two score articles in periodicals and reference volumes.

(Sources: Personnel Folder, St. Louis Records Center; Personnel Card File, Office of Education Personnel Office, U.S. Office of Education, *Educational Directory, 1925, et seq.;* Cattell and Ross (ed.), *Leaders in Education* (Lancaster, Pa., 1948), p. 422.)

GRIGSBY, RALL ILLINGSWORTH. Born November 22, 1897, in Greencastle, Indiana; A.B., Cornell College, Mount Vernon, Iowa (1918, 1949) ; A.M., Drake University, Des Moines, Iowa (1928) ; high school teacher in Illinois and Iowa, 1919–23; secondary school principal, Des Moines, Iowa, 1923–29; Assistant Superintendent of Schools, Des Moines, Iowa, 1929–39.

Mr. Grigsby entered on service with the Office of Education on May 1, 1939, as a technical consultant. On September 9, 1942 he was appointed Special Assistant to the Commissioner and on November 4, 1945, promoted to Assistant Commissioner. On May 5, 1947, he became Director of the Division of Auxiliary Services and on April 12, 1949, Deputy Commissioner. His direct relationship with the Division of Higher Education came in 1952 when he served as Acting Head between the resignation of Dr. Gallagher on August 1 and the appointment of Dr. Armstrong as Acting Head on September 15.

Dr. Grigsby was appointed Assistant Commissioner for School Assistance on March 17, 1954.

(Sources: Kardex, Office of Education Personnel Office; *Who's Who in America*, XXX, p. 1109; "Studebaker Resigns; Grigsby Acting Commissioner," *Higher Education*, V, No. 1, September 1, 1948, pp. 1–3.)

HAMILTON, FREDERIC RUTHERFORD. Born July 31, 1881, in Richland Center, Wisconsin; Ph.B., Ph.M., University of Wisconsin, Madison (1906, 1917); Ph.D., Columbia University, New York (1924); Superintendent of Schools in Wisconsin, 1901–12; Extension Division, University of Wisconsin, 1912–14; Director of Extension Division, University of Kansas, Lawrence, 1914–19; President of Marshall College, Huntington, West Virginia, 1919–23; Associate in Education, Columbia University, 1923–24; President of Bradley Polytechnic Institute, Peoria, Illinois, 1925–42.

Dr. Hamilton was appointed to the position of Principal Specialist in Higher Education on December 9, 1942. He served in a consultant capacity until May 31, 1943, when he resigned to return to full-time duty as President of Bradley Polytechnic Institute.

(Sources: U.S. Office of Education, *Educational Directory, 1942–43;* Personnel Folder, St. Louis Records Center; Cattell and Ross (Ed.), *Leaders in Education* (Lancaster, Pa., 1948), p. 444.)

HAWLEY, CLAUDE EDWARD. Born November 11, 1914, in Milwaukee, Wisconsin; A.B., Ph.D., University of Chicago, Illinois (1935, 1939); Research Assistant in Public Administration, University of Chicago, 1936–39; Instructor in Business and Public Administration, University of Missouri, Columbia, 1939–40; Assistant Professor, and Professor of Social Science, University of Florida, Gainesville, 1940–46; Professor of Political Science, Northwestern University, Evanston, Illinois, summers of 1946 and 1947; Associate Professor of Public Administration and Political Science, University of Southern California, Los Angeles, 1946–48; Field Secretary to the Mayor of Los Angeles, 1947–48; Army Officer during World War II, 1942–46.

Dr. Hawley joined the Division of Higher Education as Asso-

ciate Chief for Social Sciences in June 1948. He transferred to the
United States Information Agency as Deputy Director, Information Center Services, in September 1951.

Dr. Hawley is the author of approximately fifty articles relating
to social science and public administration. They have been published in a wide variety of scholarly journals and periodicals. With
Dr. John Russell, he wrote a long study of *Public Higher Education in Kentucky* in 1951.

(Sources: Biographical Résumé prepared by Dr. Hawley for the author,
November 6, 1959; U.S. Office of Education, *Educational Directory, 1949–50,
et seq.; Who's Who in American Education*, XVIII, p. 495.)

HIGSON, JOHN H. Born 1886 in England; studied at Sedbergh
College, Sedbergh, Yorkshire, England; received "Society of Arts
and Accountants Certificate" in England; Certified Public Accountant in the United States.

Mr. Higson was appointed Specialist in Charge of Land-Grant
College Statistics replacing Mr. Floyd B. Jenks on January 3,
1914. After investigating several Negro colleges in the Southern
States his appointment was terminated on March 15 of the same
year. Following his service with the Bureau of Education, Mr.
Higson did some accounting work in southern colleges (Tennessee,
Alabama, Mississippi, and Arkansas) with payment being made
by the institutions concerned.

(Sources: Letter, Higson to P. P. Claxton, December 22, 1913; Personnel
Folder, St. Louis Records Center; Claxton, P. P., *Statement . . . 1914*,
pp. 3–4.)

HOLLIS, ERNEST VICTOR. Born November 24, 1895, in Vardaman,
Mississippi; B.S., M.S. Mississippi State University, State College
(both in 1918) ; A.M., Ph.D. Columbia University, New York (1922,
1938) ; Honorary degrees from Shurtleff College, Alton, Illinois,
Bucknell University, Lewisburg, Pennsylvania, and Temple Uni-
versity, Philadelphia; teacher and principal in Mississippi, 1912–
15; instructor in botany, Mississippi State University, 1918–19;
President, Georgia State Teachers College, Statesboro, 1920–26;
Head, Education Department, State Teachers College, Morehead,
Kentucky, 1927–35; lecturer in education, College of the City of
New York, 1936–40; Coordinator, Commission on Teacher Educa-
tion, American Council on Education, Washington, D.C. 1940–44;
Visiting Professor, Columbia University, Duke University, and
Northwestern University, 1935–41.

Dr. Hollis joined the Office of Education as a Specialist in
Higher Education on January 26, 1944. On June 14, 1946, he was

made Specialist for State-wide Programs and on December 1, 1946, Chief of the Veterans' Educational Facilities Program. On June 13, 1948, Dr. Hollis became Associate Chief for Administration in the Division and on June 6, 1954, Chief for Administration. He was appointed Director of the College and University Administration Branch, Division of Higher Education, on January 18, 1957.

Prominent among the large number of publications by Dr. Hollis are *Philanthropic Foundations and Higher Education* (1938) ; *The College and Teacher Education* (1944), and *Social Work Education in the United States* (with Alice Taylor, 1951.)

(Sources: Biographical Résumé prepared by the professional staff of the Division of Higher Education; Kardex, Office of Education Personnel Office; U.S. Office of Education, *Educational Directory, 1943–44, et seq.; Who's Who in America*, XXX, p. 1312.)

IFFERT, ROBERT EARL. Born December 28, 1899 in Greenville, Pennsylvania; attended Slippery Rock State Normal School, Pennsylvania and Allegheny College, Meadville, Pennsylvania (1916–19, 1920–21) ; B.S., M.A., University of Pittsburgh, Pennsylvania (1922, 1927) ; Teacher and Principal, Pennsylvania high schools, 1919–25; Research Associate and Instructor in Educational Measurements and Statistics, University of Pittsburgh, 1925–33; Special Assistant to the Superintendent of Public Instruction, Harrisburg, Pennsylvania, 1933–36; Assistant Director, CCC–NYA study, American Youth Commission, American Council on Education, Washington, D.C.

Mr. Iffert entered Federal Service in 1941 as Special Representative for vocational training of war production workers. He joined the Division of Higher Education on January 26, 1946, as Resident Education Officer with the Veterans' Educational Facilities Program. On September 21, 1947, he was promoted to Assistant Chief of that program, and on October 11, 1953, to Specialist for Faculty and Facilities in the Division.

(Sources: Kardex, Office of Education Personnel Office; Biographical Résumé prepared by the professional staff of the Division of Higher Education; U.S. Office of Education, *Educational Director, 1947–48, et seq.;* Cattell and Ross (ed.), *Leaders in Education* (Lancaster, Pa., 1948), p. 540.)

JARACZ, WILLIAM A. Born September 2, 1916; Instructor in Marketing at the University of Pennsylvania, Philadelphia.

Jaracz joined the Division of Higher Education on May 21, 1951 as a Research Assistant on a temporary assignment to help with the inventory of physical facilities and human resources. On July 1, 1951, he was made an Educationist and on March 3 of the

following year he became a Statistician in Program Development
and Coordination. He remained with the Office of Education until
March 31, 1956, when he joined the staff of the National Science
Foundation.

(Sources: Personnel Card File, Office of Education Personnel Office;
*Higher Education*, VIII, No. 1, September 1, 1951, p. 10.)

JARVIS, CHESTER D. Born March 29, 1876, in London, Ontario,
Canada; B.S.A., Ontario Agricultural College, Guelph (1899);
Ph.D., Cornell University, Ithaca, New York (1908); Assistant
Horticulturalist, Ontario Agricultural College, 1899–1904; Horticulturalist, Storrs, Connecticut, Agricultural Experiment Station,
1906–13; Director, Connecticut Agricultural Extension Service,
1913–14.

Dr. Jarvis was appointed "Special Collaborator" in the Bureau
of Education on January 16, 1915. On October 8, 1917, he was
appointed Temporary Specialist in Agricultural Education. The
appointment was made permanent on April 22, 1918.

He resigned on March 31, 1921 following a leave of absence of
four months because of poor health and began farming in
Grimsby, Ontario, Canada.

(Sources: Personnel Folder, St. Louis Records Center; Ltr., Jarvis to
Claxton, October 24, 1914; U.S. Office of Education, *Educational Directory*,
*1918–19, et seq.*)

JENKS, FLOYD B. Born July 7, 1876, in Vermillion County, Indiana;
B.S. in Ag., Purdue University, Lafayette, Indiana (1898); manager of dairy farm in Nebraska, 1899; taught in Indiana,
1900–08; instructor in agricultural education, Massachusetts Agricultural College, 1908–10; Assistant Professor of Agricultural
Education, Massachusetts Agricultural College, 1910–11.

Appointed Specialist in Charge of Land-Grant College Statistics
on December 11, 1911. Resigned on August 31, 1913 to become
Professor of Agricultural Education, University of Vermont,
Burlington.

(Sources: Personnel Folder, St. Louis Records Center, Claxton, P. P.,
*Statement . . . 1914*, pp. 3–4.)

JOHN, WALTON COLCORD. Born January 30, 1881, in Ridott, Illinois;
A.B., Kenner Institute, Mexico City, Mexico; A.B., A.M., Ph.D.,
George Washington University, D.C.; Principal of private high
school in Dramante, Argentina, 1908–13; Assistant, Department
of Education, Seventh Day Adventist Church, 1915–18; Instructor
in Spanish, George Washington University, D.C., 1913–18.

Dr. John was appointed Specialist in Charge of Land-Grant College Statistics on March 11, 1918, replacing Benjamin F. Andrews. On February 12, 1921, he was promoted to the position of Specialist in Rural and Technical Education and on July 1, 1924, he was made Specialist in Higher Education. Dr. John was made Senior Specialist in Higher Education on December 1, 1931. He prepared most of the early reports on Howard University. He died in office on June 16, 1942.

(Sources: Personnel Folder, St. Louis Records Center, U.S. Office of Education, *Educational Directory, 1918–19, et seq.; Education for Victory,* I, No. 10, July 15, 1942, p. 2.)

JOHNSTON, MARJORIE CECIL. Born December 27, 1904, in Luray, Missouri; B.A., M.A., Ph.D., University of Texas, Austin (1927, 1931, 1939); additional study at the National University of Mexico, Mexico City, Radcliffe College, Cambridge, Massachusetts, and the University of New Mexico, Albuquerque; teacher of Spanish in Texas, 1927–37; critic teacher and demonstration teacher, University of Texas, 1935–41; instructor in Spanish, Stephens College, Missouri, 1940–42; Director of Foreign Languages and Professor of Spanish, American Institute for Foreign Languages, and Professor of Spanish, American Institute for Foreign Trade, Phoenix, Arizona, 1946–49.

Dr. Johnston began her career with the Office of Education in 1942 when she was a consultant in the teaching of Spanish in the Division of Inter-American Educational Relations. She left in 1946 to take the position in Phoenix, Arizona, noted above. She returned in 1950 as a Specialist in Latin American Education, Division of International Education. From May 2, 1951 to September 1952, Dr. Johnston served as Acting Chief, Comparative Education Branch, Division of Higher Education. In September she was transferred to the Division of International Education and in 1956 to the Division of State and Local School Systems.

Dr. Johnston has cooperated in writing or editing seven Spanish textbooks and has contributed essays to a large number of scholarly works and learned journals.

(Sources: Biographical Résumé prepared by Dr. Johnston for the author; U.S. Office of Education, *Educational Directory, 1950–51, et seq.; Who's Who of American Women,* I, p. 660.)

JUDD, CHARLES HUBBARD. Born February 20, 1873 in Bareilly, India; A.B., Wesleyan University, Connecticut, (1894); Ph.D., University of Leipzig, Germany, (1896); Instructor in Philosophy,

Wesleyan University, 1896–98; Professor of Psychology, New York University, 1898–1901; Professor of Psychology and Pedagogy, University of Cincinnati, Ohio, 1901–02; Instructor, Assistant Professor, Professor of Psychology and Director of Psychology Laboratory, Yale University, New Haven, Connecticut, 1902–09; Professor and Head of Department of Education and Director, School of Education, University of Chicago, Illinois, 1909–1938.

On July 1, 1913, Dr. Judd was appointed Specialist in Higher Education on a temporary basis. The appointment was to expire on August 31, but was extended to September 15, 1913. Following this brief period of service he returned to the University of Chicago but served as a "Special Collaborator" at $1.00 per year from January 15, 1914 to June 30, 1919. On at least two other occasions Dr. Judd served the Office. From November 4, 1929 to June 30, 1932, he was appointed an "Expert Consultant in Secondary Education without Salary" although paid travel expenses to prepare a report on the training of teachers for elementary and secondary schools in certain European countries. In 1940 he assisted as a Director in the educational program of the National Youth Administration.

Dr. Judd died July 18, 1946 in Santa Barbara, California.

(Sources: Claxton, P. P., *Statement . . . 1914*, pp. 3–4; Memo re appointment of Charles H. Judd from Claxton, January 14, 1914; Personnel Folder, St. Louis Records Center; "Forums, Correspondence," Alexandria Federal Records Center; *Who's Who in America*, XXIV, p. 1239.)

KALBACH, LEWIS A. Although never a member of the Division of Higher Education, Kalbach should be noted because of his early work in compiling information on colleges and universities.

He was born on December 12, 1866 in Hamburg, Pennsylvania. Following three years of education at the United States Naval Academy, Annapolis, Maryland, he was appointed a copyist in the Bureau on April 22, 1887. He gained attention early in his career with the Bureau when in 1888–89 he compiled the first complete table of courses of study from more than 100 colleges and universities of the country in classics, mathematics, astronomy, English, modern languages, philosophy, chemistry, physics, biology, geology, mineralogy, history, political economy, and "technics."

On May 16, 1907 Mr. Kalbach was appointed a Specialist in Charge of Land-Grant College Statistics. On July 1, 1909 he became Chief Clerk of the Bureau, a position which roughly corresponds to the present day position of Deputy Commissioner. Except for a period of approximately three years, September 1917 to July 1920, when he was Director of Statistics, Mr. Kalbach held the position of Chief Clerk until his retirement on December 1, 1935, after 48 years of distinguished service.

(Sources: Harris, W. T., *Report* . . . *1888–89*, p. lii; Dawson, N. T., *Report* . . . *1887–88*, p. 1120; Personnel Folder; St. Louis Records Center.)

KOON, KLINE MORGAN. Born January 30, 1894, in Shinnston, West Virginia; B.S., West Virginia University, Morgantown (1915); A.M., Teachers College, Columbia University, New York (1918); Ph.D., Ohio State University, Columbus (1931); Principal of high schools in West Virginia, 1920–28; Assistant Director of Ohio School of the Air, 1929–31.

Dr. Koon joined the Office of Education on September 8, 1931, as Senior Specialist in Education by Radio. He resigned on September 8, 1937. In his letter of resignation to Commissioner Studebaker he said, "in view of the fact that with the ever-increasing responsibilities and opportunities, I have been forced to work with more and more restrictions and handicaps, I do not feel that it will be mutually advantageous to continue in my present condition."

(Sources: Memo from Koon to Studebaker, May 22, 1937; Memo Sec. Ickes to Zook, March 2, 1934; Personnel Folder, St. Louis Records Center; U.S. Office of Education, *Educational Directory 1935, et seq.*)

LAYTON, ELIZABETH (PATTERSON). Born October 17, 1896, in Stockholm, Sweden and appointed to the Bureau of Education as a Clerk on July 18, 1918; remained in administrative work until May 2, 1948 when she was appointed a Research Assistant in the Division of Higher Education. Mrs. Layton retired with the rank of Research Assistant on July 30, 1954.

(Sources: Personnel Card File, Office of Education Personnel Office; U.S. Office of Education, *Education Directory, 1948–49, et seq.*)

LINDEGREN, ALINA MARIE. Born January 9, 1887, in Vasa, Finland; Diploma from State Normal School, Superior, Wisconsin; Ph.B., M.A., Ph.D., University of Wisconsin, Madison (1921, 1922, 1928); teacher in Superior, Wisconsin, 1906–20; professor, Oxford College for Women, Ohio, 1925–28; member of Department of History, Superior State Teachers College, Superior, Wisconsin, 1928–31.

Dr. Lindegren joined the Office of Education on November 2, 1931, as Specialist in European School Systems. Her service with the Division of Higher Education was quite brief lasting from February 9, 1951, when she transferred from the Division of

International Educational Relations, until July 15, 1952, when she transferred to the Division of International Education.

Dr. Lindegren died while in office on January 25, 1957, six days prior to her scheduled retirement.

(Sources: Personnel Folder, St. Louis Records Center; Personnel Card File, Office of Education Personnel Office; U.S. Office of Education, *Educational Director, 1950–51, et seq.;* Cattell and Ross (ed.), *Leaders in Education* (Lancaster, Pa., 1948), p. 649.)

LUND, JOHN. Born February 10, 1891, in Nordreland, Norway; A.B., Clark University, Worcester, Massachusetts (1913) ; M.A., Columbia University, New York (1914) ; Ph.D., Yale University, New Haven, Connecticut, (1938) ; instructor in Suffield School, Connecticut, 1914–15; principal, Lanier School, Eliot, Maine, 1915–17; high school teacher, Bridgeport, Connecticut, 1917–18; Superintendent of Schools in Connecticut, 1918–34; instructor and graduate student, New York University, 1934–35; lecturer and graduate student, Yale University, 1936–37; State Director of Connecticut Educational and Recreation Program of the W.P.A. with later service in the national program in Washington, 1937–39.

Dr. Lund joined the Office of Education as a Specialist in School Administration, Division of Higher Education, on March 16, 1940. He remained with the Division until August 24, 1943 when he entered military service. On July 1, 1946, he returned to the Office of Education as a Specialist for State School Administration but on September 2, 1946, he transferred to the War Department (Department of the Army). He returned to the Office of Education on July 1, 1947, and remained until April 1, 1951, when he joined the Institute of Inter-American Affairs. He was assigned to Mexico and remained there until March of 1956.

(Sources: Personnel Folder, St. Louis Records Center; Cattell and Ross (ed.), *Leaders in Education* (Lancaster, Pa., 1948), p. 670; U.S. Office of Education, *Educational Directory, 1941, et seq.*)

MACLEAN, GEORGE EDWIN. Born August 31, 1950, in Rockville, Connecticut; A.B., A.M., LL.D., Williams College, Williamstown, Massachusetts (1871, 1874, 1895) ; B.D., Yale University, New Haven (1874) ; Ph.D., University of Leipzig, Germany (1883) ; Presbyterian Minister, 1874–81; Professor of English Language and Literature, University of Minnesota, Minneapolis, 1883–95; Chancellor, University of Nebraska, Lincoln, 1895–99; President, State University of Iowa, Iowa City, 1899–1911.

Dr. MacLean was given a temporary appointment on May 2, 1913, following the resignation of Dr. Babcock. He was assigned the duty of visiting universities and colleges of Great Britain and Ireland. From 1914 through 1916 he studied institutions of higher education in those countries. Following this he was with the United States Educational Commission in the United Kingdom and served as Director of the British Division of the American University Union in Europe. He returned to the United States in 1923 and died in Washington, D.C. on May 5, 1938.

(Sources: Claxton, P. P., *Statement . . . 1913*, p. 5; Personnel Folder (Judd, Charles Hubbard), St. Louis Records Center; *Who Was Who in America*, I, p. 765.)

McCLINTOCK, JAMES E. Born 1881 or 1882, in Whigsville, Ohio; B.S., Ohio State University, Columbus (1906); teacher in Ohio, 1900–01; Deputy Inspector of Orchards and Nurseries in Ohio, 1904; Special Assistant in Bureau of Soils, Ohio Department of Agriculture, and Supervisor of the Department of Agricultural Extension, College of Agriculture, Orono, Maine, 1906–09.

On July 1, 1909, McClintock was appointed Specialist in Land-Grant College Statistics vice Kalbach. He entered on duty in August and spent a large part of his time travelling throughout the New England and Southern States visiting land-grant colleges. He resigned on March 31, 1910 to take a position with the International Correspondence Schools, Scranton, Pennsylvania.

(Sources: Brown, E. E., *Report . . . 1909*, p. 28; Personnel Folder, St. Louis Records Center.)

McNEELY, JOHN HAMILTON. Born May 19, 1882, in Evansville, Indiana; Culver Military Academy, Culver, Indiana (1899–1901); student at University of Virginia, Charlottesville (1901–03); M.A., George Washington University, D. C., and work on Ph.D.; Reporter, News Editor and Managing Editor, Evansville *Journal*, Indiana, 1903–17; U.S. Army, 1917–19; newspaper correspondent in Washington, D.C. 1920–22; Clerk in U.S. Post Office Department, 1922–23.

Mr. McNeely remained in the Federal Service after entering the Post Office Department in 1922. On March 5, 1923, he transferred to the Department of the Interior in a clerical position and entered into professional status through excellent publicity work. He was appointed Specialist in Higher Education on May 1, 1936, and remained in this position until his death in office on August 11, 1940.

(Sources: U.S. Office of Education, *Educational Directory, 1932, et seq.;* Personnel Folder, St. Louis Records Center.)

MARSHALL, KENDRIC NICHOLS. Born June 17, 1899, in Portsmouth, New Hampshire; B.A., Harvard University, Cambridge, Massachusetts (1921); M.A. and completion of course and residence requirements for Ph.D., Harvard University (1934–    ); graduate study at Institute of International Studies, Geneva, Switzerland and University of Paris, France (1926); history master, schools in Connecticut and Massachusetts, 1922–26; lecturer in Political Science, Lingman University, Canton, China, 1927–30; instructor in government and tutor in the Division of History, Government and Economics, Harvard University, Cambridge, Massachusetts, 1930–40; President of Chevy Chase Junior College, Washington, D.C., 1940–42.

Mr. Marshall began his service with the Office of Education on September 2, 1942 as Director of the Student War Loans Program, Division of Higher Education. In February 1945, he transferred to the United Nations Relief and Rehabilitation Administration as Assistant Chief, Far Eastern Division, and Chief, China Branch. He was in Shanghai, China, serving as Regional Director, UNRRA, from November 1945 to November 1946. On December 6, 1946, he rejoined the Office of Education as Chief, Near and Far Eastern Section, Division of International Educational Relations. In April 1947, Mr. Marshall was made Director of that Division. He resigned on April 6, 1951 to become Chief of the UNESCO Mission to Thailand, returning to the Office of Education as a Specialist in the Financial Aid Branch, Division of Higher Education, on October 9, 1958.

(Sources: Biographical Résumé loaned author by Mr. Marshall; Kardex, Office of Education Personnel Office; U.S. Office of Education, *Educational Directory, 1942–43, et seq.*)

MONAHAN, ARTHUR COLEMAN. Born March 24, 1877, in Framingham, Massachusetts; B.S., Massachusetts Agricultural College, Amhurst (1900); taught at the College and in public high schools, serving also as a high school principal in Massachusetts, 1900–1910.

On July 1, 1910, Mr. Monahan became Specialist in Rural and Agricultural Education in the Bureau of Education. He remained in the Bureau, serving with the Division of Higher Education, until January 8, 1918, when he left for service in the Army.

In 1921 he was relieved from duty with the rank of Major and he became Director of the Educational Bureau, National Catholic Welfare Council. He remained with the Council until 1932, serving as an editor and educational advisor. Following this he served with the United States Office of Indian Affairs and retired with residence in Washington, D.C.

(Source: *Who's Who in America*, XXII, p. 1570).

MOOR, RALPH CARL. Mr. Moor was born on December 18, 1912, and saw military service in the Second World War. He was appointed on October 1, 1951 as a Program Representative in the College Housing Loan Section, College and University Administration Branch, Division of Higher Education. He remained in this capacity until November 9, 1952, when he took a field position in Atlanta, Georgia, with the Division of Veterans Educational Services. A reduction in force in 1953 required him to leave Federal Service on April 3.

(Sources: Personnel Card File, Office of Education Personnel Office; U.S. Office of Education, *Educational Directory, 1951-52*.)

NELSON, JULIUS. Born August 15, 1910. At the time he was given a temporary assignment at the Office of Education he was an instructor in Business Education at the University of Baltimore, Maryland.

He joined the Office on May 21, 1951 as an Educationist with the Division of Higher Education to help with the Controlled Materials Plan of the National Production Authority as it affected institutions of higher education. On July 1, 1951, he was made a Research Assistant and on September 14 of that year he resigned to enter private industry.

(Sources: *Higher Education*, VIII, No. 1, September 1, 1951, p. 10; Personnel Card File, Office of Education Personnel Office.)

PATTERSON, JOHN CLARKE. Born March 25, 1894, in Montell, Texas; A.B., A.M., University of Texas, Austin (1921, 1928); Ph.D., Duke University, Durham, North Carolina (1930); U.S. Army Officer, 1917–19; Instructor in Walde High School, Texas, 1921–23; Commandant of Cadets, Schreener Institute, Kerrville, Texas, 1923–28; Professor of History and International Affairs, Westminster College, Fulton, Missouri, 1930–38; Director of Latin American Studies, The American University, Washington, D.C., 1938–39; Director of School of Public Affairs and Graduate School, The American University, 1939–40.

Dr. Patterson joined the Division of Higher Education on November 12, 1940 as a Senior Specialist. He remained with Higher Education until August 24, 1942, when he was made Chief, Branch of Inter-American Educational Relations, Division of International Educational Relations. He resigned on January 15,

1946 to become Consultant on Area and Language Studies, American Institute for Foreign Trade, Phoenix, Arizona. He later served as Dean of the Institute.

(Sources: U.S. Office of Education, *Educational Directory, 1941, et seq.;* Personnel Folder, St. Louis Records Center; *Who's Who in America,* XXVII, p. 1887.)

PHALAN, JOHN LAURENCE. Born August 28, 1907, in Boston, Massachusetts; A.B., Boston College, Newton, Massachusetts (1937) ; M.A., Ed.D., Harvard University, Cambridge, Massachusetts (1940, 1944) ; Ph.D., Boston University, Boston (1948) ; Instructor in Economics, Boston College, 1937–41; Field Inspector, Economist, Analyst, U.S. Department of Labor, Boston and New York, 1941–45; Regional Economist with Office of Price Administration and Office of Housing Expediter, Boston, 1945–47; Professor of Economics, Middlebury College, Vermont, 1947.

Dr. Phalan was appointed Specialist for Economics, Division of Higher Education, on December 15, 1947. He remained in Washington until January 5, 1950, when he took a position as Economist in the Boston Field Office of the Housing and Home Finance Agency of the Federal Government. He left Federal Service on June 30, 1953, because of a reduction in force.

(Sources: Personnel Folder, St. Louis Records Center; Personnel Card File, Office of Education Personnel Office; U.S. Office of Education, *Educational Directory, 1947–48, et seq.*)

POTTER, ANDREY ABRAHAM. Born August 5, 1882, in Vilna, Russia ; S.B., Massachusetts Institute of Technology, Boston (1903) ; D. Eng., Kansas State College, Manhattan (1925) ; D. Sc. Northeastern University, Boston, Massachusetts (1936) ; employed by General Electric Corporation, 1903–05, 1913; Assistant Professor, Professor, Dean, Kansas State College, 1905–20; appointed Dean of School of Engineering, Purdue University, Lafayette, Indiana, 1920.

Dr. Potter took leave of absence from Purdue University from mid-1940 through early 1945. During this period of time he was with the Engineering, Science and Management War Training Program, serving as first head ("Expert Consultant") of the Program, from July to November 1940, later as the Senior Advisor. After his services were no longer needed he returned to Purdue University.

(Sources: *Who's Who in Engineering,* 1954, p. 1918; Armsby, H. H., *Engineering and Management War Training—Final Report,* (Washington, 1946) pp. 10, 17.)

RATCLIFFE, ELLA BURGESS. Born September 2, 1876, in Doncaster, Maryland; entered Federal Service with the Civil Service Commission in August 1906; service with the Navy Department, Bureau of Plant Industry, and Department of Justice, 1908–10. Miss Ratcliffe joined the Bureau of Education as a Copyist on August 28, 1911. From then until her retirement in 1946 she remained with the Bureau and Office except for a brief period as Under-clerk with the Geological Survey in April and May of 1913. Nearly all of her service was with the Division of Higher Education, first as a Clerk and later as a Stenographer. In September 1930, Miss Ratcliffe was appointed to the position of Chief Educational Assistant, a sub-professional rating. She retired on September 30, 1946, as an Educationist.

(Sources: Personnel Folder, St. Louis Records Center; U.S. Office of Education, *Educational Directory, 1916–17, et seq.*)

REID, HELEN DWIGHT. Born November 7, 1901, in Glasgow, Scotland; A.B., Vassar College, Poughkeepsie, New York (1922); M.A., Ph.D., Radcliffe College, Cambridge, Massachusetts (1924, 1933); Instructor and Associate Professor of Government and Diplomatic History, University of Buffalo, New York, 1924–39; lecturer in Politics, Bryn Mawr College, Pennsylvania, 1940–44; Associate in International Education, American Association of University Women, Washington, D.C., 1944–47; visiting lecturer and professor at several institutions of higher education during short periods of time from 1938 through 1947.

Dr. Reid joined the Office of Education on December 1, 1947, as Chief, European Educational Relations Section, Division of International Educational Relations. When the Division of International Educational Relations was abolished in February 1951, she became Chief of Comparative Education in the Division of Higher Education. In June of the same year, Dr. Reid was redesignated as Chief for Education about International Affairs, Division of Higher Education, and on August 17, 1952, she became Specialist for Political Science in the Division. She was reassigned as Assistant to the Chief of the Division of International Education on December 21, 1952. On March 29, 1954, Dr. Reid left the Office of Education to take an overseas assignment with the Foreign Operations Administration.

Dr. Reid has contributed sections and chapters to several books on foreign affairs and diplomacy. She has also contributed to a large number of learned journals and served as Chairman of the Board of Editors of *World Affairs* as well as a member of several other committees dealing with international relations and higher education.

(Sources: Personnel Card File, Office of Education Personnel Office; Biographical Résumé supplied author by Educational Office, ICA; U.S. Office of Education, *Educational Directory, 1950–51, et seq.;* *Who's Who in America,* XXX, p. 2287.)

RORK, JOHN BIEHL. Born February 17, 1905, in Albany, New York; B.S., M.B.A., University of Denver, Colorado (1932, 1957) ; Accountant, University of Denver, 1932–37; Accountant, Colorado-Utah Coal Company, Denver, Colorado, 1937; Chief ·Accountant, Purchasing Agent, Assistant Business Manager, Assistant to the Treasurer, University of Denver, 1937–51.

Mr. Rork joined the Office of Education on July 23, 1951, as a Consultant, Division of Civilian Education Requirements. On November 17, 1952, he was assigned to the College Housing Program, Division of Higher Education, as a Program Representative. He returned briefly to the University of Denver as Assistant Business Manager, April-October 1953, returning to the College Housing Program on October 21 of that year. In 1957 he was appointed Specialist for College and University Facilities and the following year became Specialist for Campus Planning.

Most of Mr. Rork's articles and publications have been in the fields of cost and financing, and planning of physical plants.

(Sources: Kardex, Office of Education Personnel Office; Biographical Résumé prepared by professional staff of the Division of Higher Education; U.S. Office of Education, *Educational Directory, 1952–53, et seq.*)

SANDERS, JENNINGS BRYAN. Born March 18, 1901, in Martin County, Indiana; A.B., Franklin College, Indiana (1933) ; A.M., Ph.D., University of Chicago, Illinois (1925, 1928) ; member of history staff at University of Chicago; taught history at Denison University, Granville, Ohio, and University of Alabama, University (suburb of Tuscaloosa), Alabama, 1926–35; Professor of History and Head of Department of History, University of Tennessee, Knoxville, 1935–43; President of Memphis State College (now Memphis State University), Tennessee, 1943–46; Visiting Professor, University of Washington, Seattle, Washington, 1946–47.

Dr. Sanders was appointed Specialist for History in the Division of Higher Education on January 5, 1948. He remained with the Division of Higher Education, devoting his attention largely to education in history and the other social sciences until his resignation on April 10, 1959, to engage in independent research and writing.

In addition to numerous articles on history and history teaching, Dr. Sanders wrote a textbook on Colonial America, *Early American History, 1492–1789* (1938), an essay on John Fiske for the memorial volume, *Jernegan Essays on American Historiography* (1937), and two volumes on the administration and activities of the American Continental Congress.

(Sources: Information supplied the author by Dr. Sanders, October 13, 1959; Personnel Card File, Office of Education Personnel Office; U.S. Office of Education, *Educational Directory, 1947–48, et seq.;* Cattell (ed), *Directory of American Scholars* (New York, 1957), p 654.)

SASSANI, ABUL H. K. Born September 6, 1906, in Tabriz, Iran; B.S., M.S., University of Idaho, Moscow (1937) ; Ph.D., University of Missouri, Columbia (1940) ; additional graduate study at University of Chicago, Illinois, and University of Minnesota, Minneapolis; lecturer on life and culture of the countries of the Near East, 1940–42; Examiner and Consultant, U.S. Office of Censorship, New York City, 1942–43; Occupational Analyst, War Manpower Commission, 1943–44; Training Editor, Reports Officer, and Consultant on various assignments with the War Department and Department of the Army, 1945–48.

Dr. Sassani joined the Office of Education on February 2, 1948, as a Specialist in Near and Far Eastern Education in the Division of International Educational Relations. When the Division of International Educational Relations was abolished in February 1951, Dr. Sassani, with the other members of the Division, was transferred to the Division of Higher Education. He served as the head of Near Far East and Africa Branch. When the Division of International Education was established in 1952, Dr. Sassani was transferred to it.

(Sources: Memo from Abul Sassani to author, October 22, 1959; U.S. Office of Education, *Educational Directory, 1950–51, et seq.*)

SEATON, ROY ANDREW. Born April 17, 1884, in Glasco, Kansas; B.S., M.S., Kansas State College, Manhattan (1904, 1910) ; S.B. in M.E., Massachusetts Institute of Technology, Cambridge (1911) ; Sc.D., Northeastern University, Boston, Massachusetts (1942) ; Instructor and Assistant Professor of Mathematics, Kansas State College, 1904–06; Instructor and Assistant Professor of Mechanical Engineering, Kansas State College, 1906–10; Professor of Applied Mechanics and Machine Design, Kansas State College, 1910–20; Dean of School of Engineering and Architecture and Director of the Engineering Experiment Station, Kansas State College, 1920–49.

Dean Seaton joined the Division of Higher Education in 1940 replacing Dean Potter as Director of the Engineering, Science, and Management War Training Program on November 25, 1940.

He was succeeded in the position of Director by Dean George W. Case on June 24, 1942.

Dean Seaton returned to Kansas State College. He was made Dean Emeritus in 1949.

(Sources: *Who's Who in Engineering*, 1954, p. 2151; Armsby, H. H. *Engineering, Science, and Management War Training—Final Report* (Washington, 1946), pp. 17–18.)

THOMAS, JOHN TREVOR. Born June 29, 1913, in Nottingham, England; B.Sc. and additional work at University of South Dakota, Vermillion (1939); book store manager, University of Omaha, Nebraska, 1940–41; World War II service as an officer, 1941–45; Assistant Business Manager, University of Omaha, 1946–47; Business Manager, South Dakota School of Mines and Technology, Rapid City, 1947–51.

Mr. Thomas served as a contract employee advising for the Civilian Education Requirements Program from April 27 to June 30, 1951. On July 2, 1951, he was appointed Civilian Education Requirements Officer and on September 22, 1952, Assistant Director of Liaison, Division of Civilian Education Requirements. He resigned April 24, 1953, to return to his position with the South Dakota School of Mines and Technology.

(Sources: Personnel Card File, Office of Education Personnel Office; Personnel Folder, St. Louis Records Center; U.S. Office of Education, *Educational Directory, 1950–51, et seq.*)

THOMPSON, GRANVILLE KEITH. Born November 21, 1920; A.A., Graceland College, Lamoni, Iowa (1940); M.B.A., University of Chicago, Illinois (1942); U.S. Army, 1942–45; additional study at University of Chicago, 1946–47; Office Manager, Division of Roentgenology, University of Chicago, 1945–47; Business Manager, Graceland College, 1947–51.

Appointed Specialist for Business Management, Division of Higher Education on July 2, 1951. Resigned on February 11, 1955 to take a position with the New York management firm of Cresap, McCormick, and Paget.

(Sources: Personnel Card File, Office of Education Personnel Office; Personnel Folder, St. Louis Records Center; U.S. Office of Education, *Educational Directory, 1950–51, et seq.*)

UPDEGRAFF, HARLAN. Born 1874 in Sigourney, Iowa; Ph.B., Cornell College, Mount Vernon, Iowa (1894); A.M., Ph.D., Columbia University, New York (1898, 1908); LL.D., Syracuse University, New York (1926); taught in public schools in Iowa and Baltimore, and at Columbia University to 1907.

Dr. Updegraff joined the Bureau of Education as Chief of the Alaska Division in 1907. In 1910 he became Chief of the Division of School Administration, a position which he held for two years. Dr. Updegraff was never a member of the Division of Higher Education but he served as an adviser and promoter of higher educational activity in the Bureau prior to establishment of that Division.

Following his service with the Bureau, Dr. Updegraff was associated with several institutions of higher education including Northwestern University, Evanston, Illinois, the University of Pennsylvania, Philadelphia, Cornell University, and the University of California, Berkeley. He served as President of Cornell College from 1923 to 1927. Dr. Updegraff died on April 14, 1953.

(Source: *Who's Who in America*, XXVIII, p. 2720.)

UPTON, FREDERICK E. Mr. Upton, from New Jersey, entered the Bureau of Education on January 3, 1886. He became the Specialist in Charge of Land-Grant College Statistics on July 1, 1902. He remained in this work until May 9, 1907. His successor in land-grant college statistical work was Lewis Kalbach.

On February 12, 1910, Mr. Upton was promoted to the position of Editor with the Bureau but he was forced to resign on April 9 of the same year because of poor health.

(Sources: U.S. Office of Education, *Commissioner of Education . . . Annual Statements, 1887–1907* (Brown, E. E., *Statement for 1906–07*, p. 39); Personnel Folder, St. Louis Records Center.)

VAN DYKE, GEORGE E. Born November 4, 1896, in Knoxville, Arkansas; B.S., M.S., University of Illinois, Urbana (1926, 1928); graduate work at University of Chicago, Illinois (1929–32) and Northwestern University, Evanston, Illinois (1934–35); Technical Secretary, American Council on Education, Washington, D.C., 1935–36; Secretary and Treasurer, Case School of Applied Science, Cleveland, Ohio, 1936–41; Treasurer, Syracuse University, New York, 1941–49.

Mr. Van Dyke was appointed Specialist for Business Management, Division of Higher Education, on April 1, 1949. This was his second period of service with the Office having served as Junior Specialist in Secondary School Administration from July 25, 1930 to June 30, 1932. He remained with the Division of Higher Education until June 18, 1951, giving as his reason "Insufficient salary on present position. Acceptance of better-paying position."

(Sources: Personnel Folder, St. Louis Records Center; Personnel Card File, Office of Education Personnel Office; U.S. Office of Education, *Educational Directory, 1948–49, et seq.*)

VAN ZWOLL, JAMES ADRIAN. Born November 15, 1909, in Rochester, New York; A.B., Calvin College and Seminary, Grand Rapids, Michigan (1933); A.M., Ph.D., University of Michigan, Ann Arbor (1937, 1942), secondary school teacher, Michigan, 1934–38; Administrative Intern, Board of Education, Detroit, Michigan, 1940–41; Assistant Superintendent of Schools, Port Huron, Michigan, 1942–43; U.S. Navy, 1943–46; Lecturer, General School Administration, University of Michigan, 1946–47; Assistant Professor, State University of Iowa, Iowa City, 1947–48; appointed Professor, University of Maryland, College Park, 1948.

Dr. Van Zwoll was appointed Consultant to assist in analyzing and interpreting applications for college housing loans on July 5, 1951. He completed his service on July 31 and on September 4 he was appointed Civilian Education Requirements Officer in the School Housing Section of the Division of State and Local School Systems. He returned to the University of Maryland on September 12, 1952. Since that time he has twice served as a Consultant to the College Housing Loan Program; May–June 1953, and May–December 1957.

(Sources: *Higher Education*, VIII, No. 1, September 1, 1951, p. 10; Cattell and Ross (ed.), *Leaders in Education* (Lancaster, Pa., 1948), p. 1097; Personnel Card File, Office of Education Personnel Office.)

WATSON, BERNARD BENNETT. Born May 17, 1911, in Philadelphia, Pennsylvania; A.B., Temple University, Philadelphia (1932); Ph.D., California Institute of Technology, Pasadena (1935); graduate study at Wharton School, University of Pennsylvania, Philadelphia (1940); Instructor, Assistant Professor, Associate Professor of Physics, Arizona State College, Tempe, 1935–41; Assistant Physicist, National Bureau of Standards, Washington, D.C., 1941; Assistant Professor of Physics, University of Pennsylvania, 1941–47; Senior Research Fellow in Physics, California Institute of Technology, 1947–48; Associate Professor of Physics, Temple University, 1948–49.

Dr. Watson was appointed Specialist for Physics, Division of Higher Education, on July 1, 1949. He remained with the Division until February 10, 1952. At that time he transferred to the Defense Manpower Administration as a Scientific and Professional Manpower Specialist in Washington. He left Federal Service on June 30, 1953 to become Operations Analyst and Group Chairman, Operations Research Office, The Johns Hopkins University, Baltimore, Maryland.

Dr. Watson has written several articles on physics. He is the author of a textbook, *Problems in College Physics*, and co-author of *Randal Morgan Laboratory Notes*, Series III.

(Sources: Personnel Folder, St. Louis Records Center, Personnel Card File, Office of Education Personnel Office; U.S. Office of Education, *Educational Directory, 1949–50, et seq.;* Ltr. Dr. Watson to author dtd. November 19, 1959.)

WILKINS, THERESA BIRCH. Born November 24, 1906; B.A., Fisk University, Nashville, Tennessee (1927); M.A., Columbia University, New York (1939); graduate study at University of Chicago, Illinois, Columbia University, and the United States Department of Agriculture Graduate School, Washington, D.C.; Registrar, Fisk University, 1927–30; Registrar, Dillard University, New Orleans, Louisiana, 1935–44; Registrar, Hampton Institute, Virginia, 1947–48.

Mrs. Wilkins had served as a Research Assistant in Negro Education with the Office of Education from 1930 to 1933. She served in the Division of Higher Education in a clerical position from July 1944 to September 1946, resigning to study at Columbia University. On March 1, 1948, she returned to the Office as a Research Assistant in the Division. From then on she continued her service with the Division, devoting her attention largely to the preparation of the *Educational Directory, Part 3: Higher Education,* an annual publication, and *Accredited Higher Institutions,* a quadrennial publication.

(Sources: Kardex, Office of Education Personnel Office; Memo from Theresa Wilkins to author, October 15, 1959; U.S. Office of Education, *Educational Directory, 1947–48, et seq.*)

WILSON, ROBERT JAMES. Born February 13, 1906, in Sharpsburg, Pennsylvania; A.B., Westminster College, Fulton, Missouri (1929); M.A., Ed.D., Teachers College, Columbia University, New York (1941, 1952); Instructor, Hammond High School, Indiana, 1931–42, military service, 1942–45; Purdue University Teachers Institute, Lafayette, Indiana, 1945–47; Instructor, Brooklyn Polytechnic Institute, New York, 1949–50.

Mr. Wilson joined the Division of Higher Education on May 28, 1951, shortly before completing his doctorate at Columbia. He was appointed as an Educationist to assist with the Controlled Materials Plan of the National Production Authority as it affected institutions of Higher Education. On July 1, 1951, he was made a Research Assistant and on November 1 of that year a Project Analyst in the Division of Civilian Educational Requirements. He resigned on December 20, 1952, to accept a position with the Department of the Navy. He was appointed Training Officer, Bureau of Yards and Docks, in the Department of the Navy.

(Sources: *Higher Education,* VIII, No. 1, September 1, 1951, p. 10; Personnel Card File, Office of Education Personnel Office; *Who's Who in American Education*, XVIII, p. 1239.)

WOOD, WILLIAM RANSOM. Born February 3, 1907, in Morgan County, Illinois; A.B., Illinois College, Jacksonville, Illinois (1927) ; M.A., University of Illinois, Urbana (1928) ; Ph.D., State University of Iowa, Iowa City (1939) ; Secondary school teacher and coach, Wakefield High School, Michigan, 1929–35; First Assistant in English, State University of Iowa, 1935–39; Chairman of English Department in Evanston, Illinois, High School, 1939–43; Officer in U.S. Navy, 1943–46; Assistant Superintendent and Director of Community College, Evanston Township High School and Community College, 1946–50.

Dr. Wood was appointed on February 1, 1950 to the position of Specialist for Junior Colleges and Lower Divisions, Division of Higher Education. He remained in this position until March 26, 1954, except for a brief period of service from January to March 1953, as Program Planning Officer. Dr. Wood resigned in 1954 to become Dean of Statewide Development of Higher Education and Professor of English, University of Nevada, Reno.

Dr. Wood's writings include several textbooks in English instruction and approximately 100 professional articles in educational journals.

(Sources: Personnel Folder, St. Louis Records Center; Personnel Card File, Office of Education Personnel Office; U.S. Office of Education, *Educational Directory, 1949–50, et seq.; Who's Who in America*, XXX, p. 3043.)

# The Suppressed Babcock Report
# and
# Commissioner Claxton's Explanation

A CLASSIFICATION
OF UNIVERSITIES AND COLLEGES
WITH REFERENCE
TO BACHELOR'S DEGREES

*By* KENDRIC CHARLES BABCOCK
*Specialist in Higher Education*
*Bureau of Education*

WASHINGTON
GOVERNMENT PRINTING OFFICE
1911

213

## *Classification of Universities and Colleges*
## *with Reference to Bachelor's Degrees*

The classification of universities and colleges presented in this circular is the result of an attempt to estimate the work and status of a large group of institutions whose graduates in considerable numbers have sought admission to graduate schools and to professional schools requiring either a bachelor's degree or some part of an undergraduate course for admission to regular standing. No effort has been made to include all of the institutions listed as colleges by the Bureau of Education nor should it be assumed that this classification represents a final judgment of the bureau relative to the institutions named. The preparation of this tentative classification was undertaken at the urgent suggestion of the deans of graduate schools at their meeting held in connection with the meeting of the Association of American Universities at Charlottesville, Va., in November, 1910. The circular is sent out at this time semi-confidentially for their use, in the hope that the frank and thorough-going criticisms by those who may make use of its lists will materially assist the Bureau of Education in its preparation of a classified list of a large number of institutions for regular publication, within the next year or two years, within which time the Division of Higher Education should have arrived at a reasonable, well-informed, and definite judgment.

The basis for the judgment expressed in this classification and in the one proposed is not merely a study of catalogues, registers, reports, and statistical statements of the institutions concerned. Information and opinions from widely different sources have been sought and used. The Specialist in Higher Education during the past six months made personal visits to nearly all of the large institutions having graduate schools; he has studied their practice in dealing with applicants holding degrees from other institutions, both before and after admission to graduate status; he has conferred with deans, presidents, and committees on graduate study; and he has inspected the credentials and records of several thousands of graduate students taking courses during the last five years, in order to ascertain how such students stood the test of transplanting. In several cases the deans placed at the disposal of the specialist their own classified lists of institutions. Some of these lists were merely the accumulations of rulings of various officers of varying standards running over many years; others, as in the case of the University of Chicago, represented a recent attempt at rating the worth of degrees from colleges having students in the particular graduate school concerned.

The institutions thus visited were: Johns Hopkins University, University of Pennsylvania, Bryn Mawr College, Princeton University, Columbia University, New York University, Vassar College, Yale University, Harvard University, Cornell University, University of Michigan, University of Chicago, Northwestern University, University of Wisconsin, University of Illinois, Indiana University, and Ohio State University. On visits to State universities special endeavor was made to ascertain their practice in dealing with undergraduates entering the State university from the other colleges and universities in their respective States, as well as with the graduates of these contributing institutions.

Special mention should also be made of helpful interviews with the officials of the Carnegie Foundation for the Advancement of Teaching, and of the General Education Board; with the first assistant commissioner of education of New York State, who is charged with oversight of colleges, professional and technical schools; with similar State education officers of Illinois, Virginia, North Carolina, and South Carolina; and with the heads of several agencies for teachers who have supplied members of faculties to the small institutions and have dealt with large numbers of graduates desiring positions as teachers.

The rating of institutions in this classification is based upon the course which might be followed by the ambitious student proceeding under normal conditions: (1) An earnest student of good ability and health who has complied with the requirements for a bachelor's degree in a standard college (one requiring the usual four years of high school work, or at least 14 units, for admission, and four years of well-distributed college work for graduation, in charge of a competent faculty of not less than six persons giving their whole time to college work). (2) Whose work includes a solid foundation for the courses which he desires to take for the advanced degree. (3) Who enters upon graduate work within a year or two after taking his bachelor's degree, without intervening special study and without such advantages as might arise from teaching subjects of a special nature in high school or college, thereby making up in some part deficiencies in his college preparation for graduate work. Since many of the smaller colleges do their soundest and most efficient work in classical lines, the names of several such institutions are placed in Class II, but with the limitation that this recognition of their work is confined to students trained in the particular line of study mentioned in the parenthesis, as A, for the traditional classical or distinctively arts course.

It is of course assumed that the line of study pursued for the higher degree is closely allied to the work done as an undergraduate, and not widely divergent as would be the case if a graduate from the classical course desired to take a masters' degree in forestry.

## Class I

Institutions whose graduates would ordinarily be able to take the master's degree at any of the large graduate schools in one year after receiving the bachelor's degree, without necessarily doing more than the amount of work regularly prescribed for such higher degree.

## Class II

Institutions whose graduates would probably require for the master's degree in one of the strong graduate schools somewhat more than one year's regular graduate work. This would mean a differential which might be represented by one or two extra year-courses, by one or more summer school sessions, or by a fourth or fifth quarter. In accordance with the practice of some graduate schools a brilliant student with a brilliant record from the strong institutions in this class (those marked *) might be admitted probationally to regular candidacy, and if he gives satisfactory evidence of his ability to do the prescribed work during the first term or semester he might be given an individual rerating in the middle of the year and granted the higher degree on the completion of the regular minimum amount of work.

## Class III

Institutions whose standards of admission and graduation are so low, or so uncertain, or so loosely administered, as to make the requirement of two years for the master's degree probable. The alternative for this requirement of two years might be one year in undergraduate status, terminating with a bachelor's degree, and a second year in regular candidacy for a higher degree with the ordinary amount of work. The older private institutions, such as Harvard University and Yale University, usually prefer not to give their bachelor's degree after a single year in residence.

## Class IV

Institutions whose bachelor's degree would be approximately two years short of equivalency with the standard bachelor's degree of a standard college as described above. It should be said in connection with this class that the information upon which to base judgment of individual institutions is less sufficient and satisfactory, and in larger proportion drawn from catalogues, than is the case for the other classes, since a relatively smaller proportion of the graduates of institutions in this class appears in the registration in graduate and professional schools. Presumably a much larger number of institutions will appear in this class when work upon the classification of colleges and universities has further progressed. Many of these institutions make the claim that certain of their graduates have taken the master's degree in one year at some one of the great graduate schools, but in practically all such cases the original deficiency has been measurably supplied by summer schools, teaching, field work, or practical experience extending over several years.

*Classification of Universities and Colleges With Reference to Bachelor's Degrees*

| Class I | Class II | Class III | Class IV |
|---|---|---|---|
| Amherst College. | Adelphi College.<br>Agnes Scott College.<br>Alabama, University of.<br>Albion College.<br>Alfred University.<br>Allegheny College.<br>Alma College (A).<br>Arizona, University of (engineering).<br>*Armour Institute (engineering).<br>Augustana College (A). | Adrian College.<br>Albright College.<br>Amity College.<br>Antioch College.<br>Arkansas, University of. | Alabama Polytechnic Institute.<br>Ashland College.<br>Atlanta University.<br>Atlanta Baptist College. |
| Barnard College.<br>Beloit College.<br>Bowdoin College.<br>Brown University. | *Baker University.<br>*Bates College.<br>Baylor University.<br>Bethany College (Kansas). | Baldwin University.<br>Bellevue College (Omaha).<br>Berea College.<br>Bethany College (West Virginia). | |
| Bryn Mawr College. | *Boston College.<br>*Boston University.<br>Brooklyn Polytechnic Institute.<br>*Bucknell University.<br>Buchtel College (science).<br>Butler College. | Blackburn College.<br>Bridgewater College. | |

*Classification of Universities and Colleges With Reference to Bachelor's Degrees—continued*

| Class I | Class II | Class III | Class IV |
|---|---|---|---|
| California, University of. Catholic University of America. Chicago, University of. Colgate University. Colorado, University of. Columbia University. Cornell University. | Carleton College (Minnesota). *Case School of Applied Science (engineering). Colorado Agricultural College (science and engineering). Central College (A) (Missouri). Central University of Iowa (?). Central University (Kentucky). *Cincinnati, University of. Clark College (Massachusetts). Coe College. Colby College. *Colorado College. Colorado School of Mines (mining engineering). *Cornell College. | Carroll College. Carthage College. Chattanooga, University of. Charles City College. Charleston, College of. Converse College. Cotner University. | Campbell College. Carson and Newman College. Cedarville College. Citadel (South Carolina Military College). Clemson Agricultural College. Cox College. Cumberland University. |
| Dartmouth College. | Davidson College (A). *Denison University. Denver, University of. *De Pauw University. Des Moines College. Detroit University (A). *Dickinson College. Doane College. *Drake University. *Drury College. | Dakota Wesleyan University. Delaware College. | Defiance College. |

*Classification of Universities and Colleges With Reference to Bachelor's Degrees—continued*

| Class I | Class II | Class III | Class IV |
|---|---|---|---|
| | Earlham College (A).<br>Elmira College.<br>Emory College (A).<br>Emporia College (A). | Elon College.<br>Emory and Henry College.<br>Eureka College.<br>Ewing College. | Franklin College (Ohio). |
| | Fairmont College.<br>Fargo College.<br>Franklin College (A) (Indiana).<br>Franklin and Marshall College (A). | Findlay College.<br>Fisk University.<br>Florida, University of.<br>Florida State College for Women. | |
| Goucher College.<br>Grinnell College. | George Washington University.<br>Georgetown College (A).<br>Georgetown University (A).<br>Georgia, University of.<br>Gustavus Adolphus College (A). | German Wallace College.<br>Grand Island College.<br>Greenville College.<br>Guilford College. | Georgia School of Technology.<br>Greensboro Female College. |
| Hamilton College.<br>Harvard University.<br>Harverford College. | Hamline University.<br>Hanover College (A).<br>Hillsdale College (A).<br>Hobard College (A).<br>*Hope College (A).<br>*Holy Cross College. | Hampden-Sidney College.<br>Heidelberg University.<br>Hendrix College.<br>Highland Park College.<br>Hiram College.<br>Howard University. | Hardin College.<br>Hedding College. |
| Illinois, University of.<br>Indiana University.<br>Iowa, State University of. | Idaho, University of.<br>Illinois College (A).<br>Iowa State College (science-recent degrees).<br>Iowa State Teachers College. | Illinois Wesleyan University.<br>Iowa Wesleyan University. | |

*Classification of Universities and Colleges With Reference to Bachelor's Degrees—continued*

| Class I | Class II | Class III | Class IV |
|---|---|---|---|
| Johns Hopkins University. | James Millikin University. | Juniata College. | |
| Kansas, University of. | Kalamazoo College (A). | Kingfisher College. | Kansas State Agricultural College. |
| Knox College. | Kentucky, State University of. | | |
| | Kenyon College (A). | | |
| Lafayette College. | Lake Erie College (A). | Leander Clark College. | |
| Leland Stanford, Jr., University. | Lawrence College. | Lebanon University. | |
| Lake Forest College. | Lebanon Valley College (A). | Louisiana State University. | |
| Lehigh University. | Lewis Institute (engineering). | Loyola College. | |
| | Lombard University (A). | | |
| | Luther College (A). | | |
| Massachusetts Institute of Technology. | Macalester College. | McKendree College. | Maryland Agricultural College. |
| Michigan, University of. | *Maine, University of. | McMinnville College. | Mississippi Agricultural and Mechanical College. |
| Minnesota, University of. | Manhattan College. | McPherson College. | Mississippi College. |
| Missouri, University of. | Marietta College. | Marquette University. | Michigan College of Mines. |
| Mount Holyoke College. | *Massachusetts Agricultural College (science). | Maryville College (Tennessee). | Milligan College. |
| | *Miami University. | Mercer University. | |
| | *Middlebury College. | Meredith College. | |
| | Mills College (A) (recent degrees). | Michigan Agricultural College (science). | |
| | Missouri Valley College (A). | Millsaps College. | |
| | *Monmouth College (A) (recent degrees). | Milwaukee-Downer College. | |
| | Montana, University of. | Mooreshill College. | |
| | Morningside College. | Mt. Union College (A). | |
| | Muhlenberg College (A). | Muskingum College (A). | |

*Classification of Universities and Colleges With Reference to Bachelor's Degrees—continued*

| Class I | Class II | Class III | Class IV |
|---------|----------|-----------|----------|
| Nebraska, University of. | Nevada, University of (science and mining engineering). | Nebraska Wesleyan University. | New Mexico School of Mines. |
| Northwestern University (Illinois). | New Hampshire College of Agriculture and Mechanic Arts. | New Mexico, University of. | North Carolina Agricultural and Mechanical College. |
| | New Mexico Agricultural and Mechanical College (science). | North Dakota Agricultural College. | Northwestern University (Wisconsin). |
| | *New York, College of the City of. | Northwestern College (Illinois). | |
| | New York, Normal College of the City of (degrees since 1905). | | |
| | New York State Normal College (degrees since 1905). | | |
| | *New York University. | | |
| | *North Carolina, University of. | | |
| | *North Dakota, University of. | | |
| | Notre Dame, University of. | | |
| Oberlin College. | Occidental College | Ohio Northern University (degrees since 1910). | Oregon State Agricultural College. |
| Ohio State University | Ohio University. | Ottawa University. | Oklahoma Agricultural and Mechanical College. |
| | *Ohio Wesleyan University. | Ouachita College. | |
| | Olivet College (A). | | |
| | Oklahoma, University of. | | |
| | Oregon, University of. | | |
| | Otterbein University. | | |
| Pennsylvania, University of. | Penn College (A). | Pacific, College of the. | Pennsylvania Military College. |
| Princeton University. | Park College. | | |

*Classification of Universities and Colleges With Reference to Bachelor's Degrees—continued*

| Class I | Class II | Class III | Class IV |
|---|---|---|---|
| Purdue University (science and engineering). | *Parsons College.<br>Pennsylvania College (A).<br>Pennsylvania State College (science and engineering).<br>Pittsburg, University of (recent degrees).<br>*Pomona College. | | |
| Radcliffe College.<br>Rensselaer Polytechnic Institute (civil engineering). | Randolph-Macon College.<br>Randolph-Macon Woman's College.<br>*Richmond College (A).<br>Ripon College.<br>*Roanoke College (A).<br>Rockford College.<br>*Rochester, University of.<br>*Rose Polytechnic Institute (engineering).<br>*Rutgers College. | Rhode Island College of Agriculture and Mechanic Arts. | |
| Smith College.<br>Stevens Institute of Technology (mechanical engineering). | St. John's College (A). (Maryland).<br>St. Lawrence University.<br>St. Olaf College (A).<br>Sheffield Scientific School.<br>*South, University of the (A).<br>Southern California, University of (A). | Shurtleff College.<br>Simpson College.<br>South Carolina, University of.<br>South Dakota State College of Agriculture and Mechanic Arts.<br>Southwestern College (Kansas). | Scio College.<br>South Carolina Military College (Citadel). |

Classification of Universities and Colleges With Reference to Bachelor's Degrees—continued

| Class I | Class II | Class III | Class IV |
|---|---|---|---|
| Texas, University of. | South Dakota, University of. | Susquehanna University. | |
| Tufts College. | Southwestern University. | | |
| | Stetson (John B.) University. | | |
| | *Swarthmore College. | | |
| | *Syracuse University. | | |
| | Tarkio College (A). | Tabor College. | Texas Agricultural and Mechanical College. |
| | Temple University (A) (recent degrees). | Texas Christian University. | Tri-State College. |
| | Tennessee, University of. | | |
| | Trinity College (Connecticut). | | |
| | Trinity College (North Carolina) (recent degrees). | | |
| | Trinity University. | | |
| | Tulane University. | | |
| | *Union University. | Union College (Nebraska) | Union Christian College. |
| | Ursinus College (A). | Upper Iowa University. | Utah, Agricultural College of. |
| | Utah, University of. | | |
| Vermont, University of. | | Valparaiso University. | Vincennes University. |
| Vanderbilt University. | | | Virginia Polytechnic Institute. |
| Vassar College. | | | |
| Virginia, University of. | | | |
| Washington, University of. | *Wabash College. | Wesleyan University of West Virginia. | Wartburg College. |
| Washington University. | Wake Forest College (recent degrees). | Westminster College (Pennsylvania). | Waynesburg College. |
| Wellesley College. | Washburn College. | | Wilmington College (Ohio). |
| Wesleyan University. | | | |

*Classification of Universities and Colleges With Reference to Bachelor's Degrees—continued*

| Class I | Class II | Class III | Class IV |
|---|---|---|---|
| Western Reserve University | Washington and Jefferson College (A). | Wheaton College. | |
| Williams College. | Washington and Lee University (A). | Whitworth College. | |
| Wisconsin, University of. | Wells College. | Wittenberg College | |
| | Western Maryland College. | | |
| | Western College for Women. | | |
| | West Virginia, University of. | | |
| | Whitman College. | | |
| | *William Jewell College. | | |
| | Wilson College. | | |
| | Willamette University (A). | | |
| | Wofford College. | | |
| | *Wooster, University of. | | |
| | *Worcester Polytechnic Institute (science and engineering). | | |
| | Wyoming, University of. | | |
| Yale University (except Sheffield Scientific School). | Yankton College. | | |

UNITED STATES BUREAU OF EDUCATION

SPECIAL PUBLICATION_____WHOLE NUMBER 501

# AN EXPLANATORY STATEMENT

## In Regard To

# "A Classification of Universities and Colleges With Reference to Bachelor's Degrees"

*By*

P. P. CLAXTON
*Commissioner of Education*

WASHINGTON
1912

*An Explanatory Statement in Regard to*
*"A Classification of Universities and Colleges*
*with Reference to Bachelor's Degrees."*

According to returns made to the United States Bureau of Education for the year 1910–11, there were in that year in the universities and technological schools of this country 10,858 students doing graduate work. Of these, 8,369, or 77 percent, were enrolled in 25 institutions, and 9 other institutions enrolled 539, or 5 percent of the total. Thus 82 percent of all the graduate students in the country were enrolled in 34 institutions, and only 18 percent in the remaining 568 institutions reporting to this bureau. The number of graduate students is rapidly increasing. And since the cost of equipment and teaching force for effective graduate work is comparatively very great, the concentration of work of this kind in a few of the richer institutions will doubtless increase rapidly from year to year. In the same year several thousand other students were enrolled in the professional schools whose standards of admission require the bachelor's degree from a standard college, or the completion of some definite portion of the work required for graduation in the same. These thousands of graduate students and students with advanced standing in academic and professional schools come from four or five hundred colleges, old and new, large and small, public and private, rich and poor, in all parts of the country and with standards varying as widely as the conditions under which they work and the needs of the people they serve.

The deans and other responsible officers of the graduate and professional schools naturally wish to deal justly with the large numbers of students applying annually for admission, and at the same time to maintain their own standards. But, from the very nature of the case, they can not examine students applying for admission as a child is examined for admission to a grade in an elementary school, nor can any one officer hope to know accurately the character of work done in each of the hundred or more colleges and schools from which men and women come seeking admission as graduate students to work for advanced academic or professional degrees. The few colleges from which students come to his institution in considerable numbers several years in succession he may soon know sufficiently well to enable him to evaluate their work with some degree of accuracy and to deal with their graduates intelligently and for the best interest both of the students and of the institution which he represents and for the maintenance of whose standards he is responsible. For an evaluation of the work of other colleges from which students come intermittently and in small numbers, he must depend on officers in schools to which more of their graduate students go, or on the judgment of disinterested persons more or less intimately acquainted with their work and standards. To the extent that such judgment is affected by the personal equation or is based on superficial or inadequate knowledge, it must of course be unsatisfactory. For these and other reasons, the deans of most of the larger graduate and professional schools have for several years held annual conferences, largely for the purpose of comparing notes and trying to arrive at some just conclusion as to the status to be given graduates of each of the several colleges from which graduate students come to their institutions in any considerable numbers.

Anyone at all familiar with this problem must understand its importance, and it is easy to see that important economies of colleges and of graduate and professional schools alike, as well as vital interests of the students, depend on its solution. For any adequate solution there is need of some accurate information in regard to the equipment, work, and standards of the colleges, just as the colleges themselves desire, need, and obtain information in regard to the equipment, work, and standards of the high schools and preparatory schools from which they draw their students.

At the conference of deans of the larger graduate and professional schools held at the University of Virginia in 1910 this question came up for special consideration, and it was decided to undertake to collect such definite information about all colleges sending considerable numbers of students on for advanced work as would enable the responsible officers of the graduate and professional schools to deal intelligently and justly with their students and at the same time protect themselves against the false representations sometimes made by students in regard to standing offered them in other graduate and professional schools.

Two methods of arriving at the desired results were possible: To appoint a committee of their own number to undertake the work, or to obtain the services of some competent and disinterested outside persons or agency. The first course was open to the objection that the judgment of any committee composed of deans or other officers of graduate and professional schools might be suspected of being influenced too much by the experiences and practices of the particular institutions from which they might be chosen. An appeal was therefore made to the United States Bureau of Education to undertake this work, in the belief that it could be done here more accurately and more acceptably than anywhere else. Dr. Brown, at that time Commissioner of Education, recognized the magnitude and difficulty of the task, but he also foresaw the good results that must come from having it well done. Therefore, after careful consideration, he agreed to have the work done by this bureau and assigned it to Dr. Kendric C. Babcock, who had recently come to the bureau as specialist in higher education. It was easily apparent that this work would require much time, skill, and patience, and that it must reach even a tentative conclusion through several stages following upon one another at rather long intervals. It was hoped, however, that the work might be allowed to proceed without undue exploitation of the earlier and necessarily imperfect results.

The enormous task of visiting and examining all the colleges concerned was clearly out of question. It could not be done in any reasonable time. Evidently, therefore, the first step was to find as nearly as possible the common or average practice of the graduate and professional schools in dealing with students coming from each of the more important colleges and to correct this by a careful study of the experiences of each of the larger graduate and professional schools with students coming from colleges within its own particular sphere and of whose work and standards its officers might well be supposed to have more accurate knowledge than the officers of other institutions could have. Each large graduate or professional school has such a sphere, which includes a larger or smaller group of colleges the majority of whose students desiring to do advanced work come to it. Its officers therefore are soon possessed of knowledge about these colleges which can not fail to be helpful to the officers of all other graduate or professional schools at which any of the students of these colleges seek admission.

By finding and making known to each of the graduate and professional schools the average practice of all, and to all the more intelligent practice of each in regard to the students of colleges in its own immediate and particular sphere, it was hoped that at least the most obvious errors in dealing with advanced and graduate students might be eliminated. This Dr. Babcock undertook to do. He visited as many of the graduate and professional schools as he could, consulted their deans and other responsible officers and examined their records of students. The information thus gained he supplemented by consulting the executive officers of all or most of the large educational boards in regard to the institutions of learning best known to them, by conference with State officers and by interviews with presidents and deans of State universities as to their experience with graduate students coming to them from other colleges in their respective States.

Reliance was also placed upon the somewhat full and accurate information which this bureau has of the colleges in all parts of the country, some of which have made marked improvement in standards and work so recently that these improvements have not yet been fully recognized even by the graduate and professional schools with which they have the closest relations. With a later stage of the work in mind, Dr. Babcock visited as many colleges as he could conveniently in connection with the performance of other duties, but none of these was examined with the purpose of making a personal and final evaluation of its work as a whole.

After 10 months of careful investigation of the kind above indicated, Dr. Babcock made a tentative grouping of 344 colleges, only a little more than half the number reporting to this bureau, but a much larger proportion of those sending graduates on for advanced work. The list was confessedly incomplete and the grouping only tentative.

"Institutions whose graduates would," according to his findings, "ordinarily be able to take the master's degree at any of the large graduate schools in one year after receiving the bachelor's degree, without necessarily doing more than the amount of work regularly prescribed for such higher degree," were listed in the first group, which contained the names of 59 colleges.

"Institutions whose graduates would probably require for the master's degree in one of the strong graduate schools somewhat more than one year's regular graduate work * * * a differential which might be represented by one or two extra year courses, by one or more summer school sessions, or by a fourth or fifth quarter" were placed in the second group, which contained the names of 161 colleges. "In accordance with the practice of some graduate schools" Dr. Babcock found "a brilliant student with a brilliant record from the strong institutions in this class might be admitted probationally to regular candidacy, and if he gave satisfactory evidence of his ability to do the prescribed work during the first term or semester he might be given an individual rerating in the middle of the year and be granted the higher degree on the completion of the regular minimum amount of work." The colleges in this list to which this practice seemed to apply were starred. Of these there were 44. This gives a total of 103 colleges whose better students may, according to this finding, hope to make the master's degree in one year without doing more than the usual amount of work, and leaves 117 whose students must to obtain this degree expect to do something more than the minimum amount of work required.

"Institutions whose standards of admission and graduation are so low, or so uncertain, or so loosely administered as to make the requirement of two years for the master's degree probable" were placed in the third class, which contained the names of 84 colleges.

"Institutions whose bachelor's degree would be approximately two years short of equivalency of the standard bachelor's degree of a standard college" were placed in the fourth group, which contained the names of 40 colleges. A "standard college" was interpreted as being "one requiring the usual four years of high-school work or at least 14 units for admission and four years of well-distributed college work for graduation, in charge of a competent faculty of not less than six persons giving their whole time to college work."

"The rating of institutions in this classification is based upon the course which might be followed by an ambitious student proceeding under normal conditions: (1) An earnest student of good ability and health who has complied with the requirements for a bachelor's degree in a standard college. (2) Whose work includes a solid foundation for the courses which he desires to take for the advanced degree. (3) Who enters upon graduate work within a year or two after taking his bachelor's degree without intervening special study and without such advantages as might arise from teaching subjects of a special nature in high school or college, thereby making up in some part deficiencies in his college preparation for graduate work."

It is "assumed that the line of study pursued for the higher degree is closely allied to the work done as an undergraduate and not widely divergent, as would be the case for a graduate from a classical course desiring to take a master's degree in forestry" or civil engineering.

The tentative grouping made on this basis Dr. Babcock submitted to me for my inspection and approval. It seemed to be as accurate as could be made without the careful criticism of the officers of the graduate and professional schools on whose judgment and practice it was largely based. Since it would be easier for them to review it if presented in the form of a printed pamphlet rather than on multigraph sheets, as was at first suggested, I requested that it be printed and treated as a proof sheet until it might be revised in the light of their criticism. This was done, and 200 copies were delivered to the Bureau of Education, practically all of which were sent to the deans of the larger graduate and professional schools in the hope that their "frank and thorough-going criticism" might assist the bureau in its preparation of a larger and more correct list later. Through an oversight the pamphlet was not marked "Proof—Confidential" as it should have been, and before the error was discovered the superintendent of documents had received copies of it for distribution to the depository libraries and for sale. This explains why the pamphlet does not have any serial number on it, nor any statement that it is a document of the United States Bureau of Education. The Bureau of Education does nothing which it wishes to conceal, but its work, like any other work, can not fairly be considered as complete when it has only been begun, and even a cursory reading of this tentative statement could not fail to reveal the fact that it was not intended for general publication, and that any such use of it was not expected.

It seems also to have been unfortunate that the groups of colleges referred to above were designated as "Class 1," "Class 2," "Class 3," and "Class 4," and that the word "classification" appeared on the title-page, since these facts have given offense to some who have doubtlessly not read the full and specific statement that the classification is "with reference to bachelor's degrees" only, on the basis, and for the purpose, and from the information set forth above, and only tentative.

No attempt was made to classify colleges on the basis of their worth and merits as educational institutions founded and maintained to serve their constituencies according to their needs and conditions, nor did it have any intention of announcing "a judgment day for our colleges," or doing anything more than that which is clearly stated above. I know many colleges listed in the second, third, or fourth group which are serving their constituencies much better than they could if, in disregard of needs, conditions, and demands, they should raise their requirements for admission and graduation so as to put them into a higher group of this classification, made on the narrow basis of the rating of their bachelor's degrees as recorded at the graduate and professional schools. Neither can the place of any institution in this tentative group be legitimately used for advertising purposes unless accompanied by a clear statement of the purpose, method, and basis of the grouping and the statement that it is only tentative and confessedly imperfect.

What further has been done? What is the further intention of the Bureau of Education in this work? Briefly, as follows:

The generous criticisms and continued investigations of a year have indicated the desirability of making the grouping in a somewhat different form and the change of about a dozen colleges to another group from that in which they were first placed. A revision of the original statement embodying these changes has been made and the galley proofs of it have been sent to the officers of the graduate and professional schools for further criticism.

When these have been returned a revised statement, which will then show as clearly as possible, not the independent judgment of the Bureau of Education or of any of its employees, but mainly the practice of the graduate and professional schools in dealing with students holding the bachelor's degree from any of the several colleges listed and presenting themselves for professional or advanced work, will be issued as a confidential proof sheet and sent to the officers of the graduate and professional schools for such assistance as it can give them in this still imperfect and tentative stage, and to the presidents of the colleges listed for their information as to how these colleges are rated at the graduate and professional schools to which their students go for advanced work, and also for the frank criticism of these presidents and of the members of the faculties of their colleges. To have sent to these presidents or to the public press the first tentative statement before it could be corrected so as to show more accurately the practice of the graduate and professional schools would have been premature and unfair to graduate schools and colleges alike.

No doubt it will be discovered, when this revised statement comes into the hands of the presidents of the colleges listed in it, that the work and standards of many of them have not been correctly evaluated, and that there has been danger, at least, that their graduates would not be given the exact amount of credit they should receive when presenting themselves for advanced work. That there has been such danger is well known, and this knowledge constituted the principal reason for undertaking this difficult and important task.

Upon request from the proper authorities of any college which seems to be rated too low or too high, the bureau will gladly undertake an examination of equipment, requirements, standards, and work and assist in any other way it can toward having the rating corrected, and it will issue new revisions of these proof sheets as often as may seem desirable. The number of men in the bureau who can give their time to this work is not sufficient to carry it forward as rapidly as we and all concerned would like, but possibly a way may be found by which competent assistance may be had, and no great harm can come from a reasonable delay if those interested will only take the trouble to inform themselves fully as to the nature and purpose of the work and then give such assistance as they can in carrying it forward. A delay of a few months, or a few years even, in the accomplishment of a task of this kind and magnitude is not so important as that it may finally be done honestly, faithfully, and intelligently.

There can be little doubt, on the other hand, that some colleges will find they have defects of which they have not been aware.

The frank, but unbiased, criticism from the outside, which should be welcomed by all educational institutions, may reveal defects and weaknesses in equipment, requirements for admission, standards of graduation, organization, and teaching not realized by those charged with their government and conduct. Many of these will ask, as some have already done, that the bureau send some competent person to examine them thoroughly in the light of his broader knowledge of similar institutions in all parts of the country, point out frankly their particular defects, and offer such advice as he can for their improvement. The bureau will always respond to such a request to the extent of its ability, or perhaps expert and disinterested advice may be obtained from other sources. In this way many colleges may easily be brought up to the desired standard, which their officers and supporters, in the fullness of love and zeal, supposed they had already attained.

Some colleges will say, no doubt, as they should, that they are less concerned about the standing of their few graduates who go elsewhere for advanced work than about meeting the obligations placed upon them by the needs of the people they serve or the educational conditions of the States or sections in which they are located. They will rightly choose rather to serve the purposes for which they were founded and are maintained, with low standards of admission and graduation, than to prove recreant to their trust by attempting to raise these standards prematurely. They will either ask to be removed from the list because of their disregard of all standards or to be retained because of their honest desire to have their standards and purposes known as they are.

Finally, it will be possible to publish to the world a statement of the standing of colleges in respect to the value of their bachelor's degrees, which will for the time be approximately complete and correct. No such statement can ever be final. It will need careful revision from year to year as new colleges come into existence and old ones go out of existence or change their standards through growth or decay. Such revision will, however, not be so difficult after an approximately correct statement of the standing of existing colleges has once been made.

Why should the Bureau of Education have undertaken this task, and having begun it, why continue it? What adequate results are to be expected? These questions have been partially answered already.

For one thing, when the work has been completed to the extent indicated above, or to a lesser degree even, there will no longer be the danger which now exists of unjust treatment of students from one college applying for admission for graduate or advanced work in another. It must be recognized and admitted that some of this danger arises from the natural tendency to overestimate the work of old, large, and wealthy institutions as compared with that of those which are younger, smaller, or less wealthy. Only a few days ago I was told of a student who, having received a bachelor's degree from a college well known and much honored in its section, applied for admission as a graduate student working for the master's degree in a university in another section, with the expectation of being able to do the work required in one year, or in two at most. This student, however, was informed that before she could be admitted to graduate work she would have to do two years' work for the bachelor's degree of that institution. I know both of these institutions and believe the average graduate of the first should be admitted to higher standing at the second than was granted this young woman, and that its standard and work are higher and better than the authorities of the second institution seem to think. If they are not, then the authorities of the first institution, its faculty and students, the people who support it, and the State it serves should know it.

Many colleges whose standards are low and whose work is not so good as it might be will, when they have become conscious of their defects, take delight in remedying them, and their supporters will find equal pleasure in providing the necessary funds to enable them to do better work and to attain the standards to which they, in their affection and pride, imagined they had already attained. With this raising of standards of the colleges there will come a general improvement in all the schools from which they draw students and the possibility of a better and a more thorough work in all the universities and professional schools to which they send their graduates.

Sooner or later, let us hope soon, colleges whose equipment, endowment, income, purpose, or constituency will not permit them to do more than two years of college work will frankly acknowledge it, deal honestly with themselves, their students, and the people who contribute to their support, cease to give for two years of college work degrees that are generally understood to be given only as a reward of four years of such work, or to spend unwisely the larger part of their income on a very few students in the higher classes to the neglect of much larger numbers in the lower classes, face their conditions and tasks frankly and do thoroughly and well the work they can and should do without undue temptation to deceive themselves, their students, those who contribute to their support, or the general public.

It will, I believe, also be possible, without increasing the danger of a deadening, mechanical uniformity, to so standardize the work of all our colleges that a year's work in any course at any college will mean practically the same as a year's work in the same course at any other college, and that students may go from one to another freely, receiving full credit for work done and without loss of time and progress. Such interchange of students is very desirable and for many reasons must become more general than it has been in the past.

Finally, more accurate information in regard to our colleges will be accessible to foreigners, and a more just rating of them by foreign universities to which our students go will be possible, both of which ends are to be desired, especially by the smaller colleges whose size and wealth are not such as to attract foreign attention but whose work may nevertheless be of the highest type.

These last three results are not to be hoped for immediately, nor do I believe they were foreseen clearly enough to be counted as reasons for the beginning of this work which the Bureau of Education has undertaken. But that they may grow out of it, if the bureau can have for its completion the hearty cooperation of college men which it should have, seems quite possible. That it will have such cooperation when the nature and purpose of the work are fully understood, I firmly believe, for college men are honest, unselfish, and reasonable. It is their mission to find and teach the truth and their profession to do whatever they can for the good of all the people and for the sound advancement of the institutions by which the people are served. More than others they know that things are as they are and that no profit can come from any kind of deception, either of self or of others, that freedom comes from knowing the truth, and profit from its fearless and unselfish application.

The Bureau of Education has no selfish interest in this or any other work. It desires only to serve wisely and effectively. Having undertaken this task with a more or less full realization of its magnitude and difficulty and some understanding of its importance, it believes it would be open to the just accusation of recreancy to duty if it did not carry it forward faithfully toward completion. By doing this it seems quite certain it may fulfill a part of the high function for which it was established, viz, "for the purpose of collecting such statistics and facts as shall show the condition and progress of education in the several States and Territories, and of diffusing such information * * * as shall aid the people of the United States in the establishment and maintenance of efficient schools and school systems and otherwise promote the cause of education throughout the country."

P. P. CLAXTON,
*Commissioner.*

# A List of Publications of the Office of Education Relating to the Field of Higher Education

This list has been compiled from official lists prepared by the United States Office of Education and has been checked by the author for relationship and relevancy to higher education. It provides a clue as to the major interests of the Office of Education in the field of higher education from 1867 to 1953.

The list has been divided into two sections. The first lists publications prepared by, or sponsored and supervised by, the Office of Education prior to the establishment of the position of a specialist in higher education. The second lists publications after the establishment of that position. Within each section publications are listed by type.

The following general observations should be made concerning this list:

1. The *Annual Reports* and *Statements* of the Commissioner of Education usually contained a large amount of material relating to the condition of higher education in the United States. These are listed for that reason. In addition, many *Annual Reports* had appendices or chapters relating to special topics in higher education. These are listed in detail. Chapters dealing with statistics only (such as those found in the *Annual Reports* from 1888–89 through 1917) are not listed.

2. Separate statistical summaries on higher education are listed. The *Biennial Survey of Education* which first appeared in 1921 (Bulletin, 1919, No. 88) covering the years 1916–18 has several chapters relating to higher education statistics. These are not listed separately, nor are statistical chapters in the *Annual Report*.

3. Starting in 1912 a separate publication entitled *Educational*

*Directory* made an annual appearance. Prior to that time a short directory usually formed a part of the *Annual Report.* From 1912 to 1930 a directory of facts about institutions of higher education was a chapter of the *Directory.* In 1931 that portion relating to higher education became Part II of the *Directory;* two years later it became Part III. It was still published separately as Part III in 1953. This was one of the most important publications of the Office relating to higher education containing a wealth of information about institutions. It was prepared by the Division of Higher Education but is not listed separately since it was an annual recurring publication.

4. Studies and surveys of foreign education are not listed unless they relate entirely to higher education.

5. Capitalization and punctuation of titles are as shown in official lists prepared by the Office of Education.

6. The figure following the title is either the year of publication or the number of the publication if in a numbered series; i.e. (Bulletin) 1906, No. 2.


## Publications Prior to 1911

ANNUAL REPORTS OF THE COMMISSIONER OF EDUCATION
>    *Note:* The introductory remarks of the Commissioner of Education usually contained some summary information on higher education. Exact titles of the *Annual Reports* vary from year to year. See Bibliography for detailed publication data.

1867–68 (Henry Barnard)
1870 (John Eaton) Appendices 13 "Medical education in the United States;" 14 "Normal Schools;" and 16 "An American University."
1871 (John Eaton) Appendices 4 "National schools of science" (D.C. Gilman) ; and 11 "Cooper Union" (D. O'C. Townley).
1872 (John Eaton)
1873 (John Eaton)
1874 (John Eaton)
1875 (John Eaton)
1876 (John Eaton)
1877 (John Eaton)
1878 (John Eaton)
1879 (John Eaton)
1880 (John Eaton)
1881 (John Eaton)

1882–83 (John Eaton)

1883–84 (John Eaton)

1884–85 (John Eaton)

1885–86 (Nathaniel Dawson) Appendices 3 "Training of Teachers;" 6 "Superior and Professional Instruction;" 11 "The promotion of higher political education" (Herbert B. Adams); and 12 "University extension in England" (Herbert B. Adams).

1886–87 (Nathaniel Dawson) Appendices 6 "Training of Teachers;" 9 "Superior instruction;" 10 "Professional instruction;" 11 "Degrees conferred;" 13 "Business colleges; nurses' training schools;" and 21 "Papers on educational subjects . . . Medical colleges and the medical profession" (Charles Warren).

1887–88 (Nathaniel Dawson) Appendices 9 "The Training of teachers;" 11 "Superior instruction;" 12 "Professional instruction;" 13 "Degrees conferred;" 16 "Commercial and business colleges; nurses' training schools;" and 20 "Papers on educational subjects . . . Higher education in the Northwest territory" (G. W. Knight).

1888–89 (William T. Harris) First *Annual Report* to be issued in two volumes.

Volume I: Chapter II "The inception and the progress of the American normal-school curriculum to 1880;" Chapter 13 "Professional work in the normal schools of the United States;" Chapter 21A "The university of the future" (R. G. Moulton); and Chapter 21B "Fellowships in colleges and universities."

(Volume II, establishing a precedent which was to last until the *Annual Report for 1918,* consisted largely of statistical tables relating to all levels of education. Starting in 1919 the compilation of statistics was made a separate publication and began appearing biannually. It was designated as the *Biennial Survey of Education.*)

1889–90 (William T. Harris)

Volume I: Chapter 17 "Foreign universities."

Volume II: Chapter 4 "Higher education of women;" Chapter 5 "Colleges and universities of the United States;" Chapter 6 "Length of college curriculum;" Chapter 7 "Graduate departments of universities;" Chapter 8 "University and school extension;" Chapter 9 "Comparative diagrams illustrating the statistics of professional education during the decade 1880–90" (Wellford Addis); and Chapter 10 "Curricula of professional schools" (Wellford Addis).

1890–91 (William T. Harris)
>    Volume I: Chapter 13 "Legal education in the United States;" Chapter 14 "Legal education in Europe;" Chapter 15 "Legal education in Canada, Australia, Spanish America, Japan, and China;" Chapter 16 "Bibliography of legal education" (Wellford Addis); and Chapter 17 "Colleges of agriculture and the mechanic arts" (R. H. Alvey).
>
>    Volume II: Chapter 22 "Higher education;" Chapter 23 "Professional instruction;" and Chapter 31 "Facilities in experimental psychology in the colleges of the United States" (W. O. Krohn).

1891–92 (William T. Harris)
>    Volume I: Chapter 6 "Training of teachers in Germany, Austria, and Switzerland" (L.R. Klemm); and Chapter 10 "German universities" (W. Lexis).
>
>    Volume II: Chapter 19 "Universities and colleges;" Chapter 20 "Colleges for women;" Chapter 21 "The place of university extension in American education" (W. T. Harris); Chapter 22 "The relation of the independent colleges to the system of state schools;" Chapter 23 "Rensselaer polytechnic institute" (P. C. Ricketts); Chapter 24 "The United States military academy at West Point" (E. S. Holden); and Chapter 29 "The history of summer schools in the United States" (W. W. Willoughby).

1892–93 (William T. Harris)
>    Volume I, Part II: Chapter 5 "Medical instruction in the United States as presented by French specialists;" Chapter 7 "American technological schools" (A. Riedler); and Chapter 8 "Higher education of women in Russia" (Serge Wolkonsky).
>
>    Volume II: Chapter 5 "Pecuniary aid for students in universities and colleges;" Chapter 6 "University extension;" and Chapter 7 "Medical education" (A. E. Miller).

1893–94 (William T. Harris)
>    on training of teachers."
>
>    Volume II: Chapter 1 "Colleges of agriculture and the mechanic arts;" Chapter 2 "Forestry education" (C. W. Parks); Chapter 3 "Geology in the colleges and universities of the United States" (T. C. Hopkins); Chapter 6 "University extension;" and Chapter 7 "Professional education" (A. E. Miller).

1894–95 (William T. Harris)
>    Volume I: Chapter 15 "Higher education in Russia, Austria

and Prussian Poland" (Hermann Schoenfeld) ; Chapter 17 "Facilities for the university education of women in England" (Martha F. Crow): and Chapter 21 "Coeducation; compulsory attendance; American students in foreign universities; continuation and industrial schools."

Volume II: Chapter 25 "Admission to college by certificate;" Chapter 26 "Technological instruction in the land-grant colleges" (Wellford Addis) ; Chapter 27 "Instruction in sociology in institutions of learning" (Daniel Fulcomer) ; Chapter 28 "Professional Education" (A. E. Miller) ; and Chapter 29 "Medical schools of the United States" (Marcel Baudouin).

1895–96 (William T. Harris)

Volume II: Chapter 22 "Higher and secondary education in the United States" (Gabriel Compayre) ; Chapter 27 "Colleges endowed by Congress for the benefit of agriculture and the mechanic arts" (Wellford Addis) ; and Chapter 32 "Foreign universities."

1896–97 (William T. Harris)

Volume I: Chapter 10 "The curriculum of the land-grant colleges" (Wellford Addis) ; Chapter 11 "Requirements for admission to freshman class in colleges, universities, and schools of technology;" Chapter 14 "Discussion of educational topics by President Francis A. Walker, of the Massachusetts Institute of Technology, with some account of his life;" Chapter 18 "Entrance requirements for engineering colleges;" and Chapter 20 "Some recent contributions of biology, sociology, and metallurgy to the curriculum of colleges endowed by the Federal government for the benefit of agriculture and the mechanic arts" (Wellford Addis).

Volume II: Chapter 23 "Federal and state aid to establish higher education" (Wellford Addis) ; Chapter 25 "The learned professions and social control" (Wellford Addis) ; and Chapter 28 "Foreign universities."

1897–98 (William T. Harris)

Volume I: "Courses of study in medical schools" (In Commissioner's Introduction) ; Chapter 2 "Summer schools in England, Scotland, France, and Switzerland" (H. B. Adams) ; and Chapter 23 "Dental education in the United States."

Volume II: Chapter 27 "University types and ideals;" Chapter 28 "State supervision of degree-conferring institutions;" Chapter 31 "Bible study in American colleges;"

Chapter 32 "The Bible in the public schools and state universities;" and Chapter 39 "Foreign universities and other institutions of higher education."

1898–99 (William T. Harris)

Volume I: Chapter 9 "The Royal normal college for the blind, London, together with incidents in the life of its founder and president, Dr. F. J. Campbell, a native of Tennessee, U. S. A." (John Eaton) ; Chapter 13 "The Western literary institute and college of professional teachers" (B. A. Hinsdale and Mary L. Hinsdale) ; Chapter 14 "The United States naval academy at Annapolis; its organization and methods of training" (E. S. Holden) ; and Chapter 18 "University extension in Great Britain" (H. B. Adams).

Volume II: Chapter 34 "Foreign universities and other institutions of higher education;" and Chapter 48 "Contributions to the history of normal schools in the United States" (M. A. Newell).

1899–1900 (William T. Harris)

Volume I: Chapter 5 "Educational extension in the United States" (H. B. Adams) ; and Chapter 10 "The readjustment of the collegiate to the professional course" (S. E. Baldwin).

Volume II: Chapter 24 "The legislative career of Justin S. Morrill" (G. W. Atherton).

1900–1901 (William T. Harris)

Volume I: Chapter 18 "Third annual conference of the Association of Catholic colleges;" Chapter 22 "Relations of the National government to higher education and research" (C. D. Walcott) ; Chapter 23 "The Carnegie institution of Washington, D. C.;" and Chapter 25 "Higher commercial education."

Volume II: Chapter 30 "Foreign universities and other foreign institutions of higher education;" and Chapter 45 "Instruction in mining engineering."

1902 (William T. Harris)

Volume I: Chapter 1 "General laws relating to agricultural and mechanical land-grant colleges;" Chapter 3 "The college-bred negro [sic] ;" Chapter 12 "Admission to college on certificate of secondary schools;" Chapter 19 "Foreign universities and other foreign institutions of higher education;" Chapter 23 "Length of the college course;" and Chapter 24 "Oxford University" (Articles by W. T. Harris; J. W. Hoyt, J. B. Firth and others).

Volume II: Chapter 48 "Changes in the age of college graduation" (W. S. Thomas).

1903 (William T. Harris)

Volume I: Chapter 2 "General laws relating to agriculture and mechanical land-grant colleges;" Chapter 5 "American universities" (C. F. Thwing); Chapter 10 "The present status of the certification of teachers in the United States" (W. R. Jackson); Chapter 15 "Foreign universities and other foreign institutions of higher education in 1903;" Chapter 19 "Manual, industrial, and technical education in the United States" (C. M. Woodward); Chapter 20 "Coeducation in the schools and colleges of the United States" (Anna T. Smith); and Chapter 22 "The state normal schools of the United States" (E. O. Lyte).

1904 (William T. Harris)

Volume I: Chapter 3 "Regulations relating to pensions and insurance in all German universities;" Chapter 5 "The University of Paris during the middle ages" (J. W. Hoyt); and Chapter 13 "Higher education in England as affected by the law of 1902."

Volume II: Chapter 21 "Education at the St. Louis exposition—Universities and colleges of the United States;" and Chapter 38 "Foreign universities and other foreign institutions of higher education in 1904."

1905 (Elmer Ellsworth Brown)

Volume I: Chapter 1 "The reports of the Mosely educational commission" (W. T. Harris); Chapter 2 "Extracts from the report of the Mosely educational commission to the United States of America, October-December, 1903;" Chapter 3 "Statement of proceedings instituted to execute the Rhodes scholarship trust;" and Chapter 6 "Higher education for business men in the United States and Germany" (J. Jastrow).

1906 (Elmer Ellsworth Brown)

Volume I: Chapter 5 "Foreign universities and other foreign institutions of higher education in 1905;" and Chapter 8 "The education and professional position of nurses" (M. Adelaide Nutting).

1907 (Elmer Ellsworth Brown)

Volume I: Chapter 1 "The work of the Bureau of Education."

1908 (Elmer Ellsworth Brown)

Volume I: Chapter 2 "Recent educational legislation;" Chapter 5 "The modern aspect of higher education in Spanish-

American countries;" and Chapter 10 "Foreign universities and other foreign institutions of higher education in 1907."
1909 (Elmer Ellsworth Brown)
   Volume I: Chapter 2 "Educational legislation, Sixtieth Congress, second session;" and Chapter 14 "List of college and student periodicals currently received by the libraries in the District of Columbia."
1910 (Elmer Ellsworth Brown)
   Volume I: Chapter 2 "Educational legislation."

(The *Annual Reports,* starting with 1889–89, had a large collection of statistics relating to higher education classified usually in the following groups: "Institutions for higher education," "Professional schools," "Agricultural and mechanical colleges," "Normal schools," "Commercial and business schools," and "Schools for nurses." Nomenclature occasionally changed but these chapters covered the same statistical information year by year. They were found in Volume II of the *Annual Report.*)

ANNUAL STATEMENTS OF THE COMMISSIONER OF EDUCATION
   *Note:* Like the *Annual Report,* each *Annual Statement* contained some information on higher education.

1887 (Nathaniel Dawson)
1889–89 (Nathaniel Dawson)
1890 (William T. Harris)
1891 (William T. Harris)
1892 (William T. Harris)
1893 (William T. Harris)
1894 (William T. Harris)
1895 (William T. Harris)
1896 (William T. Harris)
1897 (William T. Harris)
1898 (William T. Harris)
1899 (William T. Harris)
1900 (William T. Harris)
1901 (William T. Harris)
1902 (William T. Harris)
1903 (William T. Harris)
1904 (William T. Harris)
1905 (William T. Harris)
1906 (Elmer Ellsworth Brown)
1907 (Elmer Ellsworth Brown)
1908 (Elmer Ellsworth Brown)

1909 (Elmer Ellsworth Brown)
1910 (Elmer Ellsworth Brown)

OFFICIAL CIRCULARS AND CIRCULARS OF INFORMATION

*State colleges and schools of science applied to agriculture and mechanic arts* (Supplement to Henry Barnard's *First Report, 1867–68*. Official Circular No. 6).

*Report on Female Education* (Supplement to Henry Barnard's *First Report, 1867–68*. Official Circular No. 8).

*State normal schools, and other institutions for the professional training of teachers* (Supplement to Henry Barnard's *First Report, 1867–68*. Official Circular No. 12).

*German and other foreign universities* (Herman Jacobsen), 1872.

1. *An inquiry concerning the vital statistics of college graduates* (Charles Warren) ; 2. *Distribution of college students in 1870–71* (Charles Warren) ; 3. *Facts of vital statistics in the United States with tables and diagrams* (J. M. Toner), 1872.

*Account of college commencements for the summer of 1873, in Maine, New Hampshire, Vermont, Massachusetts, Rhode Island, Connecticut, New York, New Jersey, and Pennsylvania*, 1873, No. 3.

*List of publications by members of certain college faculties and learned societies in the United States, 1867–1872*, 1873, No. 4.

*Account of college commencements during 1873 in the western and southern states*, 1873, No. 5.

*The training of teachers in Germany*, 1878, No. 1.

*Papers, addresses, discussions, and other proceedings of the Department of Superintendence of the National Educational Association, at the meeting held at Washington, D. C., February 4, 5, 6, 1879; the proceedings of the Department of Superintendence of the National Educational Association for 1877; and the proceedings of the Conference of the presidents and other delegates of the state universities and state colleges of Ohio for 1877*, 1879, No. 2.

*College libraries as aids to instruction*, 1880, No. 1.

*A report on the teaching of chemistry and physics in the United States* (Frank Wigglesworth Clarke), 1880, No. 6.

*The inception, organization, and management of training schools for nurses*, 1882, No. 1.

*The University of Bonn* (Edmond Dreyfus-Brisac), 1882, No. 3.

*Teachers' Institutes* (compiled by James H. Smart), 1885, No. 2.

*Physical training in American colleges and universities* (Edward Mussey Hartwell), 1885, No. 5.

*The College of William and Mary, a contribution to the history of higher education, with suggestions for its national promotion* (Herbert Baxter Adams), 1887, No. 1 (Contributions to American educational history, No. 1).

*The study of history in American colleges and universities* (Herbert B. Adams), 1887, No. 2.

*Thomas Jefferson and the University of Virginia; with authorized sketches of Hampden-Sidney, Randolph-Macon, Emory-Henry, Roanoke, and Richmond colleges, Washington and Lee university, and Virginia military institute* (Herbert B. Adams and others), 1888, No. 1 (Contributions to American educational history, No. 2).

*The history of education in North Carolina* (Charles Lee Smith), 1888, No. 2 (Contributions to American educational history, No. 3).

*History of higher education in South Carolina, with a sketch of the free school system* (Colyer Meriwether), 1888, No. 3 (Contributions to American educational history, No. 4).

*Education in Georgia* (Charles Edgeworth Jones), 1888, No. 4 (Contributions to American educational history, No. 5).

*History of education in Florida* (George Gary Bush), 1888, No. 7 (Contributions to American educational history, No. 6).

*Higher education in Wisconsin* (William F. Allen and David E. Spencer) 1889, No. 1 (Contributions to American educational history, No. 7).

*History of education in Alabama, 1702–1889* (Willis G. Clark), 1889, No. 3 (Contributions to American educational history, No. 8).

*The history of federal and state aid to higher education in the United States* (Frank W. Blackmar), 1890, No. 1 (Contributions to American educational history, No. 9).

*Higher education in Indiana* (James Albert Woodburn), 1891, No. 1 (Contributions to American educational history, No. 10).

*History of higher education in Michigan* (Andrew C. McLaughlin), 1891, No. 4 (Contributions to American educational history, No. 11).

*The history of higher education in Ohio* (George W. Knight and John R. Commons), 1891, No. 5 (Contributions to American educational history, No. 12).

*History of higher education in Massachusetts* (George Gary Bush), 1891, No. 6 (Contributions to American educational history, No. 13).

*Rise and growth of the normal-school idea in the United States* (J. P. Gordy), 1891, No. 8.

*Biological teaching in the colleges of the United States* (John P. Campbell), 1891, No. 9.

*Benjamin Franklin and the University of Pennsylvania* (ed. by Francis Newton Thorpe), 1892, No. 2.

*The history of education in Connecticut* (Bernard C. Steiner), 1893, No. 2 (Contributions to American educational history, No. 14).

*The history of education in Delaware* (Lyman P. Powell), 1893, No. 3 (Contributions to American educational history, No. 15).

*Higher education in Tennessee* (Lucius Salisbury Merriam), 1893, No. 5 (Contributions to American educational history, No. 16).

*Higher education in Iowa* (Leonard F. Parker), 1893, No. 6 (Contributions to American educational history, No. 17).

*History of higher education in Rhode Island* (William Howe Tolman) 1894, No. 1 (Contributions to American educational history, No. 18).

*History of Education in Maryland* (Bernard C. Steiner), 1894, No. 2 (Contributions to American educational history, No. 19).

*The history of education in Louisiana* (Edwin Whitfield Fay), 1898, No. 1 (Contributions to American educational history, No. 20).

*Higher education in Missouri* (Marshall S. Snow), 1898, No. 2 (Contributions to American educational history, No. 21).

*History of education in New Hampshire* (George Gary Bush), 1898, No. 3 (Contributions to American educational history, No. 22).

*History of education in New Jersey* (David Murray), 1899, No. 1 (Contributions to American educational history, No. 23).

*History of education in Mississippi* (Edward Mayes), 1899, No. 2 (Contributions to American educational history, No. 24).

*History of higher education in Kentucky* (Alvin Fayette Lewis). 1899, No. 3 (Contributions to American educational history, No. 25).

*History of education in Arkansas* (Josiah H. Shinn), 1900, No. 1 (Contributions to American educational history, No. 26).

*Higher education in Kansas* (Frank W. Blackmar), 1900, No. 2 (Contributions to American educational history, No. 27).

*The University of the State of New York: history of higher education in the State of New York* (Sidney Sherwood), 1900, No. 3 (Contributions to American educational history, No. 28).

*History of education in Vermont* (George Gary Bush), 1900, No. 4 (Contributions to American educational history, No. 29).

*History of education in West Virginia* (A. R. Whitehall), 1902, No. 1 (Contributions to American educational history, No. 30).

*The history of education in Minnesota* (John N. Greer), 1902, No. 2 (Contributions to American educational history, No. 31).

*Education in Nebraska* (Howard W. Caldwell), 1902, No. 3 (Contributions to American educational history, No. 32).

*A history of higher education in Pennsylvania* (Charles H. Haskins and William I. Hull), 1902, No. 4 (Contributions to American educational history, No. 33).

*History of higher education in Colorado* (James Edward Le Rossignol), 1903, No. 1 (Contributions to American educational history, No. 34).

*History of education in Texas* (J. J. Lane), 1903, No. 2 (Contributions to American educational history, No. 35).

*History of higher education in Maine* (Edward W. Hall), 1903, No. 3 (Contributions to American education history, No. 36).

BULLETINS

*German views of American education, with particular reference to industrial development, collated from the reports of the Royal Prussian industrial commission of 1904* (William N. Hailmann), 1906, No. 2.

*State school systems: legislation and judicial decisions relating to public education, October 1, 1904, to October 1, 1906* (Edward C. Elliott), 1906, No. 3.

*Agricultural education including nature study and school gardens* (James Ralph Jewell), 1907, No. 2.

*On the training of persons to teach agriculture in the public schools* (Liberty Hyde Bailey), 1908, No. 1.

*Statistics of state universities and other institutions of higher education partially supported by the state, for the year ended June 30, 1908*, 1908, No. 1.

*Admission of Chinese students to American colleges* (John Fryer), 1909, No. 2.

*Instruction in the fine and manual arts in the United States: a statistical monograph* (Henry Turner Bailey), 1909, No. 6.

*Education for efficiency in railroad service* (J. Shirley Eaton),
    1909, No. 10.
*Statistics of state universities and other institutions of higher
    education partially supported by the state, for the year ended
    June 30, 1909,* 1909, No. 11.
*Statistics of State universities and other institutions of higher
    education partially supported by the State, 1909–10,* 1910,
    No. 6.

MISCELLANEOUS PUBLICATIONS

*Statistics of colleges and collegiate institutions in the United
    States,* 1871.
*Report on the national schools of science* (D. C. Gilman), 1872.
*Contributions to the annals of medical progress and medical
    education in the United States before and during the War of
    Independence* (Joseph M. Toner), 1874.
*International exhibition, Philadelphia, 1876. Collection to illus-
    trate the history of colleges, universities, professional schools,
    and schools of science,* 1875.
*Historical sketch of Mount Holyoke seminary* (Mary O. Nut-
    ting), 1876.
*Historical sketch of Union college* (F. B. Hough), 1876.
*Contributions to the history of medical education and medical
    institutions in the United States of America, 1776–1876*
    (N. S. Davis), 1877.
*Sale of diplomas,* 1880.
*Medical colleges in the United States,* 1881.
*Recognized medical colleges in the United States,* 1881.
*Comparative statistics of elementary, secondary, and superior
    education in sixty principal countries,* 1882.
*Sketch of the Philadelphia normal school for girls,* 1882.
*Historical sketches of the universities and colleges of the United
    States* (University of Missouri) (ed. by Franklin B. Hough),
    1883.
*Statistics regarding national aid to education,* 1885.
*Art and industry. Education in the industrial and fine arts in
    the United States. Part III. Industrial and technical training
    in voluntary associations and endowed institutions* (Isaac
    Edwards Clarke), 1897.
*Art and industry. Education in the industrial and fine arts in
    the United States. Part IV. Industrial and technical training
    in schools of technology and in U. S. land grant colleges*
    (Isaac Edwards Clarke), 1898.

*Honorary degrees as conferred in American colleges* (Charles Forster Smith), 1890.

## Publications 1911–1953

ANNUAL REPORTS OF THE COMMISSIONER OF EDUCATION
*Note:* Exact titles of the *Annual Reports* vary from year to year. See Bibliography for detailed publication data.

1911 (Philander P. Claxton)
Volume I: Chapter 1 "A brief survey of educational progress during the decade 1900 to 1910" (F. B. Dresslar) ; Chapter 2 "Higher education in the United States" (K. C. Babcock) ; Chapter 11 "Training of vocational teachers in Germany" (E. G. Cooley) ; and Chapter 20 "Recent movements in higher and secondary education in Germany" (Wilhelm Munch).

1912 (Philander P. Claxton)
Volume I: Chapter 3 "Higher education" (K. C. Babcock).

1913 (Philander P. Claxton)
Volume I: Chapter 2 "Higher education" (K. C. Babcock) ; Chapter 3 "Progress in medical education" (N. P. Colwell) ; Chapter 4 "Dental education" (E. C. Kirk) ; and Chapter 24 "Progress of teacher training" (C. H. Johnston).

1914 (Philander P. Claxton)
Volume I: Chapter 7 "Higher education" (S. P. Capen) ; Chapter 8 "Progress of the year in medical education" (N. P. Colwell) ; Chapter 9 "Medical education in the homeopathic school of medicine" (W. A. Dewey) ; Chapter 10 "Recent progress in legal education" (H. M. Bates) ; and Chapter 17 "Professional art schools" (Florence N. Levy).

1915 (Philander P. Claxton)
Volume I: Chapter 6 "Higher education" (S. P. Capen) ; Chapter 7 "The training of teachers" (S. C. Parker) ; Chapter 8 "Medical education" (N. P. Colwell) ; and Chapter 13 "Education for social work" (Edith Abbott).

1916 (Philander P. Claxton)
Volume I: Chapter 8 "Higher education" (S. P. Capen) ; Chapter 10 "Medical education" (N. P. Colwell) ; Chapter 11 "Legal education" (H. N. Bates) ; Chapter 12 "Engineering education" (C. R. Mann), and Chapter 22 "Extension education" (J. L. McBrien).

1917 (Philander P. Claxton)
Volume I: Chapter 1 "Education and the war;" and Chapter 3 "General activities of the Bureau."

(This volume of the *Annual Report* marks the transition stage from the practice of issuing two volumes a year to the policy of issuing a *Biennial Survey of Education*. Prior to the policy which was established with the publication of Bulletin No. 88— first *Biennial Survey*—the second volume of the *Annual Report* contained statistical summaries.)

1918 (Philander P. Claxton)
(In this and subsequent *Reports* the information on higher education is included in a general discussion of the Office of Education activities.)
1919 (Philander P. Claxton)
1920 (Philander P. Claxton)
1921 (John J. Tigert)
1922 (John J. Tigert)
1923 (John J. Tigert)
1924 (John J. Tigert)
1925 (John J. Tigert)
1926 (John J. Tigert)
1927 (John J. Tigert)
1928 (John J. Tigert)
1929 (William J. Cooper)
1930 (William J. Cooper)
1931 (William J. Cooper)
1932 (Bess Goodykoontz, Acting Commissioner)
1933–1939 (Reports of the activities of the Office of Education appeared only in the *Annual Report of the Secretary of the Interior*. Report for 1933 by George Zook; 1934 by Bess Goodykoontz, Acting Commissioner; and 1935–1939 by John W. Studebaker.)
1940 (John W. Studebaker)
1941 (John W. Studebaker)
1943 (John W. Studebaker) (Covers fiscal years 1941–42; 1942–43)
1944 (John W. Studebaker)
1945–1952 (*Reports* published as part of the *Annual Report, Federal Security Agency. Reports* for 1945–1947 by John W. Studebaker; 1948 by Rall Grigsby, Acting Commissioner; and 1949–1952 by Earl J. McGrath.)
1953 *et seq.* published as *Annual Report of the United States*

*Department of Health, Education, and Welfare,* Samuel M. Brownell, Commissioner of Education, 1953–1956.

ANNUAL STATEMENTS OF THE COMMISSIONER OF EDUCATION

1911 (Philander P. Claxton)
1912 (Philander P. Claxton)
1913 (Philander P. Claxton)
1914 (Philander P. Claxton)
1915 (Philander P. Claxton)
1916 (Philander P. Claxton)
1917 (Philander P. Claxton)
1918 (Philander P. Claxton)
1919 (Philander P. Claxton)
1920 (Philander P. Claxton)

BIENNIAL SURVEY OF EDUCATION

(Starting with the first *Survey,* covering the years 1916–18, several chapters are devoted to statistics relating to higher education.)

BULLETINS

*Opportunities for graduate study in agriculture* (A. C. Monaham), 1911, No. 2.
*Age and grade census of schools and colleges,. A study of retardation and elimination* (George D. Strayer), 1911, No. 5.
*Graduate work in mathematics in universities and in other institutions of like grade in the U. S.* (International commission on the teaching of mathematics), 1911, No. 6.
*Undergraduate work in mathematics in colleges of liberal arts and universities* (International commission on the teaching of mathematics), 1911, No. 7.
*Examinations in mathematics* (International commission on the teaching of mathematics), 1911, No. 8.
*Mathematics in the technological schools of collegiate grade in the U.S.* (International commission on the teaching of mathematics), 1911, No. 9.
*Training of teachers of elementary and secondary mathematics* (International commission on the teaching of mathematics), 1911, No. 12.
*Statistics of State universities and other institutions of higher education partially supported by the State, 1910–11,* 1911, No. 19.
*Course of study for the preparation of rural-school teachers* (Fred Mutchler and W. J. Craig), 1912, No. 1.

*Mathematics at West Point and Annapolis* (International commission on the teaching of mathematics), 1912, No. 2.

*Educational status of nursing* (M. Adelaide Nutting), 1912, No. 7.

*Professional distribution of college and university graduates* (Baily B. Burritt), 1912, No. 19.

*Latin-American universities and special schools* (Edgar W. Brandon), 1912, No. 30.

*Statistics of State universities and other institutions of higher education partially supported by the State, 1912,* 1912, No. 33.

*Training courses for rural teachers* (A. C. Monahan and R. H. Wright), 1913, No. 2.

*Present standards of higher education in the United States* (George E. MacLean), 1913, No. 4.

*College Entrance Requirements* (Clarence D. Kingsley), 1913, No. 7.

*Georgia Club at the State normal school, Athens, Ga., for the study of rural sociology* (E. C. Branson), No. 23.

*Accredited secondary schools in the U. S.* (Kendric C. Babcock), 1913, No. 29.

*Statistics of State universities and other institutions of higher education partially supported by the State, 1913,* 1913, No. 60.

*University extension in the U. S.* (Louis E. Reber), 1914, No. 19.

*Library instruction in universities, colleges, and normal schools* (Henry R. Evans), 1914, No. 34.

*Training of teachers in England, Scotland, and Germany* (Charles H. Judd), 1914, No. 35.

*Education for the home* (Benjamin R. Andrews)
*Part II: 5, Normal schools; 6, Technical institutions,* 1914, No. 37, *Part III: Colleges and universities,* 1914, No. 38.

*City training schools for teachers* (Frank A. Manny), 1914, No. 47.

*Statistics of State universities and State colleges, 1914,* 1914, No. 50.

*Study of the colleges and high schools in the North Central association,* 1915, No. 6.

*Accredited secondary schools in the U. S.* (S. P. Capen), 1915, No 7.

*Present status of the honor system in colleges and universities* (Bird T. Baldwin), 1915, No. 8.

*Legal education in Great Britain* (H. S. Richards), 1915, No. 18.

*Opportunities for foreign students at colleges and universities in the U. S.* (Samuel P. Capen), 1915, No. 27.

*University and the municipality* (National association of municipal universities), 1915, No. 38.

*Training of elementary school teachers in mathematics in the countries represented in the International commission on the teaching of mathematics* (I. L. Kandel), 1915, No. 39.

*Statistics of State universities and State colleges,* 1915, 1916, No. 6.

*Problems involved in standardizing State normal schools* (Charles H. Judd and Samuel C. Parker), 1916, No. 12.

*State higher educational institutions of Iowa,* 1916, No. 19.

*Accredited secondary schools in the U. S.* (Samuel P. Capen), 1916, No. 20.

*Survey of educational institutions of the State of Washington,* 1916, No. 26.

*State higher educational institutions of North Dakota,* 1916, No. 27.

*Educational survey of Wyoming* (A .C. Monahan and Katherine M. Cook), 1916, No. 29.

*University training for public service* (A report of the meeting of the Association of urban universities), 1916, No. 30.

*Registration and student records for smaller colleges* (Benjamin F. Andrews), 1916, No. 33.

*Cooperative system of education, College of Engineering, University of Cincinnati* (Clyde W. Park), 1916, No. 37.

*Negro education* (Prepared in cooperation with the Phelps-Stokes funds under the direction of Thomas Jesse Jones), 1916, No. 37 (Vol. I) ; No. 38 (Vol. II).

*Recent movements in college and university administration* (Samuel P. Capen), 1916, No. 46.

*Statistics of State universities and State colleges, 1916,* 1916, No. 50.

*Higher technical education in foreign countries* (Anna T. Smith and W. S. Jesien), 1917, No. 11.

*Studies in higher education in Ireland and Wales* (George E. McLean), 1917, No. 15.

*Studies in higher education in England and Scotland* (George E. McLean), 1917, No. 16.

*Accredited higher institutions* (Samuel P. Capen), 1917, No. 17.

*Report of a survey of the University of Nevada,* 1917, No. 19.

*Training of teachers of mathematics for the secondary schools of the countries represented in the International commission on the teaching of mathematics* (Raymond C. Archibald), 1917, No. 27.

*Institutions in the U. S. giving instruction in agriculture, 1915–16* (A. C. Monahan and C. H. Dye), 1917, No. 34.

*Vocational teachers for secondary schools. What the land-grant colleges are doing to prepare them* (Chester D. Jarvis), 1917, No. 38.

*Educational conditions in Arizona* (Report of a survey by the U. S. Bureau of Education), 1917, No. 44.

*Statistics of State universities and State colleges, 1917,* 1917, No. 55.

*Curriculum of the woman's college* (Mabel L. Robinson), 1918, No. 6.

*Bureau of extension of the University of North Carolina* (Louis R. Wilson and Lester A. Williams), 1918, No. 7.

*Land grant of 1862 and the land-grant colleges* (Benjamin F. Andrews), 1918, No. 13.

*Facilidades Ofrecidas a los estudiantes extranjeros en los colegios y universidades de los Estados Unidos de la America del Norte* (Samuel P. Capen), 1918, No. 16.

*Instructions in journalism in institutions of higher education* (James M. Lee), 1918, No. 21.

*Rural-teacher preparation in State normal schools* (Ernest Burnham), 1918, No. 27.

*American agricultural colleges. Study of their organization and their requirements for admission and graduation* (Chester D. Jarvis), 1918, No. 29.

*Resources and standards of colleges of arts and sciences* (Samuel P. Capen), 1918, No. 30.

*Courses of stury for the preparation of teachers of manual arts* (Albert F. Siepert), 1918, No. 37.

*Statistics of agricultural and mechanical colleges, 1916–17* (Benjamin F. Andrews), 1918, No. 41.

*Educational surveys* (Edward F. Buchner), 1918, No. 45.

*Medical Education, 1916–18* (N. P. Colwell), 1918, No. 46.

*Statistics of State universities and State Colleges, 1918,* 1918, No. 51.

*Adjustment of the teaching load in a university* (Leonard V. Koos), 1919, No. 15.

*Engineering education* (F. L. Bishop), 1919, No. 19.

*Survey of higher education, 1916–18* (Samuel P. Capen and Walton C. John), 1919, No. 22.

*Junior college* (F. M. McDowell), 1919, No. 34.

*Private commercial and business schools, 1917–18* (H. R. Bonner), 1919, No. 47.

*Application of commercial advertising methods to university extension* (Mary B. Orvis), 1919, No. 51.

*Administration of correspondence-study departments of universities and colleges* (Arthur J. Klein), 1919, No. 56.

*Commercial engineering. Report of a conference, 1919* (Glen L. Swiggett), 1919, No. 58.

*Public discussion and information service of university extension* (Walton S. Bittner), 1919, No. 61.

*Class extension work in the universities and colleges of the U. S.* (Arthur J. Klein), 1919, No. 62.

*Training teachers of agriculture* (American association for the advancement of agricultural teaching, 1919), 1919, No. 66.

*Nurse training schools, 1917–18* (H. R. Bonner), 1919, No. 73.

*Statistics of normal schools, 1917–18* (L. E. Blauch and H. R. Bonner), 1919, No. 81.

*University extension movement* (W. S. Bittner), 1919, No. 84.

*Statistics of State universities and State colleges, 1919,* 1919, No. 87.

*Note:* first *Biennial Survey of Education,* containing detailed information on higher education, appeared as Bulletins No. 88 to 91 in the 1919 series.

*Requirements for the bachelor's degree* (Walton C. John), 1920, No. 7.

*Agricultural and mechanical colleges, including statistics for 1917–18* (Walton C. John), 1920, No. 8.

*Correspondence study in universities and colleges* (Arthur J. Klein), 1920, No. 10.

*Training teachers for Americanization. A course of study for normal schools and teachers' institutes* (John J. Mahoney et al.), 1920, No. 12.

*Salaries in universities and colleges in 1920,* 1920, No. 20.

*Statistics of universities, colleges, and professional schools, 1917–18* (H. R. Bonner), 1920, No. 34.

*Facilities for foreign students in American colleges and universities* (Samuel P. Capen), 1920, No. 39.

*Curriculum of the college of agriculture* (Carl R. Woodward), 1920, No. 40.

*Education for highway engineering and highway transport* (Report of the Conference on highway engineering and highway transport education, Washington, May 14–15, 1920. F. L. Bishop and Walton C. John), 1920, No. 42.

*Statistics of State universities and State colleges, 1920*, 1920, No. 48.

*Opportunities for study at American graduate schools* (George F. Zook and Samuel P. Capen), 1921, No. 6.

*Present status of music instruction in colleges and high schools, 1919–20* (Osbourne McConathy), 1921, No. 9.

*Pharmaceutical education* (Wortley F. Rudd and P. F. Fackenthall), 1921, No. 11.

*Medical education, 1918–20* (N. P. Colwell), 1921, No. 15.

*Education in homeopathic medicine during the biennium 1918–20* (W. A. Dewey), 1921, No. 18.

*Developments in nursing education since 1918* (Isabel M. Stewart), 1921, No. 20.

*Higher education, 1918–20* (George F. Zook), 1921, No. 21.

*State laws and regulations governing teachers' certificates* (Katherine M. Cook), 1921, No. 22.

*Training for foreign service* (Glen L. Swiggett), 1921, No. 27.

*Standards in graduate work in education* (Leonard V. Koos), 1921, No. 38.

*Business training and commercial education* (Glen L. Swiggett), 1921, No. 43.

*Education in forestry*, 1921, No. 44.

*Education for highway engineering and highway transport* (Pyke Johnson and Walton C. John), 1921, No. 47.

*Engineering education after the war* (Arthur M. Greene, Jr.), 1921, No. 50.

*Statistics of nurse training schools, 1919–20* (H. R. Bonner), 1921, No. 51.

*Statistics of State universities and State colleges, 1921*, 1921, No. 53.

*Preparation of teachers of the social studies for the secondary schools* (Edgar Dawson), 1922, No. 3.

*Statistics of private commercial and business schools, 1919–20* (H. R. Bonner), 1922, No. 4.

*Report of the higher educational institutions of Arkansas* (George F. Zook), 1922, No. 7.

*Statistics of teachers colleges and normal schools, 1919–20* (H. R. Bonner), 1922, No. 8.

*Accredited secondary schools in the U. S.* (George F. Zook), 1922, No. 9.

*Residence of students in universities and colleges* (George F. Zook), 1922, No. 18.

*National conference of junior colleges, 1920, and first annual meeting of American association of junior colleges, 1921* (George F. Zook), 1922, No. 19.

*Higher education in Australia and New Zealand* (Charles F. Thwing), 1922, No. 25.

*Philanthropy in the history of American higher education* (Jesse B. Sears), 1922, No. 26.

*Statistics of agricultural and mechanical colleges for 1919 and 1920* (Walton C. John), 1922, No. 27.

*Statistics of universities, colleges, and professional schools, 1919–1920,* 1922, No. 28.

*Accredited higher institutions* (George F. Zook), 1922, No. 30.

*University summer schools* (James C. Egbert), 1922, No. 31.

*Statistics of land-grant colleges year ended June 30, 1921* (L. E. Blauch), 1922, No. 34.

*Report of a survey of the University of Arizona,* 1922, No. 36.

*History of the Manual Training School of Washington University* (C. P. Coates), 1923, No. 3.

*Medical education, 1920–22* (N. P. Colwell), 1923, No. 18.

*Hampton normal and agricultural institute* (Walton C. John, Introduction by William Howard Taft), 1923, No. 27.

*Higher education, 1920–22* (George F. Zook), 1923, No. 34.

*Report of survey of State institutions of higher learning in Kansas* (G. F. Zook, L. D. Coffman, A. R. Mann), 1923, No. 40.

*Statistics of State universities and State colleges, 1922,* 1923, No. 49.

*Statstics of land-grant colleges, 1922* (L. E. Blauch), 1924, No. 6.

*Statistics of teachers colleges and normal schools, 1921–22,* 1924, No. 10.

*Objectives in commercial engineering* (Conference report), 1924, No. 16.

*Statistics of universities, colleges, and professional schools, 1921–22,* 1924, No. 20.

*Practices and objectives in training for foreign service* (Conference Report), 1924, No. 21.

*Technique of procedure in collegiate registration* (C. T. Avery), 1924, No. 22.

*Statistics of State universities and State colleges, 1922–23,* 1924, No. 26.

*Fiscal support of State universities and colleges* (C. H. Thurber), 1924, No. 28.

*Land-grant college education, 1910 to 1920, Part I. History and educational objectives*, 1924, No. 30.

*Trend of college entrance requirements, 1913–1922* (H. C. McKown), 1924, No. 35.

*Land-grant college education, 1910 to 1920. Part II. Liberal arts and sciences*, 1924, No. 37.

*Land-grant college education, 1910 to 1920. Part III. Agriculture*, 1925, No. 4.

*Land-grant college education, 1910 to 1920. Part IV. Engineering and mechanic arts*, 1925, No. 5.

*Statistics of land-grant colleges, 1923* (W. J. Greenleaf), 1925, No. 19.

*Statistics of land-grant colleges, 1924* (W. J. Greenleaf), 1925, No. 26.

*Statistics of teachers colleges and normal schools*, 1925, No. 28.

*Land-grant college education, 1910 to 1920. Part V. Home economics*, 1925, No. 29.

*Medical education* (N. P. Colwell), 1925, No. 31.

*Progress of dental education* (F. C. Waite), 1925, No. 39.

*Land-grant colleges, June 30, 1925* (W. J. Greenleaf), 1925, No. 44.

*Statistics of universities, colleges, and professional schools, 1923–24*, 1925, No. 45.

*Recent progress in legal education* (A. Z. Reed), 1926, No. 3.

*General university extension* (T. H. Shelby), 1926, No. 5.

*Accredited higher institutions* (Ella B. Ratcliffe), 1926, No. 10.

*Residence and migration of university and college students* (G. F. Zook), 1926, No. 11.

*Statistics of private business and commercial schools, 1924–25*, 1926, No. 14.

*Higher education, 1922–24* (Arthur J. Klein), 1926, No. 20.

*Medical education, 1924–26* (N. P. Colwell), 1927, No. 9.

*Physical education in American colleges and universities* (Marie M. Ready), 1927, No. 14.

*Statistics of teachers colleges and normal schools, 1925–26*, 1927, No. 30.

*Higher education, 1924–26* (Arthur J. Klein), 1927, No. 34.

*Preparation of teachers* (Wm. M. Robinson), 1927, No. 36.

*Land-grant colleges, June 30, 1926* (Walter J. Greenleaf), 1927, No. 37.

*Statistics of universities, colleges, and professional schools, 1925–26*, 1927, No. 40.

*Accredited higher instittuions*, 1927, No. 41.

*Statistics of nurse training schools, 1926–27,* 1928, No. 2.
*College and university extension helps in adult education,* 1928, No. 3.
*Professional preparation of teachers for rural schools,* 1928, No. 6.
*Survey of Negro colleges and universities,* 1928, No. 7.
*Educational surveys* (A. J. Klein, *et al.*), 1928, No. 11.
*Land-grant colleges and universities, 1927* (W. J. Greenleaf), 1928, No. 14.
*Self-help for college students* (Walter J. Greenleaf), 1929, No. 2.
*Accredited higher institutions, 1927–1928* (Ella B. Ratcliffe), 1929, No. 7.
*Medical education, 1926–1928* (N. P. Colwell), 1929, No. 10.
*Higher education, 1926–1928* (Arthur J. Klein), 1929, No. 11.
*Land-grant colleges and universities, 1928* (Walter J. Greenleaf), 1929, No. 13.
*Statistics of teachers colleges and normal schools, 1927–1928* (Frank M. Phillips), 1929, No. 14.
*Teacher Training, 1926–1928* (Benjamin W. Frazier), 1929, No. 17.
*Legal education, 1925–1928* (Alfred Z. Reed), 1929, No. 31.
*Statistics of universities, colleges, and professional schools, 1927–1928* (Frank M. Phillips), 1929, No. 38.
*Bibliography of junior colleges* (Walter C. Eells), 1930, No. 2.
*Survey of land-grant colleges and universities* (Arthur J. Klein), (2 Volumes), 1930, No. 9.
*College and university extension helps in adult education, 1928–1929* (L. R. Alderman), 1930, No. 10.
*Accredited higher institutions, 1929–1930* (Ella B. Ratcliffe), 1930, No. 19.
*Statistics of private commercial and business schools, 1928–29* (Maris M. Proffitt), 1930, No. 25.
*Land-grant colleges and universities, 1929* (Walter J. Greenleaf), 1930, No. 28.
*Survey of state-supported institutions of higher learning in Arkansas,* 1931, No. 6.
*Survey of public higher education in Oregon* (Survey commission: Arthur J. Klein, Fred J. Kelly, George A. Works), 1931, No. 8.
*Research in higher education,* 1931, No. 12.
*Scholarships and Fellowships* (Ella B. Ratcliffe), 1931, No. 15.
*History of the municipal university in the U.S.* (R. H. Eckelberry), 1932, No. 2.

*National survey of secondary education,* 1932, No. 17 (5 of 28 monographs relate to higher education).

*Land-grant colleges and universities, 1931* (Walter J. Greenleaf), 1932, No. 20.

*Background study of Negro college students* (Ambrose Caliver), 1933, No. 8.

*National survey of the education of teachers* (6 volumes) (G. L. Betts, *et al.*), 1933, No. 10.

*Institutions of higher education in Norway* (Alina M. Lindegren), 1934, No. 2.

*Supervision exercised by states over privately controlled institutions of higher education* (John H. McNeely), 1934, No. 8.

*History of education in Washington* (Frederick E. Bolton and Thomas W. Bibb), 1934, No. 9.

*Privately controlled higher education in the U.S.* (Fred J. Kelly and Ella B. Ratcliffe), 1934, No. 12.

*Institutions of higher education in Denmark* (Alina M. Lindegren), 1934, No. 13.

*Prediction of success in college* (David Segel), 1934, No. 15.

*Accredited higher institutions, 1934* (Ella B. Ratcliffe), 1934, No. 16.

*Problem of duplication, as attacked in certain state surveys of higher education* (John H. McNeely), 1934, No. 19.

*Graduate study in universities and colleges in the U.S.* (Walton C. John), 1934, No. 20.

*Federal student aid program* (Fred J. Kelly and John H. McNeely), 1935, No. 14.

*Junior colleges* (Walter J. Greenleaf), 1936, No. 3.

*Instruction in hygiene in institutions of higher education* (J. F. Rogers), 1936, No. 7.

*Graduate work in engineering in universities and colleges in the U.S.* (Walton C. John and H. P. Hammond), 1936, No. 8.

*Scholarships and fellowships available at institutions of higher education* (Ella B. Ratcliffe), 1936, No. 10.

*Poland's institutions of higher education* (Severin K. Turosienski), 1936, No. 14.

*Authority of state executive agencies over higher education* (John H. McNeely), 1936, No. 15.

*Insurance and annuity plans for college staffs* (Sherman E. Flanagan), 1937, No. 5.

*Student health services in institutions of higher education* (James Frederick Rogers), 1937, No. 7.

*College salaries 1936,* (Walter J. Greenleaf), 1937, No. 9.

*Economic status of college alumni,* 1937, No. 10.

*College student mortality* (John H. McNeely), 1937, No. 11.

*Some factors in the adjustment of college students* (David Segel and Maris M. Proffitt), 1937, No. 12.

*University unit costs* (John H. McNeely), 1937, No. 21.

*Continuity of college attendance* (Fred J. Kelly), 1937, No. 24.

*College projects for aiding students* (Fred J. Kelly and Ella B. Ratcliffe), 1938, No. 9.

*Accredited higher institutions, 1938* (Ella B. Ratcliffe), 1938, No. 16.

*Hospital schools in the United States* (Clele Lee Matheison), 1938, No. 17.

*Higher educational institutions in the scheme of State government* (John H. McNeely), 1939, No. 3.

*The graduate school in American democracy* (Isaiah Bowman), 1939, No. 10.

*Collegiate accreditation by agencies within States* (Fred J. Kelly, Benjamin W. Frazier, John H. McNeely, and Ella B. Ratcliffe), 1940, No. 3.

*Fiscal control over State higher education* (John H. McNeely), 1940, No. 8.

*Education and service conditions of teachers in Scandinavia, the Netherlands, and Finland* (Alina M. Lindegren), 1940, No. 9.

*Financial aids for college students* (Fred J. Kelly and Ella B. Ratcliffe), 1940, No. 11.

*Placement services in colleges and universities* (Lulu B. Anderson), 1940, No. 12.

*Education of teachers. Selected bibliography: October 1, 1935 to January 1, 1941* (Benjamin W. Frazier), 1941, No. 2.

*Education of school administrators* (John Lund), 1941, No. 6.

*Handbook of college entrance requirements* (William W. Hinckley), 1941, No. 13.

*Opportunities for the preparation of teachers in health education. A Survey of 20 teachers colleges,* 1942, No. 1.

*Education of teachers for improving majority-minority relationships. Course offerings for teachers to learn about racial and national minority groups* (Ambrose Caliver), 1944, No. 2.

*Accredited higher institutions, 1944* (Ella B. Ratcliffe), 1944, No. 3.

*Data for statewide planning of veterans' education* (Ernest V. Hollis), 1945, No. 4.

*Higher education looks ahead* (Ernest V. Hollis and Ralph C. M. Flynt), 1945, No. 8.

*Engineering, science, and management war training: Final Report* (Henry H. Armsby), 1946, No. 9.

*Student war loans program: Final report* (Ralph C. M. Flynt), 1946, No. 14.

*Statistics of land-grant colleges and universities: Year ended June 30, 1944* (Lloyd E. Blauch and Francis G. Cornell), 1946, No. 16.

*Vocational education of college grade,* 1946, No. 18.

*Statistics of land-grant colleges and universities: Year ended June 30, 1945* (Maude Farr), 1947, No. 1.

*Teaching as a career* (Benjamin W. Frazier), 1947, No. 11.

*Statistics of land-grant colleges and universities: Year ended June 30, 1946* (Maude Farr), 1947, No. 14.

*Education of Negro leaders. Influences affecting graduate and professional studies* (Ambrose Caliver), 1948, No. 3.

*Statistics of land-grant colleges and universities: Year ended June 30, 1947* (Maude Farr), 1948, No. 8.

*Accredited higher institutions, 1948* (Theresa B. Wilkins), 1949, No. 6.

*Statistics of land-grant colleges and universities: Year ended June 30, 1948* (Maude Farr), 1949, No. 8.

*A survey of cooperative engineering education* (Henry H. Armsby), 1949, No. 15.

*Orientation and English instruction for students from other lands* (Program of the Washington D.C. orientation center for foreign students and trainees of Wilson Teachers College) (Margaret L. Emmons), 1950, No. 8.

*Statistics of land-grant colleges and universities: Year ended June 30, 1949* (Maude Farr), 1950, No. 11.

*Toward better college teaching* (Fred J. Kelly), 1950, No. 13.

*Statistics of land-grant colleges and universities: Year ended June 30, 1950* (Maude Farr and Robert C. Story), 1951, No. 4.

*Land-grant colleges and universities: What they are and the relations of the Federal Government to them,* 1951, No. 15.

*Scholarships and fellowships available at institutions of higher education* (Theresa B. Wilkins), 1951, No. 16.

*Statistics of land-grant colleges and universities: Year ended June 30, 1951* (Maude Farr and Robert C. Story), 1952, No. 2.

*Accredited higher institutions, 1952* (Theresa B. Wilkins), 1952, No. 3.

*Higher education in France. A handbook of information concerning fields of study in each institution* (Edith Kahler), 1952, No. 6.

*Land-grant colleges and universities: A Federal-State partnership* (Fred J. Kelly), 1952, No. 21.

*Statistics of land-grant colleges and universities: Year ended June 30, 1952* (Maude Farr and Robert C. Story), 1953, No. 1.

CIRCULARS (MIMEOGRAPHED)

*Financial support of colleges and universities, 1927–28* (Walter J. Greenleaf), No. 6, 1930.

*Collegiate courses in transportation, 1928* (J. O. Malott), No. 11, 1930.

*Collegiate courses in business organization and management, 1928* (J. O. Malott), No. 13, 1930.

*Collegiate courses in marketing and merchandising, 1928* (J. O. Malott), No. 14, 1930.

*Medical education* (W. J. Greenleaf), No. 19, 1930.

*Journalism* (W. J. Greenleaf), No. 20, 1930.

*Legal education* (W. J. Greenleaf), No. 22, 1930.

*Librarianship* (W. J. Greenleaf), No. 23, 1930.

*Architecture* (W. J. Greenleaf), No. 24, 1930.

*Electrical engineering* (W. J. Greenleaf), No. 25, 1930.

*Civil Engineering* (W. J. Greenleaf), No. 27, 1930.

*Mechanical engineering* (W. J. Greenleaf), No. 30, 1931.

*Dentistry* (W. J. Greenleaf), No. 33, 1931.

*Expenditures in publicity-controlled junior colleges, 1928* (H. G. Badger), No. 40, 1931.

*Summer session opportunities for parent education* (Ellen C. Lombard), No. 45, 1932.

*University and college courses in radio* (C. M. Koon), No. 53, 1932.

*Economic outlook in higher education for 1932–33* (Henry G. Badger), No. 58, 1932.

*Higher education in foreign countries: its history and present status. A list of references* (J. F. Abel), No. 77, 1933.

*Collegiate courses in advertising, 1932* (J. O. Malott), No. 90, 1933.

*Collegiate courses in transportation, 1932* (J. O. Malott), No. 91, 1933.

*Directory of collegiate bureaus of business research, 1933* (J. O. Malott), No. 92, 1933.

*Collegiate courses in accounting and business statistics* (J. O. Malott), No. 94, 1933.

*Collegiate courses in banking and finance, 1932* (J. O. Malott), No. 95, 1933.

*Collegiate courses in business law, 1932* (J. O. Malott), No. 96, 1933.

*Collegiate courses in foreign trade and foreign service, 1932*
(J. O. Malott), No. 97, 1933.
*Collegiate courses in insurance, 1932* (J. O. Malott), No. 98,
1933.
*Collegiate courses in marketing and merchandising, 1932* (J. O.
Malott), No. 99, 1933.
*Collegiate courses in business organization and management,
1932* (J. O. Malott), No. 100, 1933.
*Collegiate courses in realty, 1932* (J. O. Malott), No. 101, 1933.
*Collegiate courses in secretarial sciences, 1932* (J. O. Malott),
No. 102, 1933.
*Evening classes in business subjects offered by colleges and
universities, 1932* (J. O. Malott), No. 104, 1933.
*Correspondence courses in business subjects offered by colleges
and universities, 1932* (J. O. Malott), No. 105, 1933.
*Cooperative part-time courses in business offered by colleges
and universities, 1932* (J. O. Malott), No. 106, 1933.
*Extension classes in business subjects offered by colleges and
universities, 1932* (J. O. Malott), No. 107, 1933.
*Education of teachers and the financial crisis* (Katherine M.
Cook), No. 110, 1933.
*Economic outlook in higher education for 1933–34* (H. G.
Badger), No. 121, 1933.
*Preliminary report, land-grant colleges and universities, 1933*
(W. J. Greenleaf), No. 126, 1933.
*Home economics offerings in institutions of higher education,
1932–1933* (Louise O. Pettit and A. H. Gibbs), No. 134,
1934.
*Preliminary report. Land-grant colleges and universities, year
ended June 30, 1934* (W. J. Greenleaf), No. 136, 1934.
*P. W. A. allotments for non-federal educational institutions*, No.
144, 1935.
*Economic outlook in higher education for 1935–36* (H. G.
Badger), No. 148, 1935.
*Preliminary report. Land-grant colleges and universities, year
ended June 30, 1935* (W. J. Greenleaf), No. 149, 1935.
*Salaries in land-grant colleges, not including institutions for
Negroes, 1935* (W. J. Greenleaf), No. 157, 1936.
*College receipts and expenditures 1935–36* (H. C. Badger and
F. J. Kelly), No. 167, 1936.
*Preliminary report. Land-grant colleges and universities, year
ended June 30, 1936* (W. J. Greenleaf), No. 168, 1936.
*Preliminary report. Land-grant colleges and universities, year*

*ended June 30, 1937* (W. J. Greenleaf), No. 172, n.d. (probably 1937).

*College receipts and expenditures, 1936–37 (Preliminary sampling report)* (Henry G. Badger and Frederick J. Kelly), No. 174, 1937.

*College income and expenditures, 1937–38 (Preliminary sampling report)* (Henry G. Badger and Frederick J. Kelly), No. 175, 1938.

*Preliminary report. Land-grant colleges and universities, year ended June 30, 1938* (Maude Farr), No. 176, n.d. (probably 1938).

*College income and expenditures, 1938–39 (Preliminary sampling report)* (Henry G. Badger and Frederick J. Kelly), No. 182, 1939.

*Preliminary report. Land-grant colleges and universities, year ended June 30, 1938* (Maude Farr), No. 183, n.d. (probably 1939).

*Institutions of higher education accredited by State departments of education and State universities, 1940–41*, No. 185, n.d. (probably 1941).

*Preliminary report. Land-grant colleges and universities, year ended June 30, 1940* (Maude Farr), No. 187, n.d. (probably 1940).

*College income and expenditures, 1939–40 (Preliminary sampling report)* (Henry G. Badger and Frederick J. Kelly), No. 188, 1940.

*Survival rates of pupils (5th grade through college)* (Emery M. Foster), No. 193, 1940.

*College salaries, 1939–40* (Maude Farr and Blanche K. Choate), No. 195, n.d. (probably 1940).

*Age and College year of men students, 1940–41* (Emery M. Foster), No. 198, n.d. (probably 1941).

*Land-grant colleges and universities, year ended June 30, 1941 (Preliminary report)*, (Maude Farr), No. 206, n.d. (probably 1941).

*College income and expenditures, 1940–41 (Preliminary sampling report)* (Henry G. Badger), No. 207, 1941.

*Teacher placement, registration, announcement, and related services, 1942* (Benjamin W. Frazier), No. 209, 1942.

*Teacher certification in wartime, 1942* (Benjamin W. Frazier), No. 213, 1942.

*Statistics of the education of Negroes (a decade of progress)* (David T. Blose and Ambrose Caliver), No. 215, 1943.

*Estimated college staff, enrollments, and graduates, 1941–42 and enrollments and staff for 1942–43* (Margaret J. S. Carr and Henry G. Badger), No. 216, 1943.

*Effect of the war upon college personnel* (Henry G. Badger and Benjamin W. Frazier), No. 217, 1943.

*Land-grant colleges and universities, year ended June 30, 1942 (Preliminary report)* (Maude Farr), No. 220, 1943.

*College income and expenditures, 1941–42* (Henry G. Badger), No. 222, 1943.

*Income and expenditures of institutions of higher education, 1939–40 and 1941–42* (Maude Farr), No. 223, 1943.

*Some Federal agencies cooperating with higher institutions in war and post-war activities* (Benjamin W. Frazier), No. 226, 1944.

*Effects of the war upon colleges, 1943–44* (Henry G. Badger and Benjamin W. Frazier), No. 228, 1944.

*Land-grant colleges and universities, year ended June 30, 1943* (Maude Farr), No. 229, 1944.

*College salaries, 1941–42* (Maude Farr), No. 232, 1945.

*Graduate degrees: July 1, 1946—June 30, 1947. A report prepared at the request of the President's Commission on Higher Education,* No. 235, 1947.

*Estimated expenditures for educational and general purposes in institutions of higher education, and income from student fees: Fiscal year 1946–47. A report prepared for the President's Commission on Higher Education,* No. 236, 1947.

*Fall enrollment in higher educational institutions* (Robert C. Story and Betty J. Kelly), No. 238, 1947.

*Innovations in curriculum organization and instructional methods in colleges and universities. Bibliography* (Elizabeth N. Layton), No. 240, 1948.

*Library statistics of colleges and universities with enrollments of 5,000 students or more, 1946–47,* No. 243, 1948.

*Significant dates in the early history of institutions for the higher education of women in the United States* (Elizabeth N. Layton), No. 244, 1948.

*Earned degrees conferred by higher educational institutions, 1947–48* (Robert C. Story), No. 247, 1948.

*1948 Fall enrollment in higher educational institutions* (Robert C. Story), No. 248, 1948.

*Survey of salaries and occupational attitudes of faculty personnel of higher education, 1947–48* (Robert C. Story and Ann Gucwa), No. 254, 1949.

*Summary of statistics of higher education, 1945–46* (Henry G. Badger), No. 256, 1949.

*Surveys of higher education in the United States, 1937–1949* (Elizabeth N. Layton), No. 257, 1949.

*Summer session enrollment in higher educational institutions, 1948 and 1949* (Robert C. Story), No. 261, 1949.

*Earned degrees conferred by higher educational institutions, 1948–49* (Robert C. Story), No. 262, 1949.

*Statistical summary of higher education, 1947–48: Faculty, students, and degrees in higher education, 1947–48* (Henry G. Badger), No. 263, 1949.

*1949 Fall enrollment in higher educational institutions* (Robert C. Story), No. 264, 1949.

*Engineering enrollments and degrees, 1949* (Robert C. Story and Henry H. Armsby), No. 266, 1950.

*Undergraduate and graduate degrees in history conferred in 1948–49: Analyses and comparisons* (Jennings B. Sanders), No. 267, 1950.

*Finances in higher education: Statistical summary for 1947–48* (Henry G. Badger), No. 268, 1950.

*Geographical distribution of college students, 1949–50. A summary report* (Robert C. Story), No. 279 (a), 1950.

*1950 Fall enrollment in higher educational institutions* (Robert C. Story), No. 281, 1950.

*Earned degrees conferred by higher educational institutions, 1949–50* (Robert C. Story), No. 282, 1950.

*Earned degrees conferred by higher educational institutions, 1949–50. Summary report* (Robert C. Story), No. 282 (a), 1950.

*Faculty salaries in land-grant colleges and universities, 1949–50* (Maude Farr), No. 283, 1951.

*The college introductory course in United States history* (Jennings B. Sanders), No. 284, 1950.

*Engineering enrollments and degrees, 1950* (Robert C. Story and Henry H. Armsby), No. 287, 1951.

*How the college introductory course in United States history is organized and taught* (Jennings B. Sanders), No. 288, 1951.

*Statistics of Negro colleges and universities: Students, Staff, and finances, 1900–1950* (Henry G. Badger), No. 293, 1951.

*Degrees in history conferred in 1949–50* (Jennings B. Sanders), No. 295, 1951.

*Undergraduate economics in higher educational institutions, 1951,* No. 297, 1951.

*Office of Education estimates of enrollments for 1951–52 as compared with those of 1950–51* (Emery M. Foster), No. 299, 1951.

*Faculty, students, and degrees in higher education: Statistical summary for 1949–50* (Margaret J. S. Carr), No. 326, 1951.

*College introductory courses on the history of Europe, the Western World, or World Civilization with special reference to the 95 land-grant colleges and State universities* (Jennings B. Sanders), No. 327, 1951.

*Fall enrollment in higher educational institutions* (Robert C. Story), No. 328, 1951.

*Finances in higher education: Statistical summary for 1949–50* (Maude Farr), No. 332, 1951. ,

*Earned degrees conferred by higher educational institutions, 1950–51* (Robert C. Story), No. 333, 1952.

*Earned degrees conferred by higher educational institutions, 1950–51: Summary report* (Robert C. Story), No. 333(a), 1952.

*Engineering enrollments and degrees, 1951* (Robert S. Story and Henry H. Armsby), No. 338, 1952.

*ROTC units and engineering enrollments* (Henry H. Armsby), No. 342, 1952.

*Transfers to schools or colleges of engineering* (Henry H. Armsby and Robert C. Story), No. 343, 1952.

*Office of Education estimates of enrollments for 1952–53 as compared with those for 1951–52* (Emery M. Foster), No. 354, 1952.

*Faculty salaries in land-grant colleges and State universities 1951–52* (Maude Farr), No. 358, 1952.

*1952 Fall enrollment in higher educational institutions* (Robert C. Story), No. 359, 1952.

*Earned degrees conferred by higher educational institutions, 1951–52* (Robert C. Story), No. 360, 1952.

*Earned degrees conferred by higher educational institutions, 1951–52: Summary report* (Robert C. Story), No. 360(a) 1952.

*Student-body size in institutions of higher education, 1951* (Henry G. Badger), No. 361, 1952.

*Methods used by college social science departments to improve students' understanding of post-World War II international tensions* (Jennings B. Sanders), No. 362, 1952.

*Engineering enrollments and degrees, 1952* (Robert C. Story and Henry H. Armsby), No. 364, 1953.

*Transfers to schools or colleges of engineering* (Robert C. Story and Henry H. Armsby), No. 365, 1953.

*Cooperative educational programs in colleges and technical institutes* (Henry H. Armsby), No. 368, 1953.

*Library statistics of colleges and universities with enrollments of 5,000 students or more, 1951–52*, No. 370, 1953.

*Earned degrees conferred by higher educational institutions, 1952–53* (Mabel C. Rice and Neva A. Carlson), No. 380, 1953.

*Earned degrees conferred by higher educational institutions, 1952–53: Summary report* (Mabel C. Rice and Neva A. Carlson), No. 380 (a), 1953.

## COMMERCIAL EDUCATION LEAFLETS

*College entrance credits in commercial subjects* (G. L. Swiggett), No. 4, 1923.

*Statistics relating to business education in colleges and universities, 1921–22* (G. L. Swiggett), No. 6, 1923.

## GOOD REFERENCES—BIBLIOGRAPHY

*Junior colleges* (W. C. Eells), No. 31, 1935.

*Higher education: control, organization, and administration* (John H. McNeely and Martha R. McCabe), No. 49, 1936.

*Higher education: curriculum and instruction* (Ella B. Ratcliffe and Martha R. McCabe), No. 50, 1936.

*Student personnel work for counsellors and college students* (Walter J. Greenleaf), No. 51, 1936.

*. . . on changing philosophies in higher education* (Ella B. Ratcliffe and Martha R. McCabe), No. 53, 1937.

*Good references on selection of students in higher education* (Martha R. McCabe and Ella B. Ratcliffe), No. 67, 1940.

## HIGHER EDUCATION CIRCULARS

*The institutional budget* (Hollis Godfrey) (unnumbered), 1916.

*Work of American Colleges and universities during the war* (Report of a conference held at Washington, May 3, 1917, under the auspices of the committee on science, engineering, and education of the Advisory commission of the Council of national defense), No. 1, 1917.

*Work of American colleges and universities during the war* (Report of the work of the education section of the Committee on engineering and education of the Advisory commission of the Council of national defense), No. 2, 1917.

*Work of American colleges and universities during the war* (Report of a joint conference of the Education section of the Committee on engineering and education of the Advisory commission of the Council of national defense and a commission representing the universities of Canada, held at Washington, July 3–4, 1917), No. 3, 1917.

*Work of American colleges and universities during the war. Contributions of higher institutions to the war and to reconstruction,* No. 4, 1917.

*Work of American colleges and universities during the war* (Report of the work of the university section of the Committee on engineering and education of the advisory commission of the Council of national defense), No. 5, 1917.

*Work of American colleges and universities during the war* (Report on the contributions of higher institutions to the national service), No. 6, 1918.

*Work of American colleges and universities during the war. The importance of technical training in military operations* (M. E. Cooley), No. 7, 1918.

*Administrative organization of the college of agriculture* (C. D. Jarvis), No. 8, 1918.

*Work of American colleges and universities during the war. Effect of the war on student enrollment,* No. 9, 1918.

*Work of American colleges and universities during the war. Effect of the war on college budgets,* No. 10, 1918.

*Bureau of Education and the educational survey movement* (S. P. Capen), No. 11, 1918.

*Opportunities at college for returning soldiers,* No. 12, 1918.

*College catalogue* (C. D. Jarvis), No. 13, 1919.

*Advanced educational work within a government bureau* (P. G. Agnew), No. 14, 1919.

*Increases in salaries of college teachers,* No. 15, 1919.

*Rhodes Scholarships. Announcements for the U. S. of A., 1919,* No. 16, 1919.

*How much does higher education cost?* (E. B. Stevens), No. 17, 1919.

*Ohio plan for the training of teachers and the improvement of teachers in service* (W. F. Stewart), No. 18, 1919.

*Rhodes Scholarships. Announcement for the U. S. of A., 1920,* No. 19, 1920.

*Opportunities for the study of engineering at American higher institutions,* No. 20, 1920.

*Report of progress of the subcommittee on college instruction in agriculture,* No. 21, 1920.

*Opportunities for the study of medicine in the U.S.* (G. F. Zook), No. 22, 1920.

*Slavonic languages and literature in American colleges and universities* (C. W. Hazek), No. 23, 1920.

*Rhodes scholarships. Memorandum. U. S. of A.*, No. 24, 1921.
*Rhodes scholarships. Memorandum. U. S. of A.*, No. 25, 1922.
*Rhodes scholarships. Regulations for the U. S. of A.*, No. 26, 1923.
*Need of art training in college and its application in after life* (G. C. Nimmons), No. 27, 1923.
*Rhodes scholarships. Regulations for the U. S. of A.*, No. 28, 1924.
*Rhodes scholarships. Memorandum. U. S. of A.*, No. 29, 1925.
*Policies and curricula of schools of education in State Universities* (J. B. Edmonson and A. H. Webster), No. 30, 1925.
*Rhodes scholarships. Memorandum. U. S. of A.*, No. 31, 1926.
*Expenditures of State universities and State colleges, 1924–25* (W. J. Greenleaf), No. 32, 1926.
*Rhodes scholarships. Memorandum. U. S. of A.*, No. 33, 1927.
*Rhodes Scholarships. Memorandum. U. S. of A.*, No. 34, 1928.

## HOME ECONOMICS CIRCULARS

*Brief courses in home making for normal schools* (Carrie A. Lyford), No. 8, 1919.
*Higher institutions in which home economics is taught*, No. 17, 1923.
*Titles of completed research from home economics departments in 'American colleges and universities, 1918 to 1923*, No. 18, 1924.
*Home economics instruction in universities, colleges, state teachers colleges, and normal schools* (Revised by Emeline S. Whitcomb), No. 20, 1926.

## INDUSTRIAL EDUCATION CIRCULARS

*Lessons from the war and their application in the training of teachers* (W. T. Bawden), No. 1, 1919.
*Progress in the preparation of industrial teachers* (W. T. Bawden), No. 5, 1920.
*Higher standards for teachers of industrial subjects* (W. T. Bawden), No. 7, 1922.
*Preparation of teachers of manual arts and industrial subjects* (W. T. Bawden), No. 11, 1922.
*Preparation of teachers* (W. T. Bawden), No. 22, 1924.

## LIBRARY LEAFLETS

*List of references on higher education*, No. 28, 1924.
*List of references on higher education*, No. 35, 1927.

MISCELLANEOUS PUBLICATIONS

*Agricultural and mechanical colleges, 1915–16,* (B. F. Andrews), (No. 2), 1917.

*Curricula in teachers colleges and normal schools* (E. U. Rugg), (Supplementary report to the National survey of the education of teachers), (No. 15), 1933.

*Curricula for the education of teachers in colleges and universities* (W. E. Peik) (Supplementary report to the National survey of the education of teachers), (No. 16), 1933.

*An explanatory statement in regard to "A classification of universities and colleges with reference to bachelor's degrees"* (P. P. Claxton), (No. 30), 1912 (Special publication. Whole Number 501).

*Federal laws, regulations, and rulings affecting the land-grant colleges of agriculture and mechanic arts,* (No. 34), 1924.

*Federal laws, regulations, and rulings affecting the land-grant colleges of agriculture and mechanic arts,* (No. 35), 1916.

*Federal laws and rulings affecting land-grant colleges,* (No. 36), 1925.

*Federal university for the people,* (No. 37), 1926.

*List of references on higher education,* (No. 53), 1913.

*Modern foreign languages in training for foreign service,* (No. 71), 1922.

*Suggestions for the conduct of educational institutions during the continuance of the war . . . 1917,* (No. 89), 1917.

*University organization for national service and defense,* (No. 94), 1917.

*Note:* The numbers on the Miscellaneous Publications shown above are those assigned in the *List of Publications of the Office of Education, 1910–1936,* Bulletin, 1936, No. 22; the numbers on the Miscellaneous publications below are those assigned by *1937–1959 Publications,* Bulletin 1960, No. 3.

*Accredited programs in degree-granting colleges and universities* (E. Winston and M. Farr), (No. 2), 1943.

*Civil defense education activities in schools and colleges,* (No. 9), 1952. (Also listed as No. 13, 1952).

*College radio courses, Revised 1942,* (No. 16), 1942.

*College radio workshops* (Leonard Power), (No. 17), 1940.

*Colleges and universities reporting nursery schools and/or kindergarten laboratories,* (No. 18), 1942.

*Counseling college students during the defense period* (Willard W. Blaesser and Everett H. Hopkins), (No. 22), 1952.

*Listeners appraise a college station* (Alberta Curtis), (No. 58), 1940.

*The Pennsylvania State College trains for war,* (No. 74), 1944.
*School and college civilian morale service, how to participate*
(No. 88), 1941.
*Students and the Armed Forces,* (No. 96), 1952.

MISCELLANY BULLETINS

*National survey of the higher education of Negroes,* No. 6,
1942–43.
Vol I — (Ina Corinne Brown)
Vol II — (no author listed)
Vol III — (Lloyd E. Blauch and Martin D. Jenkins)
Vol IV — (Ambrose Caliver)
*Residence and migration of college students, 1949–50* (Robert
C. Story), No. 14, n.d. (probably 1951).

PAMPHLETS

*Camp in higher education* (Marie M. Ready), No. 1, 1930.
*Home economics instruction in higher institutions, including
universities, colleges, teachers colleges, normal schools, and
junior colleges, 1928–29* (Emeline S. Whitcomb and A. H.
Gibbs), No. 3, 1930.
*Federal laws and rulings affecting land-grant colleges and uni-
versities* (Walter J. Greenleaf), No. 15, 1930.
*Bibliography on the honor system and academic honesty in
American schools and colleges* (C. O. Mathews), No. 16,
1930.
*Status of the junior college instructor* (John T. Wahlquist), No.
20, 1931.
*Salaries in land-grant universities and colleges* (John H. Mc-
Neely), No. 24, 1931.
*Recent theses in education. Annotated list of 242 theses . . .
available for loan,* No. 26, 1932.
*Summer educational opportunities. Novel features of university
and college summer sessions* (Ella B. Ratcliffe), No. 27, n.d.
(probably 1932).
*Study of the educational value of military instruction in uni-
versities and colleges* (Ralph C. Bishop), No. 28, 1932.
*Official certificates, diplomas, and degrees granted in France*
(J. F. Abel), No. 29, 1932.
*Faculty imbreeding in land-grant colleges and universities*
(J. H. McNeely), No. 31, 1932.
*Institutions of higher education in Sweden* (Alina M. Linde-
gren), No. 32, 1932.

*Residence and migration of college students* (F. J. Kelly and Betty A. Patterson), No. 48, 1934.

*Cost of going to college* (W. J. Greenleaf), No. 52, 1934.

*Doctors' theses in education. A list of 797 theses deposited with the Office of Education and available for loan* (Ruth A. Gray), No. 60, 1935.

*Education of teachers: selected bibliography, June 1, 1932 to Oct. 1, 1935* (B. W. Frazier), No. 66, 1936.

*Training of elementary teachers for school health work* (J. F. Rogers), No. 67, 1936.

*Physical education in institutions of higher education* (James F. Rogers), No. 82, 1937.

*Opportunities for the preparation of teachers in the use of visual aids in instruction* (Katherine M. Cook and Florence E. Reynolds), No. 89, 1940.

*Opportunities for the preparation of teachers in conservation education* (Katherine M. Cook and Florence E. Reynolds), No. 90, 1941.

*Federal laws and rulings relating to Morrill and supplementary Morrill funds for land-grant colleges and universities administered by Federal Security Agency through U.S. Office of Education*, No. 91, 1940.

*Residence and migration of college students* (Fred J. Kelly and Ruth E. Eckert), No. 98, 1945.

PAMPHLETS (EDUCATION AND NATIONAL DEFENSE, WORLD WAR II)

*Practicing democracy in the college* (John Lund), No. 8, 1942.

*Inter-American cooperation through colleges and universities* (John C. Patterson), No. 14, 1943.

PERIODICALS

*Education for Victory* (March 3, 1942, Vol. I, No. 1, to June 20, 1945, Vol. III, No. 24), Biweekly. (Contains some information on higher education and the war).

*Higher Education* (January 1, 1945, Vol. I, No. 1, discontinued June 1964), Bimonthly until May 15, 1953, then Monthly, September to May.

*School Life* (August 1, 1918, Vol. I, No. 1, discontinued December 1964), Semimonthly until June 15, 1921; then Monthly September 1921 through June. Suspended January to June 1922. Replaced by *Education for Victory* from March 1942 to June 1945, then reissued October 1945 through July 1948, and from October 1948 to date. (Contains some material on higher education, especially prior to publication of *Higher Education*, January 1, 1945).

## PHYSICAL EDUCATION SERIES

*Professional training in physical education*, No. 9, 1928.

## RURAL SCHOOL LEAFLETS

*Courses in rural education offered in universities, colleges, and normal schools* (Katherine M. Cook), No. 37, 1925.

*Preparation of teachers for rural consolidated and village schools. Plan of observation and practice teaching used in the Louisiana state normal college* (L. J. Alleman), No. 38, 1925.

## SPECIAL SERIES

*College building needs: A survey of existing space in relation to needed buildings and the means for providing them* (Ernest V. Hollis and associates), No. 1, 1949.

## STATISTICAL CIRCULARS

*Per capita costs in teachers' colleges and state normal schools, 1925–26*, No. 9, 1927.

*Per capita costs in teacher-training institutions, 1927–28*, (F. M. Phillips), No. 11, 1929.

## TEACHERS LEAFLETS

*Americans should study foreign languages.* (Resolutions adopted by the Modern Language Association of America at the Columbus meeting), No. 94, 1920.

*Credit for professional improvement of teachers* (Bertha Y. Hebb), No. 16, 1922.


*Publications of the Former Federal Board for Vocational Education, 1917–1933, and the Vocational Division of the Office of Education, 1933–1953, Relating to Higher Education*

## VOCATIONAL BULLETINS

*Training of teachers for occupational therapy for the rehabilitation of disabled soldiers and sailors*, No. 6, 1918.

*The training of teachers of vocational agriculture* (William G. Hummel), No. 27, 1919.

*Instructor training* (Charles R. Allen), No. 62, 1921.

*Agricultural teacher training* (Theodore H. Eaton), No. 90, 1924.

*Teacher training in agriculture* (Henry M. Skidmore), No. 94, 1924.

*A study of the professional training of teachers of vocational agriculture* (Edwin Lee Holton), No. 122, 1927.

*The training of teachers for agriculture evening class work* (Will G. Crandall), No. 129, 1928.

*Training teachers of vocational agriculture in service* (Lester S. Ivins), No. 135, 1929.

*The training of teachers for trade and industrial education* (Cyril F. Klinefelter), No. 150, 1930.

*Present practices in vocational industrial teacher-training institutions of granting college credit for trade experience, for teaching experience in trade schools, and administrative experience in vocational education,* No. 152, 1930.

*Training teachers in supervised farm practice methods* (William T. Spanton), No. 165, 1932.

*Vocational teacher training in the industrial field,* No. 172, 1934.

*Working your way through college and other means of providing for college expenses (with list of selected references)* Walter J. Greenleaf), No. 210, 1941.

*The State and the preservice preparation of teachers of vocational education. (Federally aided programs),* (Herbert B. Swanson), No. 219, 1941.

MISCELLANEOUS

*Training trade and industrial instructors* (Frank Cushman), No. 11, 1924.

# Bibliography

The facilities of the following libraries were utilized in searching for information which would be germane to this history:
Department of Health, Education, and Welfare Library, including: Education Library, Law Library.
Department of the Interior Library
Bureau of the Budget Library
The Library of Congress,
    including: National Union Catalogue
The American University Library
In addition the facilities of the National Archives, Washington, D.C., and the Federal Records Centers in Alexandria, Virginia, and St. Louis, Missouri, furnished archival material.

## Primary Sources

ANNUAL REPORTS OF THE UNITED STATES COMMISSIONER OF EDUCATION
(All Annual Reports published by the Government Printing Office, Washington, D.C.)

Barnard, Henry, *First Report . . . 1868*, 1868.
Brown, Elmer Ellsworth, *Report . . . June 30, 1906*, 1907 (Two Volumes); *Report . . . June 30, 1907*, 1908 (Two Volumes); *Report . . . June 30, 1908*, 1908 (Two Volumes); *Report . . . June 30, 1909*, 1909 (Two Volumes); *Report . . . June 30, 1910*, 1910 (Two Volumes).
Claxton, Philander P., *Report . . . June 30, 1911*, 1912 (Two Volumes); *Report . . . June 30, 1912*, 1913 (Two Volumes); *Report . . . June 30, 1913*, 1914 (Two Volumes); *Report . . . June 30, 1914*, 1915 (Two Volumes); *Report . . . June 30, 1915*, 1915 (Two Volumes); *Report . . . June 30, 1916*, 1916 (Two Volumes); *Report . . . June 30, 1917*, 1917; *Report . . . June 30, 1918*, 1918; *Report . . . June 30, 1919*, 1919; *Report . . . June 30, 1920*, 1920.
Cooper, William John, *Annual Report . . . June 30, 1929*, 1929; *Annual Report . . . June 30, 1930*, 1930; *Annual Report . . . June 30, 1931*, 1931.
Dawson, Nathaniel H. R., *Report . . . 1885–86*, 1887; *Report . . . 1886–87*, 1888; *Report . . . 1887–88*, 1889.
Eaton, John, Jr., *Report . . . 1870 with Accompanying Papers*, 1870; *Report* (Volume II, *Report of the Secretary of the Interior, 1871*), 1872; *Report . . . 1872*, 1873; *Report . . . 1873*, 1874; *Report . . . 1874*, 1875; *Report . . . 1875*, 1876; *Report . . . 1876*, 1878; *Report . . . 1877*, 1879;

281

*Report* . . . *1878*, 1880; *Report* . . . *1879*, 1881; *Report* . . . *1880*, 1882; *Report* . . . *1881*, 1883; *Report* . . . *1882–83*, 1884; *Report* . . . *1883–84*, 1885; *Report* . . . *1884–85*, 1886.

Goodykoontz, Bess, (Acting Commissioner), *Annual Report* . . . *June 30, 1932*, 1932; "Office of Education" in *Annual Report of the Department of the Interior, 1934*, 1934 (pp. 254–301).

Grigsby, Rall I., (Acting Commissioner), *Annual Report of the Federal Security Agency, 1948. Office of Education*, 1948.

Harris, William Torrey, *Report* . . . *1888–89*, 1891 (Two Volumes); *Report* . . . *1889–90*, 1893 (Two Volumes); *Report* . . . *1890–91*, 1894 (Two Volumes); *Report* . . . *1891–92* (Two Volumes); *Report* . . . *1892–93*, 1895 (Two Volumes); *Report* . . . *1893–94*, 1896 (Two Volumes); *Report* . . . *1894–95*, 1896 (Two Volumes); *Report* . . . *1895–96*, 1897 (Two Volumes); *Report*. . . . *1896–97*, 1898 (Two Volumes); *Report* . . . *1897–98*, 1899 (Two Volumes); *Report* . . . *1898–99*, 1900 (Two Volumes); *Report* . . . *1899–1900*, 1901 (Two Volumes); *Report* . . . *1900–01*, 1902 (Two Volumes); *Report* . . . *1902*, 1903 (Two Volumes); *Report* . . . *1903*, 1905 (Two Volumes); *Report* . . . *1904*, 1906 (Two Volumes); *Report* . . . *1905*, 1907 (Two Volumes).

Hobby, Oveta Culp, *Annual Report of the U.S. Department of Health, Education, and Welfare, 1953*, 1954 (Report of Commissioner Samuel M. Brownell on pp. 159–198); *Annual Report of the U.S. Department of Health, Education, and Welfare, 1954*, 1955 (Report of Commissioner Samuel M. Brownell on pp. 171–192).

McGrath, Earl J., *Annual Report* . . . *1949*, 1950; *Annual Report* . . . *1950*, 1951; *Annual Report* . . . *1951*, 1952; *Annual Report* . . . *1952*, 1953.

Studebaker, John W., "Office of Education" in *Annual Report of the Secretary of the Interior* . . . *June 30, 1935*, 1935 (pp. 275–309); "Office of Education" in *Annual Report of the Secretary of the Interior* . . . *June 30, 1936*, 1936 (pp. 229–285); "Office of Education" in *Annual Report of the Secretary of the Interior* . . . *June 30, 1937*, 1937 (pp. 262–308); "Office of Education" in *Annual Report of the Secretary of the Interior* . . . *June 30, 1938*, 1938 (pp. 294–356); "Office of Education" in *Annual Report of the Secretary of the Interior* . . . *June 30, 1939*, 1939 (pp. 69–138); *Annual Report* . . . *1940*, 1941; *Annual Report* . . . *1941*, 1942; *Annual Reports, 1941–42, 1942–43*, 1943; *Annual Report* . . . *1944*, 1945; *Annual Report* . . . *Section Two* . . . *1945*, 1945; *Annual Report* . . . *Section Two* . . . *1946*, 1947; *Annual Report* . . . *Section Two* . . . *1947*, 1948.

Tigert, John J., *Report* . . . *June 30, 1921*, 1921; *Report* . . . *June 30, 1922*, 1922; *Report* . . . *June 30, 1923*, 1923; *Report* . . . *June 30, 1924*, 1924; *Report* . . . *June 30, 1925*, 1925; *Report* . . . *June 30, 1926*, 1926; *Report* . . . *June 30, 1927*, 1927; *Report* . . . *June 30, 1928*, 1928.

Zook, George F., "Office of Education" in *Annual Report of the Secretary of the Interior* . . . *June 30, 1933*, 1933 (pp. 238–289).

ANNUAL STATEMENTS OF THE UNITED STATES COMMISSIONER OF EDUCATION
(All Annual Statements published by the Government Printing Office, Washington, D.C.)

Brown, Elmer Ellsworth, *Statement* . . . *June 30, 1908*, 1908; *Statement* . . . *June 30, 1909*, 1909; *Statement* . . . *June 30, 1910*, 1910.

Claxton, Philander P., *Statement* . . . *June 30, 1911*, 1911; *Statement* . . .

*June 30, 1912*, 1912; *Statement . . . June 30, 1913*, 1913; *Statement . . . June 30, 1914*, 1914; *Statement . . . June 30, 1915*, 1915; *Statement . . . June 30, 1916*, 1916; *Statement . . . June 30, 1917*, 1917; *Statement . . . June 30, 1918*, 1918; *Statement . . . June 30, 1919*, 1919; *Statement . . . June 30, 1920*, 1920.

(U.S. Office of Education), *Commissioner of Education, Department of Interior, Annual Statement, 1887–1907*, 1887 *et seq.* (Annual Statements for 21 years in one volume).

### EDUCATIONAL DIRECTORIES OF THE OFFICE OF EDUCATION
(All Educational Directories published by the Government Printing Office, Washington, D.C.)

U. S. Bureau of Education, *Educational Directories, 1894–1908*, 1895 *et seq.; Educational Directories, 1909–1911*, 1910 *et seq.; Educational Directories, 1912–1916*, 1913 *et seq.; Educational Directories, 1916–1919*, 1917 *et seq.; Educational Directories, 1919–1920*, 1920; *Educational Directories, 1920–1925*, 1921 *et seq.; Educational Directories, 1926–1930*, 1926 *et seq.*

U. S. Office of Education, *Educational Directories, 1931–1935*, 1931 *et seq.; Educational Directories, 1936–1939*, 1936, *et seq.; Educational Directories, 1940–1941/42*, 1940 *et seq.; Educational Directories, 1942/43–1944/45*, 1943 *et seq.; Educational Directories, 1945/46–1947/48*, 1945 *et seq.; Educational Directory, 1948–49*, 1949; *Educational Directory, 1949–50*, 1950; *Educational Directory, 1950–51*, 1951; *Educational Directory, 1951–52*, 1952; *Educational Directory, 1952–53*, 1953; *Educational Directory, 1953–54*, 1954.

### BULLETINS OF THE OFFICE OF EDUCATION
(All Bulletins published by the Government Printing Office, Washington, D.C. The date of the Bulletin shows the fiscal year of publication.)

Andrews, Benjamin F., *Land-Grant of 1862 and the Land-Grant Colleges*, Bulletin, 1918, No. 13.

Armsby, Henry H., *Engineering, Science, and Management War Training —Final Report*, Bulletin, 1946, No. 9.

Babcock, Kendric C., *Accredited Secondary Schools in the United States*, Bulletin, 1913, No. 29.

Betts, G. L. *et al., National Survey of the Education of Teachers*, Bulletin, 1933, No. 10 (Six Volumes).

Blauch, Lloyd E., *Statistics of Land-Grant Colleges, Year Ended June 30, 1921*, Bulletin, 1922, No. 34.

Bowman, Isaiah, *The Graduate School in American Democracy*, Bulletin, 1939, No. 10.

Capen, Samuel P., *Accredited Higher Institutions*, Bulletin, 1917, No. 17.

Capen, Samuel P., *Accredited Secordary Schools in the United States*, Bulletin, 1915, No. 7.

Capen, Samuel P., *Resources and Standards of Colleges of Arts and Sciences*, Bulletin, 1918, No. 30.

Capen, Samuel P., and Walton C. John, *Survey of Higher Education, 1916–18*, Bulletin, 1919, No. 22.

Flynt, Ralph C. M., *Student War Loan Program—Final Report*, Bulletin, 1946, No. 14.

Hollis, E. V., *Data for State-wide Planning of Veterans' Education*, Bulletin, 1945, No. 4.

Hollis, E. V. and Ralph C. M. Flynt, *Higher Education Looks Ahead*, Bulletin, 1945, No. 8.

John, W. C., *Graduate Study in Universities and Colleges in the United States*, Bulletin, 1934, No. 20.

Kelly, Fred J., *et al.*, *Collegiate Accreditation by Agencies within States*, Bulletin, 1940, No. 13.

Kelly, Fred J., and John H. McNeely, *Federal Student Aid Program*, Bulletin, 1935, No. 14.

Kelly, Fred J., *Land-Grant Colleges and Universities: A Federal-State Partnership*, Bulletin, 1952, No. 21.

Kelly, Fred J., *Toward Better College Teaching*, Bulletin, 1950, No. 13.

Klein, Arthur J., *Correspondence Study in Universities and Colleges*, Bulletin, 1920, No. 10.

McLean, George E., *Present Standards of Higher Education in the United States*, Bulletin, 1913, No. 4.

Steiner, Bernard C., *Life of Henry Barnard, the First Commissioner of Education, 1867–70*, Bulletin, 1919, No. 8.

U.S. Bureau of Education, *List of Publications of the United States Bureau of Education, 1867–1910*, Bulletin, 1910, No. 3.

U.S. Office of Education, *Biennial Survey of Education, 1928–30*, Bulletin, 1931, No. 20 (Two Volumes).

U.S. Office of Education, *List of Publications of the Office of Education, 1910–1936*, Bulletin, 1937, No. 22.

Zook, George F., *Higher Education, 1918–20*, Bulletin, 1921, No. 21.

Zook, George F. and Samuel P. Capen, *Opportunities for Study at American Graduate Schools*, Bulletin, 1921, No. 6.

## MISCELLANEOUS UNITED STATES GOVERNMENT PUBLICATIONS

(All published by the Government Printing Office, Washington, D.C.)

Adams, Herbert B., *The College of William and Mary; A Contribution to the History of Higher Education, with Suggestions for its National Promotion*, Circular of Information, No. 1, 1887.

Adams, Herbert B., "The State and Higher Education," *Smithsonian Institution Annual Report, 1889*, 1890.

The Advisory Committee on Education, *The Federal Government and Education*, 1938.

The Advisory Committee on Education, *Report of the Committee*, 1938.

Babcock, Kendric C., *A Classification of Universities and Colleges with Reference to Bachelor's Degrees*, 1911.

Badger, Henry G., M. C. Johnson, Mabel C. Rice, and Emery Foster, *Statistics of Higher Education: 1955–56. Faculty, Students, and Degrees*, 1958.

Bawden, William E. (ed), *The National Crisis in Education: An Appeal to the People*, 1920.

Blauch, Lloyd E. (ed), *Accreditation in Higher Education*, 1959.

Blauch, Lloyd E., *To Promote the Cause of Education. A Review of Historic Background of Today's Office of Education*, 1953.

Campbell, Doak S., Frederick H. Blair, and Oswald L. Harvey, *Educational Activities of the Works Progress Administration*, 1939.

Capen, Samuel P., *The Bureau of Education and the Educational Survey Movement*, Higher Education Circular No. 11, 1918.

Claxton, Philander P., *An Explanatory Statement in Regard to "A Classi-*

*fication of Universities and Colleges with Reference to Bachelor's De-grees,"* Special Publication, Whole No. 501, 1912.

Division of Higher Education, Office of Education, *Federal Laws and Rul-ings Relating to Morrill and Supplementary Morrill Funds for Land-Grant Colleges and Universities,* Pamphlet No. 91, 1940.

Federal Security Agency and War Manpower Commission, *Final Report of the National Youth Administration, Fiscal Years 1936–1943,* 1944.

Heer, Clarence, *Federal Aid and the Tax Problem,* 1939.

Johnson, Palmer O., and Oswald L. Harvey, *The National Youth Adminis-tration,* 1938.

Judd, Charles H., *Research in the United States Office of Education,* 1939.

The National Archives, *Handbook of Federal World War Agencies and Their Records, 1917–1921,* 1943.

Poole, Hazel C. and Leah W. Ramsey, *Opening (Fall) Enrollment in Higher Education, 1959: Institutional Data,* Circular No. 606, 1959.

President's Commission on Higher Education, *Higher Education for Amer-ican Democracy: Report of the Commission,* 1947.

Quattlebaum, Charles A., *Federal Educational Activities and Educational Issues Before Congress,* 1952.

Quattlebaum, Charles A., *Federal Scholarship and Fellowship Programs and Other Government Aids to Students,* 1950 (Revised Edition).

U.S. Office of Education, *Conference Workbook on Problems of Post-War Higher Education,* 1944.

U.S. Office of Education, *Index to the Reports of the Commissioners of Education: 1867–1907,* 1909.

Warren, Charles O., *Answers to Inquiries about the U. S. Bureau of Edu-cation, Its Work and History: Prepared Under the Direction of the Com-missioner,* 1883.

Works, George A. and Barton Morgan, *The Land-Grant Colleges,* 1939.

*Handbook on Education and the War Based on Proceedings of the National Institute on Education and the War,* 1943.

*National Survey of the Higher Education of Negroes,* Miscellaneous No. 6 (Four Volumes), 1942 *et seq.*

*Work of American Colleges and Universities During the War,* Higher Ed-ucation Circulars Nos. 1–7 and 9, 1917, 1918.

OFFICIAL RECORDS

*The National Archives, Labor and Transportation Branch, Washington, D.C.* (Records Group 12).

Archives File 14: "Office of Education, Commissioner's Office, Profes-sional Education and College Standards, 1909–1928."

Archives File 26: "Office of Education, Commissioner's Office, Land-Grant Correspondence, Research on Educational Correspondence, 1921–26."

Archives File 91: "Office of Education, Monthly Reports of Division Chiefs, 1932–35."

Archives File 100: "Civilian Morale Service for Schools and Colleges, Conference July 19, 1941, etc."

Archives File 204: "Standard Reports, Higher Education."

Archives File 204–a: "Certification of Chartering and Authority to Con-fer Degrees in Colleges and Universities."

Archives File 205: "Junior Colleges, Historical."

Archives File 206: "Teacher Training—Historical."

Archives File 209-a: "Professional Education, etc."

Archives File 501: "Surveys of Public Schools, Washington, D.C., School Survey Materials, etc."

Archives File 800: "Foreign Comparative Education."

Archives File 903: "International Congresses: Sixth International Congress on Public Instruction, Zook and Kelly, etc."

Archives File 905: "Exclusion of Foreign Education in Annual Reports, etc."

*The National Archives, World War I Branch, Washington, D.C.* (Records Group 165).

"War Department Committee on Education and Special Advisory Board, 1918–1919 (C. R. Mann), Miscellaneous Papers" (three file boxes).

The National Archives, "Preliminary Inventory of the Council of National Defense Records, 1916–1921." Washington: National Archives (typeset), December 1942.

*Federal Records Center, Alexandria, Virginia* (Records Group 12).

"Accreditation of Higher Educational Institutions by State Agencies (1948), by Regional Accrediting Agencies (1946–52), by Professional Accrediting Agencies (1946–52)," Acc. No. 57–A–681, Container 27.

"Bogus Institutions," Acc. No. 57–A–681.

"Certification of Academic Credentials (January 1949–December 1954)," Acc. No. 57–A–681, Container 29.

"Education for Victory, 1942–44, etc.," Acc. No. 57–A–681, Container 3.

"Financial Assistance (General Information) (1949–1953)," Acc. No. 57–A–681.

"Forums, correspondence, etc. (1931–1947)," Acc. No. 56–A–506.

"Lanham Act, Project Folders—1948–49 and 1949–50; Maintenance and Operation Applications," (2 boxes), Acc. No. 55–A–603.

"Miscellaneous NYA Records, 1940–41," Acc. No. 55–A–68, Container 29.

"Miscellaneous NYA Records, 1943–44," Acc. No. 55–A–68, Container 30.

"National Commission on Coordination in Secondary Education, etc. (Including President's Commission on Higher Education, 1946–48)," Acc. No. 57–A–681, Container 3.

"Report of Treasurer—A & M Colleges (Morrell–Nelson)," Acc. No. 56–A–506.

"Scholarships and Fellowships (General Information) (1949–1953)," Acc. No. 57–A–681.

"Scholarships and Fellowships Provided by States (1949–50)," Acc. No. 57–A–681.

"Veterans' Educational Facilities Program, General Materials #1, 1946–1951," Acc. No. 55–A–295 (supplement), Container 1.

"Veterans' Educational Facilities Program, General Materials #2, 1946–1951 (Correspondence, etc)," Acc. No. 55–A–295 (supplement), Container 2.

*Federal Records Centers, St. Louis, Missouri*

Personnel Folders:

Wellford Addis

Howard R. Anderson

Benjamin F. Andrews

W. Earl Armstrong

Kendric C. Babcock

Willard W. Blaesser

George N. Butler
Otis W. Caldwell
Samuel P. Capen
George W. Case
William H. Conley
Walter G. Daniel
Ben W. Frazier
Otis W. Freeman
Buell G. Gallagher
Samuel L. Greene
Walter J. Greenleaf
Frederick R. Hamilton
John H. Higson
Chester D. Jarvis
Floyd B. Jenks
Walton C. John
Charles H. Judd
Lewis A. Kalbach
Frederick J. Kelly
Arthur J. Klein
Cline M. Koon
Alina M. Lindegren
John Lund
James E. McClintock
John H. McNeely
Ralph C. Moor
John C. Patterson
J. Lawrence Phalan
Ella B. Ratcliffe
John Dale Russell
Glen Lein Swiggett
John Trevor Thomas
Granville K. Thompson
Frederick E. Upton
George E. Van Dyke
Bernard B. Watson
William R. Wood
George F. Zook

*Office of Education, United States Department of Health, Education, and Welfare*
Budget Management Office Files.
*District of Columbia Code*, 1951 Edition, Part V, Law Library.
"Office of Education and the Commissioners of Education," File of material in Education Library.
National Archives Folders, Mail and Records, Administrative Management Branch, Office of the Commissioner, Office of Education.
Personnel Card File, Personnel Office, Office of Education.
Kardex (personnel card system), Personnel Office, Office of Education.

UNPUBLISHED MANUSCRIPTS AND MATERIALS OTHER THAN OFFICIAL RECORD FILES

Biographical Résumés of Staff Members, Division of Higher Education,

Office of Education, October 26, 1959 (Prepared under supervision of Dr. C. P. Dennison).

Biographical Résumés and Official Personal History Forms of:
Armsby, Mr. H. H. (prepared for author)
Badger, Mr. Henry (prepared for author)
Blauch, Dr. Lloyd E. (taken from Division of Higher Education files with permission by Dr. Blauch)
Hawley, Dr. Claude (prepared for author)
Johnston, Dr. Marjorie C. (prepared for author)
Marshall, Mr. Kendric C. (prepared for author)
Reid, Dr. Helen Dwight (loaned author from ICA Library)
Sassani, Dr. Abul H. K. (prepared for author)
Watson, Dr. Bernard (prepared for author)
Wilkins, Mrs. Theresa B. (prepared for author)

Blauch, Lloyd E., "Higher Education and the Federal Government." (paper read to Section VI at the 39th Annual Meeting of the American Council on Education, October 11–12, 1956, Chicago, Illinois).

College Housing Loan materials in possession of Dr. George Decker.

Evans, Henry Ridgely, and Edith A. Wright, "The United States Office of Education. History, Functions, and Activities, With a Brief Sketch of Each Commissioner of Education." Unfinished manuscript, typewritten format, Washington, 1939.

Foster, Emery M., "Contributions of Arthur J. Klein." Two page typed reminiscence prepared for the author, December 8, 1959.

Gaumnitz, Walter H., "Reminiscences concerning Chiefs of the Division of Higher Education." Two page typed reminiscence prepared for the author, November 17, 1959.

Harris, William Torrey, "Collection of papers and writings assembled by Office of Education Library." Papers bound in 8-vo. volume. Volume I used by author.

Herlihy, Lester B., "For Mr. Lykes' Use in Connection with the Historical Record . . ." (handwritten document), December 1959.

Marshall, Kendric N., "Federal Loans for Students." Manuscript prepared for publication in an educational journal in early 1943.

Parke, Berle, and Zelma E. McIlvain, "Office of Education, 1937–1959 Publications." Galley proofs of Bulletin, 1960, to be published in 1960.

Studebaker, John W., "Plan of Organization to Improve the Service of the U.S. Office of Education, A Three Year Program of Development." Washington, mimeographed, August 1944.

"National Defense College Training." Miscellaneous Forms and Regulations in personal file of Mr. Henry Armsby.

"A Propectus of Plans for State and National Education Conference on Peace Plans and Problems." Office of Education Memorandum, dated December 28, 1944. From Mr. Kendric Marshall's personal file.

"A Recommendation to the Chairman of the War Manpower Commission Concerning the Mobilization and Utilization of the Facilities of Higher Education for War Service Training." Prepared in U.S. Office of Education, July 10, 1942. From Mr. Kendric Marshall's personal file.

LETTERS TO THE AUTHOR

Brownell, Dr. Samuel Miller, Superintendent of Schools, Detroit, Michigan, and former Commissioner of Education, October 26, 1959.

Elliott, Dr. Edward C., President Emeritus of Purdue University, Lafayette, Indiana, December 10, 1959.

Gallagher, Dr. Buell G., President of the College of the City of New York and former Assistant Commissioner and Director of the Division of Higher Education, Office of Education, October 20, 1959.

McGrath, Dr. Earl J., Executive Officer, Institute of Higher Education, Teachers College, Columbia University, New York and Former Commissioner of Education, October 23, 1959.

Ryan, Dr. W. Carson, Professor of Education Emeritus, University of North Carolina, October 15, 1959.

Studebaker, Dr. John W., Vice President and Chairman of the Editorial Board, Scholastic Magazines, and former Commissioner of Education, October 27, 1959.

Watson, Dr. Bernard B., Operations Analyst and Group Chairman, Operations Research Office, Johns Hopkins University, Baltimore, Maryland, and former Specialist for Physics, Division of Higher Education, Office of Education, November 19, 1959.

INTERVIEWS

Anderson, Miss Lucille, Administrative Assistant to the Commissioner. (October 30, 1959).

Armsby, Mr. H. H., Chief for Engineering Education, Division of Higher Education, Office of Education. (October 27, 1959).

Armstrong, Dr. W. Earl, National Council for Teacher Accreditation. (October 20, 1959).

Ash, Mr. Lane C., Division of Vocational Education, Office of Education. (December 16, 1959).

Blauch, Dr. Lloyd C., formerly Assistant Commissioner and Director of Division of Higher Education, later Assistant Director, Register of Retired Professors. (July 21, August 20, September 29, October 13, November 5, 1959).

Caliver, Dr. Ambrose, Chief, Adult Education Section, Division of State and Local School Systems, Office of Education. (October 28, November 2, 1959).

Decker, Dr. George C., Chief, Loans to Schools Section, Aid to State and Local Schools Branch, Division of State and Local School Systems, Office of Education. (October 29, 1959).

Flynt, Mr. Ralph C. M., Assistant Commissioner and Director of Legislative Services Branch, Office of Education. (October 7, November 4, 1959).

Foster, Mr. Emery M., Chief, Research Studies and Surveys Section, Division of Statistics and Research Services, Office of Education. (November 18, 1959).

Gaumnitz, Dr. Walter H., Rural School Statistics, Research Studies and Surveys Section, Educational Statistics Branch, Division of Statistics and Research Services, Office of Education. (August 20, September 3, November 17, 1959).

Goldthorpe, Dr. J. Harold, Specialist in Student Financial Assistance, Division of Higher Education, Office of Education. (October 13, 1959).

Hollis, Dr. Ernest V., Director, College and University Administration Branch, Division of Higher Education, Office of Education. (October 27, 1959).

Iffert, Mr. Robert E., Chief, Faculty and Student Services Section, College and University Administration Branch, Division of Higher Education, Office of Education. (October 16, 1959).

Kelly, Mrs. Frederick J., Wife of the former Chief of the Division of Higher Education, Office of Education. (October 13, 1959).

Layton, Mrs. Elizabeth (Patterson), Retired Research Assistant, Division of Higher Education, Office of Education. (October 15, 1959).

Lloyd, Mr. John H., Chief, Reports Section, Publications Service, Office of Education. (October 28, 1959).

Marshall, Mr. Kendric N., Financial Aid Officer, Student Loan Section, Financial Aid Branch, Division of Higher Education, Office of Education. (October 13, November 3, 1959).

Ryan, Dr. W. Carson, Professor of Education Emeritus, University of North Carolina, (November 27, 1959).

Sanders, Dr. Jennings B., formerly Specialist for the Social Sciences, Division of Higher Education, Office of Education. (October 12, 1959).

Wilkins, Mrs. Theresa B., Research Assistant, Division of Higher Education, Office of Education. (September 29, 1959).

## Secondary Sources

### Reference Works

Bureau of the Census, *Historical Statistics of the United States, 1789–1945.* Washington: Government Printing Office, 1949.

Cattell, Jacques (ed), *American Men of Science* (Vols. I to III). New York: R. R. Bowker Co., and Lancaster, Pennsylvania: The Science Press, 1955.

Cattell, Jacques (ed), *Directory of American Scholars.* New York: R. R. Bowker Co., 1957 (3rd Edition).

Cattell, Jacques, and E. E. Ross (ed), *Leaders in Education.* Lancaster, Pennsylvania: The Science Press, 1932, 1948 (two editions).

Cook, Robert C. (ed-in-chief), *Who's Who in American Education.* Nashville, Tennessee: Who's Who in American Education, Inc., 1928 *et seq.*

Downs, Winfield S., and Edward N. Dodge (ed), *Who's Who in Engineering.* New York: Lewis Historical Pub. Co., Inc., 1954.

Graves, Eileen C. (ed), *Ulrich's Periodicals Directory, Ninth Edition.* New York: R. R. Bowker Co., 1959.

Guthrie, Anna Lorraine (ed), *et al, Reader's Guide to Periodical Literature.* Minneapolis, Minn: The H. W. Wilson Co., 1910 *et seq.* (Vols. II, 1905–09, through XXI, March 1957–February 1959).

Hansen, Harry (ed), *The World Almanac and Book of Facts, 1960.* New York: New York World-Telegram, 1960.

Johnson, Allen (ed), *et al, Dictionary of American Biography.* New York: Charles Scribner's Sons, 1928 *et seq.* (22 Vols. and Index).

Morris, Richard B. (ed), *Encyclopedia of American History.* New York: Harper and Brothers, 1953.

Towner, Isabel L. (ed), *et al, The Education Index,* New York: The H. W. Wilson Co., 1932 *et seq.* (vols. I through IX).

*Biographical Directory of the American Congress, 1774–1949.* Washington: Government Printing Office, 1950.

*Encyclopaedia Britannica.* Chicago: Encyclopaedia Britannica, Inc., 1958 (24 Volumes).

*Who's Who in America.* Chicago: A. N. Marquis and Co., 1889 *et seq.* (Vols. IV, 1906–07, through XXX, 1958–59).

*Who's Who of American Women, 1958–59* (Volume I). Chicago, Illinois: A. N. Marquis Co., 1959.

*Who Was Who in America.* Chicago, Illlinois: A. N. Marquis Co., Volume I, 1943, Volume II, 1950.

PUBLISHED WORKS

Alexander, Philip W., *John Eaton, Jr., Preacher, Soldier, and Educator,* (An Abstract of a Ph.D. Dissertation), Nashville, Tenn: George Peabody College for Teachers, 1940.

Allen, Hollis P., *The Federal Government and Education.* New York: McGraw-Hill Book Co., Inc., 1950.

American Association of Collegiate Registrars, *Bulletin: Proceedings of the Fourteenth National Convention, Minneapolis, April 13, 14, and 15, 1926.* Baltimore: The Johns Hopkins Press, July, 1926.

Bitterman, H. J., *State and Federal Grants-in-Aid.* New York: Mentzer, Bush and Co., 1938.

Brown, Francis J. (ed), *Higher Education in the National Service.* Washington: American Council on Education, 1950.

Capen, Samuel P., *The Management of Universities,* (Edited by Oscar A. Silverman). Buffalo, New York: Foster and Stewart Pub. Co., 1953.

Clark, Jane Perry, *The Rise of a New Federalism: Federal-State Cooperation in the United States.* New York: Columbia University Press, 1938.

Copeland, Lewis and Lawrence Lamm (ed), *The World's Great Speeches.* New York: Dover Publications, Inc., 1958.

Educational Policies Commission, *Federal Activities in Education.* Washington: National Education Association of the United States, 1939.

Educational Policies Commission, *Public Education and the Future of America.* Washington: National Education Association of the United States, 1955.

Eells, Walter Crosby, *Surveys of American Higher Education.* New York: The Carnegie Foundation for the Advancement of Teaching, 1937.

Fitzpatrick, Edward A., *American Education 1891–1956.* (Reprint from the March 1956 issue of *The American School Board Journal*).

Ford, Thomas Benjamin, "The Educational Contributions of the U.S. Commissioners of Education, 1867–1928." Ph.D. Dissertation, The American University, 1933 (No. 356).

Hales, Dawson, *Federal Control of Public Education: A Critical Appraisal.* New York: Bureau of Publications, Teachers College, Columbia University, 1954.

Hartley, Leslie Earle, "A Critical Study of the United States Office of Education Since 1933." Ph.D. Dissertation, University of Colorado, 1941. Borrowed through Inter-Library Loan Service.

Hill, David Spence, *Control of Tax-Supported Higher Education in the United States.* New York: The Carnegie Foundation for the Advancement of Teaching, 1934.

Judd, Charles H., "Contributions of School Surveys," *Thirty-Seventh Yearbook, National Society for the Study of Education, Part 2.* Bloomington, Indiana: Public School Publishing Co., 1937.

Kelly, Fred J. (ed), *Improving College Instruction,* (American Council on Education Studies). Washington: American Council on Education, 1951.

Kelly, Fred J. and John H. McNeely, *The State and Higher Education: Phases of Their Relationship*. New York: The Carnegie Foundation for the Advancement of Teaching in Cooperation with the U.S. Office of Education, Department of the Interior, 1933.

Key, V. O., Jr., *The Administration of Federal Grants to States*. Chicago: Public Administration Service, 1937.

Lewis, Charles Lee, *Philander Priestley Claxton, Crusader for Public Education*. Knoxville: The University of Tennessee Press, 1948.

MacDonald, A. F., *Federal Aid: A Study of the American Subsidy System*. New York: Crowell Pub. Co., 1928.

McDonald, Ralph W. (ed), *Current Issues in Higher Education, 1950*. Washington: National Education Association of the United States, 1951.

Mahoney, Robert H., "The Federal Government and Education." Ph.D. Dissertation, Catholic University of America. Privately printed, Washington, D. C., 1922.

Marsh, Clarence Stephen (ed), *Higher Education and the War*. Washington: American Council on Education, 1942.

Mason, Ethel Osgood, "John Eaton, A Biographical Sketch" in Eaton, John, *Grant, Lincoln, and the Freedmen*. New York: Longmans, Green and Co., 1907. ((pp. ix–xxxiv).

Meredith, A. B. *et al*, *Government and Educational Organization*. Washington: American Council on Education, 1937.

Monroe, Walter S. (ed), *Encyclopaedia of Educational Research*. New York: The Macmillan Co., 1950. Esp. following articles:

Armstrong, Earl W. and Raymond D. Bennett, "Teacher Education—III, Staff," pp. 1387–1390.

Blauch, Lloyd E., "Federal Relations to Education," pp. 435–448.

Blauch, Lloyd E., "United States Office of Education," pp. 1495–1498.

Hollis, Ernest V., "Graduate School," pp. 510–519.

Russell, John Dale, "Colleges and Universities," pp. 220–223, and "Colleges and Universities—III, Organization and Administration," pp. 236–249.

Mort, Paul, R., *Federal Support for Public Education*. New York: Teachers College, Columbia University, 1936.

National Advisory Committee on Education, *Federal Relations to Education*. Washington: National Advisory Committee on Education, 1931.

Part I: Committee Findings and Recommendations
Part II: Basic Facts

National Education Association of the United States, Educational Policies Commission, and American Council on Education, Problems and Policies Committee, *Federal-State Relations in Education*. Washington: National Education Association, 1945.

Public Administration Service, *A Report on an Administrative Survey of the United States Office of Education of the Federal Security Agency*. Washington: Public Administration Service, 1950.

Reeves, Floyd W., Nelson B. Henry, Frederick J. Kelly, Arthur J. Klein, and John Dale Russell, *The University Faculty*, (The University of Chicago Survey, Vol. III). Chicago: University of Chicago Press, 1933.

Reid, Robert H., *American Degree Mills*. Washington: American Council on Education, 1959.

Rodeheaver, Joseph Newton, Jr., "The Relation of the Federal Government to Civic Education. A Study of Certain Aspects of the Growth and Development of the United States Office of Education with Special Reference to Civic Education," Ph.D. Dissertation, Harvard University, 1951.

Russell, James Earl, *Federal Activities in Higher Education After the Second World War*. New York: King's Crown Press, 1951.

Russell, John Dale and Donald M. Mackenzie (ed), *Emergent Responsibilities in Higher Education*. Chicago: University of Chicago Press, 1946.

Smith, Darrell Hevenor, *The Bureau of Education. Its History, Activities and Organization*, (Institute for Government Research, Service Monographs of the United States Government, No. 14). Baltimore, Md.: The Johns Hopkins University Press, 1923.

Todd, Lewis Paul, *Wartime Relations of the Federal Government and the Public Schools, 1917–1918*. New York: Teachers College, Columbia University, 1945.

Willey, Malcolm M., *Depression, Recovery and Higher Education*. New York: McGraw-Hill Book Co., Inc., 1937.

Wright, Isaac Miles, "History of the United States Bureau of Education." A dissertation "submitted in the New York University of Pedagogy in Partial Fulfilment [sic] for the Degree of Doctor of Pedagogy."), Typewritten, 1916.

Zook, George F., "Federal Aid to Education," *Proceedings of the Seventy-second Annual Meeting Held in Washington, District of Columbia, June Thirtieth to July Sixth, 1934*. Washington: National Education Association of the United States, 1934.

Zook, George F. and M. E. Haggerty, *Principles of Accrediting Higher Institutions*. Chicago: University of Chicago Press, 1936.

*Elmer Ellsworth Brown, August 28, 1861–November 3, 1934*. New York: New York University, 1935 (privately printed).

*Journal of Proceedings and Addresses of the Forty-first Annual Conference Held at the University of Missouri, October 30–31 and November 1, 1939*. Chicago: University of Chicago Press for the Association of American Universities, 1939.

### Articles From Periodicals

Allen, Hollis P., "The Place of the Office of Education in the Federal Government," *The School Executive*, LXX, No. 1, September 1950, pp. 47–50.

Armsby, Henry H., "Federal Surplus Property and Educational Institutions," *Higher Education*, II, No. 1, September 1945, pp. 3–4.

Armsby, Henry H., "Federal Surplus War Property and Educational Institutions," *Higher Education*, I, No. 6, March 15, 1945, pp. 1–3.

Armsby, Henry H., "Recent Developments Related to Surplus Property." *Higher Education*, II, No. 5, November 1, 1945, pp. 3–4.

Badger, Henry G., "Higher Education Directory for 1947–48," *Higher Education*, IV, No. 9, January 1, 1948, pp. 105–106.

Badger, Henry G., "Higher Education Statistics: 1870 to 1952," *Higher Education*, XI, No. 1, September 1954, pp. 10–15.

Bixler, Roy W., "The Student War Loans Programs," *Higher Education*, II, No. 2, September 15, 1945, pp. 3–5.

Brown, Elmer E., "Educational Interests at Washington," *Science*, XXXIX, No. 998, February 13, 1914, pp. 239–246.

Brown, Francis J., "Conference on Higher Education in the National Service," *Higher Education*, VII, No. 6, November 15, 1950, pp. 67–69.

Butler, Nicholas M., "The Future of the Bureau of Education," *Educational Review*, XXI, No. 5, May 1901, pp. 526–529.

Capen, Samuel P., "The Colleges in a Nationalized Educational Scheme," *School and Society*, IX, No. 230, May 24, 1919, pp. 613–618.

Clark, William T., "College Level War Training Completes Four Years of Activity," *Higher Education*, I, No. 1, January 1, 1945, pp. 5–6.

Claxton, Philander P., "The National Bureau of Education," *Colorado School Journal*, XXIX, No. 7, March 1914, pp. 18–20.

Cooper, William J., "The National Advisory Committee and the Office of Education," *School and Society*, XXXV, No. 898, March 12, 1932, pp. 339–342.

Cooper, William J., "The United States Department of Education," *School and Society*, XXIX, No. 741, March 9, 1929, pp. 317–319.

Decker, George C., "College Housing Loan Programs," *Higher Education*, VIII, No. 6, November 15, 1951, pp. 69–71.

Division of Higher Education, "Fred J. Kelly Retires from the Office of Education," *Higher Education*, III, No. 2, September 16, 1946, pp. 2–3.

Draper, Andrew S., "Federal Educational Plan Needed," *Outlook*, LXXXVII, No. 5, October 5, 1907, pp. 258–262.

Dunbar, M. M., "Functions and Organization of the Bureau of Education," *School and Society*, VI, No. 154, December 8, 1917, pp. 661–668.

Edwards, Glen, "The Fight for the Bureau of Education," *Journal of Education*, LXXIII, No. 12, March 23, 1911, pp. 311–314.

Eells, Walter C., "Earned Doctorates in American Institutions of Higher Education," *Higher Education*, XII, No. 7, March 1956, pp. 109–114.

Elliott, Edward C., "Educational Advancement and the New Federalism," *Educational Review*, XXXVIII, No. 3, October 1909, pp. 217–225.

Elliott, Edward C., "A Tribute to Samuel Paul Capen," *The Educational Record*, XXXVIII, No. 1, January 1957, pp. 18–19.

Evans, Henry R., "William Torrey Harris; United States Commissioner of Education, 1889–1906," *School Life*, XV, No. 8, April 1930, pp. 144–147.

Goldthorpe, J. Harold, "Office of Education Relationships to Educational Accreditation," *Higher Education*, XI, No. 4, December 1954, pp. 51–54.

Iffert, Robert E., "Inventory of Physical Facilities and Human Resources in Colleges and Universities," *Higher Education*, VIII, No. 6, November 15, 1951, pp. 66–68.

John, Walton C., "The Office of Education's Services for Higher Education," *School Life*, XVII, No. 3, November 1931, pp. 52–53.

Johnson, E. H., "The Bureau of Education," *School and Society*, VIII, No. 197, October 5, 1918, pp. 413–414.

Johnston, Marjorie C., "Evaluation of Foreign Student Credentials: A Preliminary Report," *Higher Education*, VIII, No. 10, January 15, 1952, pp. 115–116.

Judd, Charles H., "National Problems in Education," *The Educational Record*, I, No. 2, April 1920, pp. 118–131.

Kelly, Fred J., "Another Movement Coming to a Head," *Higher Education*, I, No. 2, January 15, 1945, pp. 1–3.

Kelly, Fred J., "The Preparation of College Teachers: Report of a Conference," *Higher Education*, VI, No. 11, February 1, 1950, pp. 125–131; No. 12, February 15, 1950, pp. 143–147.

Klein, Arthur J., "Land-grant Colleges are Participating in Work of Survey," *School Life*, XIII, No. 9, May 1928, p. 180.

Kolbe, Parke R., "War Work of the United States Bureau of Education," *School and Society*, VII, No. 178, May 25, 1918, pp. 606–609.

Lindegren, Alina M., "Evaluation of Foreign Student Credentials by U. S. Office of Education," *Higher Education*, III, No. 17, May 1, 1947, pp. 1–2, 12.

Linville, Henry R., "National Leadership in Education," *Science*, XXX, No. 78, December 17, 1909, pp. 878–879.

Lloyd, John H., "Expanding the Office of Education," *The American Teacher*, XXIV, No. 8, April 1940, pp. 46–50.

Lloyd, John H., "New Assistant Commissioner for Higher Education," *Higher Education*, XII, No. 2, October 1955, pp. 17–18.

McGrath, Earl J., "Civilian Education Requirements Program," *Higher Education*, VIII, No. 6, November 15, 1951, pp. 61–66.

Magill, Hugh S., "Education and the Federal Government," *School and Society*, XIV, No. 354, October 8, 1921, pp. 259–263.

Miller, Walter, "Elmer Ellsworth Brown, the New Commissioner of Education," *Southern Educational Review*, III, No. 7, November 1906, pp. 73–78.

Oxley, Howard W., "CCC Enrollees Go to College," *School Life*, XXIV, No. 1, October 1938, pp. 25–26.

Quattlebaum, Charles A., "The Educational Activities of Federal Emergency War Agencies," *The American School Board Journal*, CX, No. 5, May 1945, pp. 23–25.

Russell, John Dale, "Plans for Development of Federal Services in Higher Education," *Higher Education*, IV, No. 2, September 15, 1947, pp. 13–14.

Russell, John Dale, "The Role of the Division of Higher Education of the United States Office of Education," *American Association of University Professors Bulletin*, XXXIII, No. 3, Autumn 1947, pp. 432–442.

Russell, John Dale, "Zeal for American Democracy," *Higher Education*, IV, No. 17, May 1, 1948, p. 193.

Smith, Anna Tolman, "Education—A National Interest," *Journal of Education*, LXXV, No. 19, May 9, 1912, p. 521.

Smith, Anna Tolman, "Expansion of the Bureau of Education," *Educational Review*, XLIII, No. 3, March 1912, pp. 310–313.

Staples, C. L., "A Critique of the U. S. Bureau of Education," *Education*, XL, No. 2, October 1919, pp. 78–97.

Studebaker, John W., "Development of the United States Office of Education," *Higher Education*, II, No. 12, February 15, 1946, pp. 1–4.

Studebaker, John W., "A Program for the Office of Education," *The Educational Record*, XVI, No. 3, July 1935, pp. 301–311.

Studebaker, John W., "The United States Office of Education," *The American Academy of Political and Social Science: Annals*, CCXXXV, No. 1, September 1944, pp. 62–68.

Studebaker, John W., "The United States Office of Education and the War," *The Educational Record*, XXIII, No. 3, July 1942, pp. 453–463.

Suzzallo, Henry, "Education in the Federal Government," *School and Society*, XXXIV, No. 885, December 12, 1931, pp. 812–813.

Tigert, John J., "Activities of the United States Bureau of Education," *School and Society*, XVI, No. 398, August 12, 1922, pp. 169–175.

Tigert, John J., "Educational Surveys as a Bureau Function," *School Life*, XIII, No. 10, June 1928, pp. 190–191.

Tigert, John J., "An Organization By the Teachers and For the Teachers," *School Life*, IX, No. 9, May 1924, pp. 195–196.

Tigert, John J., "Organization of the Bureau of Education," *School Life,* VII, No. 1, September 21, 1921, pp. 6–7.

Tigert, John J., "Organization of the Bureau of Education," *School and Society,* XIV, No. 351, September 17, 1921, pp. 180–181.

Tigert, John J., "The Relation of the Federal Bureau of Education to the State Universities and Colleges." *Transactions and Proceedings of the National Association of State Universities in the United States of America,* XIX, 1921, pp. 110–125.

Updegraff, Harlan, "The United States Bureau of Education," *The American School Board Journal,* XLIV, No. 5, May 1912, pp. 13–15, 41.

Van Dyke, George E., "Government Experience with the Student War Loan Program," *Higher Education,* VI, No. 6, November 15, 1949, pp. 61–63.

Voorhees, O. P., "A Plea for a Secretary of Education," *Journal of Education,* LXXV, No. 15, April 11, 1912, pp. 400–402.

Wilbur, Hon. Ray Lyman, "The Federal Outlook on Education," *Journal of Education,* CXV, No. 7, February 15, 1932, pp. 164–165.

Wolcott, John D., "Clearing House of Educational Research," *School Life,* XIII, No. 3, November 1927, p. 46.

Wright, Edith A., "Bureau Inaugurates Research Information Service," *School Life,* XIV, No. 5, January 1929, p. 89.

Zook, George F., "The Bureau of Education and Higher Education," *School Life,* IX, No. 9, May 1924, pp. 199–201.

Zook, George F., "President's Commission on Higher Education," *Higher Education,* III, No. 1, September 2, 1946, pp. 1–3.

"Adjustment of the College Curriculum to Wartime Conditions and Needs," *Education for Victory,* II, No. 21, May 3, 1944, p. 21.

"British Educational Mission," *School Life,* I, No. 6, October 16, 1918, p. 2.

"Bureau of Education," *The Journal of the National Education Association,* XIII, No. 5, May 1924, p. 172.

"College-level Courses in ESMWT," *Education for Victory,* I, No. 20, December 16, 1942, pp. 17–18.

"College Training Plan in Full Swing," *School Life,* I, No. 1, August 1918, p. 6.

"Conference Workbook on Problems of Post-War Higher Education," *Education for Victory,* II, No. 22, May 20, 1944, p. 14.

"Congress Assigns Another Function to the Bureau of Education," *School Life,* XIV, No. 7, March 1929, p. 127.

"Defense Mobilization Assignments in the Office of Education," *Higher Education,* VII, No. 6, November 15, 1950, p. 69.

"Diamond Jubilee of the Office of Education," *The Journal of the National Education Association,* XXXI, No. 3, March 1942, p. 82.

"Earl James McGrath Appointed Commissioner of Education," *Higher Education,* V, No. 15, April 1, 1949, pp. 169–170.

"Earl James McGrath—11th Commissioner of Education," *School Life,* XXXI, No. 8, May 1949, pp. 1–3, 14.

"Editorial Notes," *The Elementary School Teacher,* XII, No. 4, December 1911, pp. 186–188.

"The Education Bill," *School and Society,* IX, No. 218, March 1, 1919, pp. 272–277.

"Education in the Federal Government," *Journal of Home Economics,* XXIV, No. 5, May 1932, pp. 447–449.

"Educational Planning (The U.S. Office of Education)," *The School Executive.* LXVI, No. 10, June 1947, pp. 47–60.

"Enlargement of the Bureau of Education," *The School Review*, XXXI, No. 10, December 1923, pp. 721–722.

"The Federal Bureau and Educational Research," *Journal of Educational Research*, I, No. 1, January 1920, pp. 156–157.

"Federal Educational Activities," *Higher Education*, VIII, No. 5, November 1, 1951, pp. 49–55.

"For a Better Office of Education," *The American School Board Journal*, CX, No. 4, April 1945, p. 50.

"Improving College Instruction," *Higher Education*, VII, No. 10, January 15, 1951, pp. 113–116.

"An Independent U.S. Office of Education," *School and Society*, LXVIII, No. 1766, October 30, 1948, pp. 292–293.

"List of Approved Colleges Urged," *School Life*, II, No. 9, May 1, 1919, pp. 2, 4.

"New Appropriations for the Federal Office of Education," *School and Society*, XLII, No. 1096, December 28, 1935, p. 886.

"New Director of the Higher Education Division," *Higher Education*, III, No. 2, September 16, 1946, p. 1.

"Office of Education to Head New Projects," *The Journal of the National Education Association*, XXV, No. 2, February 1936, p. 42.

"Office of Education Reorganization Completed," *The Nation's Schools*, XLVII, No. 6, June 1951, p. 92.

"Program of the Division of Higher Education in the Office of Education," *Higher Education*, VIII, No. 15, April 1, 1952, pp. 169–172.

"The Reorganization of the Bureau of Education," *School and Society*, XXX, No. 774, October 26, 1929, 564–565.

"Reorganization of the Office of Education," *The School Review*, LIX, No. 5, May 1951, pp. 255–257.

"Reorganization of the U.S. Office of Education," *The School Executive*, LXIV, No. 7, March 1945, p. 31.

"Services of the Office of Education," *School and Society*, XXXVII, No. 945, February 4, 1933, pp. 142–143.

"To Strengthen and Improve Office of Education Administration," *School Life*, XXXIII, No.7, April 1951, pp. 97–101, 106–109.

"Studebaker Resigns: Grigsby Acting Commissioner," *Higher Education*, V, No. 1, September 1, 1948, pp. 1–3.

"Tangled Office of Education," *The Nation's Schools*, XLVII, No. 4, April 1951, pp. 86–88.

"Three New Office of Education Programs," *Education for Victory*, I, No. 16, October 15, 1942, p. 2.

"Toward a Stronger Office of Education," *The Journal of the National Education Association*, XXXIV, No. 3, March 1945, pp. 53–54.

"The United States Government and Negro Education," *School and Society*, XXXII, No. 882, September 27, 1930, p. 421.

"United States Office of Education," *The Journal of the National Education Association*, XVIII, No. 8, November 1929, pp. 241–242.

"The United States Office of Education," *The Journal of the National Education Association*, XXVIII, No. 9, December 1939, p. 274.

"The U.S. Office of Education," *Science*, CVIII, No. 2801, September 3, 1948. pp. 256–257.

"U.S. Office of Education Wartime Commission," *Education for Victory*, I, No. 1, March 3, 1942, pp. 3–8.

"The University Research Project of the Office of Education," *School and Society*, XLV, No. 1172, June 12, 1937, pp. 807–808.

"The Wartime Commission of the United States Office of Education," *The Elementary School Journal*, XLII, No. 8, April 1942, p. 569.

"War Training Programs Brought to a Close," *Education for Victory*, III, No. 24, June 20, 1945, pp. 4–6.